SEVEN SEAS ENTERTAINMENT PRESENTS

Monster Musume

story and art by OKAYADO

VOLUME 11

TRANSLATION
Ryan Peterson

ADAPTATION
Shanti Whitesides

LETTERING AND LAYOUT
Ma. Victoria Robado
William Ringrose

LOGO DESIGN
Courtney Williams

COVER DESIGN
Nicky Lim

PROOFREADER
Janet Houck

ASSISTANT EDITOR
Jenn Grunigen

PRODUCTION ASSISTANT
CK Russell

PRODUCTION MANAGER
Lissa Pattillo

EDITOR-IN-CHIEF
Adam Arnold

PUBLISHER
Jason DeAngelis

MONSTER MUSUME NO IRU NICHIJO VOLUME 11
© OKAYADO 2016
Originally published in Japan in 2016 by TOKUMA SHOTEN PUBLISHING
CO., LTD., Tokyo. English translation rights arranged with TOKUMA SHOTEN
PUBLISHING CO., LTD., Tokyo, through TOHAN CORPORATION, Tokyo.

Seven Seas books may be purchased in bulk for promotional, educational, or
business use. Please contact your local bookseller or the Macmillan Corporate
and Premium Sales Department at 1-800-221-7945, extension 5442, or by
e-mail at MacmillanSpecialMarkets@macmillan.com.

ISBN: 978-1-626924-66-6

Printed in Canada

First Printing: April 2017

10 9 8 7 6 5 4 3 2 1

FOLLOW US ONLINE: *www.gomanga.com*

READING DIRECTIONS

This book reads from *right to left*, Japanese style.
If this is your first time reading manga, you start
reading from the top right panel on each page and
take it from there. If you get lost, just follow the
numbered diagram here. It may seem backwards
first, but you'll get the hang of it! Have fun!!

W9-CHF-976

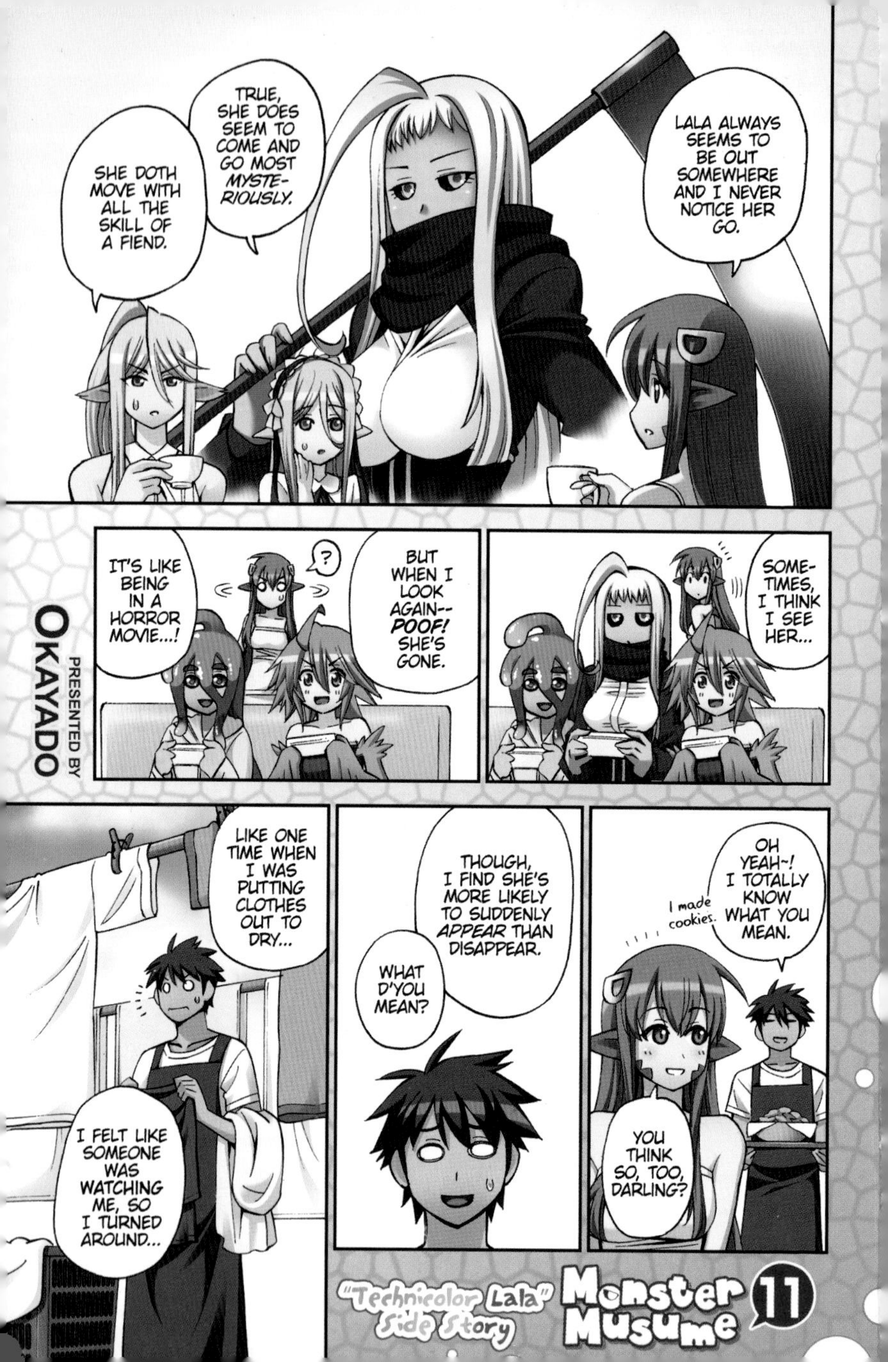
LALA ALWAYS SEEMS TO BE OUT SOMEWHERE AND I NEVER NOTICE HER GO.
TRUE, SHE DOES SEEM TO COME AND GO MOST *MYSTERIOUSLY.*
SHE DOTH MOVE WITH ALL THE SKILL OF A FIEND.
SOMETIMES, I THINK I SEE HER...
BUT WHEN I LOOK AGAIN-- *POOF!* SHE'S GONE.
?
IT'S LIKE BEING IN A HORROR MOVIE...!
PRESENTED BY OKAYADO
OH YEAH~! I TOTALLY KNOW WHAT YOU MEAN.
I made cookies.
YOU THINK SO, TOO, DARLING?
THOUGH, I FIND SHE'S MORE LIKELY TO SUDDENLY *APPEAR* THAN DISAPPEAR.
WHAT D'YOU MEAN?
LIKE ONE TIME WHEN I WAS PUTTING CLOTHES OUT TO DRY...
I FELT LIKE SOMEONE WAS WATCHING ME, SO I TURNED AROUND...
Monster Musume 11
"Technicolor Lala" Side Story

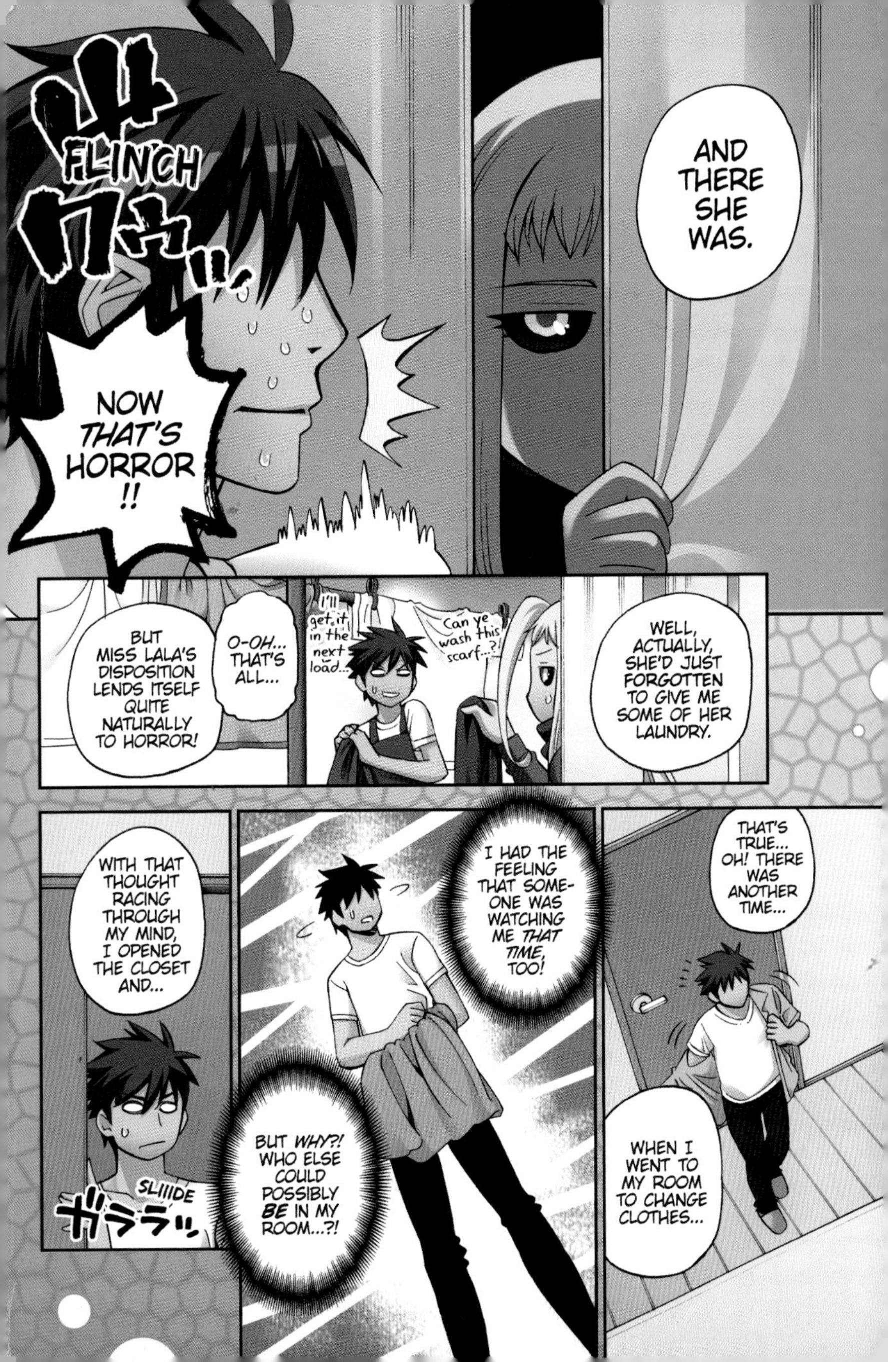
AND THERE SHE WAS.
FLINCH
NOW THAT'S HORROR!!
WELL, ACTUALLY, SHE'D JUST FORGOTTEN TO GIVE ME SOME OF HER LAUNDRY.
Can ye wash this scarf...?!
I'll get it in the next load...
O-OH... THAT'S ALL...
BUT MISS LALA'S DISPOSITION LENDS ITSELF QUITE NATURALLY TO HORROR!
THAT'S TRUE... OH! THERE WAS ANOTHER TIME...
WHEN I WENT TO MY ROOM TO CHANGE CLOTHES...
I HAD THE FEELING THAT SOME-ONE WAS WATCHING ME THAT TIME, TOO!
BUT WHY?! WHO ELSE COULD POSSIBLY BE IN MY ROOM...?!
WITH THAT THOUGHT RACING THROUGH MY MIND, I OPENED THE CLOSET AND...
SLIIIDE
ガラララッ

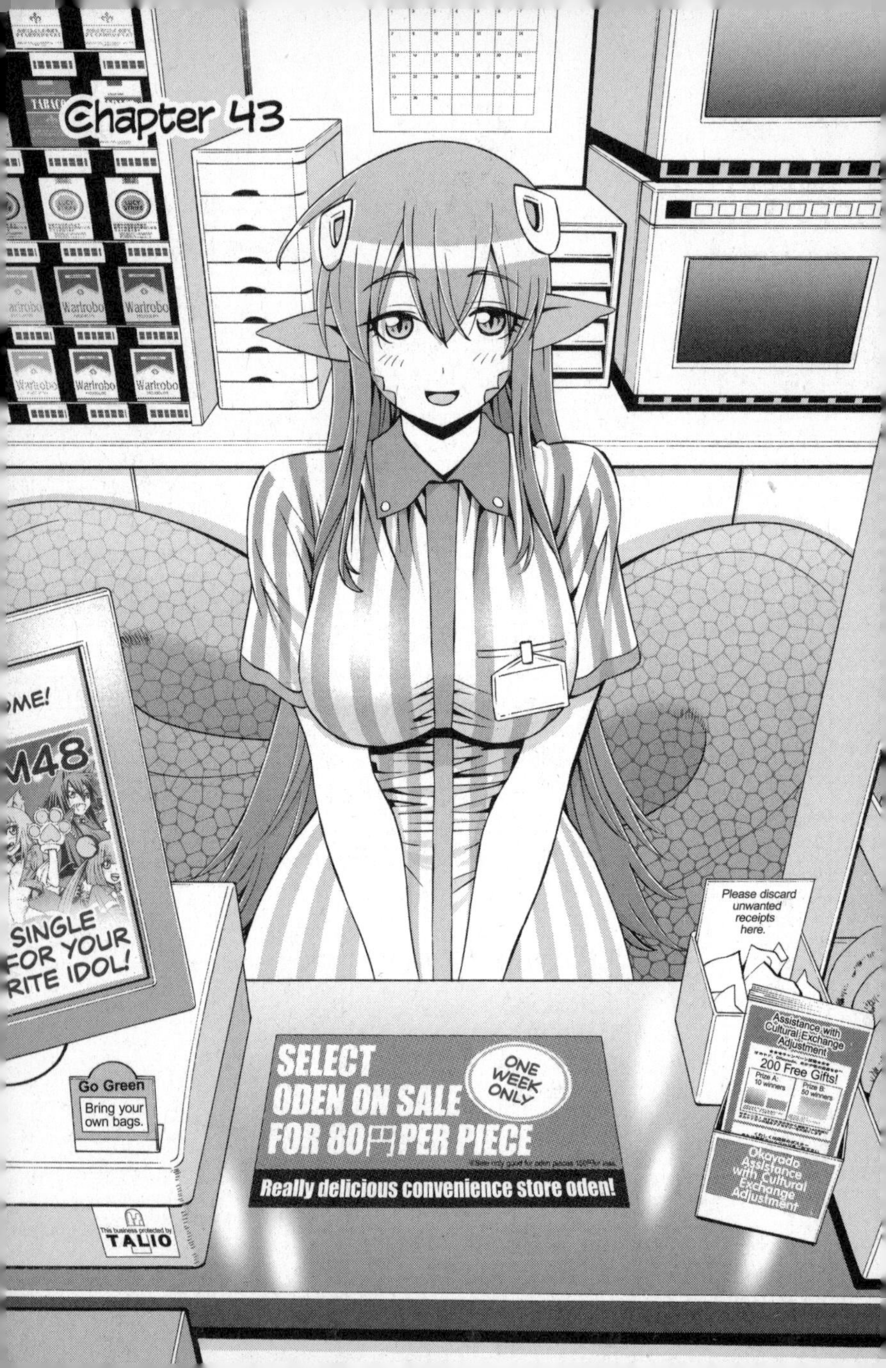
Chapter 43
SINGLE
FOR YOUR
RITE IDOL!
Go Green
Bring your own bags.
This business protected by
TALIO
SELECT
ODEN ON SALE
FOR 80円 PER PIECE
ONE WEEK ONLY
Really delicious convenience store oden!
Please discard unwanted receipts here.
Assistance with Cultural Exchange Adjustment
200 Free Gifts!
Prize A: 10 winners
Prize B: 50 winners
Okayado Assistance with Cultural Exchange Adjustment

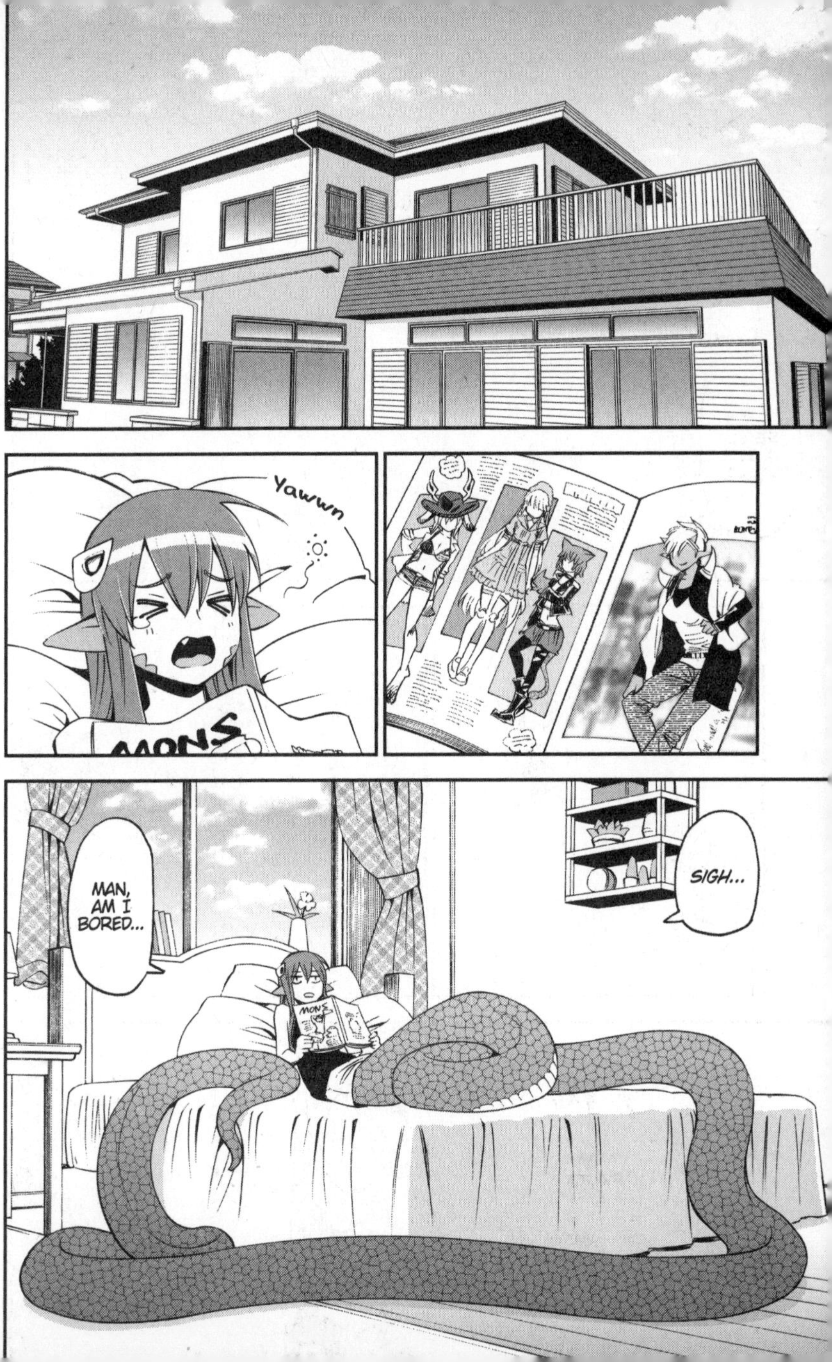
Yawwn
MONS
SIGH...
MAN, AM I BORED...

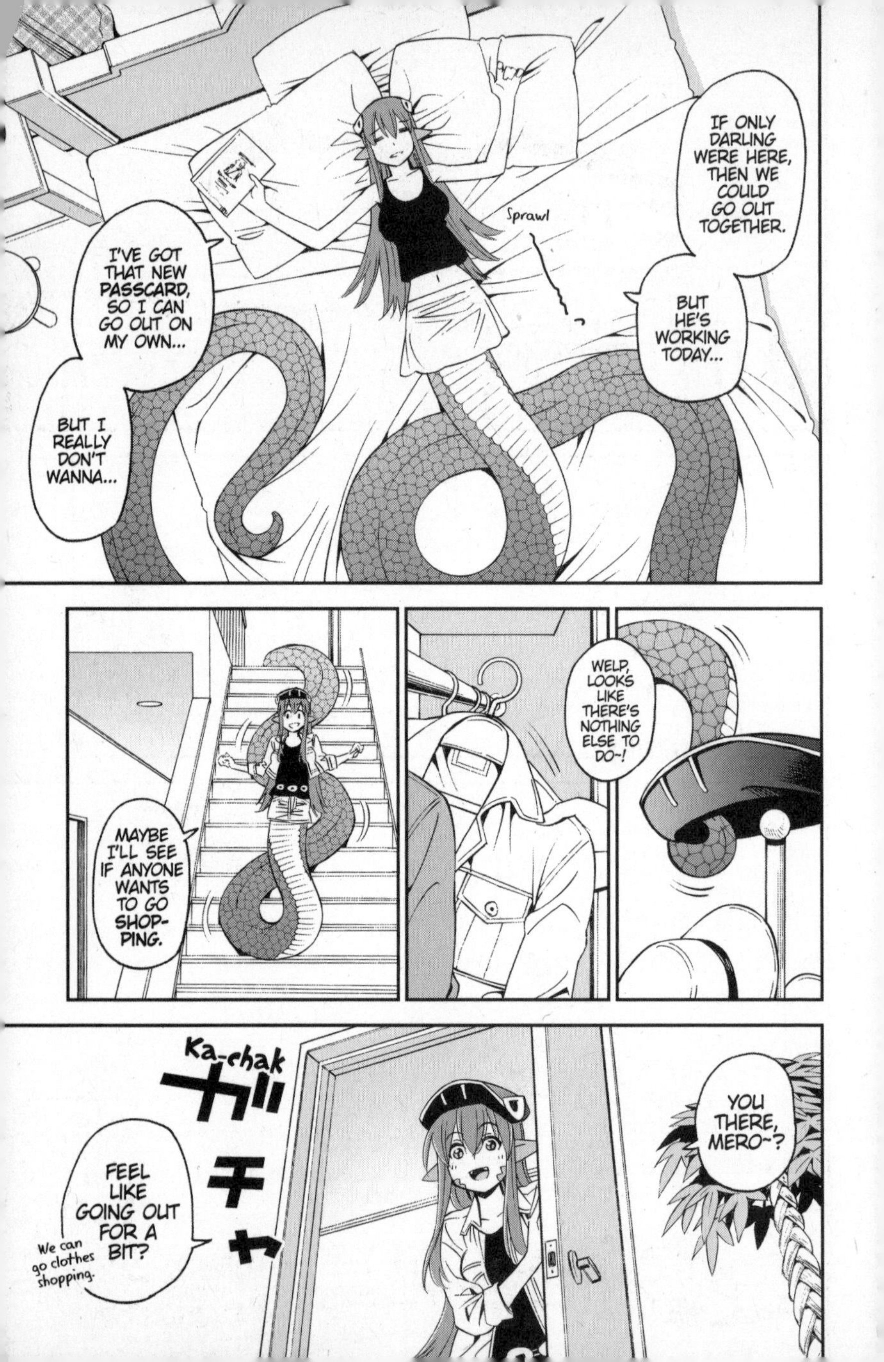

IF ONLY DARLING WERE HERE, THEN WE COULD GO OUT TOGETHER.
BUT HE'S WORKING TODAY...
Sprawl
I'VE GOT THAT NEW PASSCARD, SO I CAN GO OUT ON MY OWN...
BUT I REALLY DON'T WANNA...
WELP, LOOKS LIKE THERE'S NOTHING ELSE TO DO~!
MAYBE I'LL SEE IF ANYONE WANTS TO GO SHOP-PING.
YOU THERE, MERO~?
Ka-chak
ガチャ
FEEL LIKE GOING OUT FOR A BIT?
We can go clothes shopping.

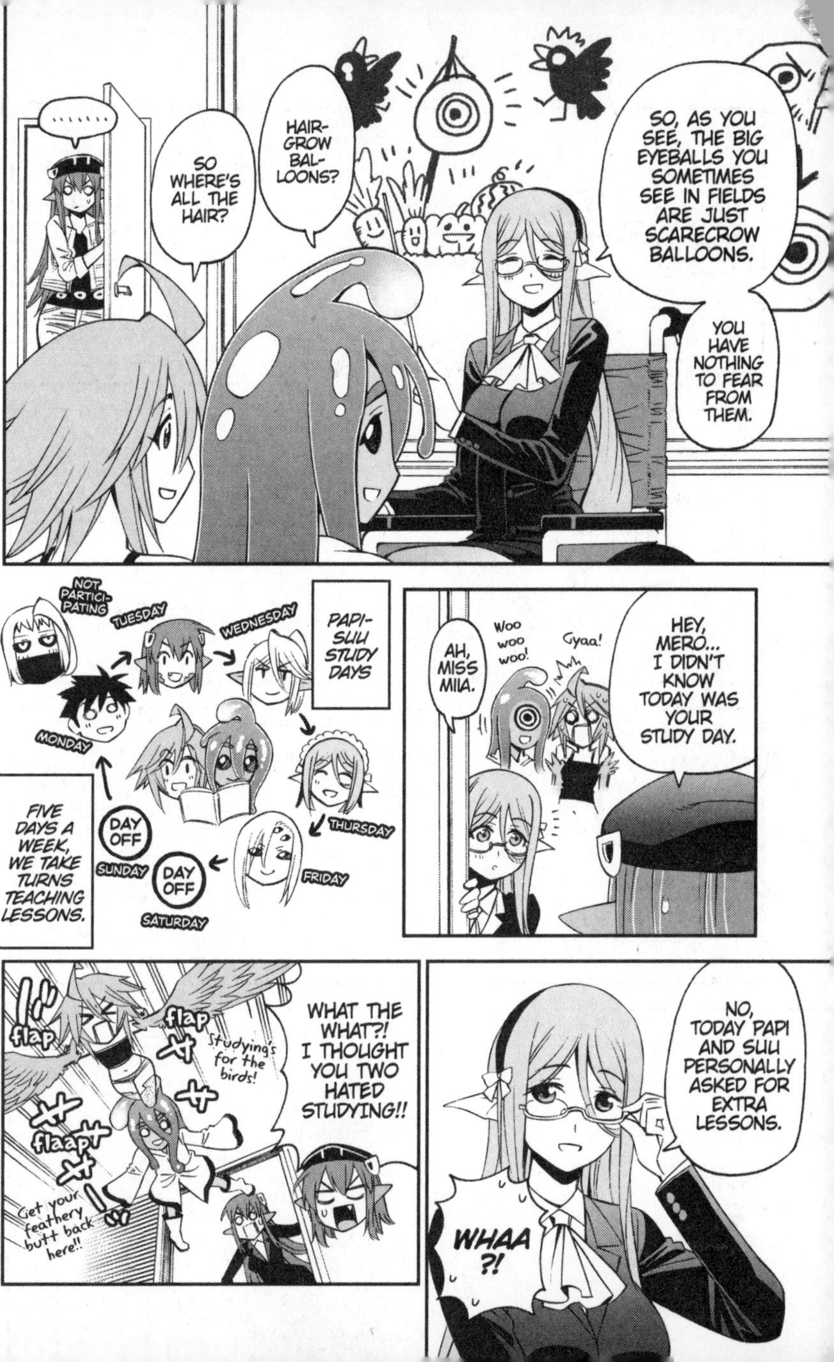
SO, AS YOU SEE, THE BIG EYEBALLS YOU SOMETIMES SEE IN FIELDS ARE JUST SCARECROW BALLOONS.
YOU HAVE NOTHING TO FEAR FROM THEM.
HAIR-GROW BALLOONS?
SO WHERE'S ALL THE HAIR?
....
HEY, MERO... I DIDN'T KNOW TODAY WAS YOUR STUDY DAY.
Gyaa!
Woo woo woo!
AH, MISS MIIA.
PAPI-SUU STUDY DAYS
NOT PARTICI-PATING
TUESDAY
WEDNESDAY
MONDAY
THURSDAY
FRIDAY
DAY OFF
SUNDAY
DAY OFF
SATURDAY
FIVE DAYS A WEEK, WE TAKE TURNS TEACHING LESSONS.
NO, TODAY PAPI AND SUU PERSONALLY ASKED FOR EXTRA LESSONS.
WHAA ?!
WHAT THE WHAT?! I THOUGHT YOU TWO HATED STUDYING!!
Studying's for the birds!
flap
flap
flaap
Get your feathery butt back here!!

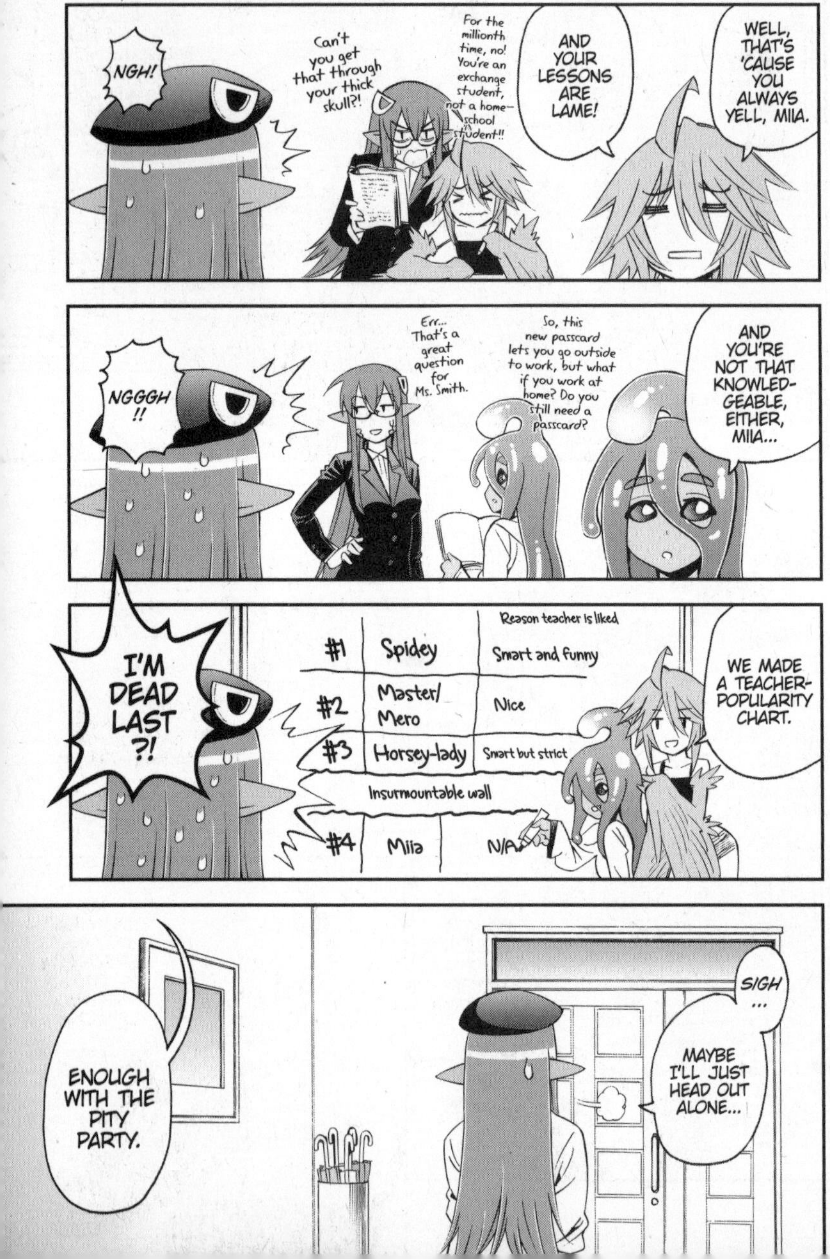
WELL, THAT'S 'CAUSE YOU ALWAYS YELL, MIIA.
AND YOUR LESSONS ARE LAME!
For the millionth time, no! You're an exchange student, not a home-school student!!
Can't you get that through your thick skull?!
NGH!
AND YOU'RE NOT THAT KNOWLEDGEABLE, EITHER, MIIA...
So, this new passcard lets you go outside to work, but what if you work at home? Do you still need a passcard?
Err... That's a great question for Ms. Smith.
NGGGH!!
WE MADE A TEACHER-POPULARITY CHART.
Reason teacher is liked
#1 Spidey Smart and funny
#2 Master/Mero Nice
#3 Horsey-lady Smart but strict
Insurmountable wall
#4 Miia N/A
I'M DEAD LAST?!
SIGH...
MAYBE I'LL JUST HEAD OUT ALONE...
ENOUGH WITH THE PITY PARTY.

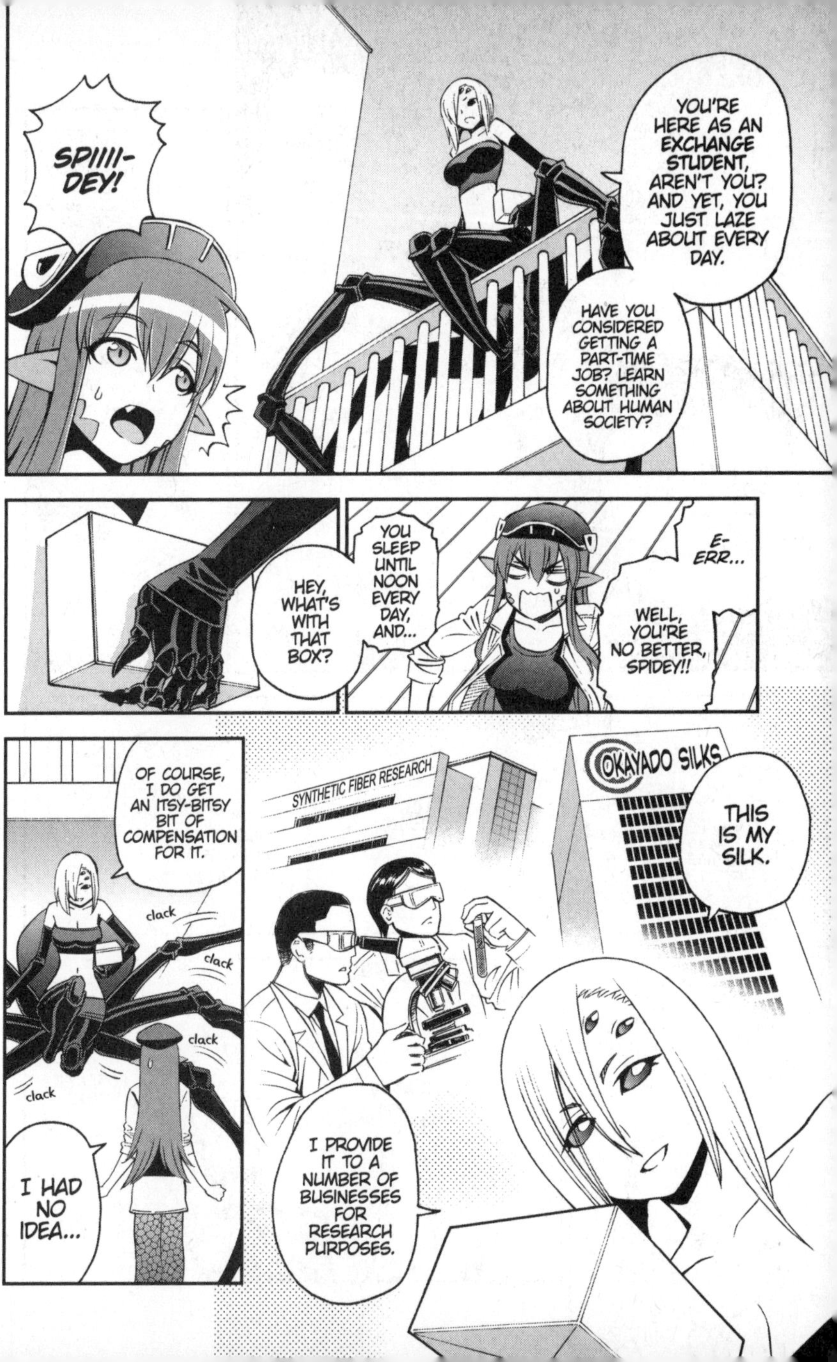

YOU'RE HERE AS AN EXCHANGE STUDENT, AREN'T YOU? AND YET, YOU JUST LAZE ABOUT EVERY DAY.
HAVE YOU CONSIDERED GETTING A PART-TIME JOB? LEARN SOMETHING ABOUT HUMAN SOCIETY?
SPIIII-DEY!
E-ERR...
WELL, YOU'RE NO BETTER, SPIDEY!!
YOU SLEEP UNTIL NOON EVERY DAY, AND...
HEY, WHAT'S WITH THAT BOX?
OKAYADO SILKS
THIS IS MY SILK.
SYNTHETIC FIBER RESEARCH
I PROVIDE IT TO A NUMBER OF BUSINESSES FOR RESEARCH PURPOSES.
OF COURSE, I DO GET AN ITSY-BITSY BIT OF COMPENSATION FOR IT.
clack
clack
clack
clack
I HAD NO IDEA...

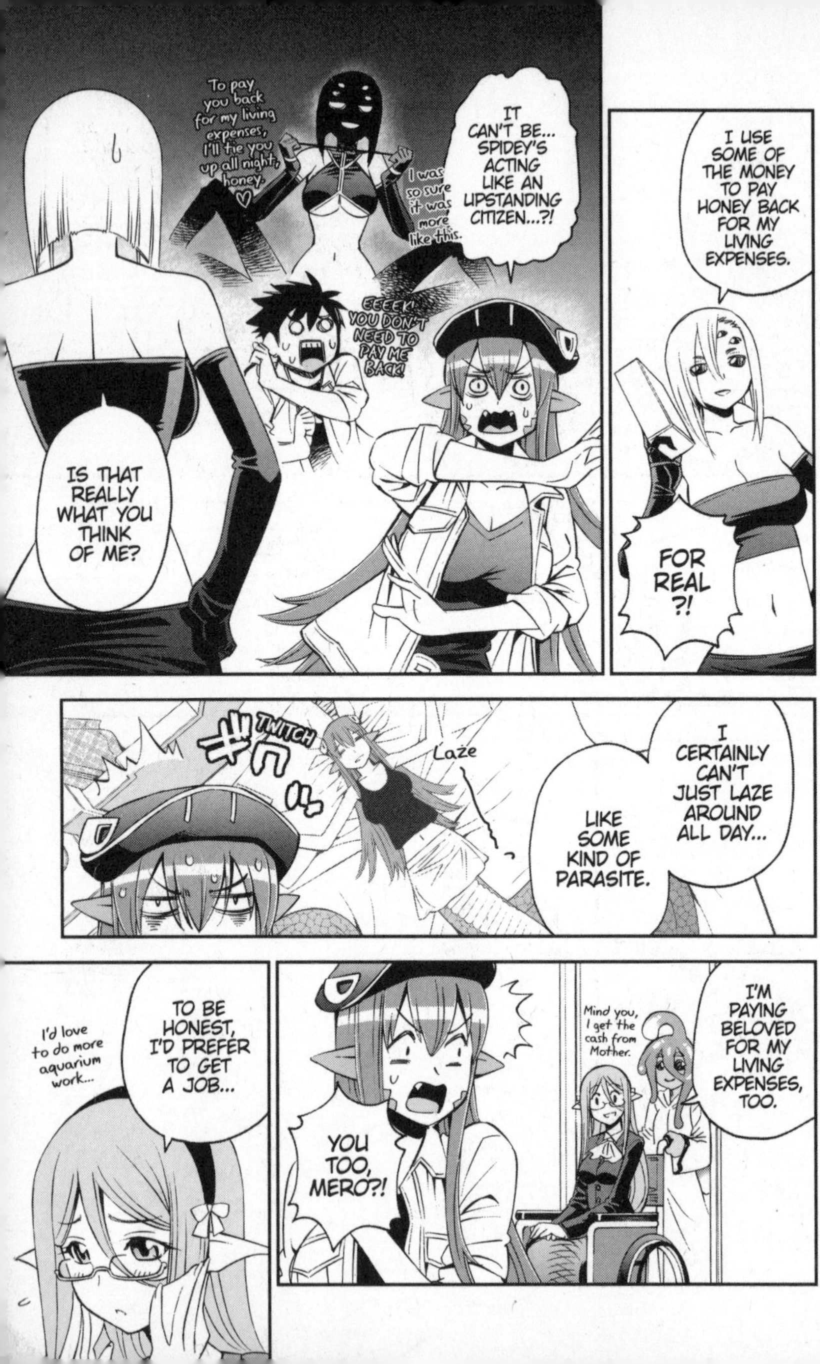
I USE SOME OF THE MONEY TO PAY HONEY BACK FOR MY LIVING EXPENSES.
FOR REAL ?!
IT CAN'T BE... SPIDEY'S ACTING LIKE AN UPSTANDING CITIZEN...?!
I was so sure it was more like this.
To pay you back for my living expenses, I'll tie you up all night, honey. ♡
EEEEK! YOU DON'T NEED TO PAY ME BACK!
IS THAT REALLY WHAT YOU THINK OF ME?
I CERTAINLY CAN'T JUST LAZE AROUND ALL DAY...
LIKE SOME KIND OF PARASITE.
Laze
TWITCH
I'M PAYING BELOVED FOR MY LIVING EXPENSES, TOO.
Mind you, I get the cash from Mother.
YOU TOO, MERO?!
TO BE HONEST, I'D PREFER TO GET A JOB...
I'd love to do more aquarium work...

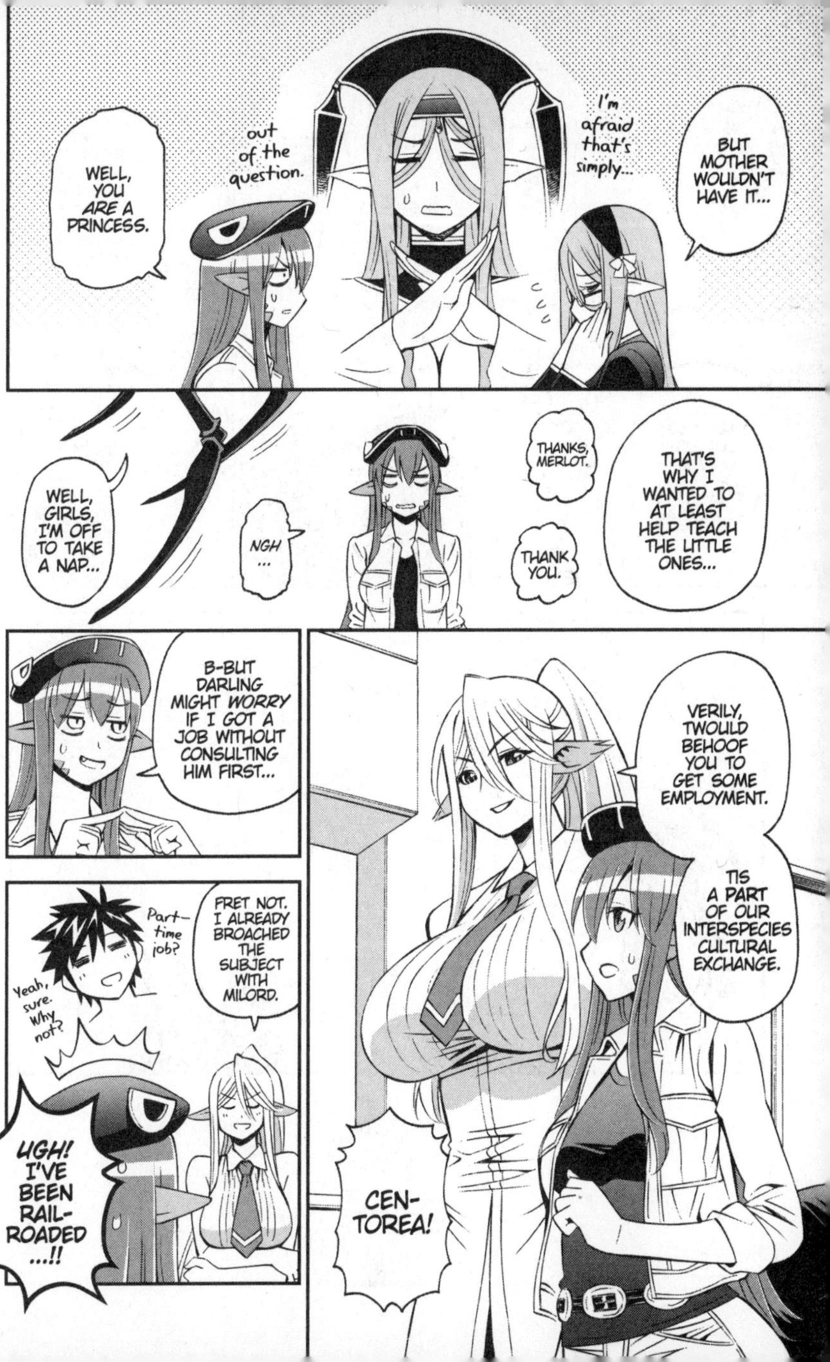
BUT MOTHER WOULDN'T HAVE IT...
I'm afraid that's simply...
out of the question.
WELL, YOU ARE A PRINCESS.
THAT'S WHY I WANTED TO AT LEAST HELP TEACH THE LITTLE ONES...
THANKS, MERLOT.
THANK YOU.
NGH ...
WELL, GIRLS, I'M OFF TO TAKE A NAP...
VERILY, TWOULD BEHOOF YOU TO GET SOME EMPLOYMENT.
TIS A PART OF OUR INTERSPECIES CULTURAL EXCHANGE.
CEN-TOREA!
B-BUT DARLING MIGHT WORRY IF I GOT A JOB WITHOUT CONSULTING HIM FIRST...
FRET NOT. I ALREADY BROACHED THE SUBJECT WITH MILORD.
Part-time job?
Yeah, sure. Why not?
UGH! I'VE BEEN RAIL-ROADED ...!!

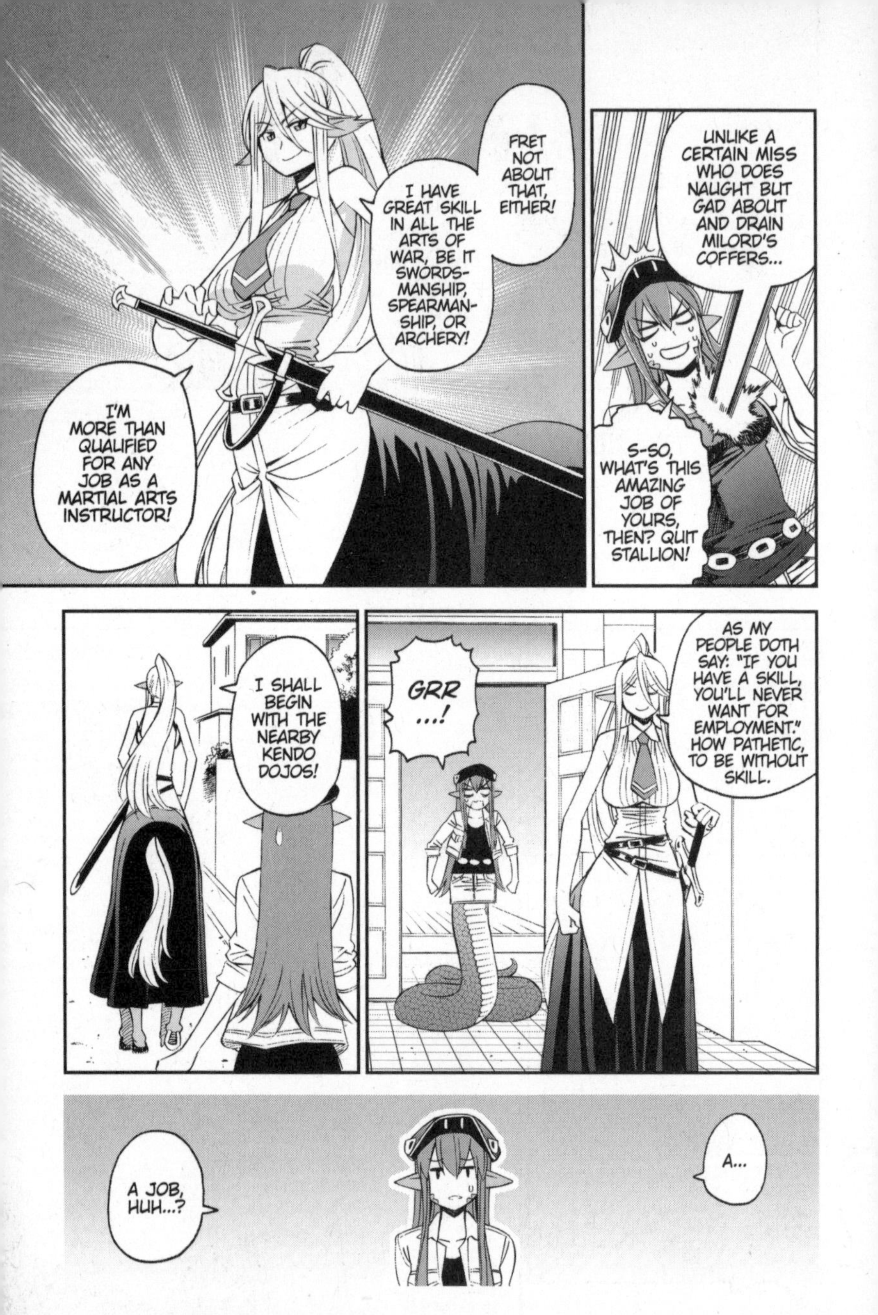
UNLIKE A CERTAIN MISS WHO DOES NAUGHT BUT GAD ABOUT AND DRAIN MILORD'S COFFERS...
S-SO, WHAT'S THIS AMAZING JOB OF YOURS, THEN? QUIT STALLION!
FRET NOT ABOUT THAT, EITHER!
I HAVE GREAT SKILL IN ALL THE ARTS OF WAR, BE IT SWORDS-MANSHIP, SPEARMAN-SHIP, OR ARCHERY!
I'M MORE THAN QUALIFIED FOR ANY JOB AS A MARTIAL ARTS INSTRUCTOR!
AS MY PEOPLE DOTH SAY: "IF YOU HAVE A SKILL, YOU'LL NEVER WANT FOR EMPLOYMENT." HOW PATHETIC, TO BE WITHOUT SKILL.
GRR ...!
I SHALL BEGIN WITH THE NEARBY KENDO DOJOS!
A...
A JOB, HUH...?

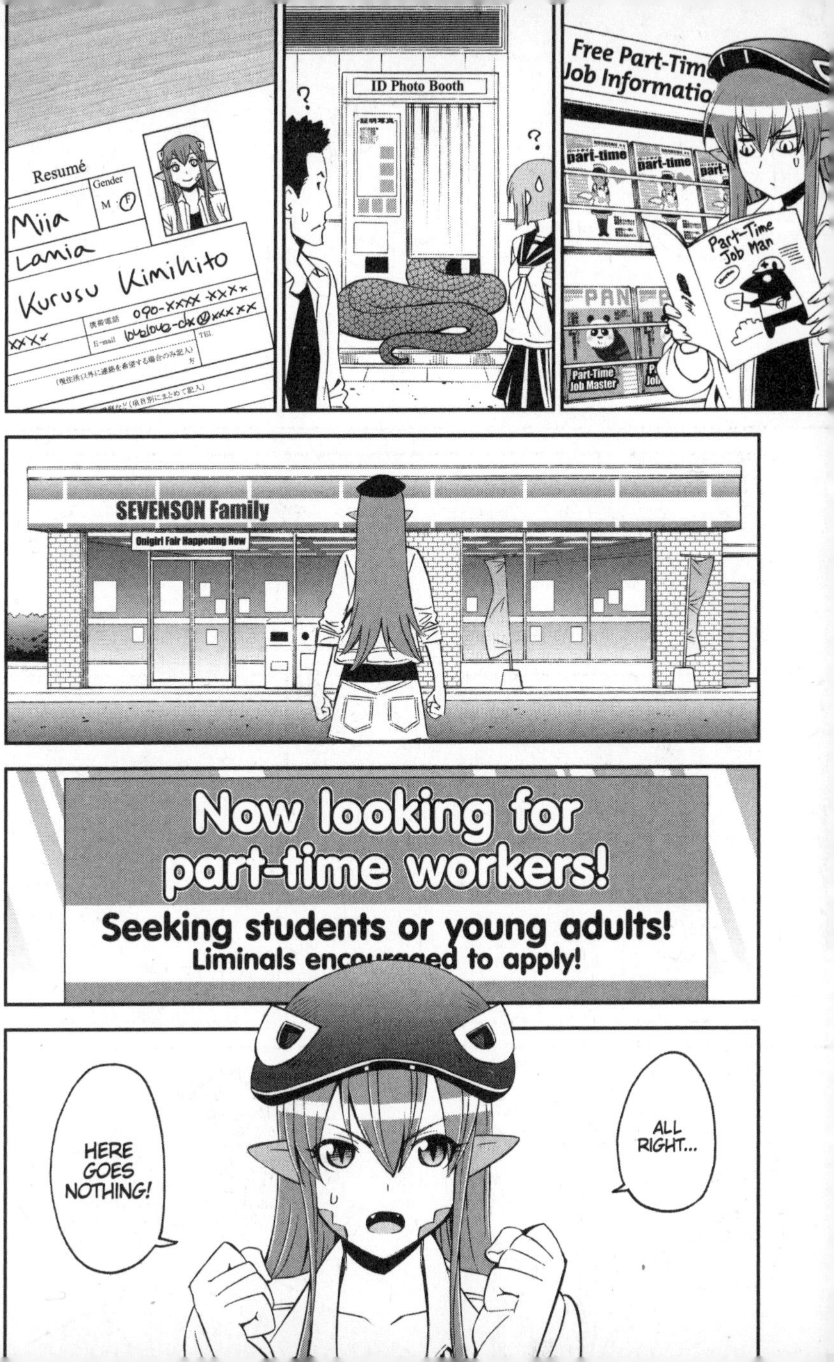
Free Part-Time Job Information
part-time
part-time
Part-Time Job Man
PAN
Part-Time Job Master
ID Photo Booth
?
?
Resumé
Gender
M · F
Miia
Lamia
Kurusu Kimihito
090-XXXX-XXXX
E-mail
TEL
SEVENSON Family
Onigiri Fair Happening Now
Now looking for part-time workers!
Seeking students or young adults!
Liminals encouraged to apply!
ALL RIGHT...
HERE GOES NOTHING!

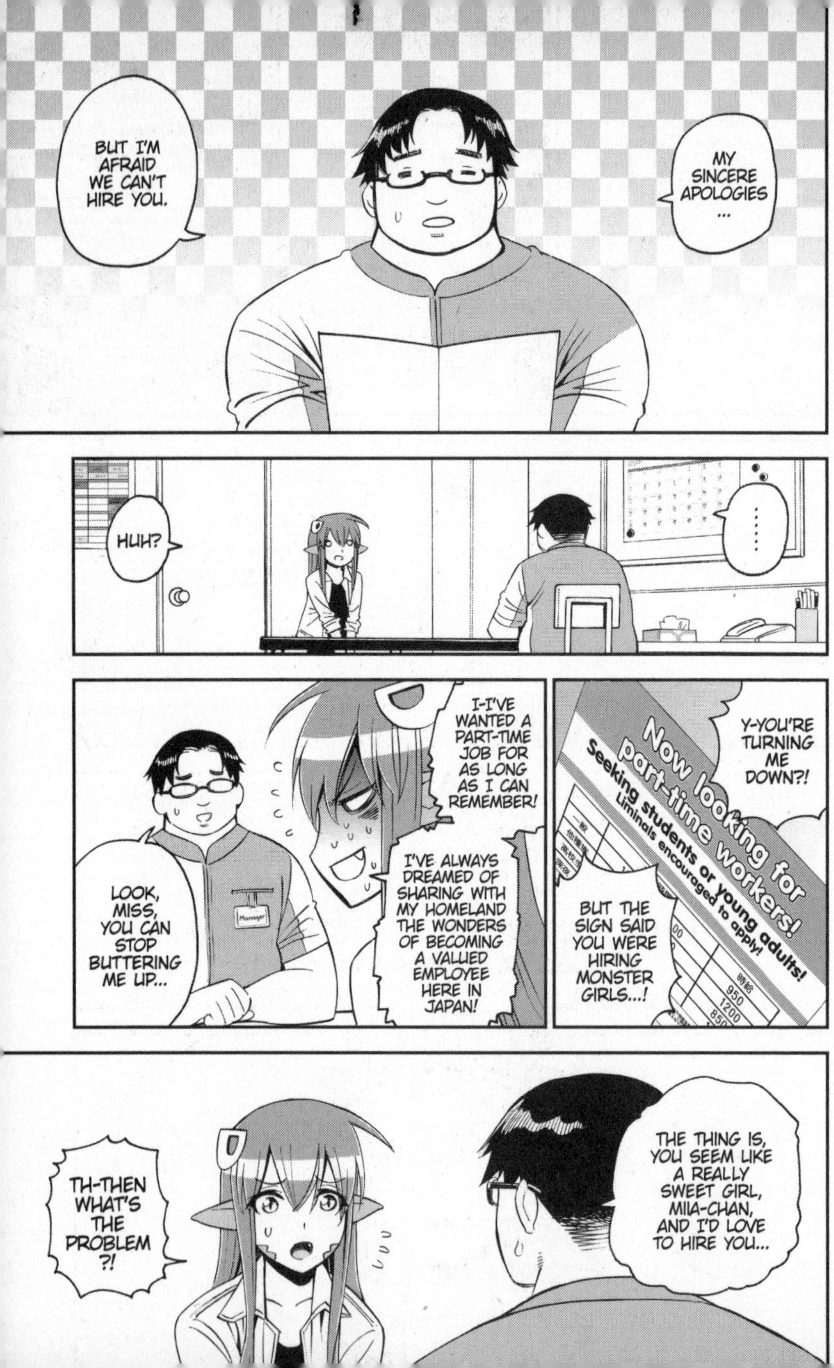
MY SINCERE APOLOGIES ...
BUT I'M AFRAID WE CAN'T HIRE YOU.
......
HUH?
Y-YOU'RE TURNING ME DOWN?!
Now looking for part-time workers!
Seeking students or young adults!
Liminals encouraged to apply!
BUT THE SIGN SAID YOU WERE HIRING MONSTER GIRLS...!
I-I'VE WANTED A PART-TIME JOB FOR AS LONG AS I CAN REMEMBER!
I'VE ALWAYS DREAMED OF SHARING WITH MY HOMELAND THE WONDERS OF BECOMING A VALUED EMPLOYEE HERE IN JAPAN!
LOOK, MISS, YOU CAN STOP BUTTERING ME UP...
Manager
THE THING IS, YOU SEEM LIKE A REALLY SWEET GIRL, MIIA-CHAN, AND I'D LOVE TO HIRE YOU...
TH-THEN WHAT'S THE PROBLEM?!

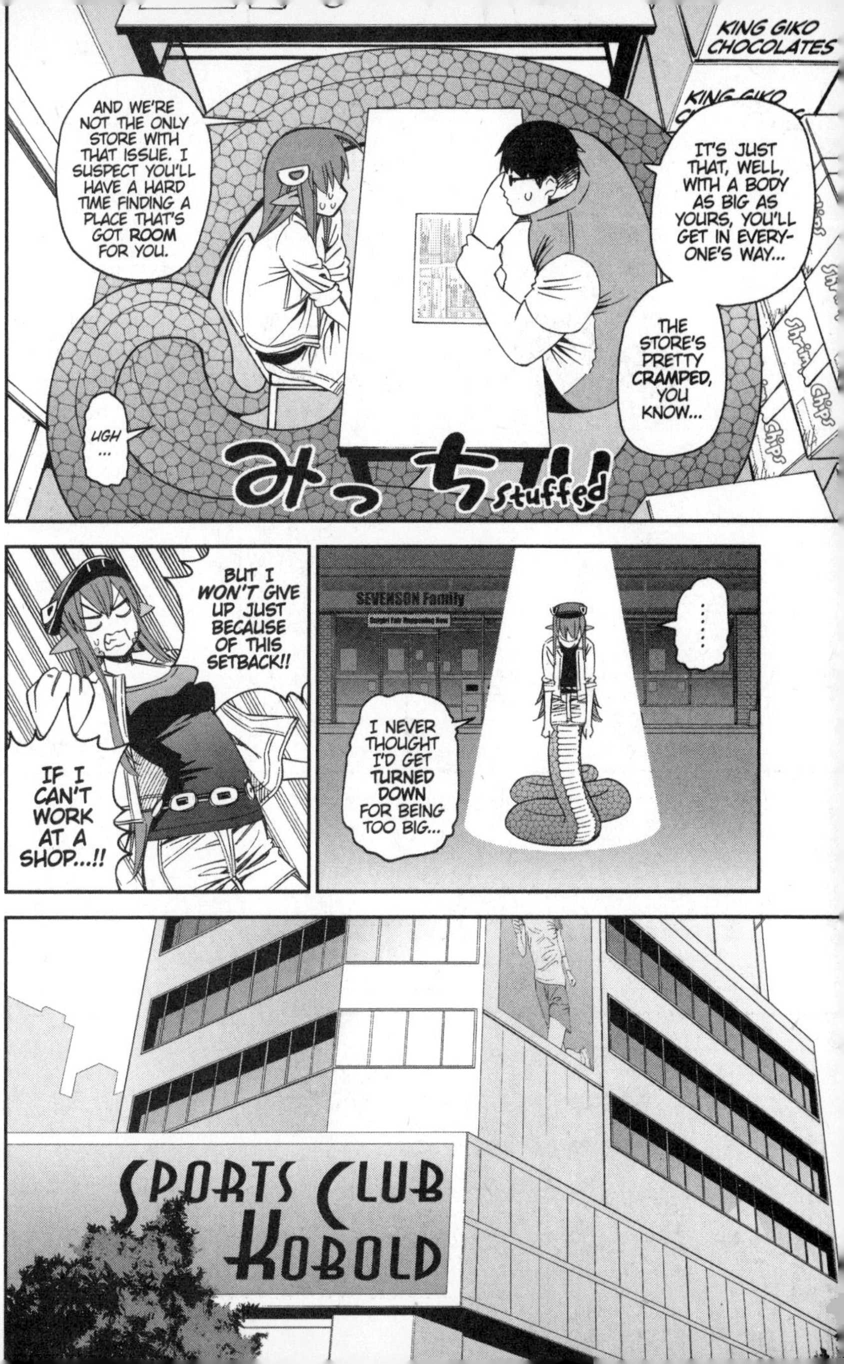
KING GIKO CHOCOLATES
IT'S JUST THAT, WELL, WITH A BODY AS BIG AS YOURS, YOU'LL GET IN EVERY-ONE'S WAY...
THE STORE'S PRETTY CRAMPED, YOU KNOW...
AND WE'RE NOT THE ONLY STORE WITH THAT ISSUE. I SUSPECT YOU'LL HAVE A HARD TIME FINDING A PLACE THAT'S GOT ROOM FOR YOU.
UGH ...
みっち stuffed
SEVENSON Family
......
I NEVER THOUGHT I'D GET TURNED DOWN FOR BEING TOO BIG...
BUT I *WON'T* GIVE UP JUST BECAUSE OF THIS SETBACK!!
IF I CAN'T WORK AT A SHOP...!!
SPORTS CLUB KOBOLD

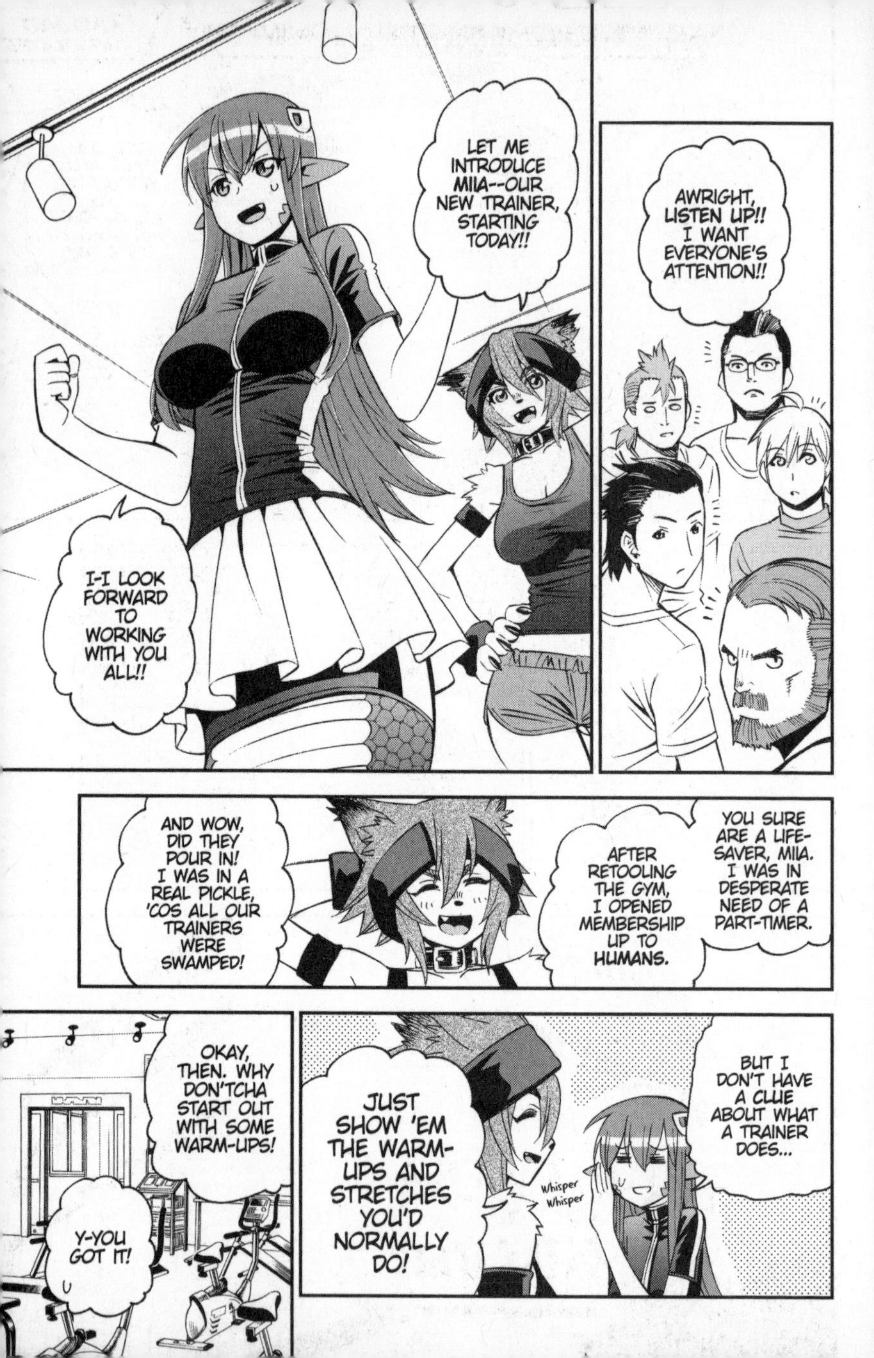
AWRIGHT, LISTEN UP!! I WANT EVERYONE'S ATTENTION!!
LET ME INTRODUCE MIIA--OUR NEW TRAINER, STARTING TODAY!!
I-I LOOK FORWARD TO WORKING WITH YOU ALL!!
YOU SURE ARE A LIFE-SAVER, MIIA. I WAS IN DESPERATE NEED OF A PART-TIMER.
AFTER RETOOLING THE GYM, I OPENED MEMBERSHIP UP TO HUMANS.
AND WOW, DID THEY POUR IN! I WAS IN A REAL PICKLE, 'COS ALL OUR TRAINERS WERE SWAMPED!
BUT I DON'T HAVE A CLUE ABOUT WHAT A TRAINER DOES...
Whisper Whisper
JUST SHOW 'EM THE WARM-UPS AND STRETCHES YOU'D NORMALLY DO!
OKAY, THEN. WHY DON'TCHA START OUT WITH SOME WARM-UPS!
Y-YOU GOT IT!

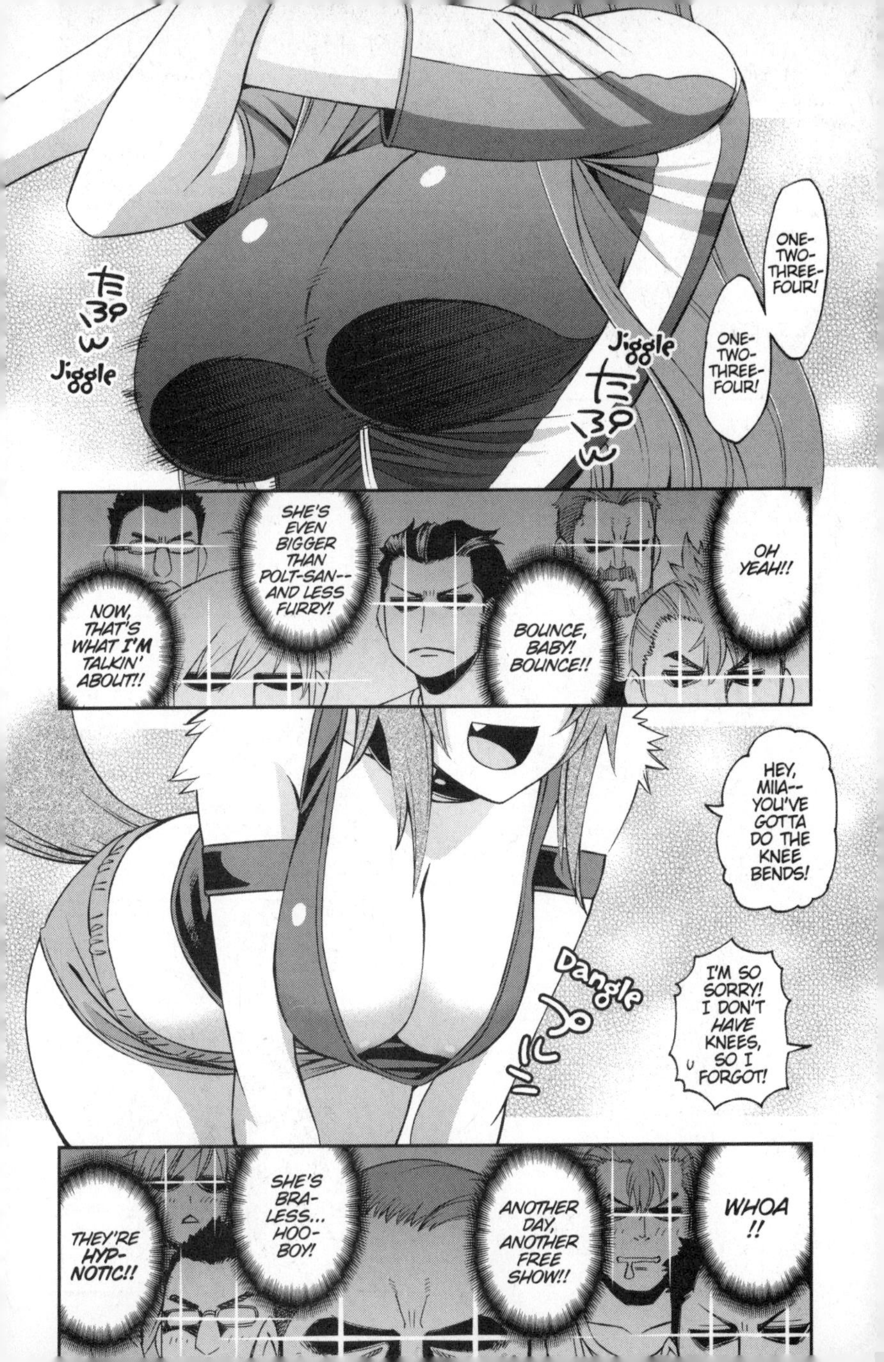
ONE-TWO-THREE-FOUR!
ONE-TWO-THREE-FOUR!
Jiggle
Jiggle
OH YEAH!!
BOUNCE, BABY! BOUNCE!!
SHE'S EVEN BIGGER THAN POLT-SAN--AND LESS FURRY!
NOW, THAT'S WHAT I'M TALKIN' ABOUT!!
HEY, MIIA--YOU'VE GOTTA DO THE KNEE BENDS!
I'M SO SORRY! I DON'T HAVE KNEES, SO I FORGOT!
Dangle
WHOA!!
ANOTHER DAY, ANOTHER FREE SHOW!!
SHE'S BRA-LESS... HOO-BOY!
THEY'RE HYP-NOTIC!!

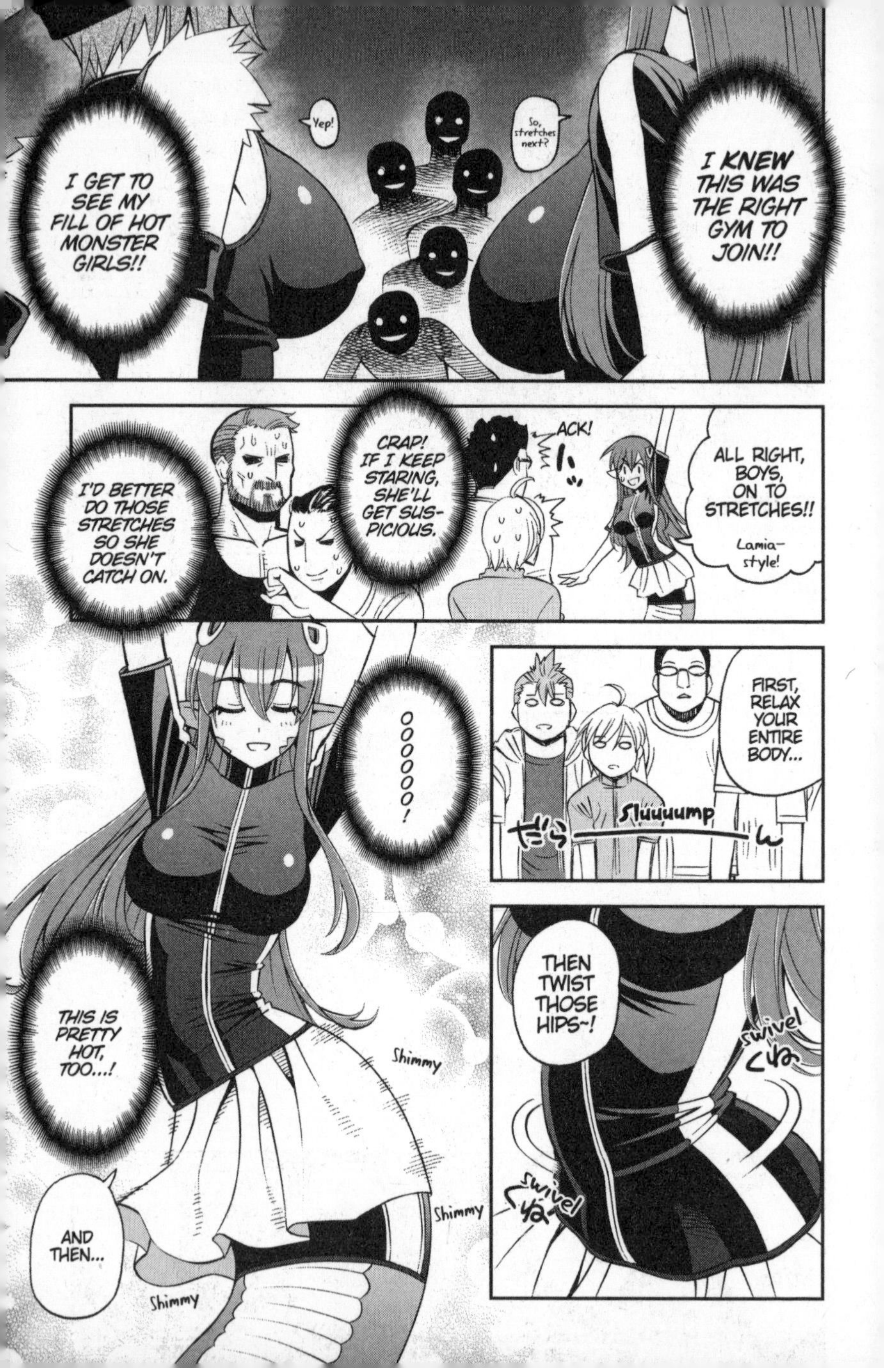
I KNEW THIS WAS THE RIGHT GYM TO JOIN!!
So, stretches next?
Yep!
I GET TO SEE MY FILL OF HOT MONSTER GIRLS!!
ALL RIGHT, BOYS, ON TO STRETCHES!!
Lamia-style!
ACK!
CRAP! IF I KEEP STARING, SHE'LL GET SUS-PICIOUS.
I'D BETTER DO THOSE STRETCHES SO SHE DOESN'T CATCH ON.
FIRST, RELAX YOUR ENTIRE BODY...
Sluuuump
THEN TWIST THOSE HIPS~!
swivel
swivel
OOOOOOO!
THIS IS PRETTY HOT, TOO...!
Shimmy
Shimmy
AND THEN...
Shimmy

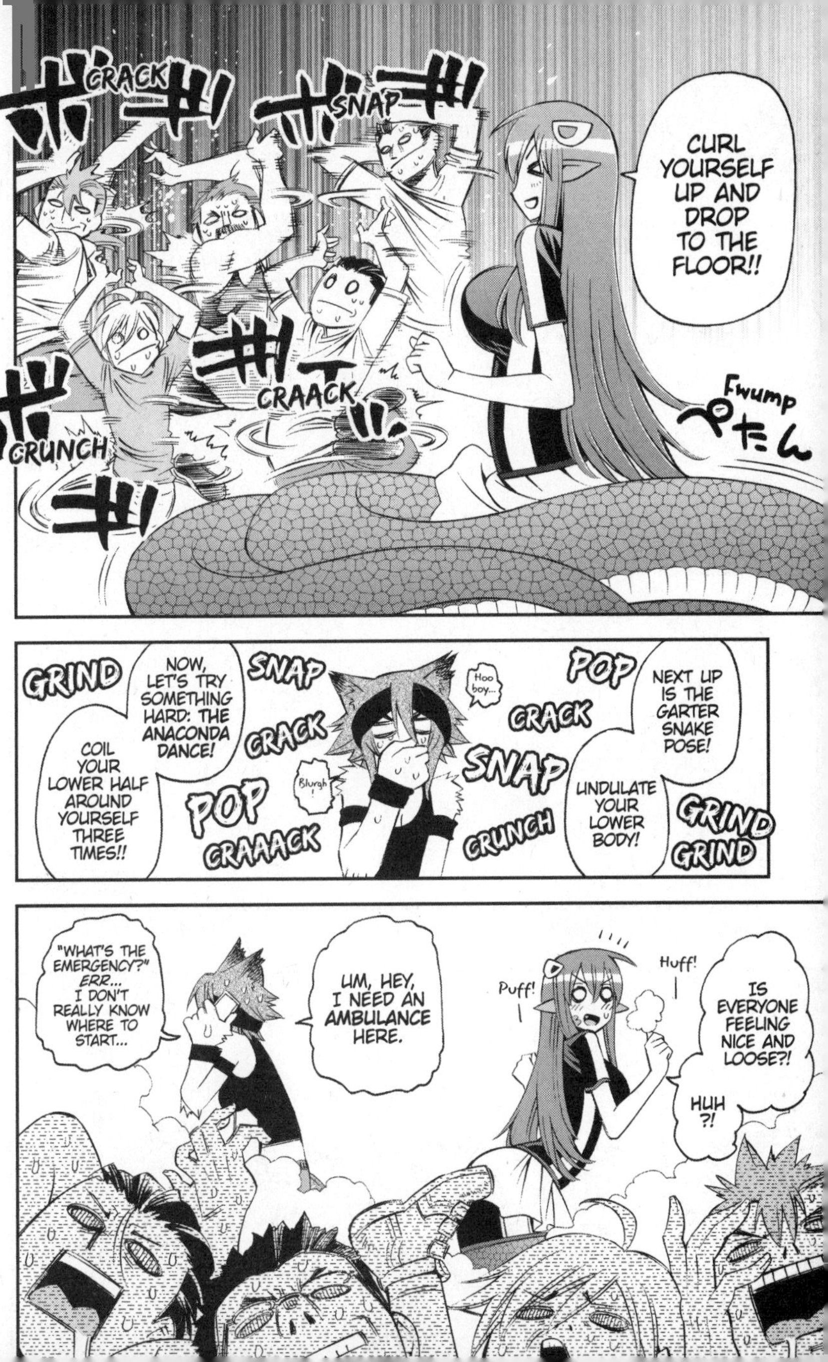
CURL YOURSELF UP AND DROP TO THE FLOOR!!
Fwump
SNAP
CRACK
CRAACK
CRUNCH
NEXT UP IS THE GARTER SNAKE POSE!
UNDULATE YOUR LOWER BODY!
POP
GRIND GRIND
CRACK
SNAP
CRUNCH
Hoo boy...
Blurgh!
NOW, LET'S TRY SOMETHING HARD: THE ANACONDA DANCE!
SNAP
CRACK
POP
CRAAACK
COIL YOUR LOWER HALF AROUND YOURSELF THREE TIMES!!
GRIND
IS EVERYONE FEELING NICE AND LOOSE?!
Huff!
Puff!
HUH?!
UM, HEY, I NEED AN AMBULANCE HERE.
"WHAT'S THE EMERGENCY?" ERR... I DON'T REALLY KNOW WHERE TO START...

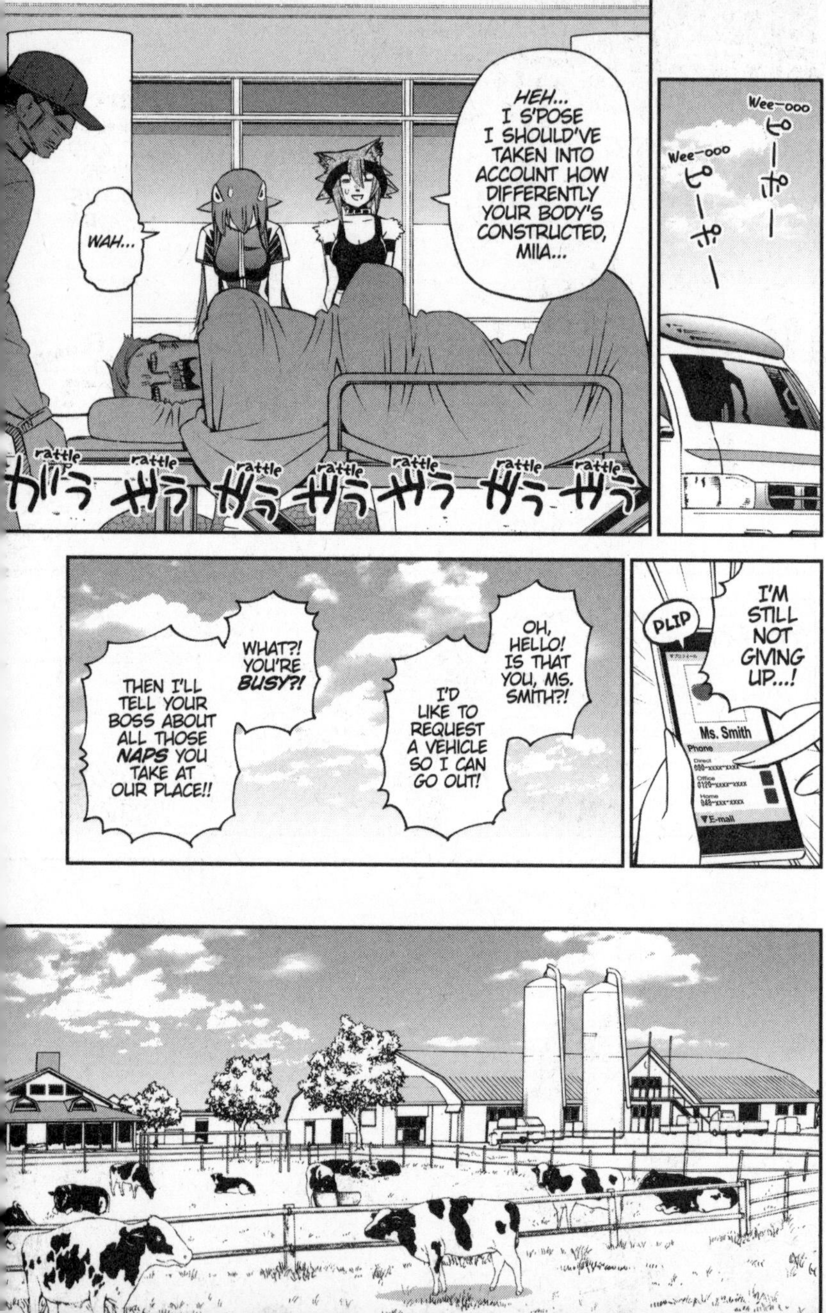
Wee-ooo
ピーポー
Wee-ooo
ピーポー
HEH... I S'POSE I SHOULD'VE TAKEN INTO ACCOUNT HOW DIFFERENTLY YOUR BODY'S CONSTRUCTED, MIIA...
WAH...
rattle ガラ
rattle ガラ
rattle ガラ
rattle ガラ
rattle ガラ
rattle ガラ
rattle ガラ
PLIP
I'M STILL NOT GIVING UP...!
Ms. Smith
Phone
Direct
090-xxxx-xxxx
Office
0120-xxxx-xxxx
Home
042-xxx-xxxx
▼E-mail
OH, HELLO! IS THAT YOU, MS. SMITH?!
I'D LIKE TO REQUEST A VEHICLE SO I CAN GO OUT!
WHAT?! YOU'RE *BUSY?!*
THEN I'LL TELL YOUR BOSS ABOUT ALL THOSE *NAPS* YOU TAKE AT OUR PLACE!!

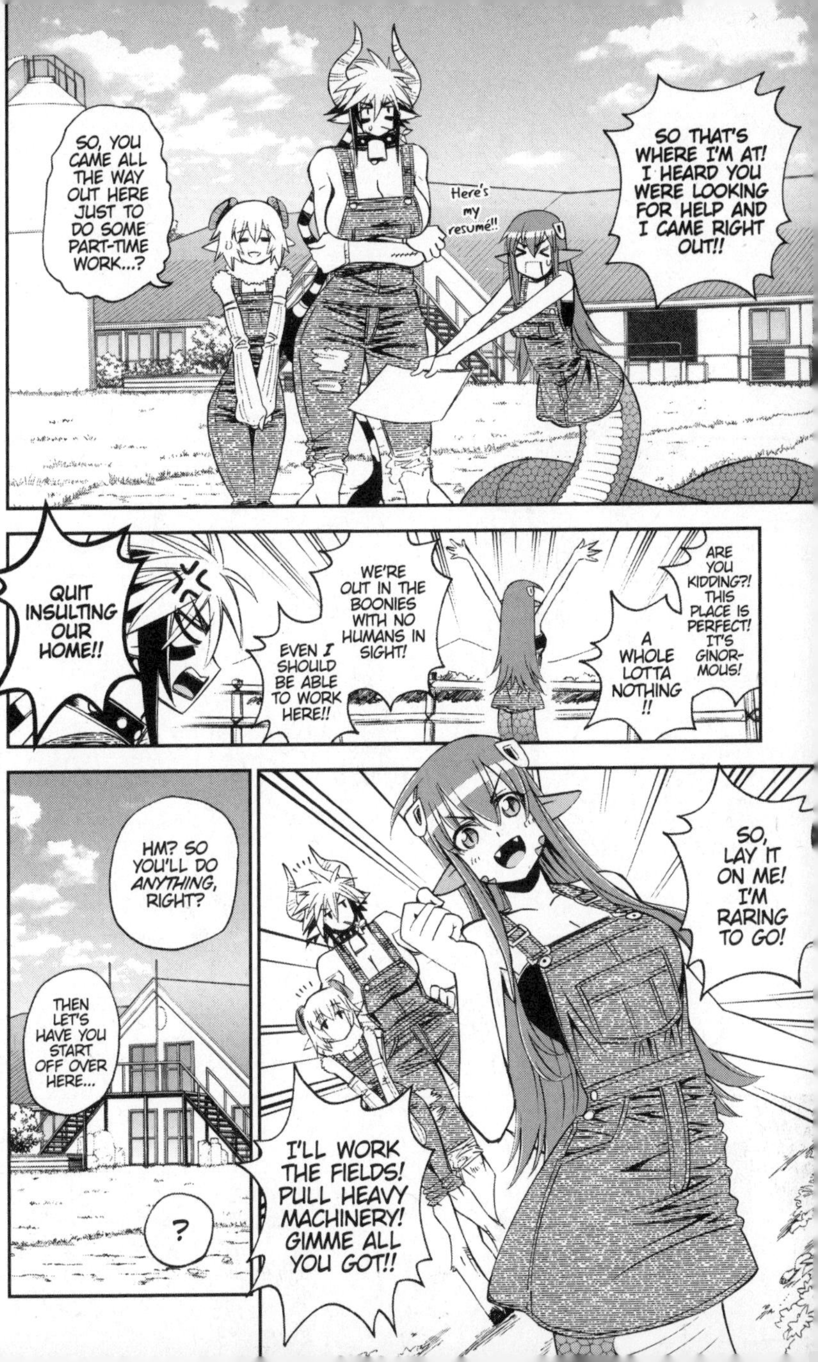
SO THAT'S WHERE I'M AT! I HEARD YOU WERE LOOKING FOR HELP AND I CAME RIGHT OUT!!
Here's my resume!!
SO, YOU CAME ALL THE WAY OUT HERE JUST TO DO SOME PART-TIME WORK...?
ARE YOU KIDDING?! THIS PLACE IS PERFECT! IT'S GINORMOUS!
A WHOLE LOTTA NOTHING!!
WE'RE OUT IN THE BOONIES WITH NO HUMANS IN SIGHT!
EVEN *I* SHOULD BE ABLE TO WORK HERE!!
QUIT INSULTING OUR HOME!!
SO, LAY IT ON ME! I'M RARING TO GO!
I'LL WORK THE FIELDS! PULL HEAVY MACHINERY! GIMME ALL YOU GOT!!
HM? SO YOU'LL DO *ANYTHING*, RIGHT?
THEN LET'S HAVE YOU START OFF OVER HERE...
?

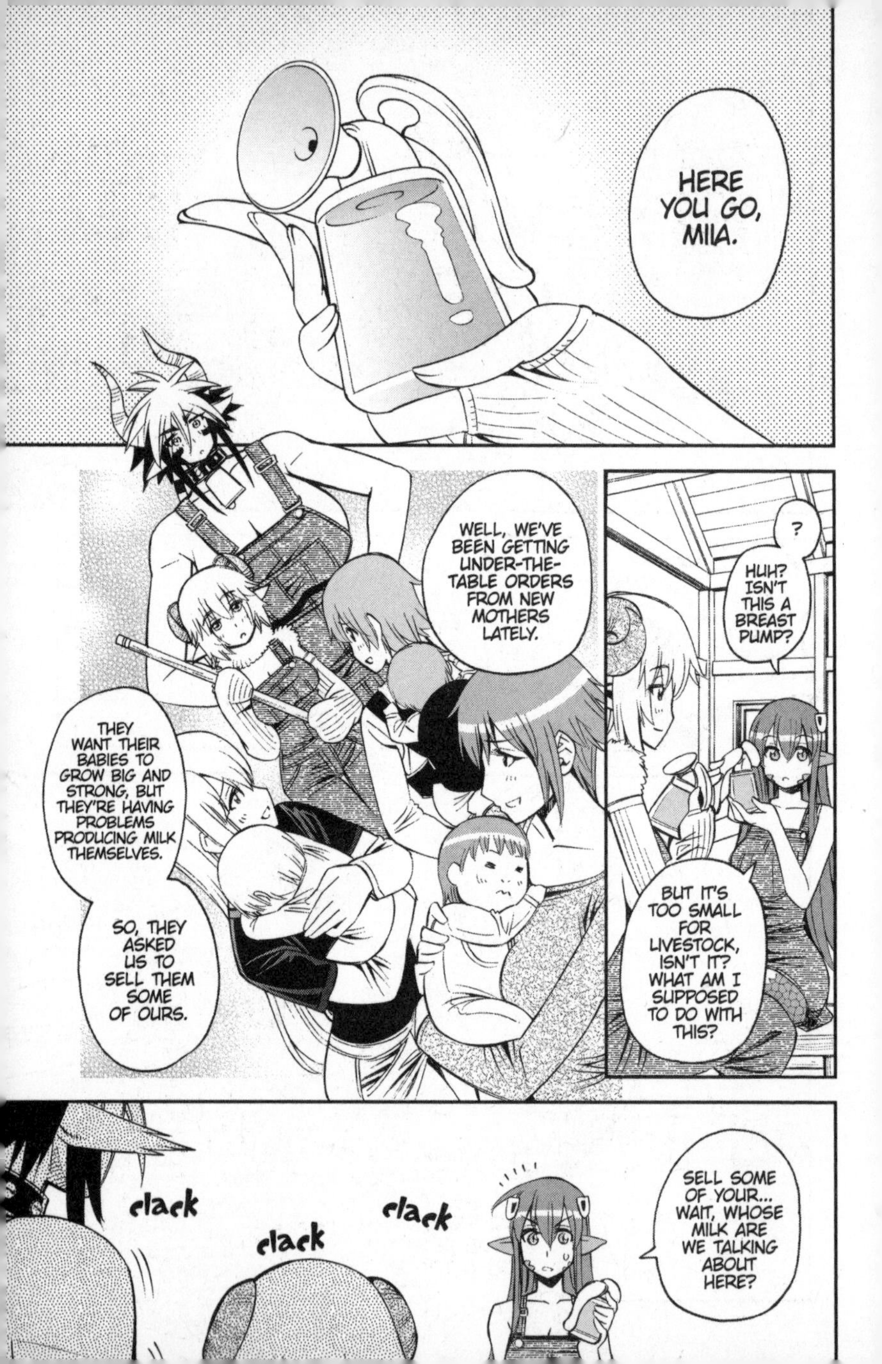
HERE YOU GO, MIIA.
?
HUH? ISN'T THIS A BREAST PUMP?
BUT IT'S TOO SMALL FOR LIVESTOCK, ISN'T IT? WHAT AM I SUPPOSED TO DO WITH THIS?
WELL, WE'VE BEEN GETTING UNDER-THE-TABLE ORDERS FROM NEW MOTHERS LATELY.
THEY WANT THEIR BABIES TO GROW BIG AND STRONG, BUT THEY'RE HAVING PROBLEMS PRODUCING MILK THEMSELVES.
SO, THEY ASKED US TO SELL THEM SOME OF OURS.
SELL SOME OF YOUR... WAIT, WHOSE MILK ARE WE TALKING ABOUT HERE?
clack
clack
clack

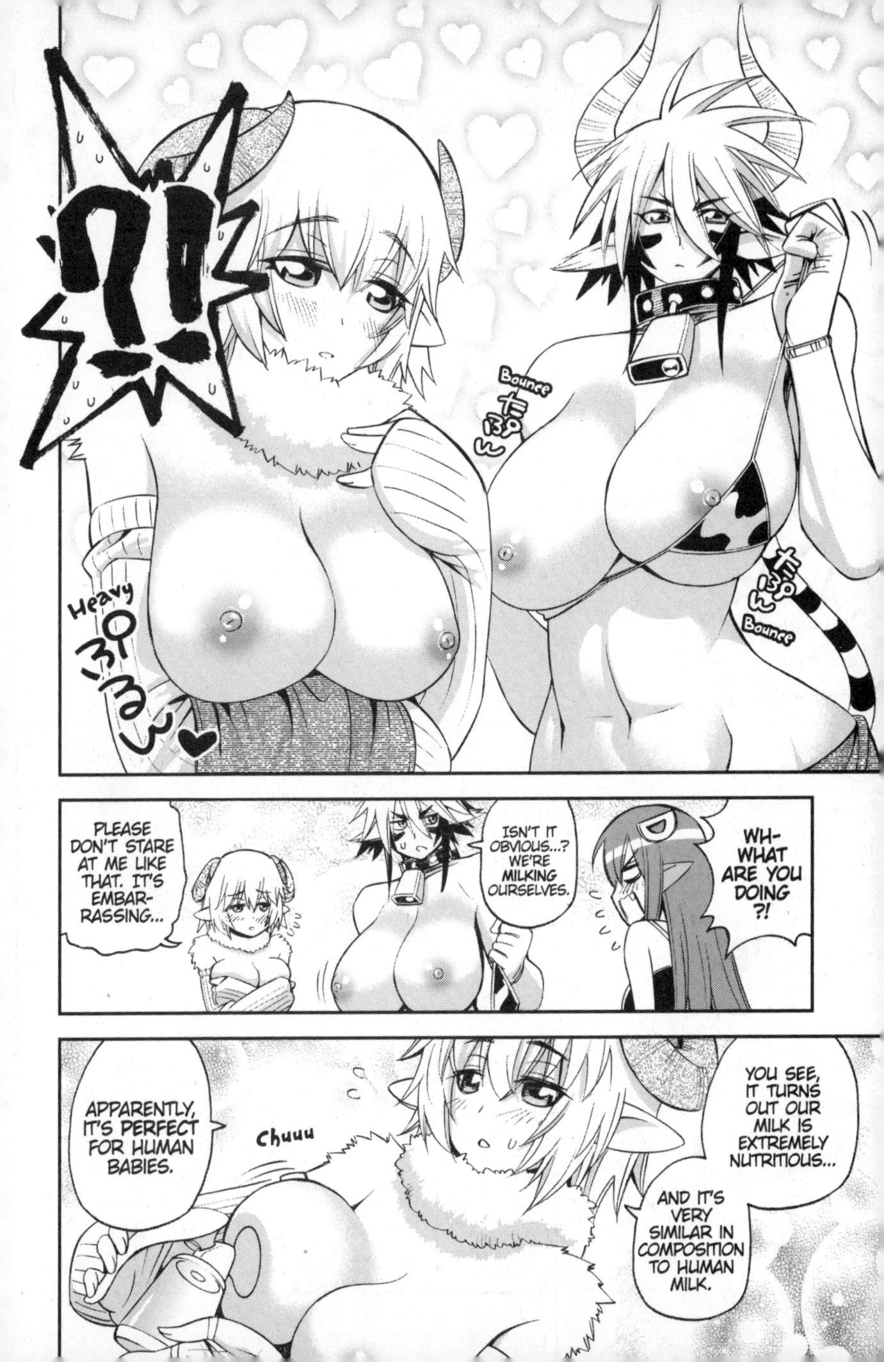
Bounce
たぷん
Bounce
たぷん
?!
Heavy
ぷるるん
WH- WHAT ARE YOU DOING ?!
ISN'T IT OBVIOUS...? WE'RE MILKING OURSELVES.
PLEASE DON'T STARE AT ME LIKE THAT. IT'S EMBARRASSING...
YOU SEE, IT TURNS OUT OUR MILK IS EXTREMELY NUTRITIOUS...
AND IT'S VERY SIMILAR IN COMPOSITION TO HUMAN MILK.
Chuuu
APPARENTLY, IT'S PERFECT FOR HUMAN BABIES.

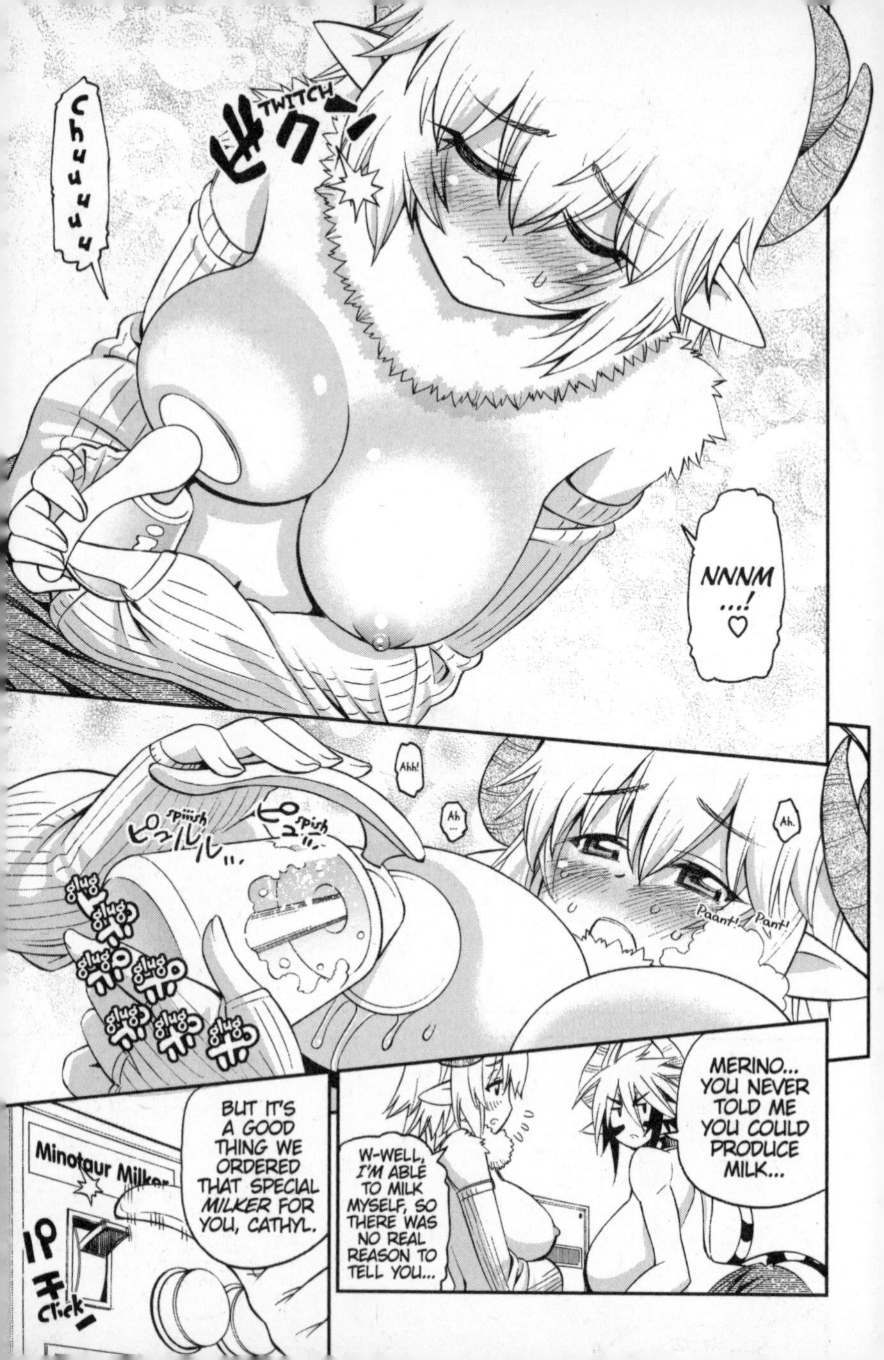
TWITCH
Chuuuuuuu
NNNM...! ♡
Ah.
Pant!
Paant!
Ah...
Ahh!
spish
spiiish
glug glug glug glug glug glug glug glug
MERINO... YOU NEVER TOLD ME YOU COULD PRODUCE MILK...
W-WELL, *I'M* ABLE TO MILK MYSELF, SO THERE WAS NO REAL REASON TO TELL YOU...
BUT IT'S A GOOD THING WE ORDERED THAT SPECIAL *MILKER* FOR YOU, CATHYL.
Minotaur Milker
click

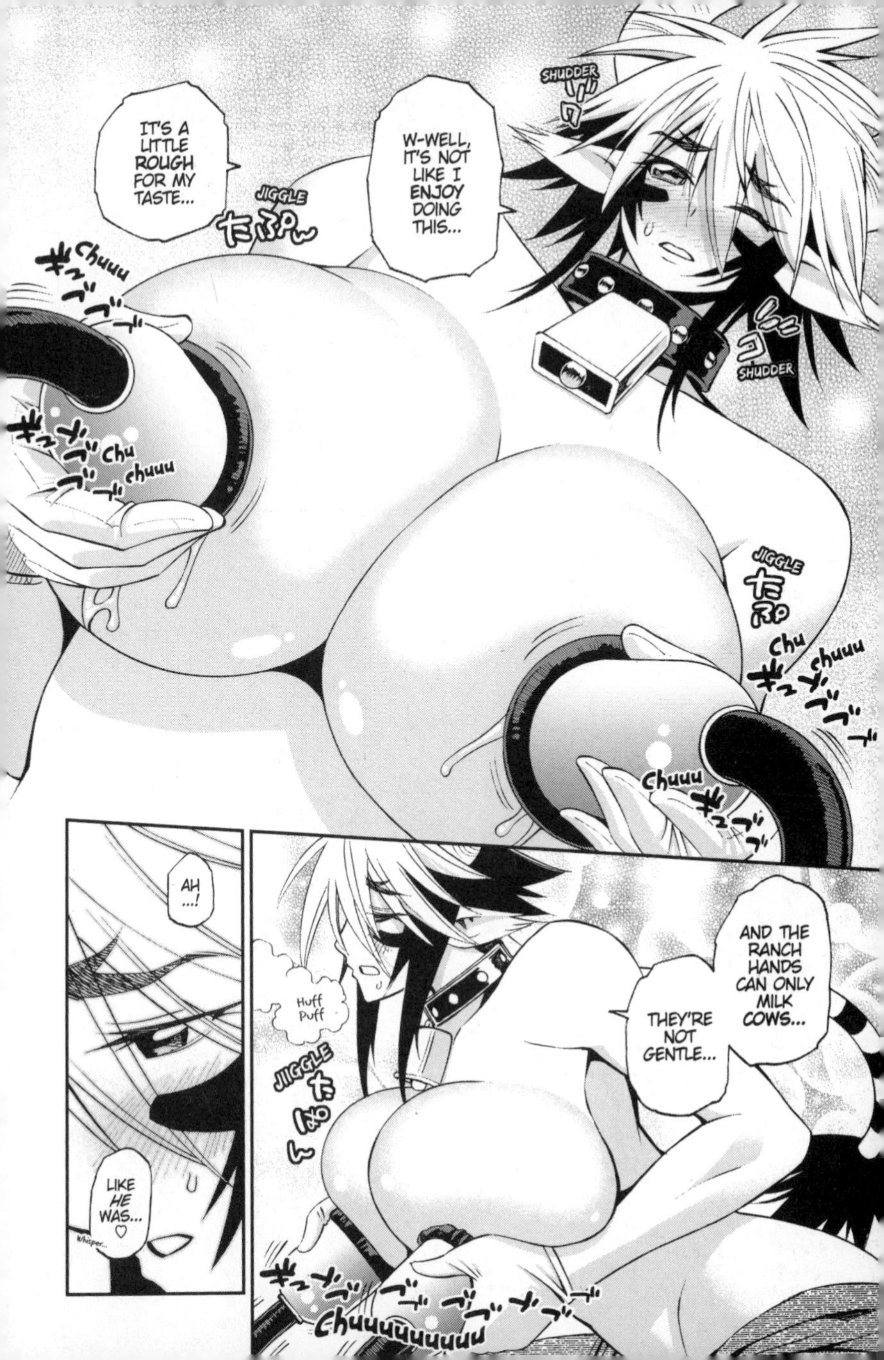
SHUDDER
W-WELL, IT'S NOT LIKE I ENJOY DOING THIS...
JIGGLE
IT'S A LITTLE ROUGH FOR MY TASTE...
Chuuu
Chu chuuu
SHUDDER
JIGGLE
Chu chuuu
Chuuu
AND THE RANCH HANDS CAN ONLY MILK COWS...
THEY'RE NOT GENTLE...
Huff Puff
JIIGGLE
Chuuuuuuuuuu
AH ...!
LIKE HE WAS...♡
Whisper...

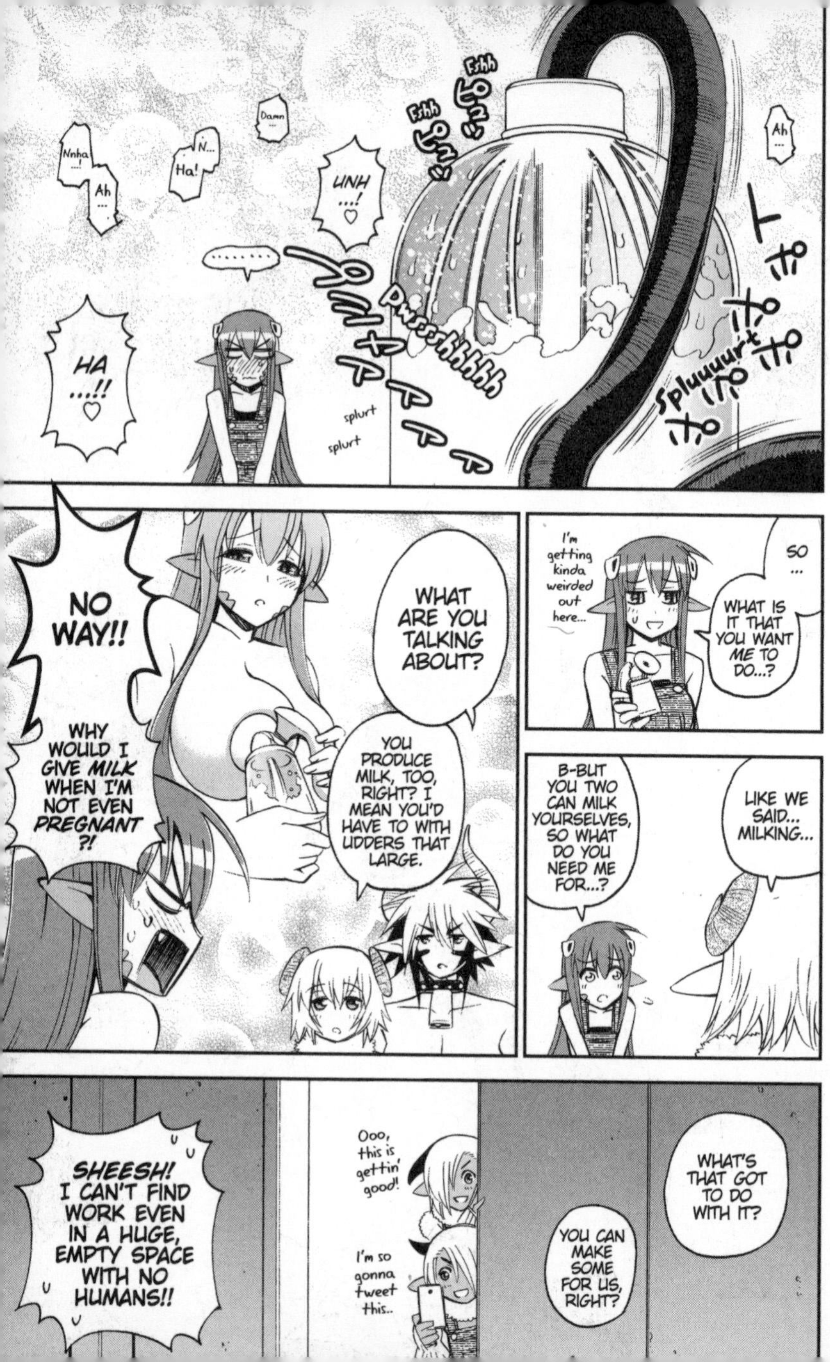
Ah ...
Fshh
Fshh
Damn ...
UNH ...! ♡
N... Ha!
Nnha ...! Ah ...
....
Spluuuurt
Pwsssshhhhhh
HA ...!! ♡
splurt
splurt
SO ... WHAT IS IT THAT YOU WANT ME TO DO...?
I'm getting kinda weirded out here...
LIKE WE SAID... MILKING...
B-BUT YOU TWO CAN MILK YOURSELVES, SO WHAT DO YOU NEED ME FOR...?
WHAT ARE YOU TALKING ABOUT?
YOU PRODUCE MILK, TOO, RIGHT? I MEAN YOU'D HAVE TO WITH UDDERS THAT LARGE.
NO WAY!!
WHY WOULD I GIVE MILK WHEN I'M NOT EVEN PREGNANT ?!
WHAT'S THAT GOT TO DO WITH IT?
YOU CAN MAKE SOME FOR US, RIGHT?
Ooo, this is gettin' good!
I'm so gonna tweet this..
SHEESH! I CAN'T FIND WORK EVEN IN A HUGE, EMPTY SPACE WITH NO HUMANS!!

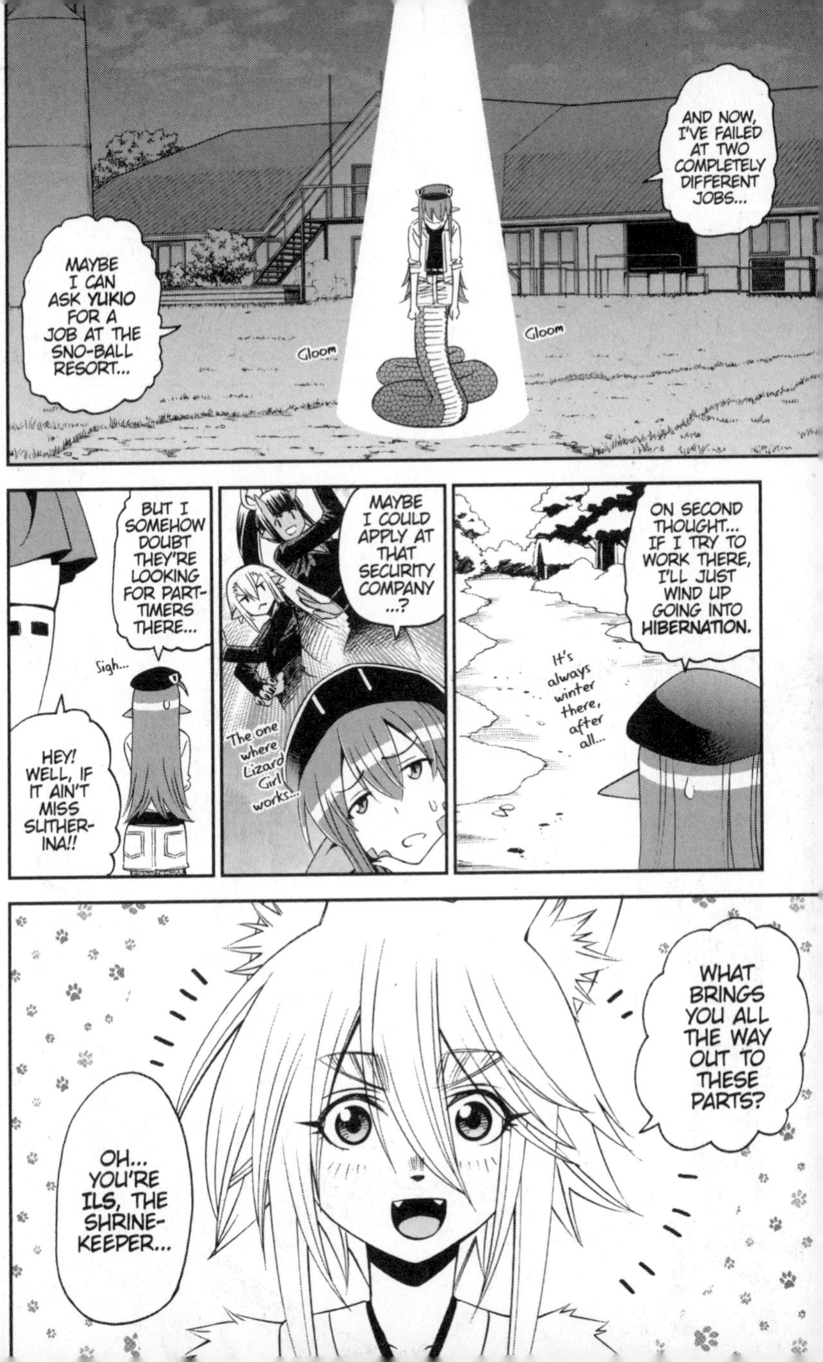
AND NOW, I'VE FAILED AT TWO COMPLETELY DIFFERENT JOBS...
Gloom
Gloom
MAYBE I CAN ASK YUKIO FOR A JOB AT THE SNO-BALL RESORT...
ON SECOND THOUGHT... IF I TRY TO WORK THERE, I'LL JUST WIND UP GOING INTO HIBERNATION.
It's always winter there, after all...
MAYBE I COULD APPLY AT THAT SECURITY COMPANY ...?
The one where Lizard Girl works...
BUT I SOMEHOW DOUBT THEY'RE LOOKING FOR PART-TIMERS THERE...
Sigh...
HEY! WELL, IF IT AIN'T MISS SLITHER-INA!!
WHAT BRINGS YOU ALL THE WAY OUT TO THESE PARTS?
OH... YOU'RE ILS, THE SHRINE-KEEPER...

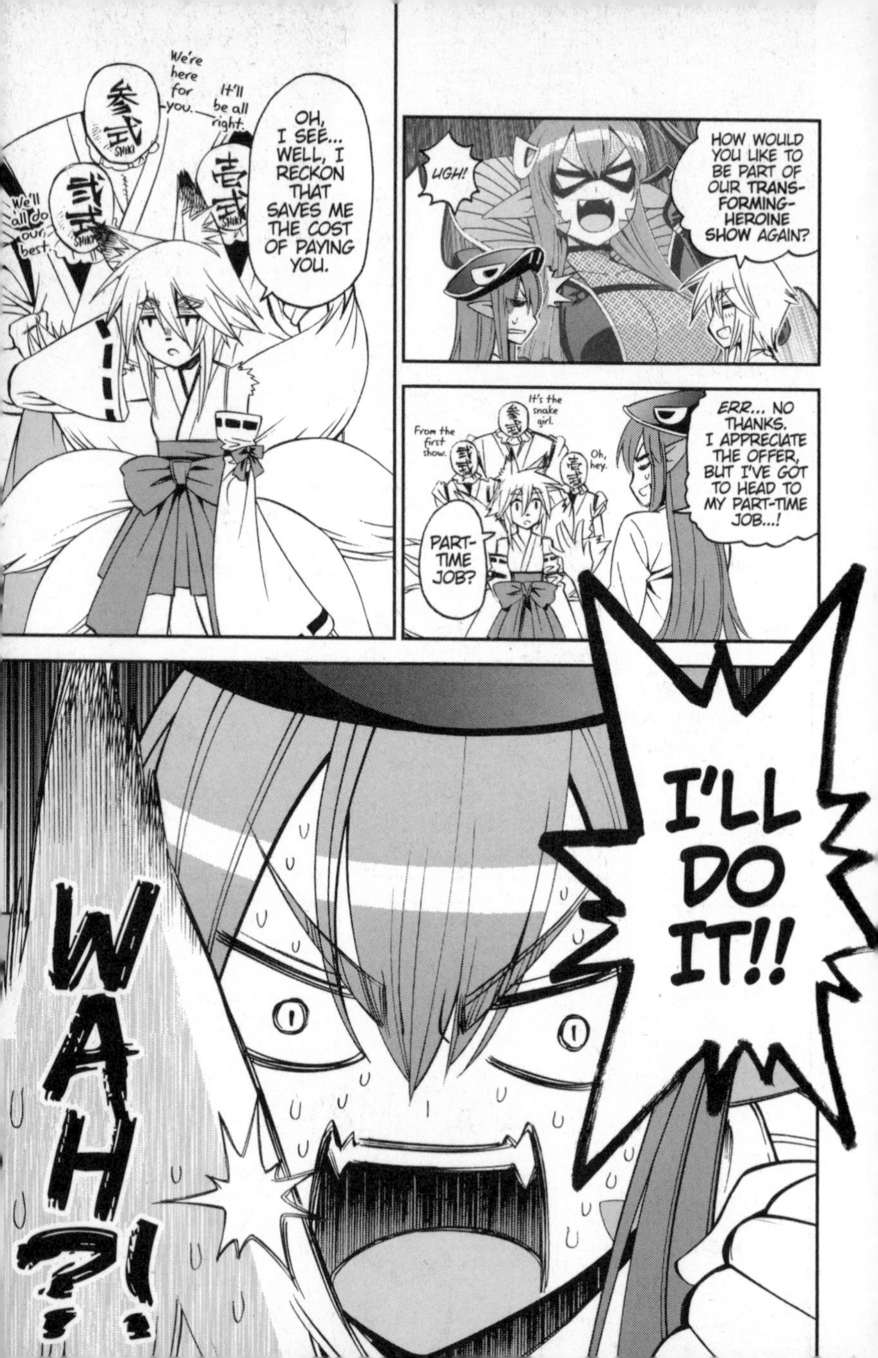
HOW WOULD YOU LIKE TO BE PART OF OUR TRANS-FORMING-HEROINE SHOW AGAIN?
UGH!
ERR... NO THANKS. I APPRECIATE THE OFFER, BUT I'VE GOT TO HEAD TO MY PART-TIME JOB...!
Oh, hey.
It's the snake girl.
From the first show.
PART-TIME JOB?
OH, I SEE... WELL, I RECKON THAT SAVES ME THE COST OF PAYING YOU.
It'll be all right.
壱式
SHIKI
We're here for you.
参式
SHIKI
We'll all do our best.
弐式
SHIKI
I'LL DO IT!!
WAH?!

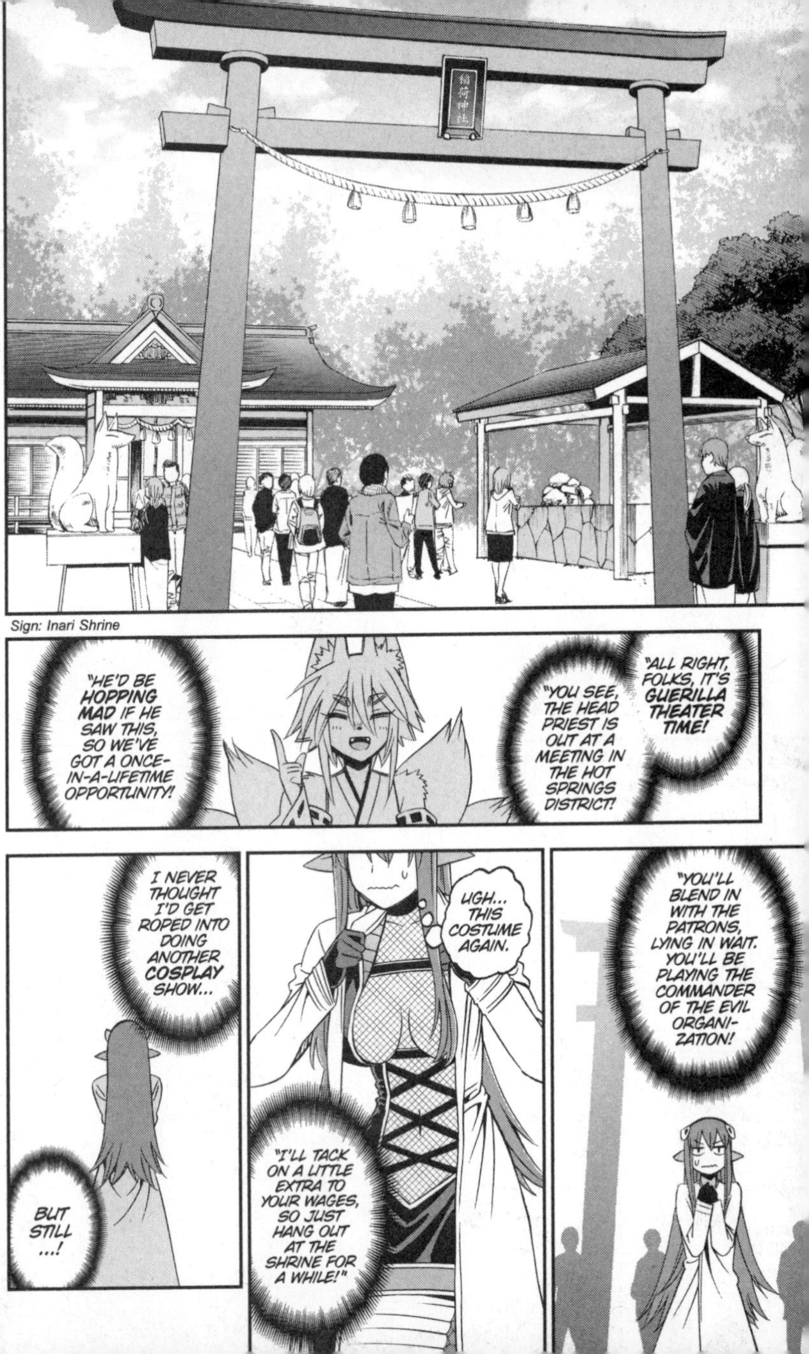
Sign: Inari Shrine
"ALL RIGHT, FOLKS, IT'S GUERILLA THEATER TIME!
"YOU SEE, THE HEAD PRIEST IS OUT AT A MEETING IN THE HOT SPRINGS DISTRICT!
"HE'D BE HOPPING MAD IF HE SAW THIS, SO WE'VE GOT A ONCE-IN-A-LIFETIME OPPORTUNITY!
"YOU'LL BLEND IN WITH THE PATRONS, LYING IN WAIT. YOU'LL BE PLAYING THE COMMANDER OF THE EVIL ORGANI-ZATION!
UGH... THIS COSTUME AGAIN.
"I'LL TACK ON A LITTLE EXTRA TO YOUR WAGES, SO JUST HANG OUT AT THE SHRINE FOR A WHILE!"
I NEVER THOUGHT I'D GET ROPED INTO DOING ANOTHER COSPLAY SHOW...
BUT STILL ...!

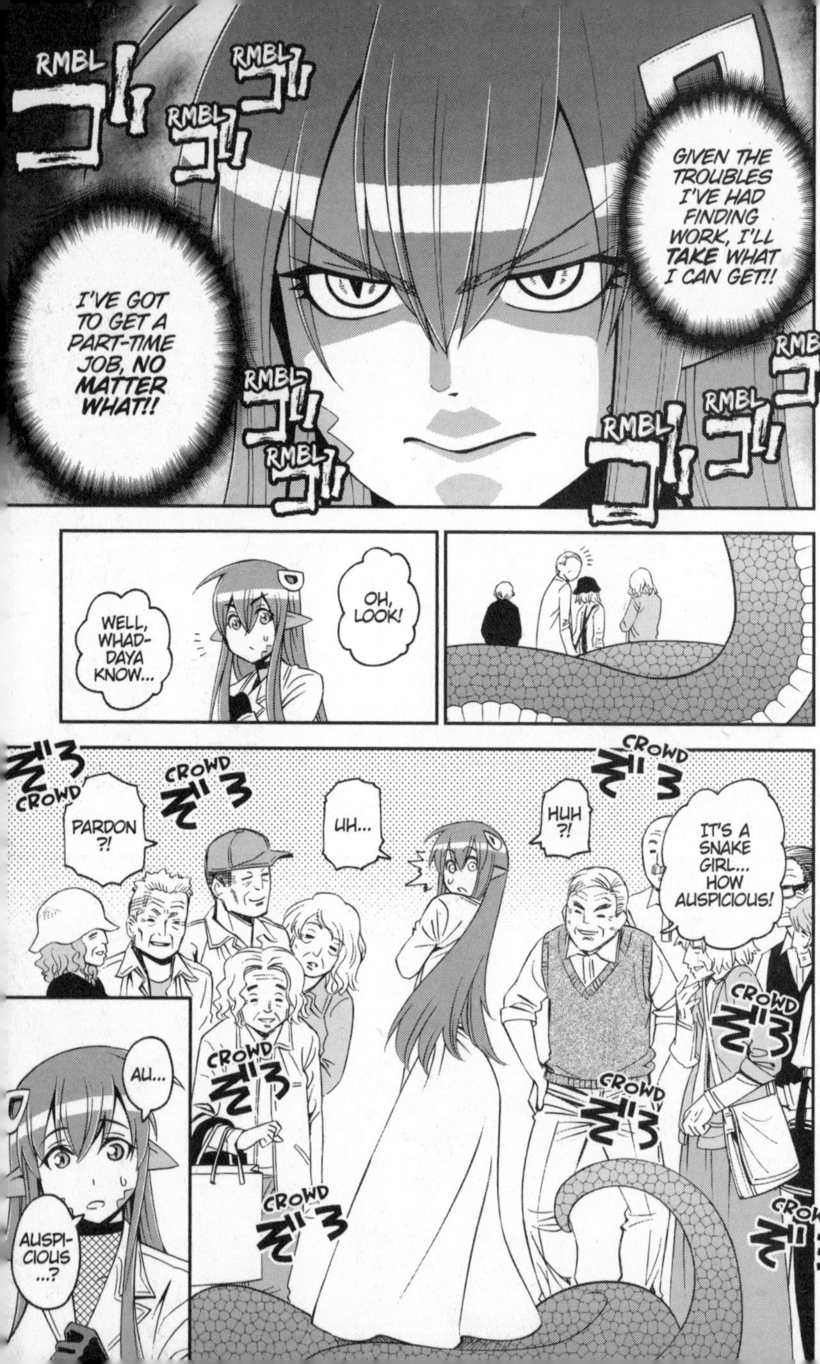
RMBL
RMBL
RMBL
GIVEN THE TROUBLES I'VE HAD FINDING WORK, I'LL TAKE WHAT I CAN GET!!
I'VE GOT TO GET A PART-TIME JOB, NO MATTER WHAT!!
RMBL
RMBL
RMBL
RMBL
RMBL
OH, LOOK!
WELL, WHADDAYA KNOW...
CROWD
IT'S A SNAKE GIRL... HOW AUSPICIOUS!
HUH ?!
UH...
CROWD
PARDON ?!
CROWD
CROWD
CROWD
CROWD
CROWD
CROWD
AU...
AUSPICIOUS...?

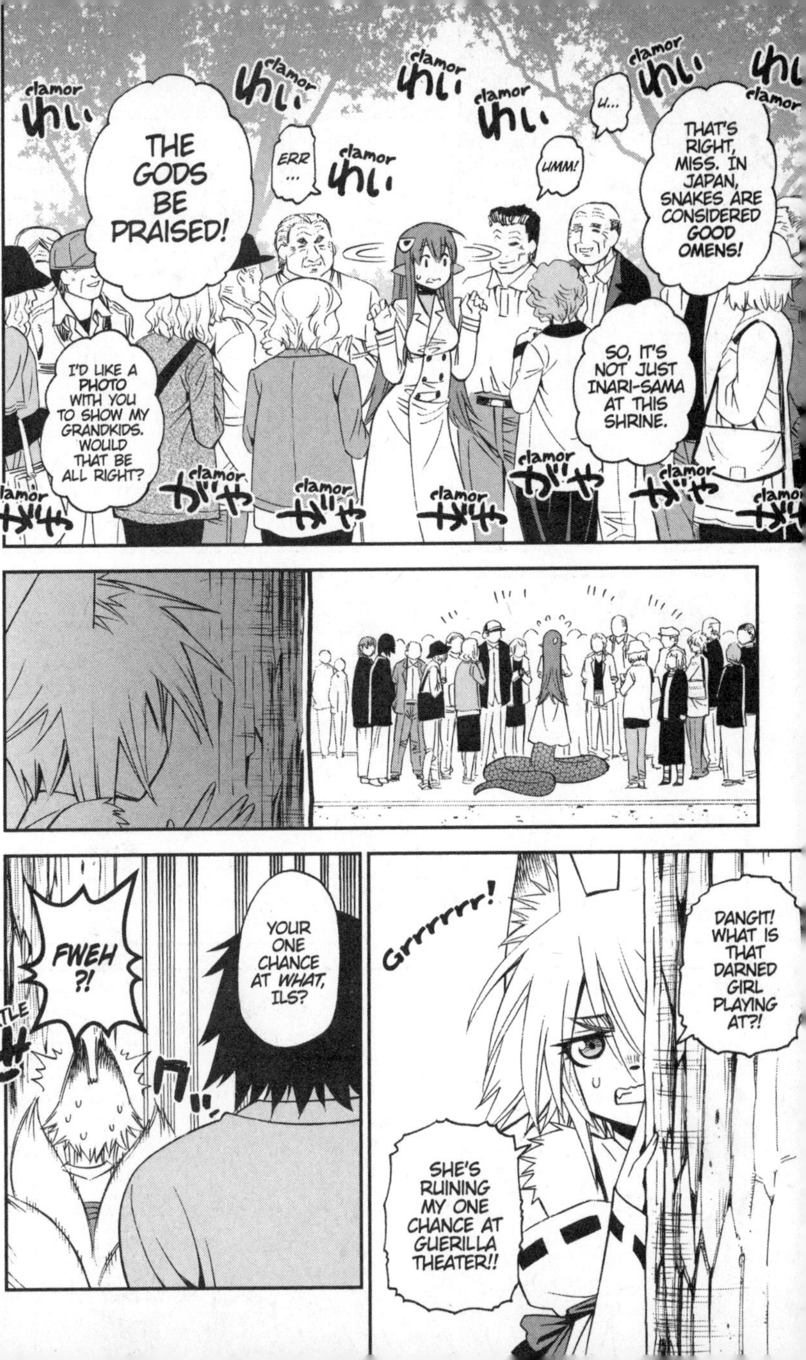
clamor
clamor
THAT'S RIGHT, MISS. IN JAPAN, SNAKES ARE CONSIDERED GOOD OMENS!
U...
clamor
UMM!
clamor
clamor
ERR ...
clamor
THE GODS BE PRAISED!
clamor
SO, IT'S NOT JUST INARI-SAMA AT THIS SHRINE.
I'D LIKE A PHOTO WITH YOU TO SHOW MY GRANDKIDS. WOULD THAT BE ALL RIGHT?
clamor
clamor
clamor
clamor
clamor
clamor
clamor
Grrrrrr!
DANGIT! WHAT IS THAT DARNED GIRL PLAYING AT?!
SHE'S RUINING MY ONE CHANCE AT GUERILLA THEATER!!
YOUR ONE CHANCE AT WHAT, ILS?
FWEH ?!
STARTLE

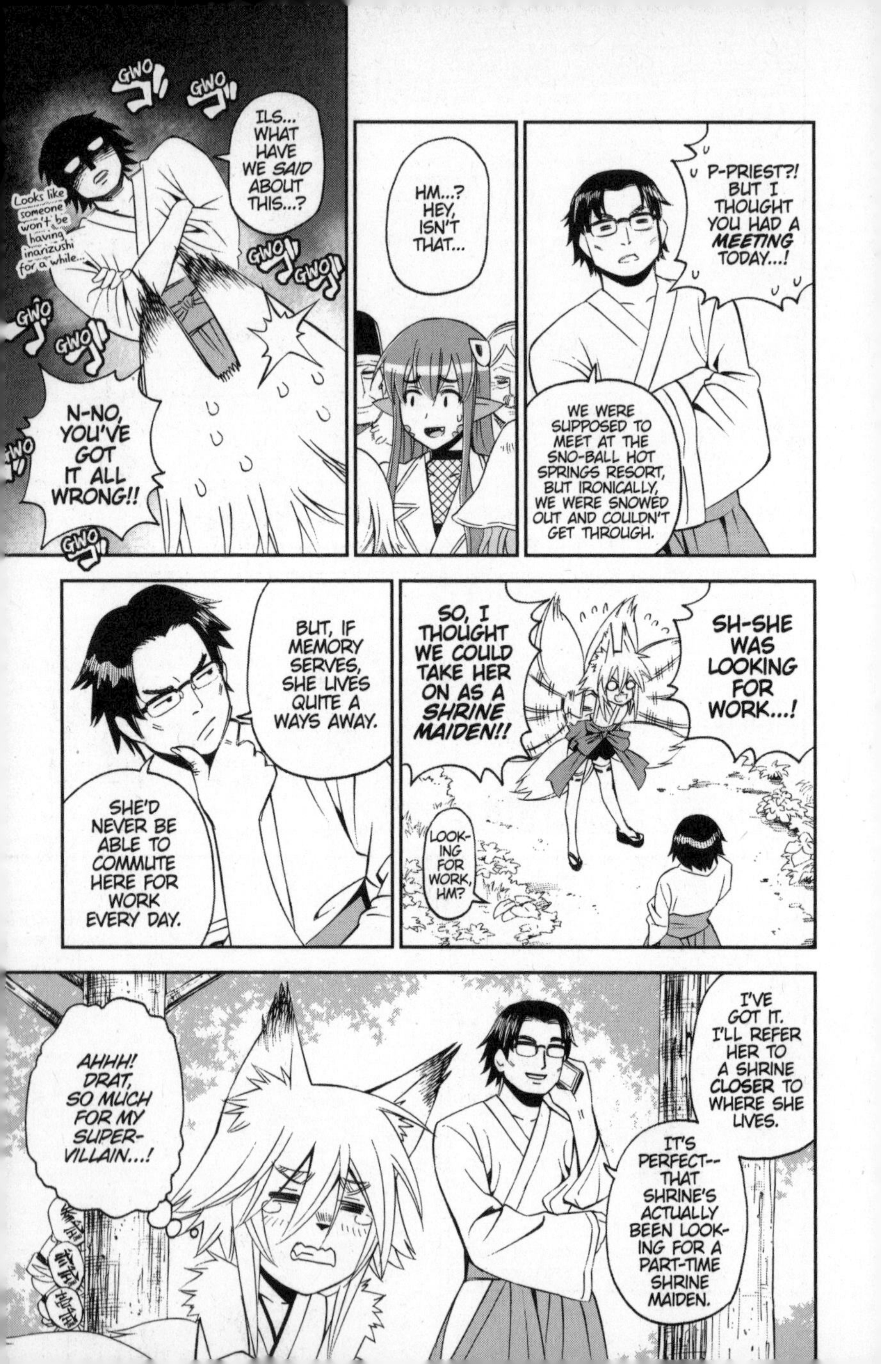
P-PRIEST?! BUT I THOUGHT YOU HAD A *MEETING* TODAY...!
WE WERE SUPPOSED TO MEET AT THE SNO-BALL HOT SPRINGS RESORT, BUT IRONICALLY, WE WERE SNOWED OUT AND COULDN'T GET THROUGH.
HM...? HEY, ISN'T THAT...
GWO
GWO
ILS... WHAT HAVE WE *SAID* ABOUT THIS...?
Looks like someone won't be having inarizushi for a while...
GWO
GWO
GWO
GWO
N-NO, YOU'VE GOT IT ALL WRONG!!
GWO
GWO
SH-SHE WAS LOOKING FOR WORK...!
SO, I THOUGHT WE COULD TAKE HER ON AS A *SHRINE MAIDEN*!!
LOOKING FOR WORK, HM?
BUT, IF MEMORY SERVES, SHE LIVES QUITE A WAYS AWAY.
SHE'D NEVER BE ABLE TO COMMUTE HERE FOR WORK EVERY DAY.
I'VE GOT IT. I'LL REFER HER TO A SHRINE CLOSER TO WHERE SHE LIVES.
IT'S PERFECT-- THAT SHRINE'S ACTUALLY BEEN LOOKING FOR A PART-TIME SHRINE MAIDEN.
AHHH! DRAT, SO MUCH FOR MY SUPER-VILLAIN...!

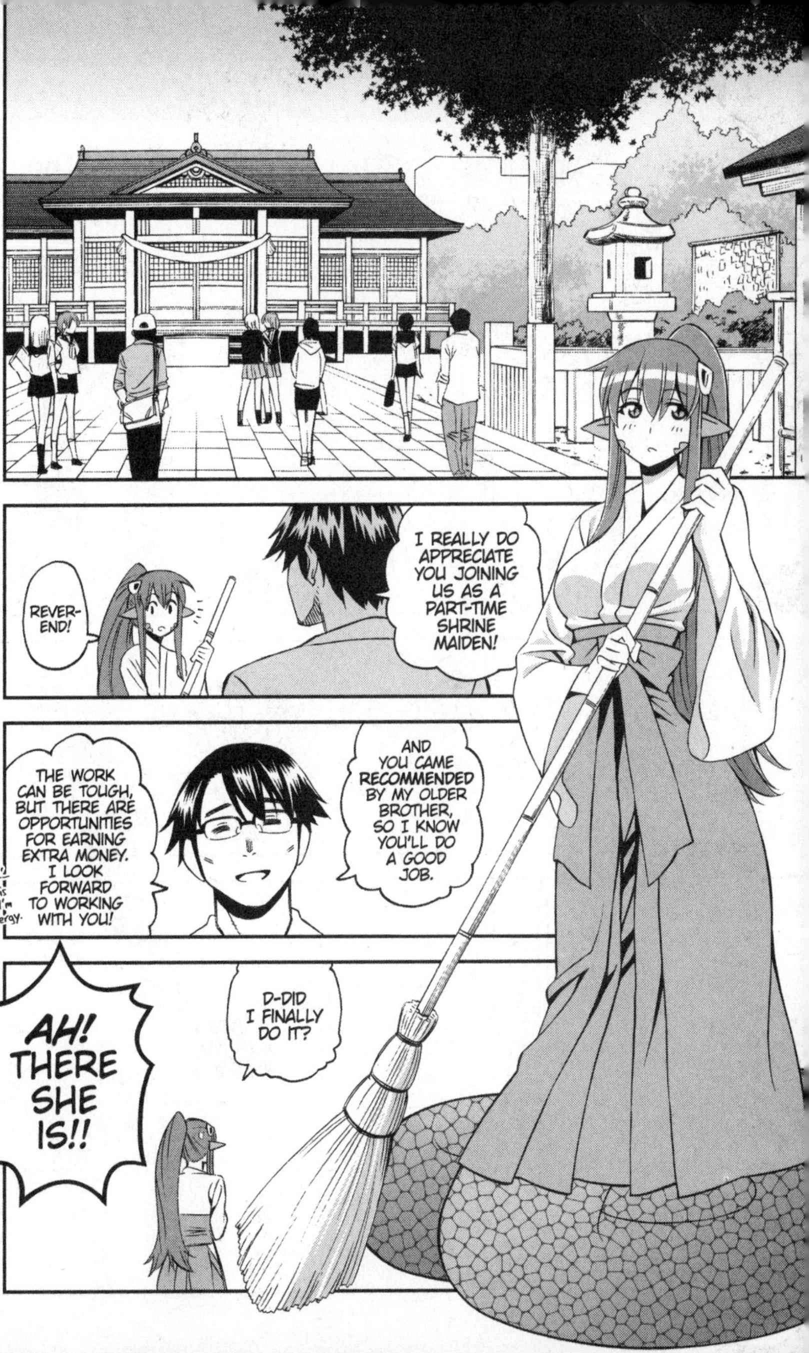
I REALLY DO APPRECIATE YOU JOINING US AS A PART-TIME SHRINE MAIDEN!
REVER-END!
AND YOU CAME RECOMMENDED BY MY OLDER BROTHER, SO I KNOW YOU'LL DO A GOOD JOB.
THE WORK CAN BE TOUGH, BUT THERE ARE OPPORTUNITIES FOR EARNING EXTRA MONEY. I LOOK FORWARD TO WORKING WITH YOU!
And please, "Priest-san" is fine. I'm not clergy.
D-DID I FINALLY DO IT?
AH! THERE SHE IS!!

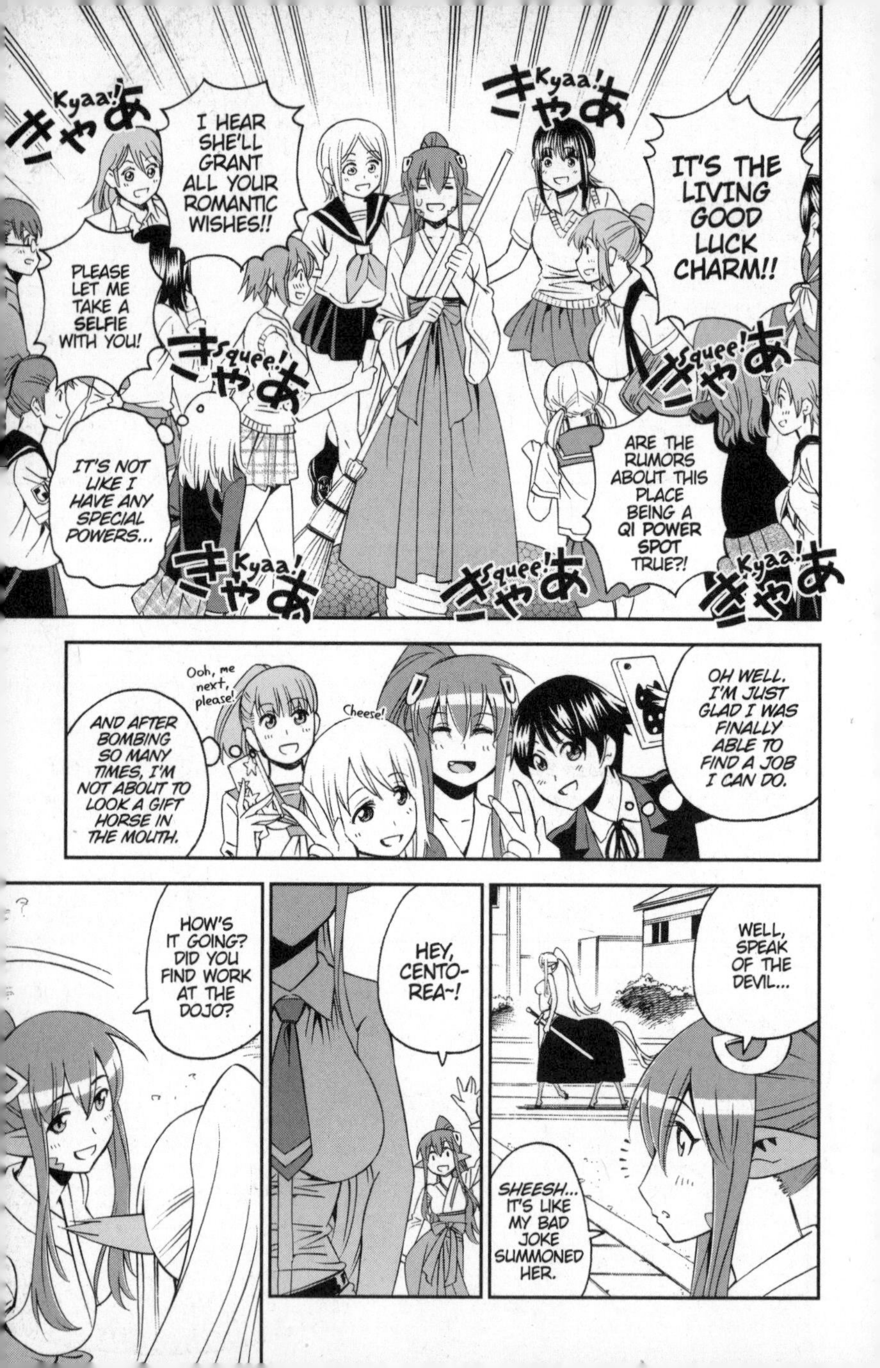
Kyaa! きゃあ
IT'S THE LIVING GOOD LUCK CHARM!!
Kyaa! きゃあ
I HEAR SHE'LL GRANT ALL YOUR ROMANTIC WISHES!!
Squee! きゃあ
ARE THE RUMORS ABOUT THIS PLACE BEING A QI POWER SPOT TRUE?!
PLEASE LET ME TAKE A SELFIE WITH YOU!
Squee! きゃあ
IT'S NOT LIKE I HAVE ANY SPECIAL POWERS...
Kyaa! きゃあ
Squee! きゃあ
Kyaa! きゃあ
OH WELL. I'M JUST GLAD I WAS FINALLY ABLE TO FIND A JOB I CAN DO.
Cheese!
Ooh, me next, please!
AND AFTER BOMBING SO MANY TIMES, I'M NOT ABOUT TO LOOK A GIFT HORSE IN THE MOUTH.
WELL, SPEAK OF THE DEVIL...
SHEESH... IT'S LIKE MY BAD JOKE SUMMONED HER.
HEY, CENTOREA~!
?
HOW'S IT GOING? DID YOU FIND WORK AT THE DOJO?

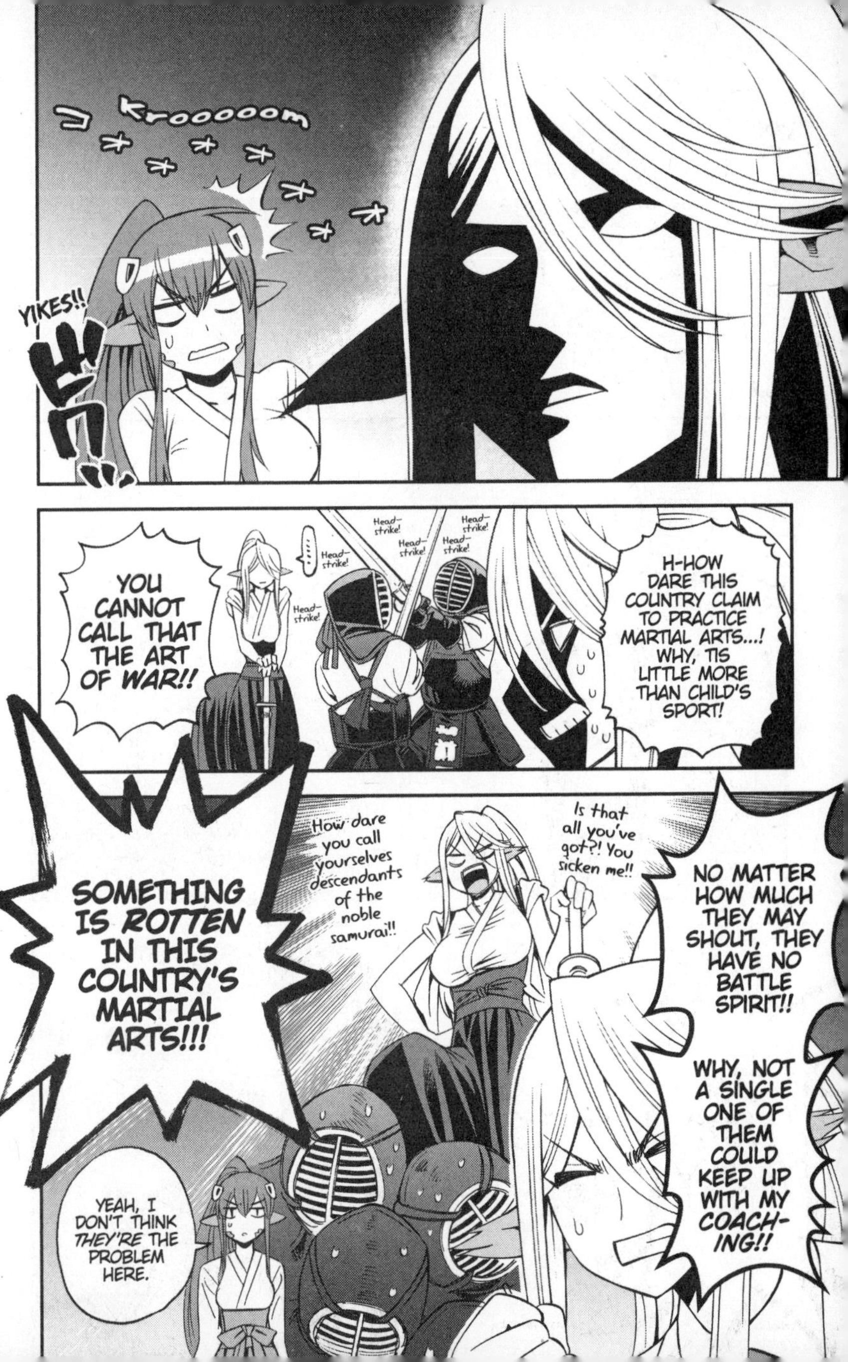

Kroooooom
YIKES!!
H-HOW DARE THIS COUNTRY CLAIM TO PRACTICE MARTIAL ARTS...! WHY, TIS LITTLE MORE THAN CHILD'S SPORT!
Head-strike!
Head-strike!
Head-strike!
Head-strike!
Head-strike!
YOU CANNOT CALL THAT THE ART OF *WAR*!!
NO MATTER HOW MUCH THEY MAY SHOUT, THEY HAVE NO BATTLE SPIRIT!!
WHY, NOT A SINGLE ONE OF THEM COULD KEEP UP WITH MY *COACHING*!!
Is that all you've got?! You sicken me!!
How dare you call yourselves descendants of the noble samurai!!
SOMETHING IS *ROTTEN* IN THIS COUNTRY'S MARTIAL ARTS!!!
YEAH, I DON'T THINK *THEY'RE* THE PROBLEM HERE.

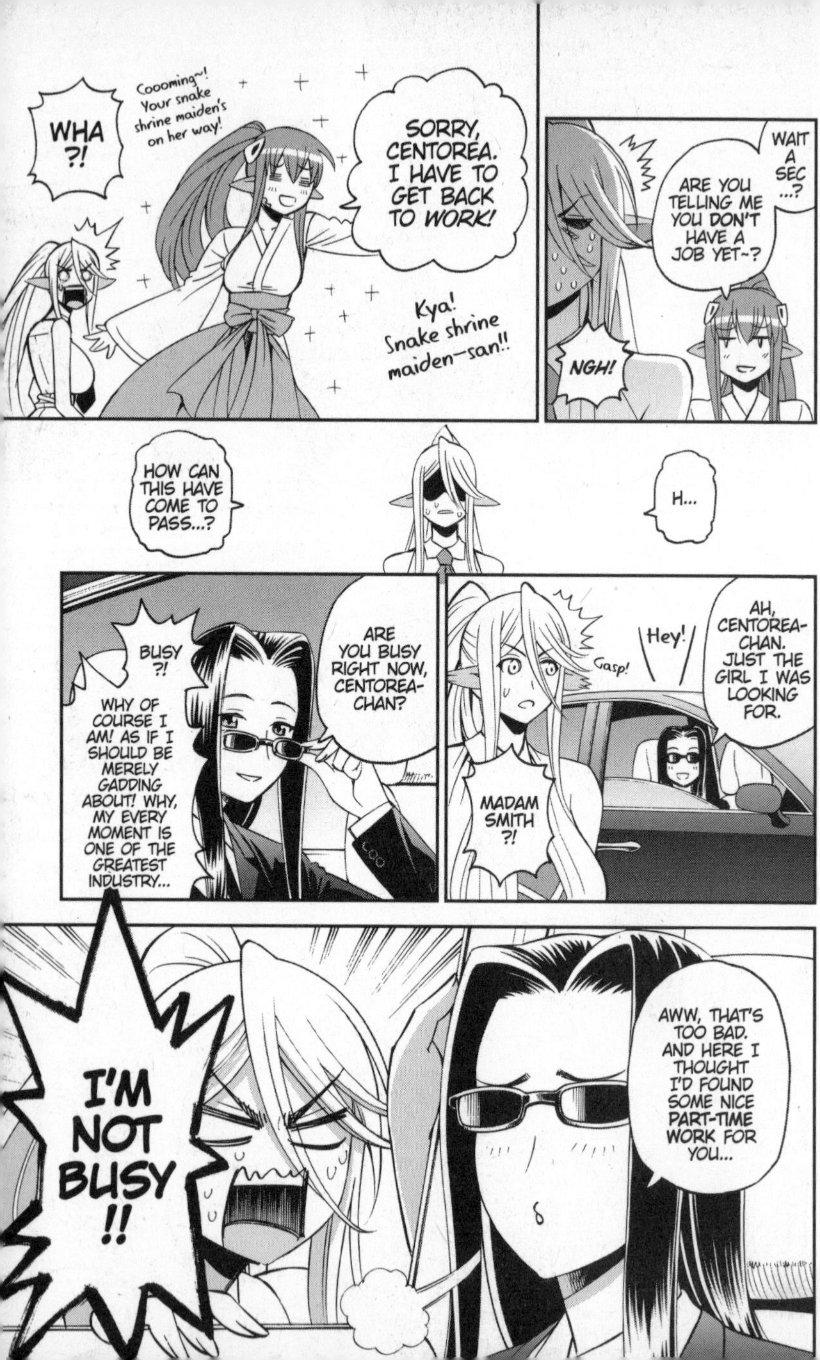

WAIT A SEC ...?
ARE YOU TELLING ME YOU DON'T HAVE A JOB YET~?
NGH!
SORRY, CENTOREA. I HAVE TO GET BACK TO WORK!
Kya! Snake shrine maiden-san!!
Coooming~! Your snake shrine maiden's on her way!
WHA ?!
H...
HOW CAN THIS HAVE COME TO PASS...?
AH, CENTOREA-CHAN. JUST THE GIRL I WAS LOOKING FOR.
Hey!
Gasp!
MADAM SMITH ?!
ARE YOU BUSY RIGHT NOW, CENTOREA-CHAN?
BUSY ?!
WHY OF COURSE I AM! AS IF I SHOULD BE MERELY GADDING ABOUT! WHY, MY EVERY MOMENT IS ONE OF THE GREATEST INDUSTRY...
AWW, THAT'S TOO BAD. AND HERE I THOUGHT I'D FOUND SOME NICE PART-TIME WORK FOR YOU...
I'M NOT BUSY !!

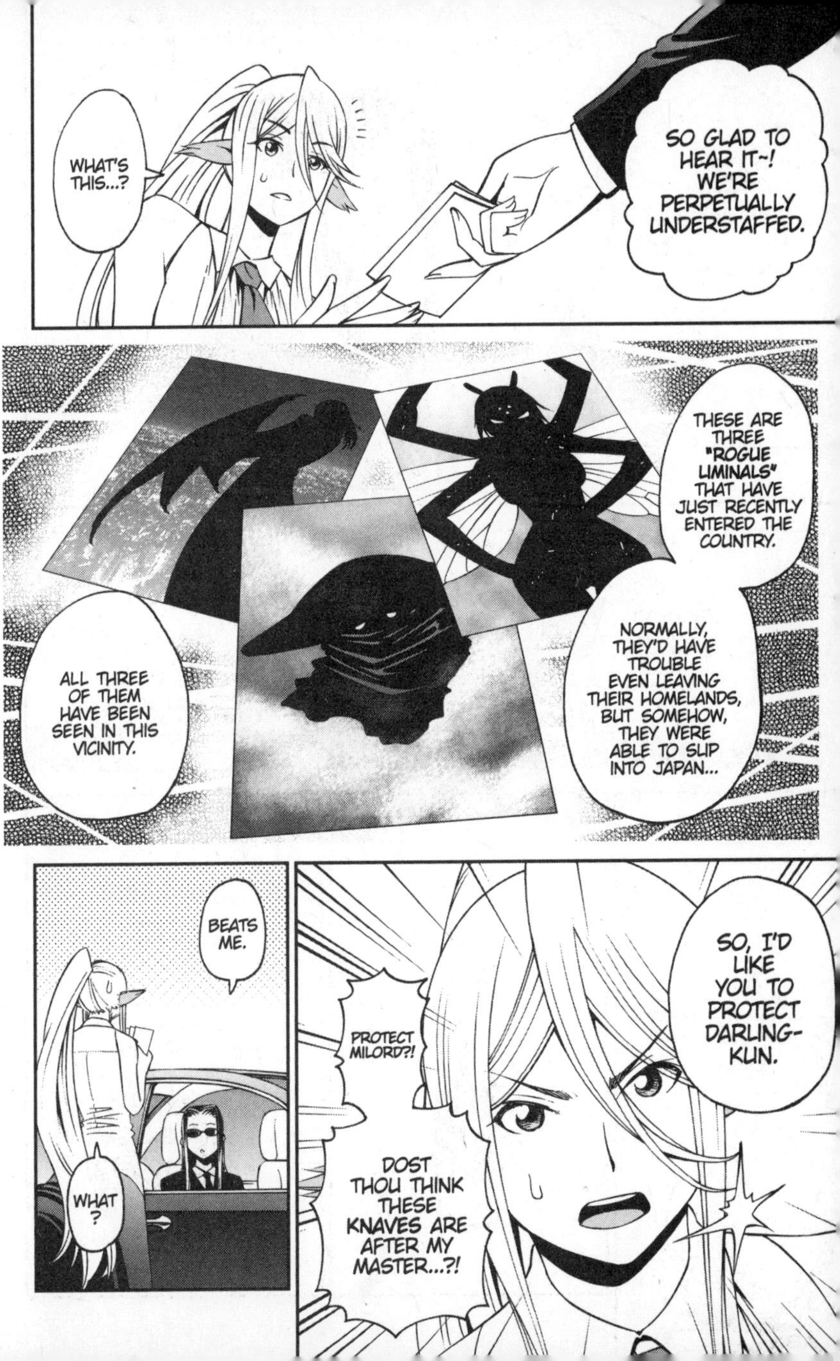
SO GLAD TO HEAR IT~! WE'RE PERPETUALLY UNDERSTAFFED.
WHAT'S THIS...?
THESE ARE THREE "ROGUE LIMINALS" THAT HAVE JUST RECENTLY ENTERED THE COUNTRY.
NORMALLY, THEY'D HAVE TROUBLE EVEN LEAVING THEIR HOMELANDS, BUT SOMEHOW, THEY WERE ABLE TO SLIP INTO JAPAN...
ALL THREE OF THEM HAVE BEEN SEEN IN THIS VICINITY.
SO, I'D LIKE YOU TO PROTECT DARLING-KUN.
PROTECT MILORD?!
DOST THOU THINK THESE KNAVES ARE AFTER MY MASTER...?!
BEATS ME.
WHAT ?

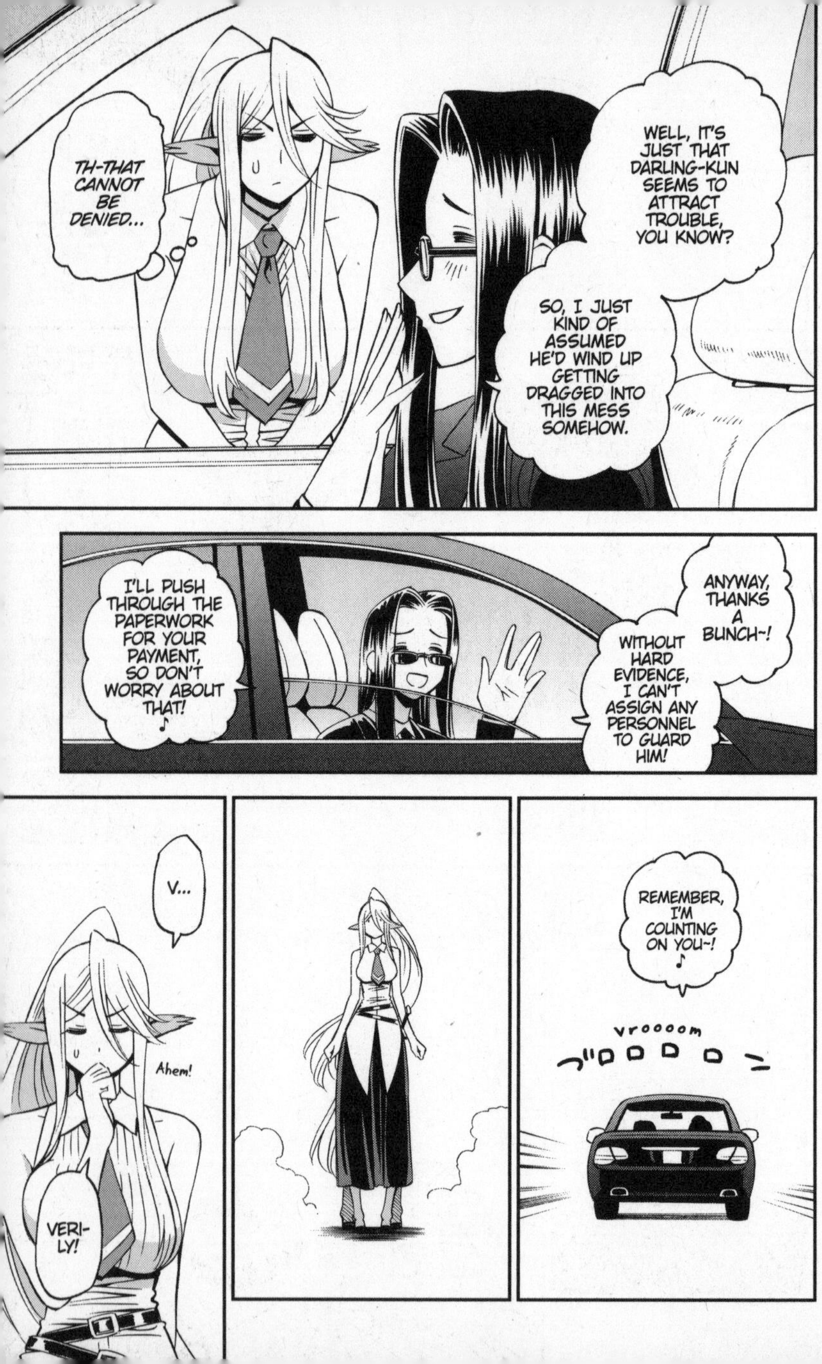

WELL, IT'S JUST THAT DARLING-KUN SEEMS TO ATTRACT TROUBLE, YOU KNOW?
SO, I JUST KIND OF ASSUMED HE'D WIND UP GETTING DRAGGED INTO THIS MESS SOMEHOW.
TH-THAT CANNOT BE DENIED...
ANYWAY, THANKS A BUNCH~!
WITHOUT HARD EVIDENCE, I CAN'T ASSIGN ANY PERSONNEL TO GUARD HIM!
I'LL PUSH THROUGH THE PAPERWORK FOR YOUR PAYMENT, SO DON'T WORRY ABOUT THAT! ♪
REMEMBER, I'M COUNTING ON YOU~! ♪
vroooom
V...
Ahem!
VERI-LY!

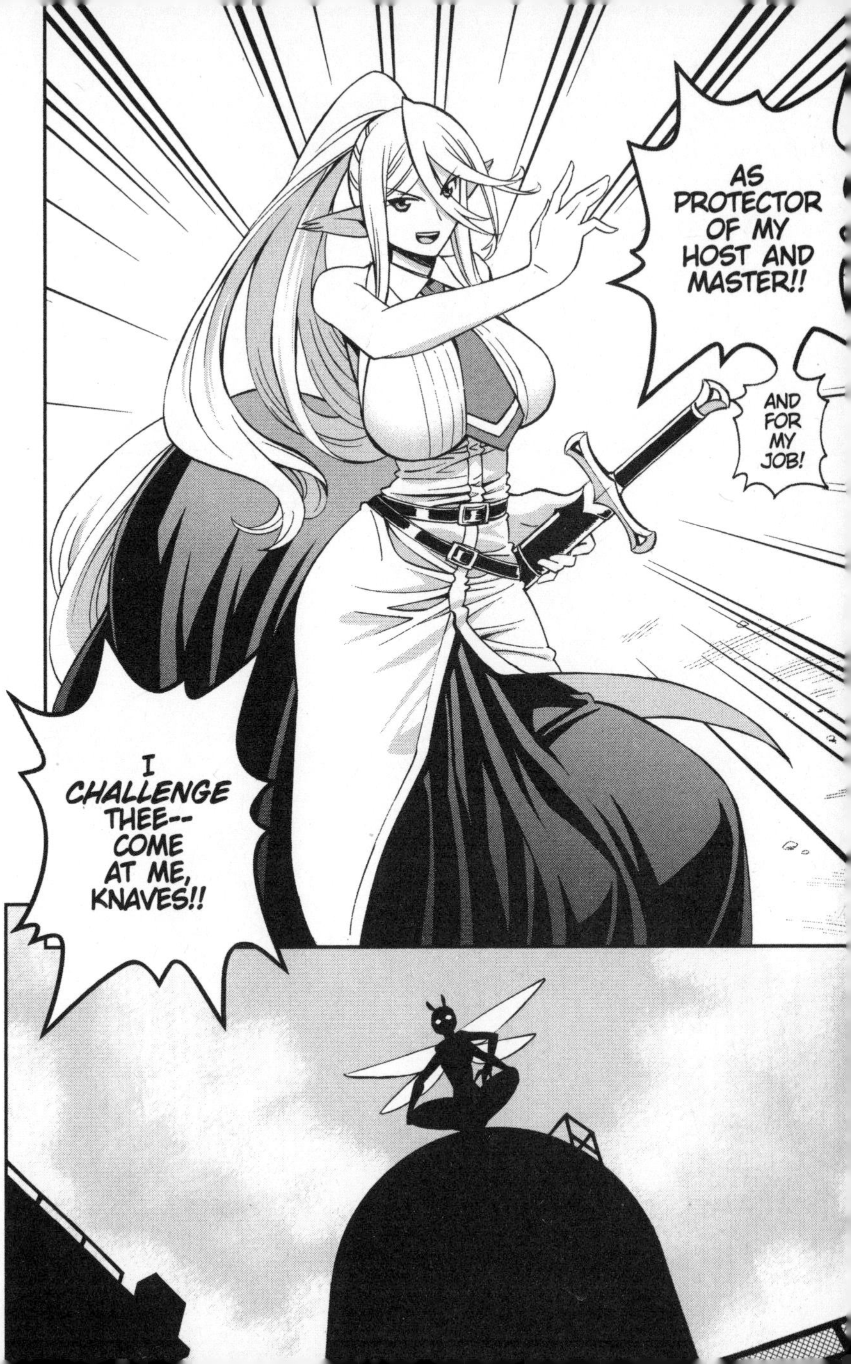
AS PROTECTOR OF MY HOST AND MASTER!!
AND FOR MY JOB!
I CHALLENGE THEE--COME AT ME, KNAVES!!

Monster Musume

Everyday Life with Monster Girls

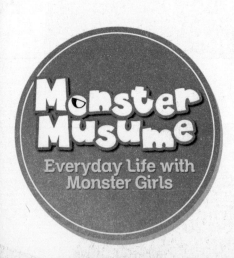

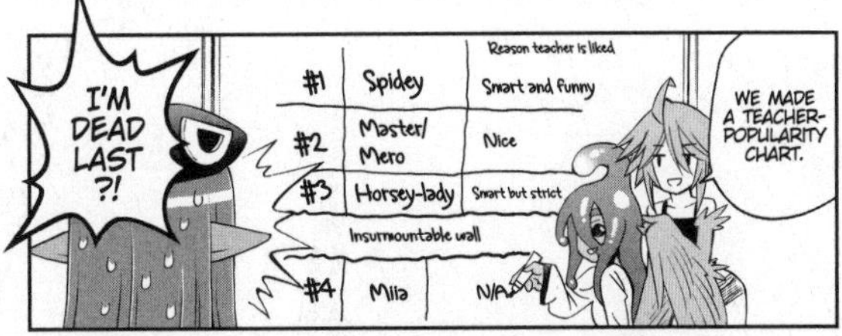
WE MADE A TEACHER-POPULARITY CHART.
Reason teacher is liked
#1
Spidey
Smart and funny
#2
Master/ Mero
Nice
#3
Horsey-lady
Smart but strict
Insurmountable wall
#4
Miia
N/A
I'M DEAD LAST ?!

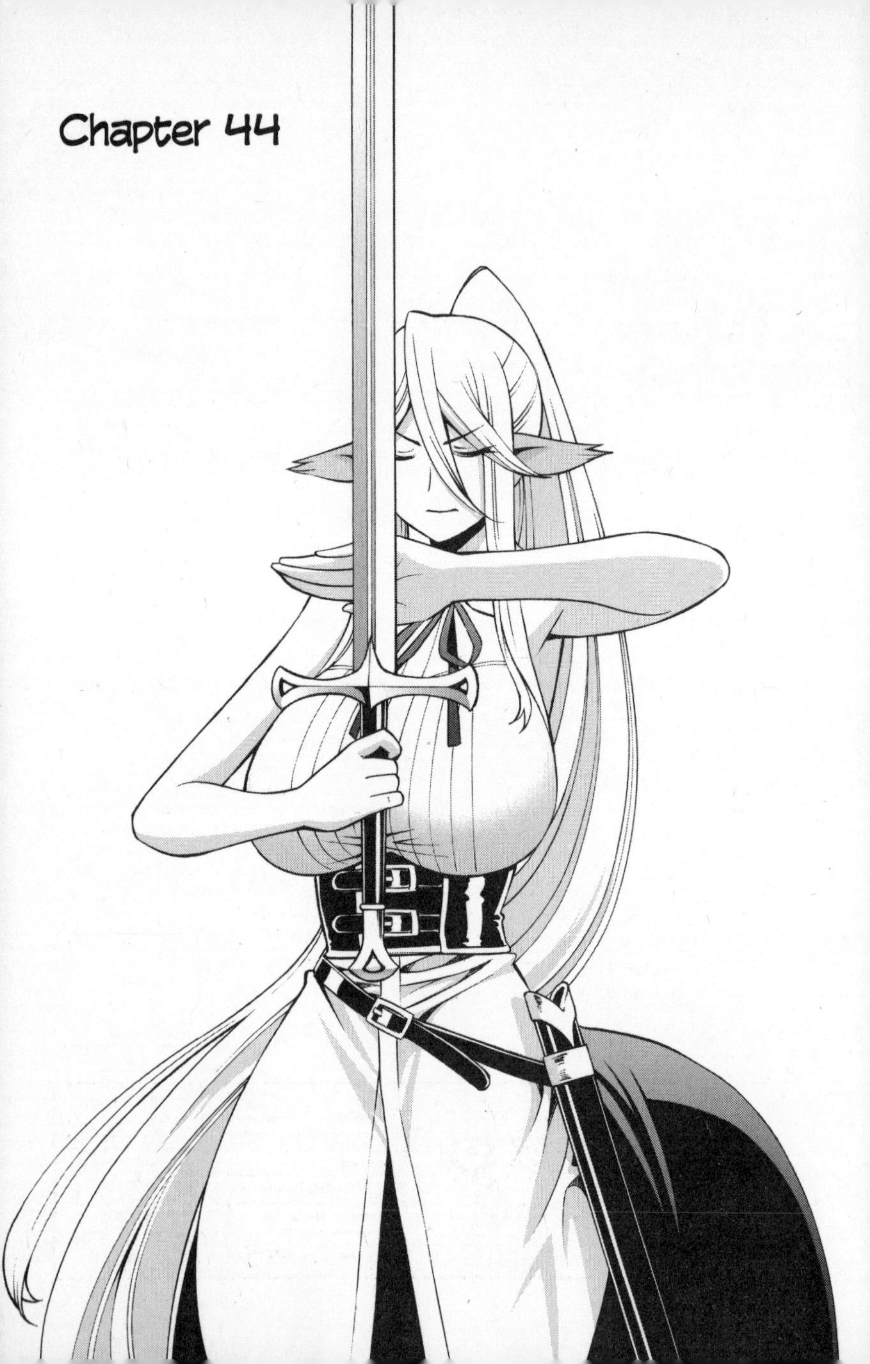
Chapter 44

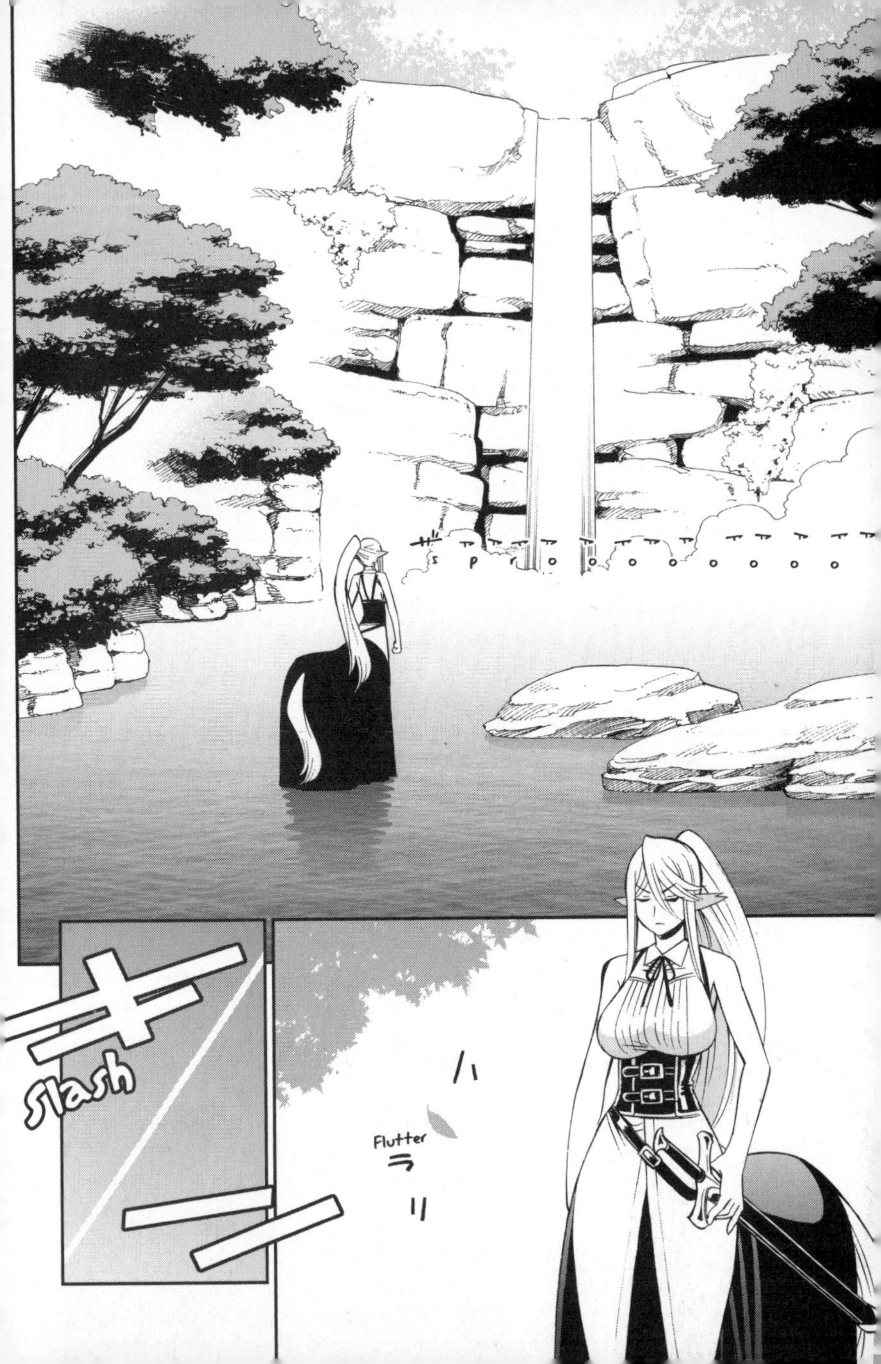
sprooooooooo
Flutter
Slash

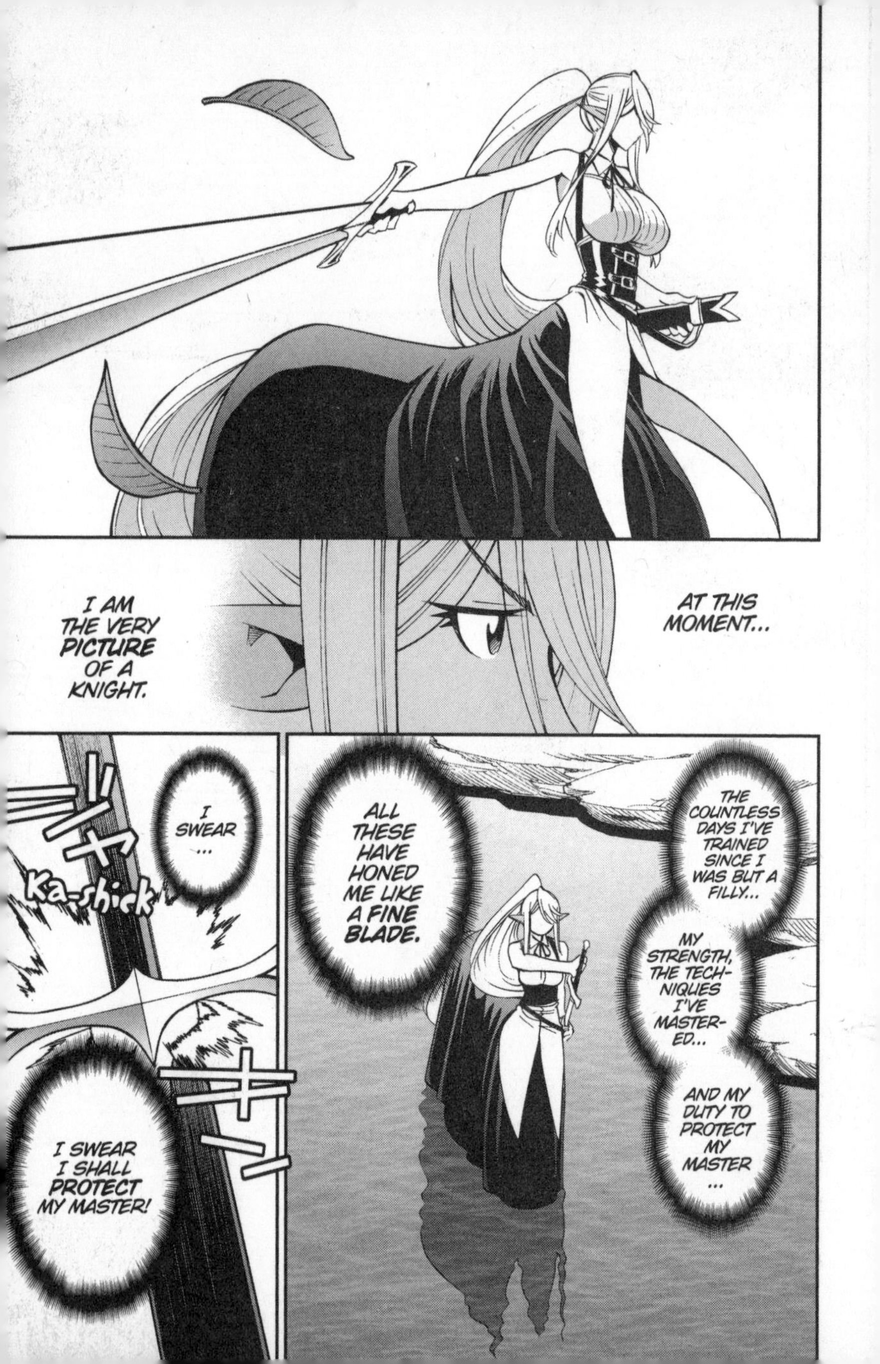
AT THIS MOMENT...
I AM THE VERY PICTURE OF A KNIGHT.
THE COUNTLESS DAYS I'VE TRAINED SINCE I WAS BUT A FILLY...
MY STRENGTH, THE TECHNIQUES I'VE MASTERED...
AND MY DUTY TO PROTECT MY MASTER...
ALL THESE HAVE HONED ME LIKE A FINE BLADE.
I SWEAR...
Ka-shick
I SWEAR I SHALL PROTECT MY MASTER!

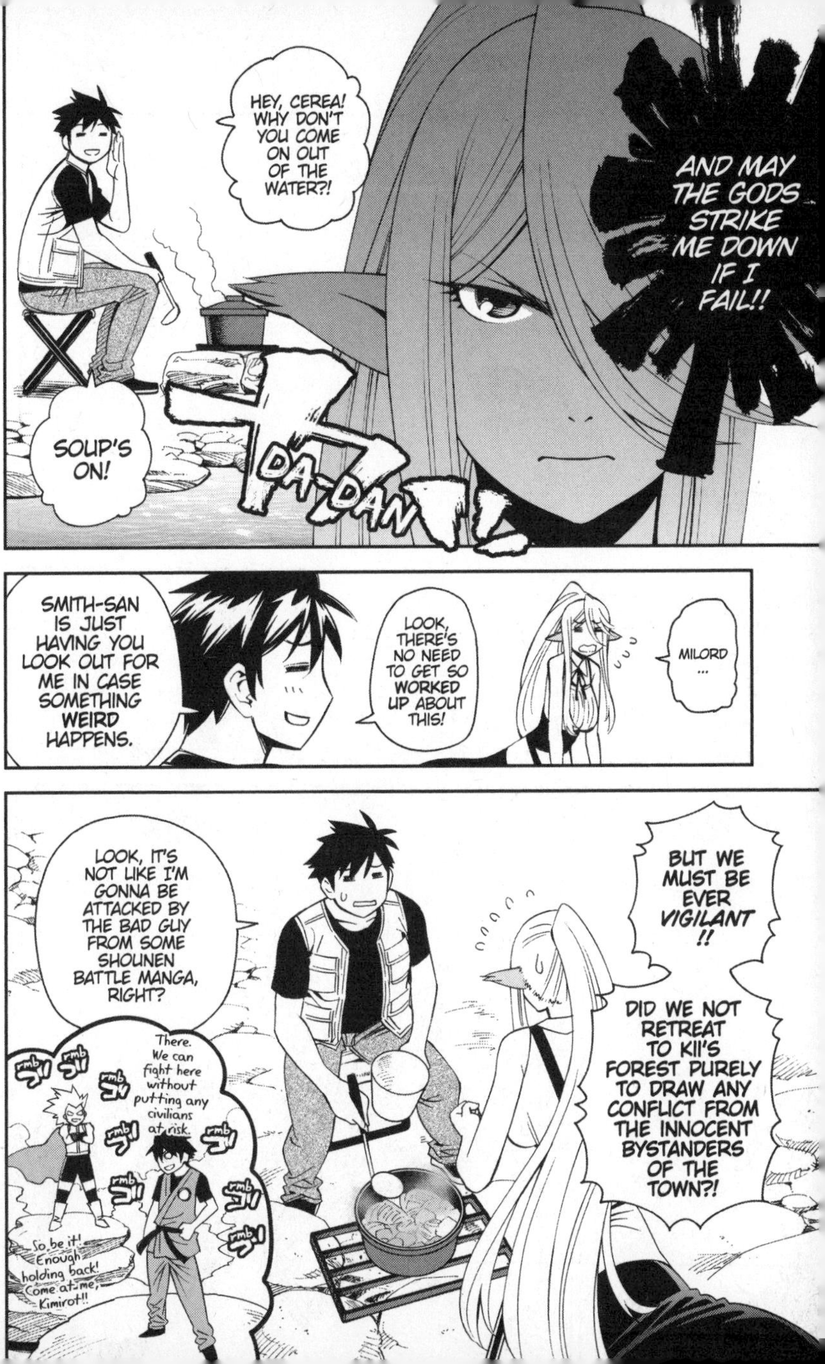
AND MAY THE GODS STRIKE ME DOWN IF I FAIL!!
DA-DAN
HEY, CEREA! WHY DON'T YOU COME ON OUT OF THE WATER?!
SOUP'S ON!
MILORD...
LOOK, THERE'S NO NEED TO GET SO WORKED UP ABOUT THIS!
SMITH-SAN IS JUST HAVING YOU LOOK OUT FOR ME IN CASE SOMETHING WEIRD HAPPENS.
BUT WE MUST BE EVER VIGILANT!!
DID WE NOT RETREAT TO KII'S FOREST PURELY TO DRAW ANY CONFLICT FROM THE INNOCENT BYSTANDERS OF THE TOWN?!
LOOK, IT'S NOT LIKE I'M GONNA BE ATTACKED BY THE BAD GUY FROM SOME SHOUNEN BATTLE MANGA, RIGHT?
There. We can fight here without putting any civilians at risk.
rmb
So be it! Enough holding back! Come at me, Kimirot!!

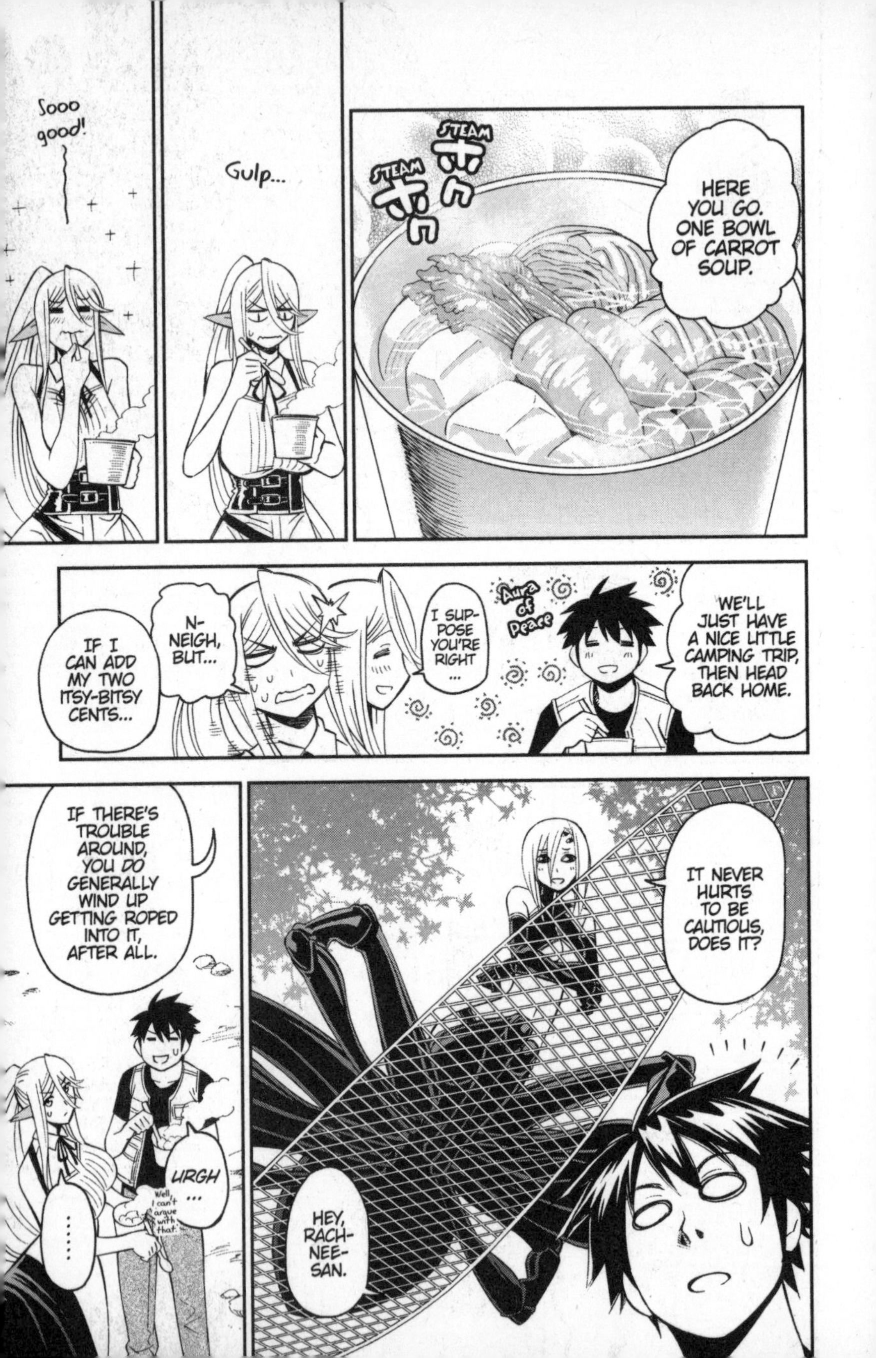
STEAM
STEAM
HERE YOU GO. ONE BOWL OF CARROT SOUP.
Gulp...
Sooo good!
WE'LL JUST HAVE A NICE LITTLE CAMPING TRIP, THEN HEAD BACK HOME.
Aura of Peace
I SUP-POSE YOU'RE RIGHT ...
N-NEIGH, BUT...
IF I CAN ADD MY TWO ITSY-BITSY CENTS...
IT NEVER HURTS TO BE CAUTIOUS, DOES IT?
HEY, RACH-NEE-SAN.
IF THERE'S TROUBLE AROUND, YOU DO GENERALLY WIND UP GETTING ROPED INTO IT, AFTER ALL.
URGH ...
Well, I can't argue with that.
......

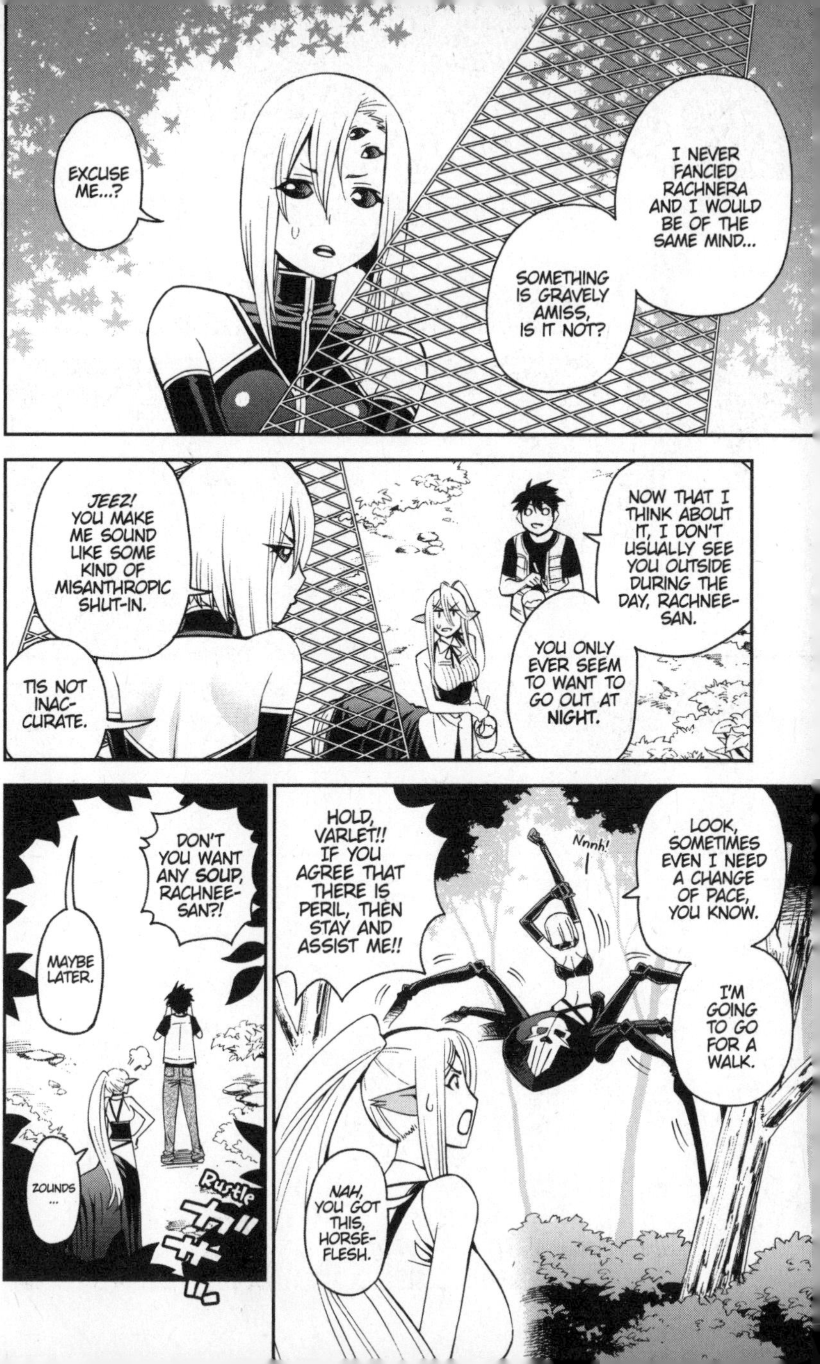
I NEVER FANCIED RACHNERA AND I WOULD BE OF THE SAME MIND...
SOMETHING IS GRAVELY AMISS, IS IT NOT?
EXCUSE ME...?
NOW THAT I THINK ABOUT IT, I DON'T USUALLY SEE YOU OUTSIDE DURING THE DAY, RACHNEE-SAN.
YOU ONLY EVER SEEM TO WANT TO GO OUT AT NIGHT.
JEEZ! YOU MAKE ME SOUND LIKE SOME KIND OF MISANTHROPIC SHUT-IN.
TIS NOT INACCURATE.
LOOK, SOMETIMES EVEN I NEED A CHANGE OF PACE, YOU KNOW.
I'M GOING TO GO FOR A WALK.
Nnnh!
HOLD, VARLET!! IF YOU AGREE THAT THERE IS PERIL, THEN STAY AND ASSIST ME!!
NAH, YOU GOT THIS, HORSE-FLESH.
DON'T YOU WANT ANY SOUP, RACHNEE-SAN?!
MAYBE LATER.
Rustle
ZOUNDS...

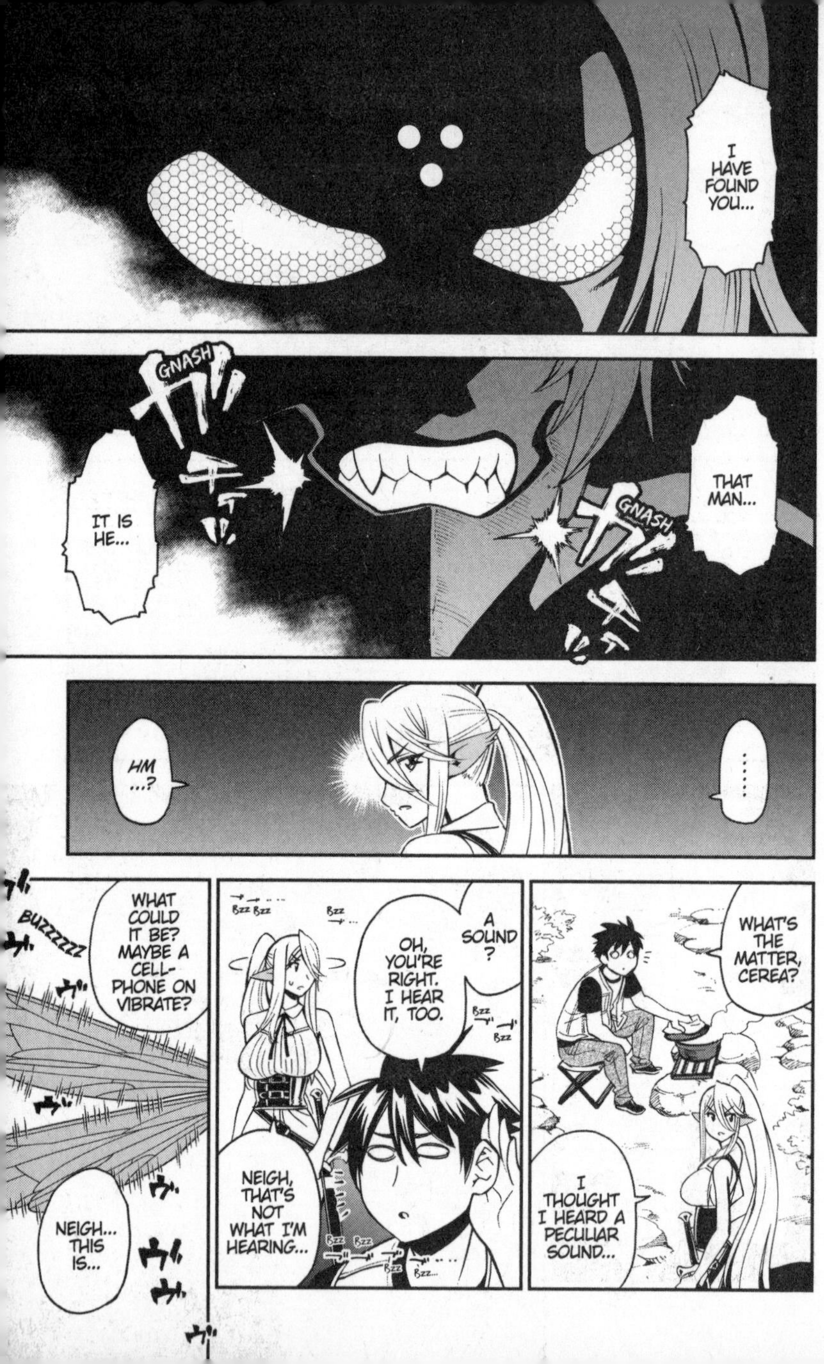
I HAVE FOUND YOU...
THAT MAN...
GNASH
GNASH
IT IS HE...
......
HM ...?
WHAT'S THE MATTER, CEREA?
I THOUGHT I HEARD A PECULIAR SOUND...
A SOUND?
OH, YOU'RE RIGHT. I HEAR IT, TOO.
Bzz Bzz
Bzz
Bzz Bzz
NEIGH, THAT'S NOT WHAT I'M HEARING...
Bzz Bzz
Bzz Bzz...
WHAT COULD IT BE? MAYBE A CELL-PHONE ON VIBRATE?
BUZZZZZZZ
NEIGH... THIS IS...

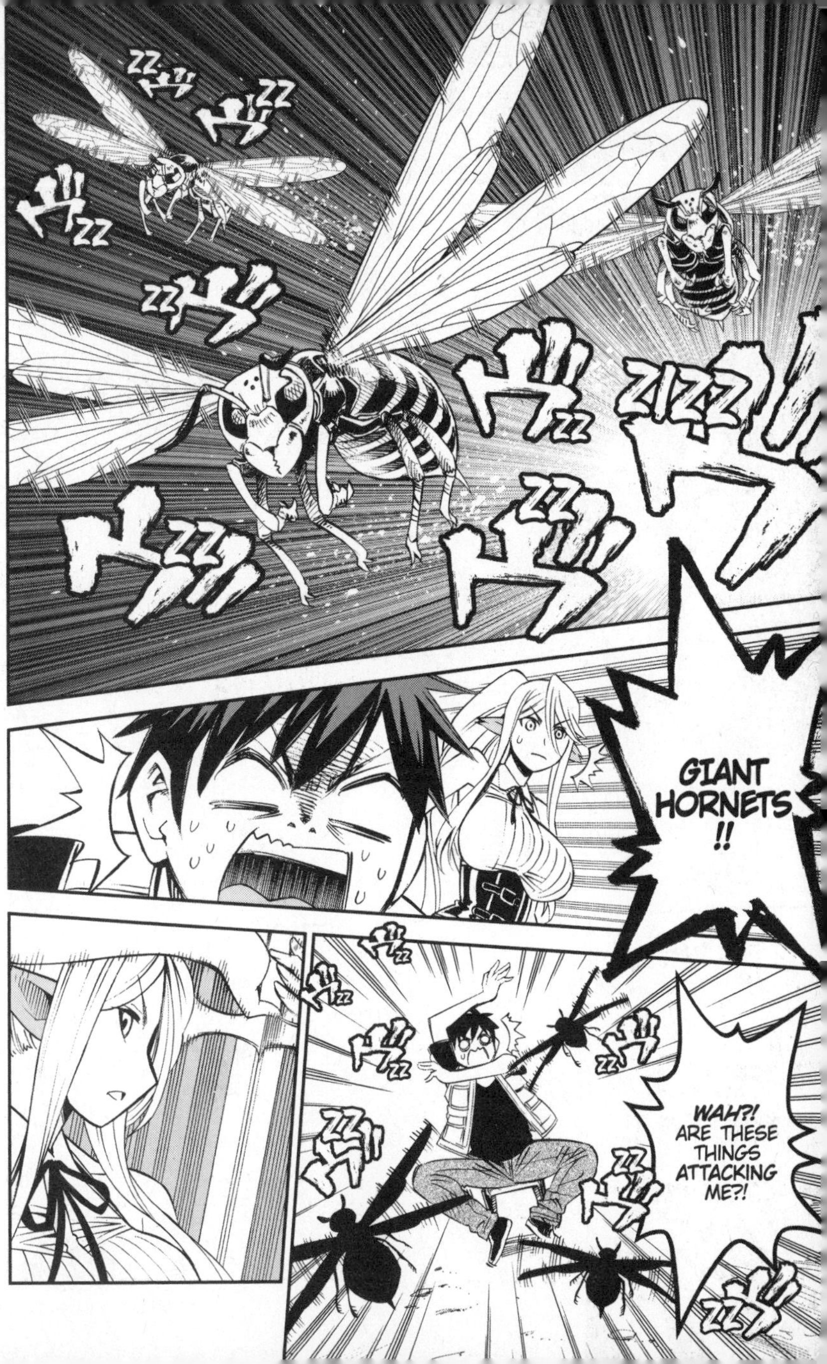
ZIZZZ
GIANT HORNETS !!
WAH?! ARE THESE THINGS ATTACKING ME?!

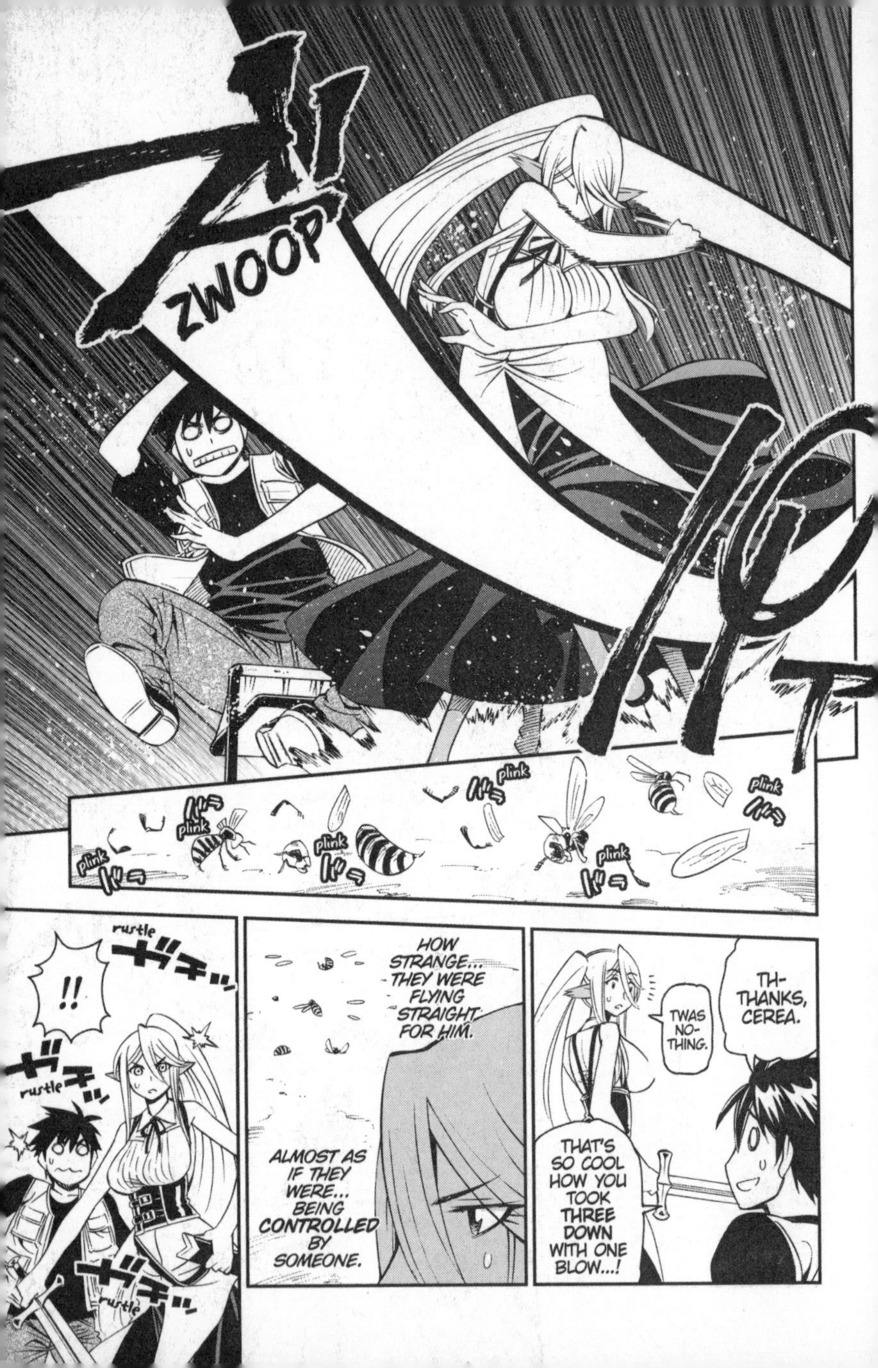
ZWOOP
plink
plink
plink
plink
plink
plink
TH-THANKS, CEREA.
TWAS NO-THING.
THAT'S SO COOL HOW YOU TOOK THREE DOWN WITH ONE BLOW...!
HOW STRANGE... THEY WERE FLYING STRAIGHT FOR HIM.
ALMOST AS IF THEY WERE... BEING CONTROLLED BY SOMEONE.
rustle
!!
rustle
rustle

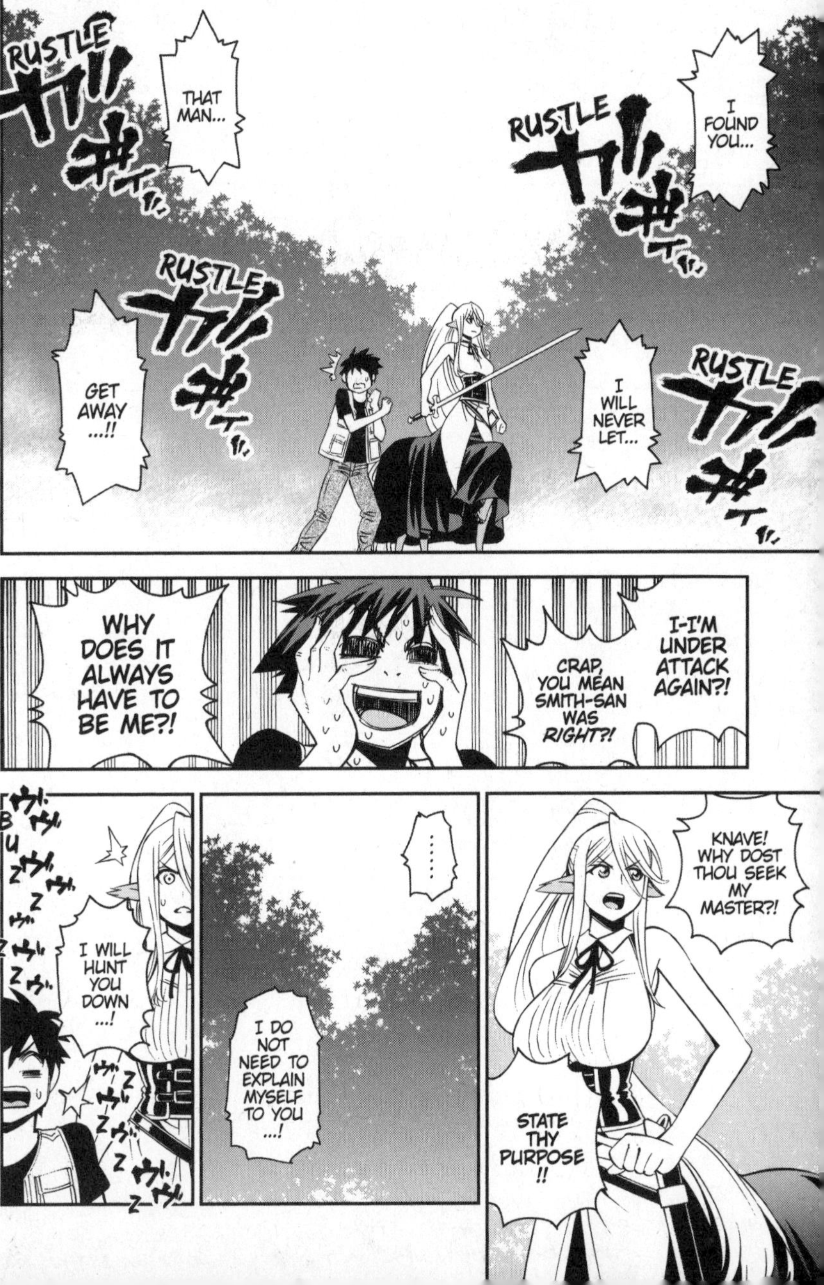
I FOUND YOU...
RUSTLE
THAT MAN...
RUSTLE
RUSTLE
I WILL NEVER LET...
RUSTLE
GET AWAY ...!!
I-I'M UNDER ATTACK AGAIN?!
CRAP, YOU MEAN SMITH-SAN WAS RIGHT?!
WHY DOES IT ALWAYS HAVE TO BE ME?!
KNAVE! WHY DOST THOU SEEK MY MASTER?!
STATE THY PURPOSE !!
......
I DO NOT NEED TO EXPLAIN MYSELF TO YOU ...!
BUZZZZ
I WILL HUNT YOU DOWN ...!

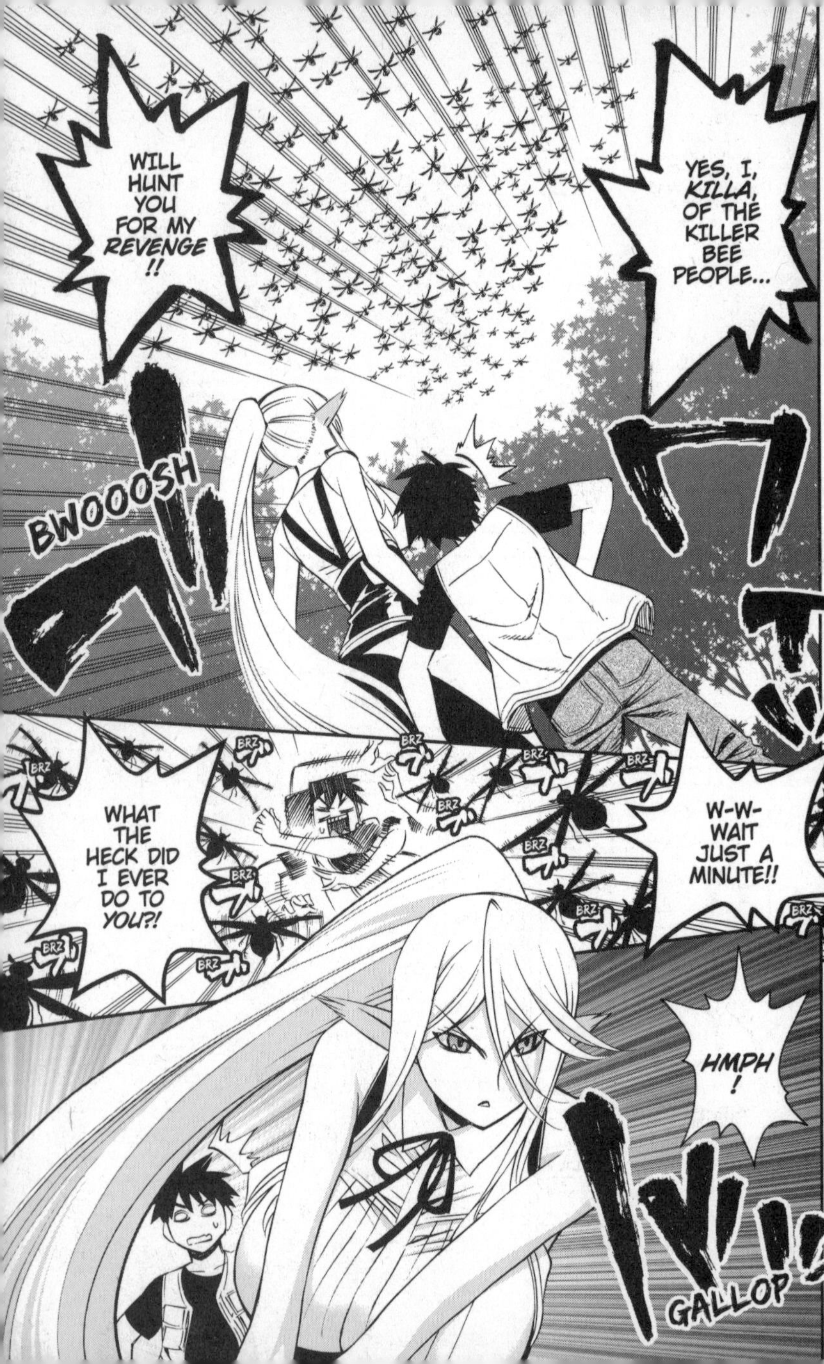
YES, I, *KILLA*, OF THE KILLER BEE PEOPLE...
WILL HUNT YOU FOR MY *REVENGE*!!
BWOOOSH
W-W-WAIT JUST A MINUTE!!
BRZ
WHAT THE HECK DID I EVER DO TO YOU?!
HMPH!
GALLOP!!

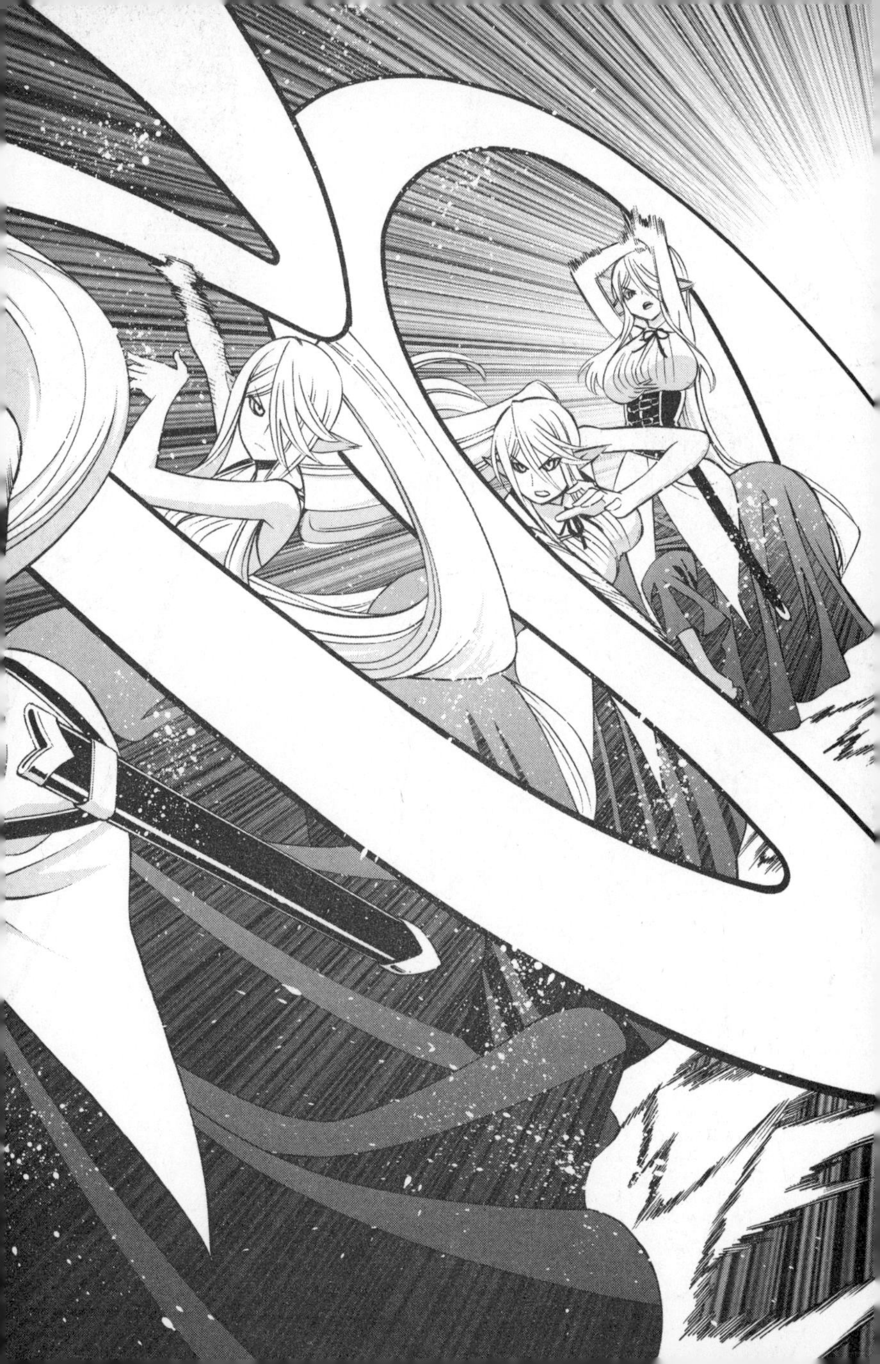

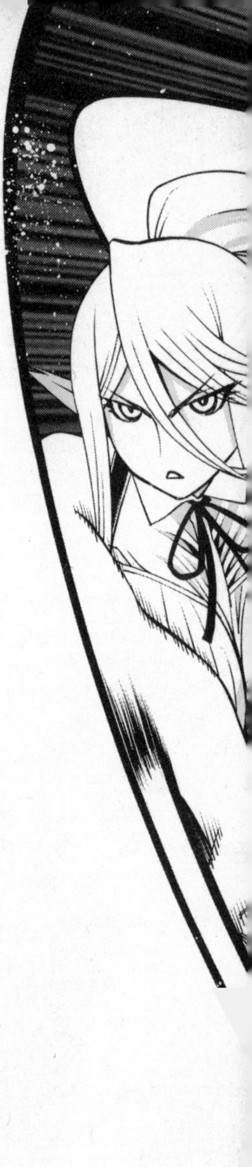

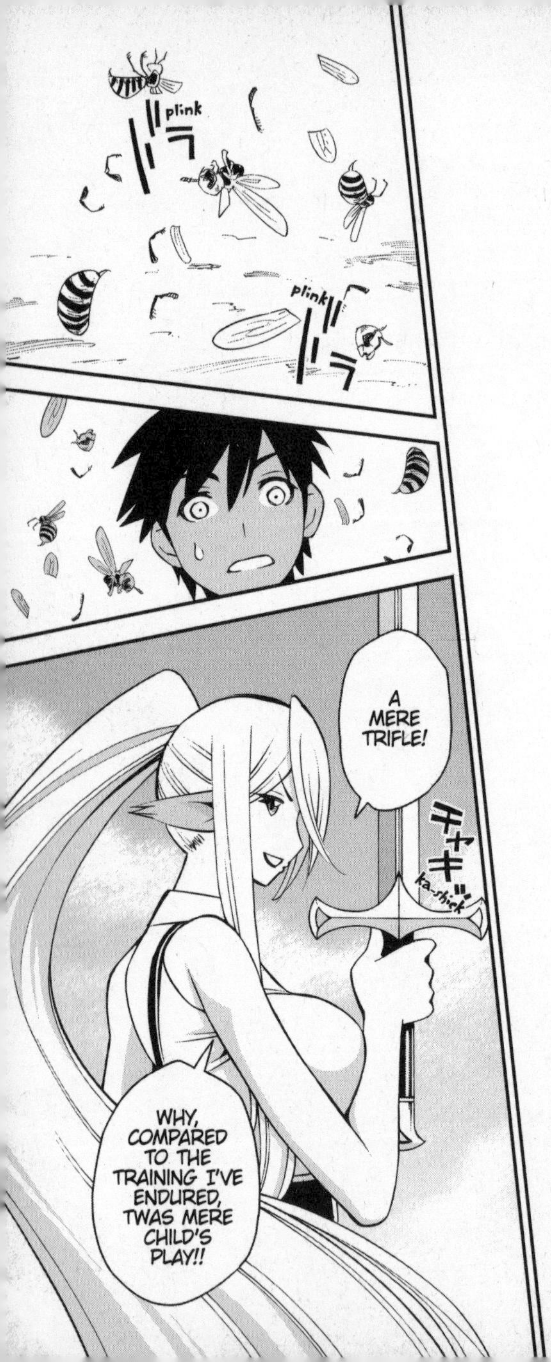
ドラ plink
plink ドラ
A MERE TRIFLE!
チャキ ka-shick
WHY, COMPARED TO THE TRAINING I'VE ENDURED, TWAS MERE CHILD'S PLAY!!

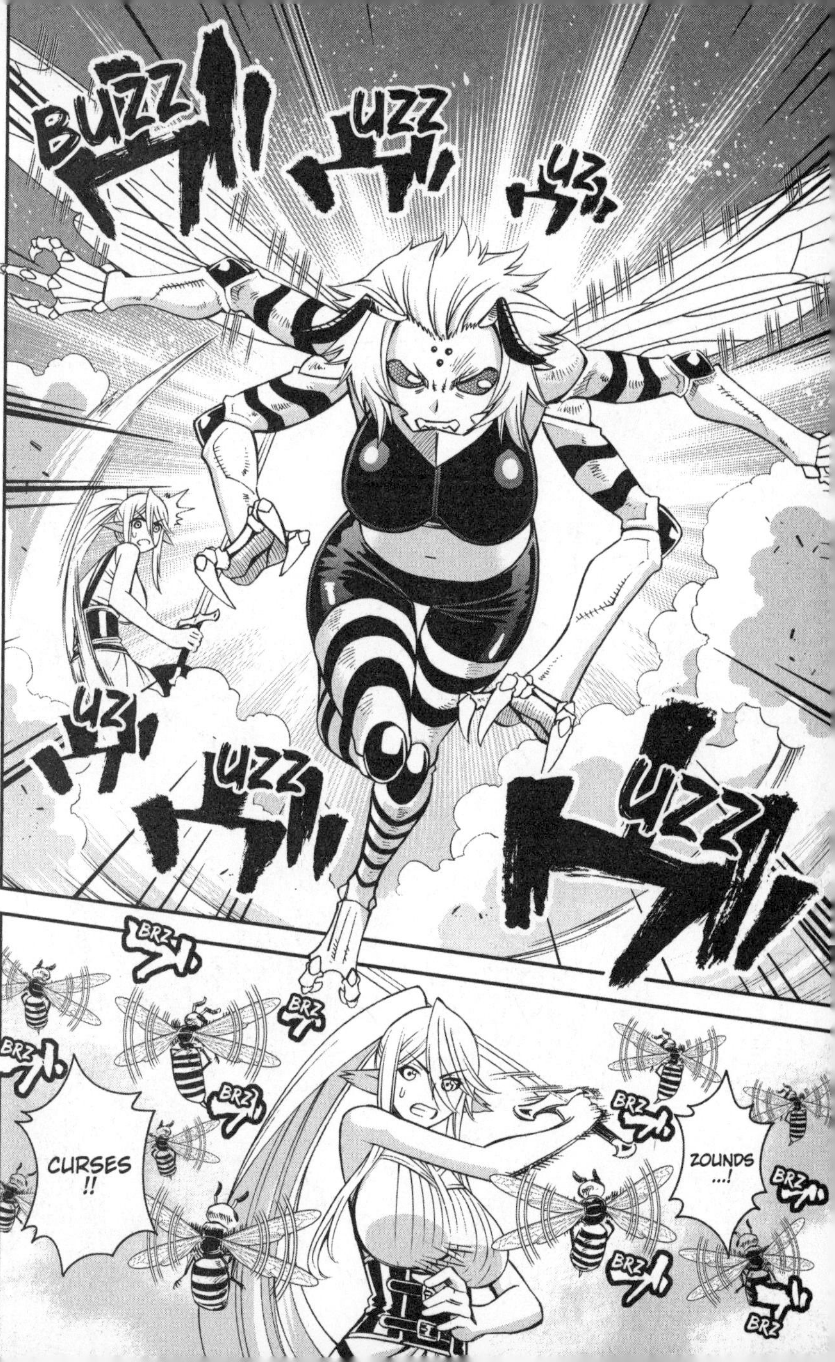
BUZZ
UZZ
UZ
UZ
UZZ
UZZ
BRZ
BRZ
BRZ
BRZ
ZOUNDS ...!
BRZ
BRZ
BRZ
BRZ
CURSES !!
BRZ
BRZ

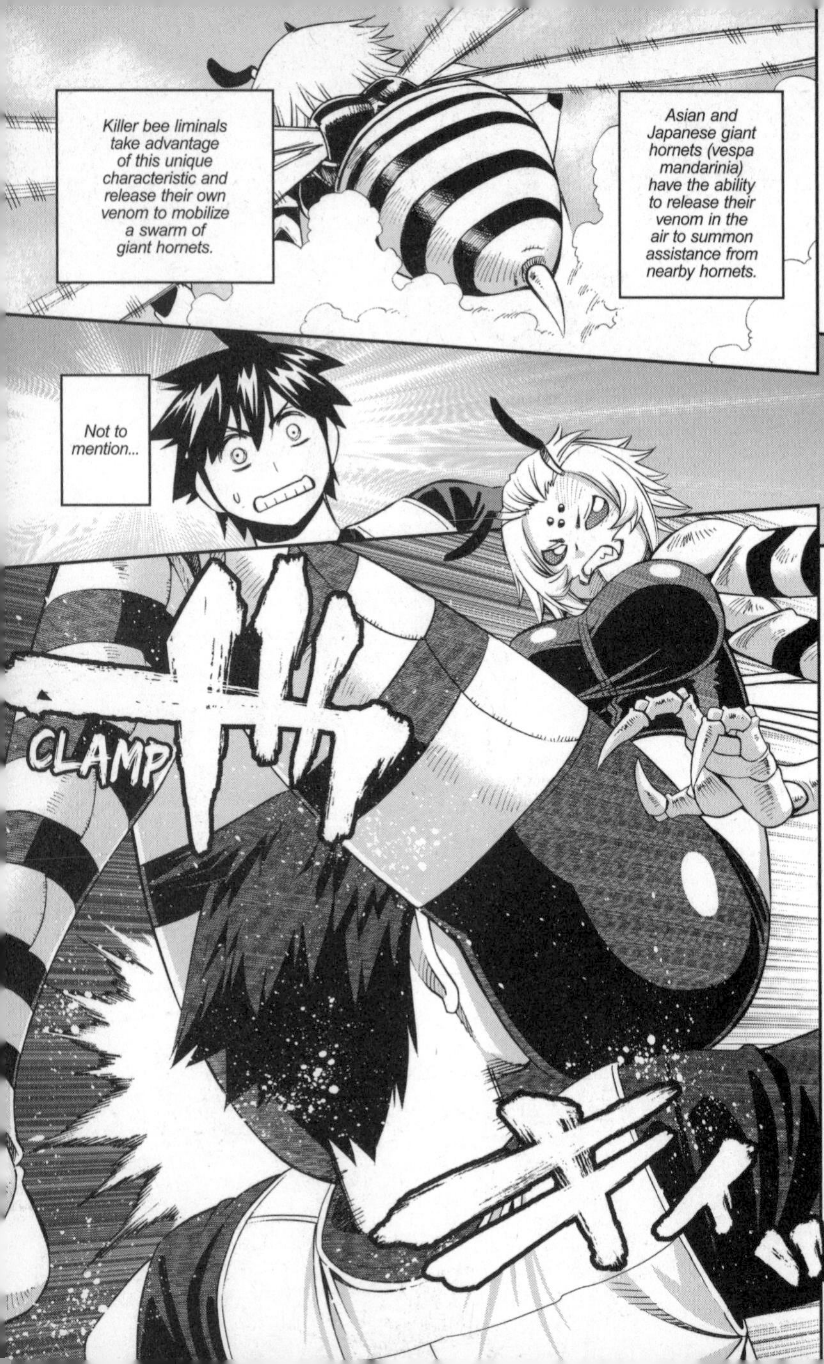
Asian and Japanese giant hornets (vespa mandarinia) have the ability to release their venom in the air to summon assistance from nearby hornets.
Killer bee liminals take advantage of this unique characteristic and release their own venom to mobilize a swarm of giant hornets.
Not to mention...
CLAMP

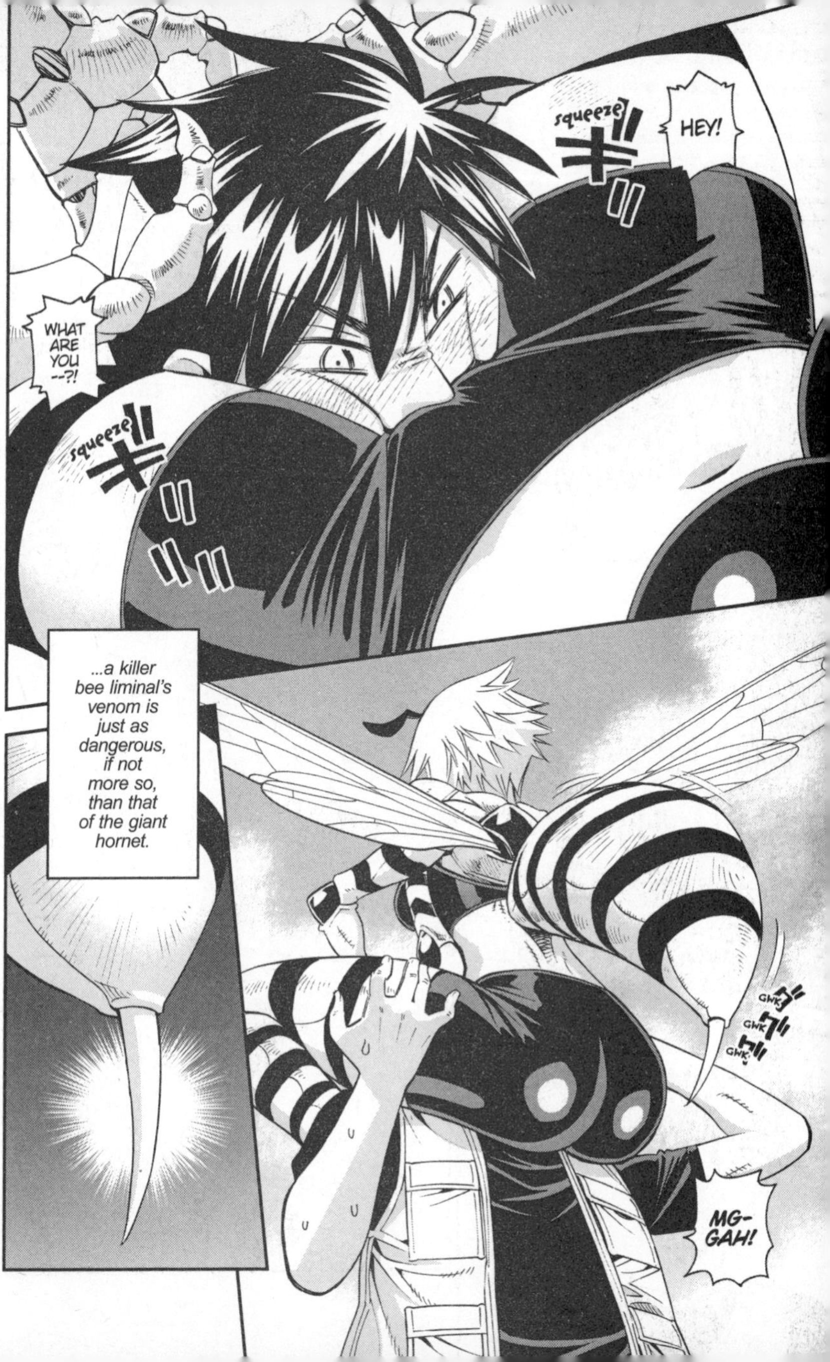
HEY!
squeeze
WHAT ARE YOU --?!
squeeze
GWK GWK GWK
MG-GAH!
...a killer bee liminal's venom is just as dangerous, if not more so, than that of the giant hornet.

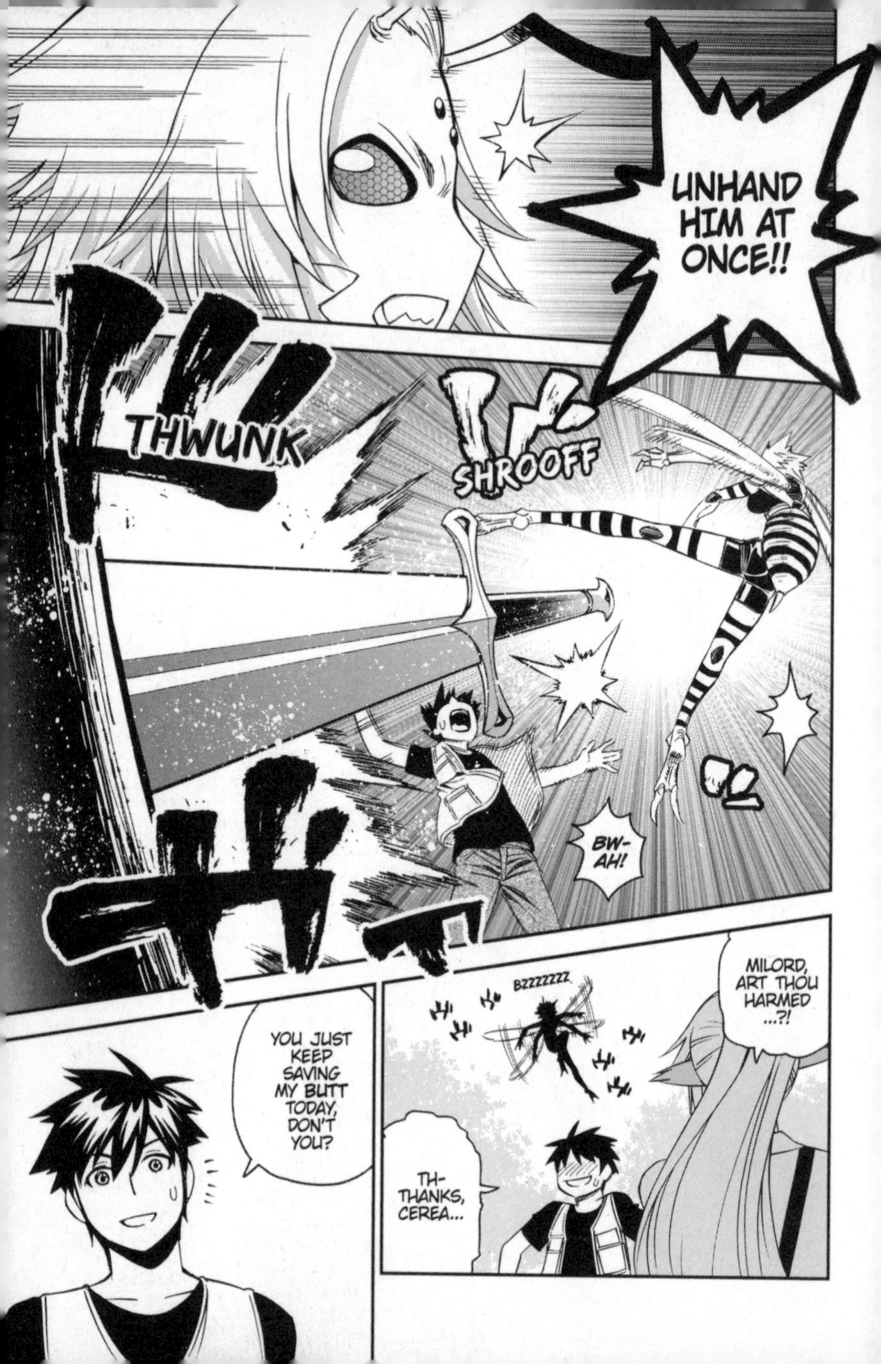
UNHAND HIM AT ONCE!!
SHROOFF
THWUNK
BW-AH!
MILORD, ART THOU HARMED ...?!
BZZZZZZZ
TH-THANKS, CEREA...
YOU JUST KEEP SAVING MY BUTT TODAY, DON'T YOU?

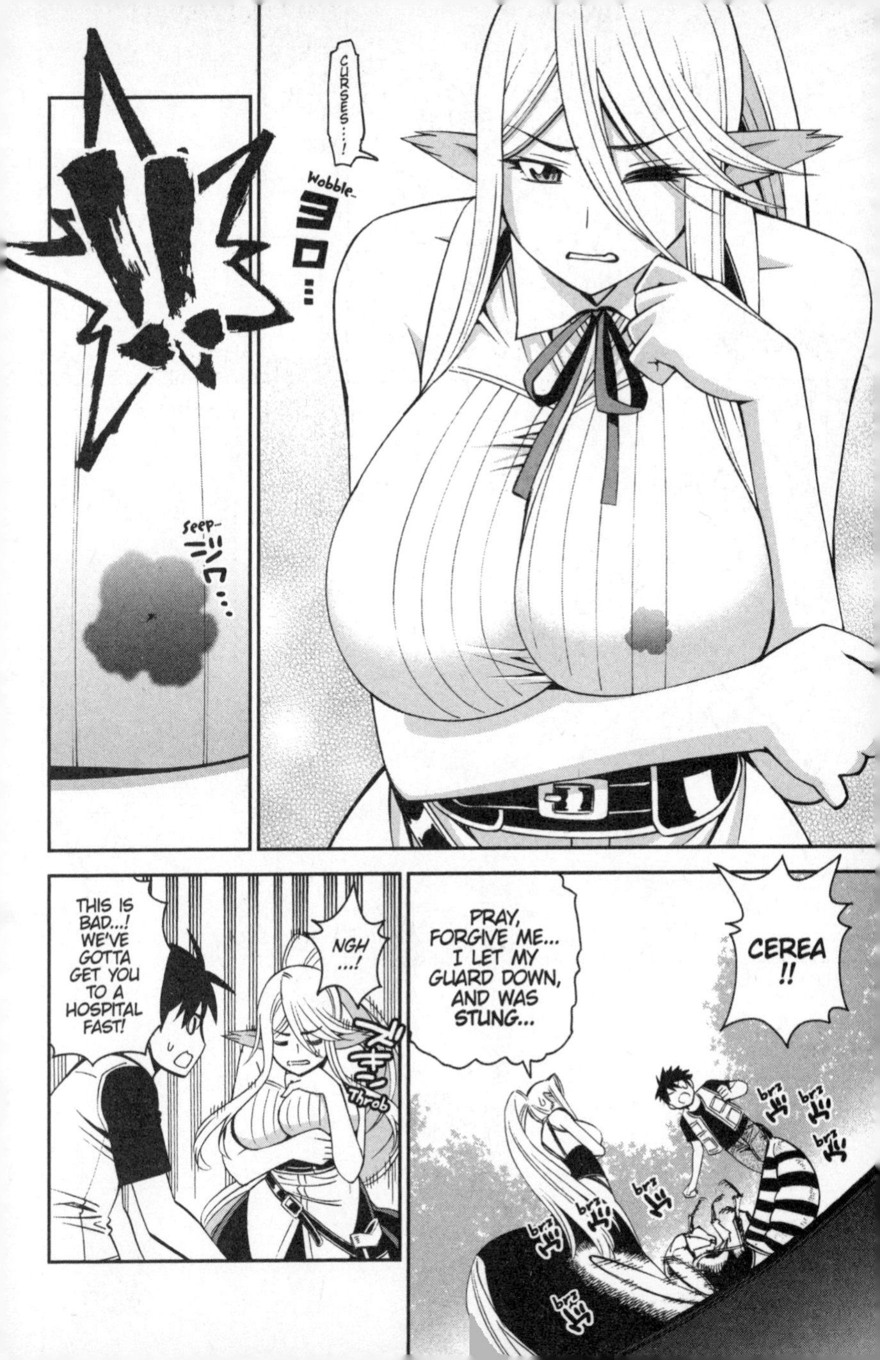
CURSES...!
Wobble
ヨロ…
Seep
CEREA!!
PRAY, FORGIVE ME... I LET MY GUARD DOWN, AND WAS STUNG...
brz brz brz brz brz brz brz brz
NGH ...!
THIS IS BAD...! WE'VE GOTTA GET YOU TO A HOSPITAL FAST!
Throb

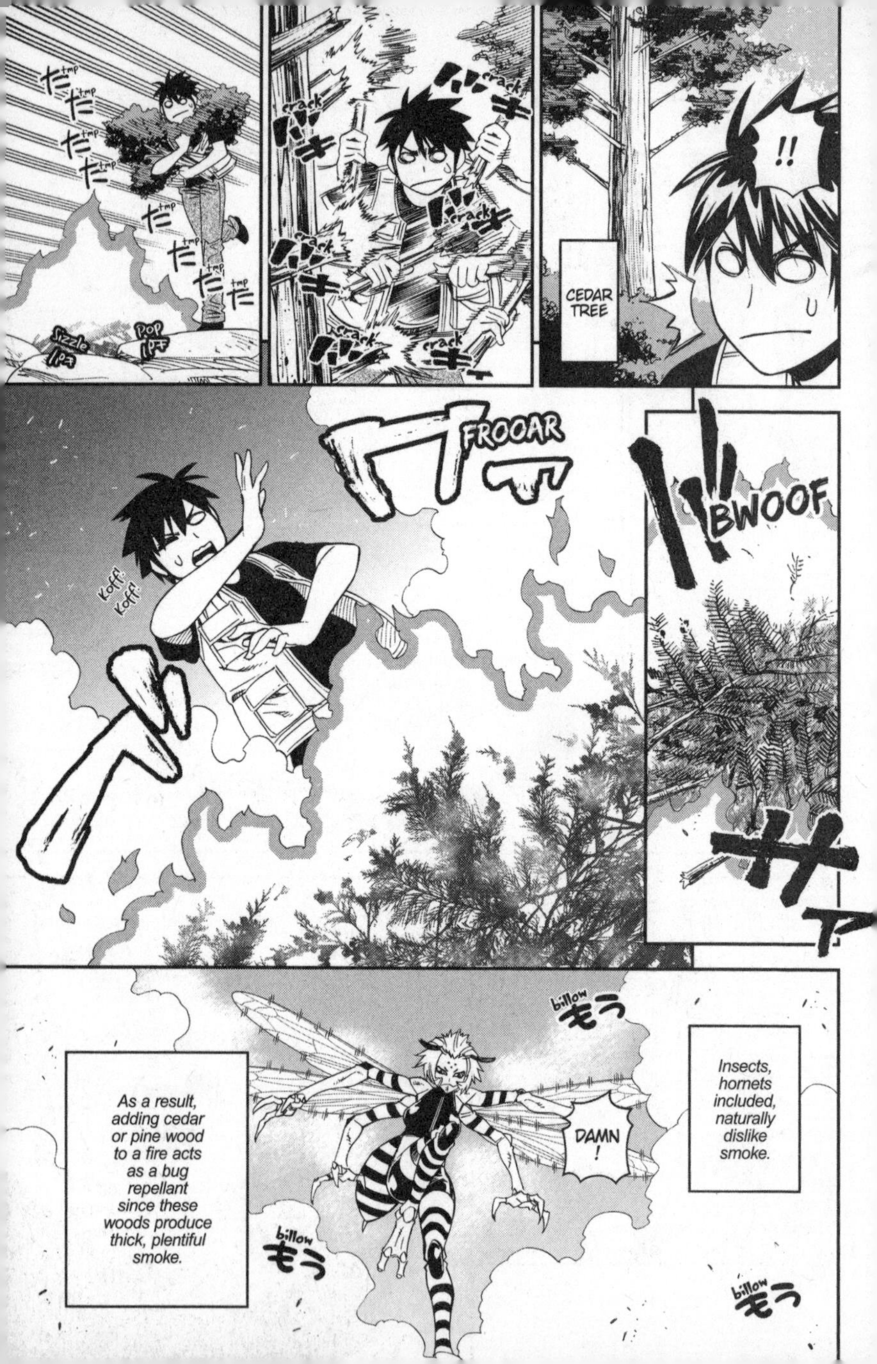

!!
CEDAR TREE
crack
crack
crack
crack
crack
crack
tmp
tmp
tmp
tmp
tmp
tmp
tmp
tmp
だ
だ
だ
だ
だ
だ
だ
だ
pop
sizzle
BWOOF
FROOAR
Koff.
Koff.
Insects, hornets included, naturally dislike smoke.
billow
もう
DAMN!
billow
もう
billow
もう
As a result, adding cedar or pine wood to a fire acts as a bug repellant since these woods produce thick, plentiful smoke.

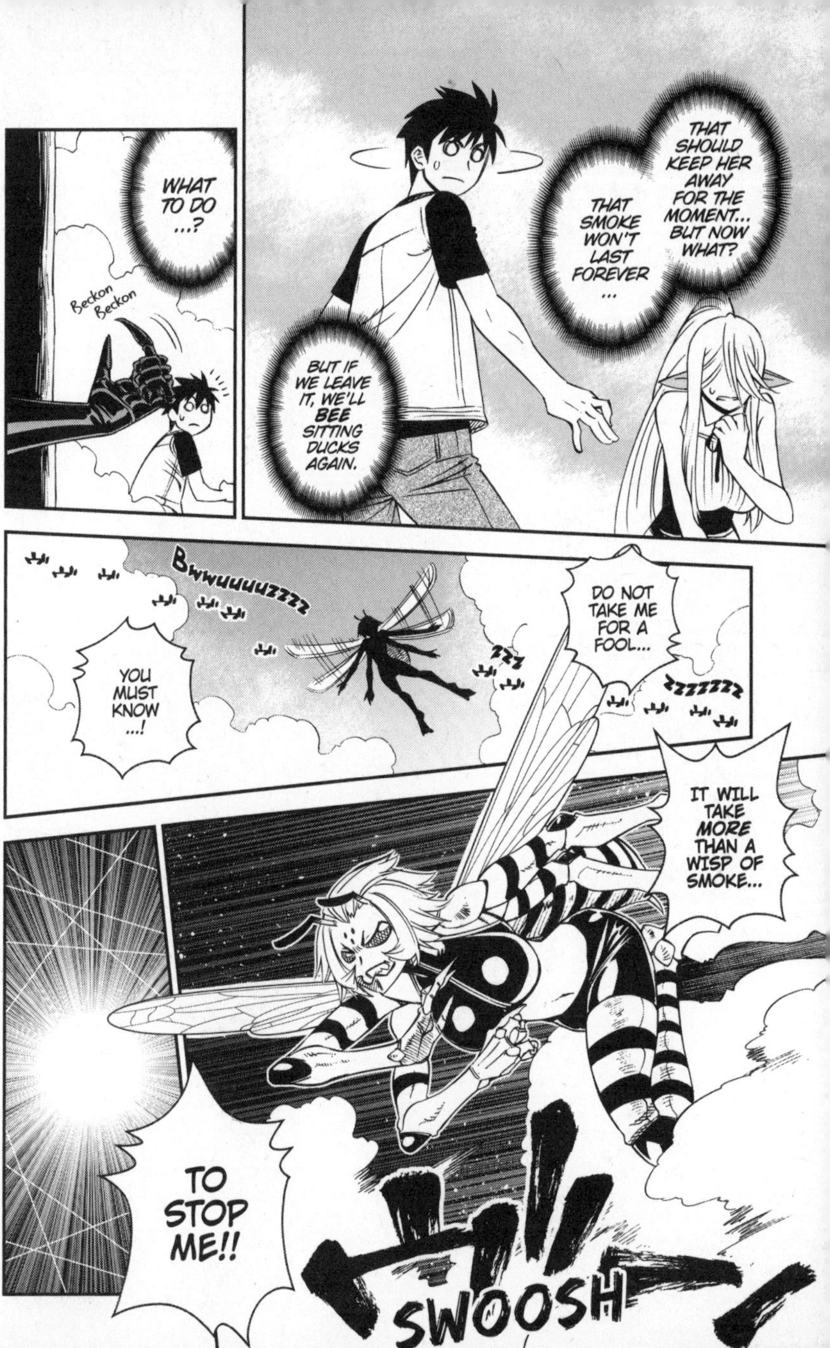
THAT SHOULD KEEP HER AWAY FOR THE MOMENT... BUT NOW WHAT?
THAT SMOKE WON'T LAST FOREVER ...
BUT IF WE LEAVE IT, WE'LL BEE SITTING DUCKS AGAIN.
WHAT TO DO ...?
Beckon Beckon
DO NOT TAKE ME FOR A FOOL...
zzzzzzz
zzz
Bwwuuuuzzzz
YOU MUST KNOW ...!
IT WILL TAKE MORE THAN A WISP OF SMOKE...
TO STOP ME!!
SWOOSH

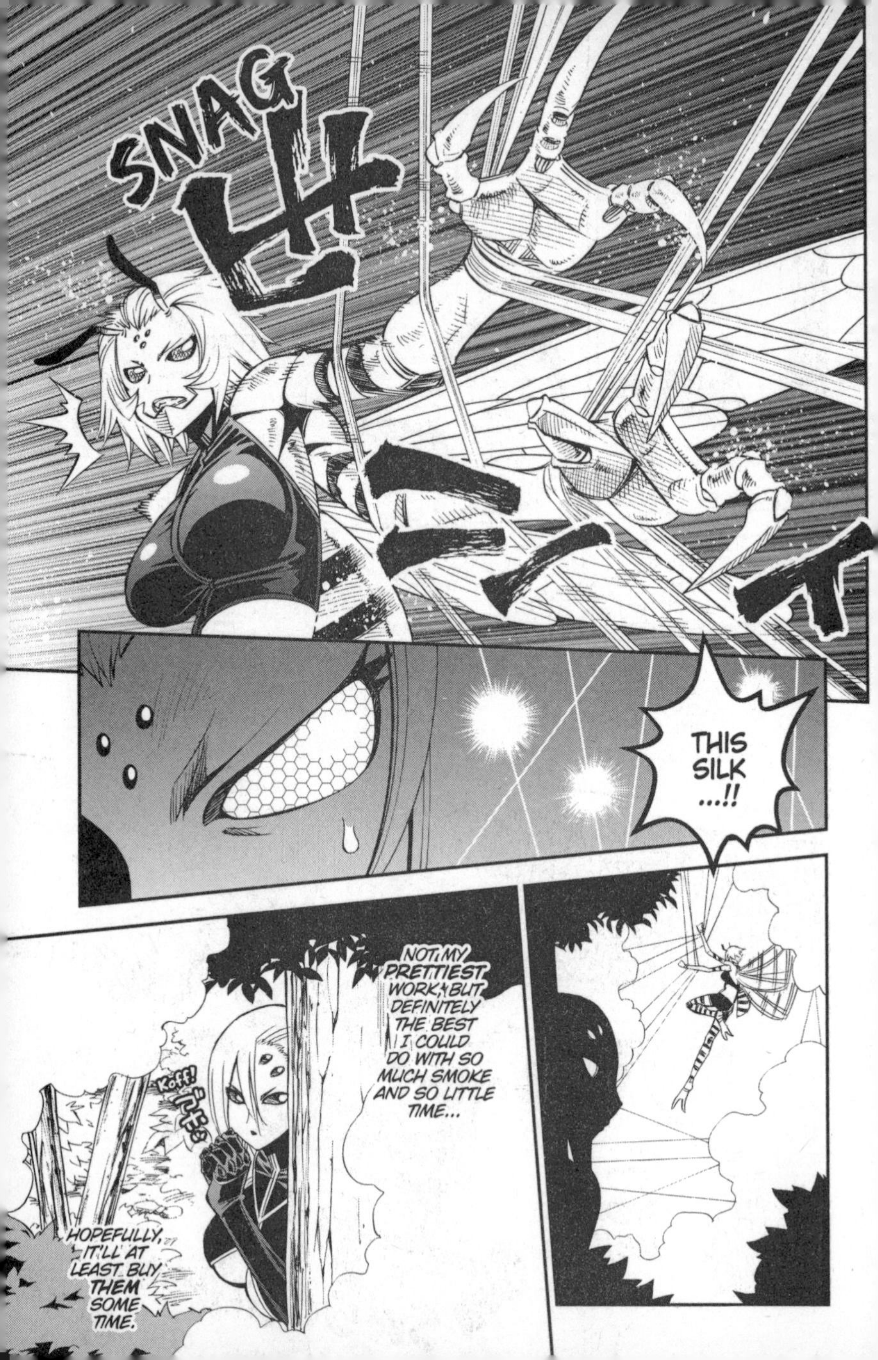
SNAG
THIS SILK ...!!
NOT MY PRETTIEST WORK, BUT DEFINITELY THE BEST I COULD DO WITH SO MUCH SMOKE AND SO LITTLE TIME...
Koff!
ごほっ
HOPEFULLY, IT'LL AT LEAST BUY THEM SOME TIME.

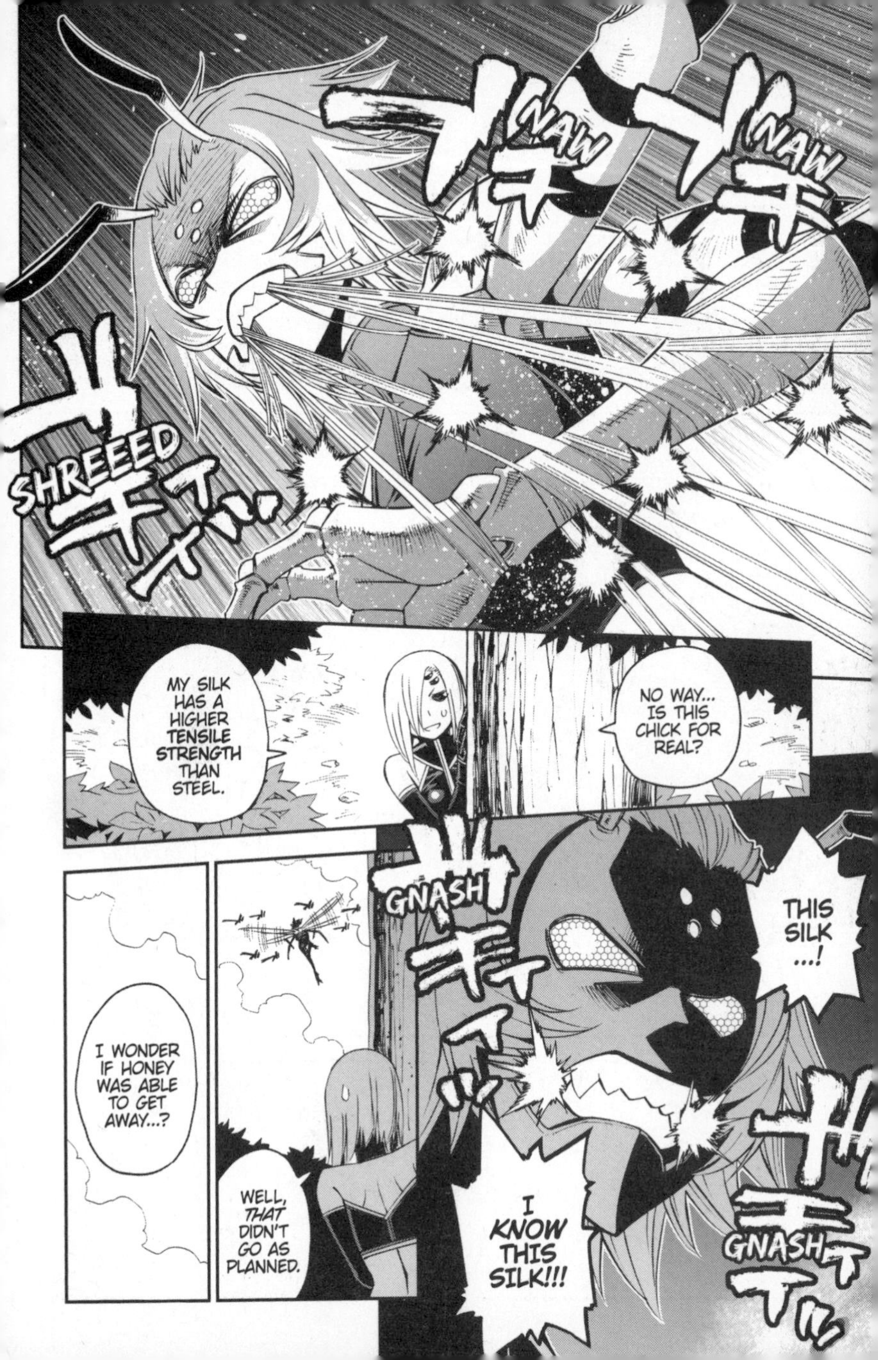
NAW
NAW
SHREEED
NO WAY... IS THIS CHICK FOR REAL?
MY SILK HAS A HIGHER TENSILE STRENGTH THAN STEEL.
THIS SILK ...!
GNASH
I KNOW THIS SILK!!!
GNASH
WELL, *THAT* DIDN'T GO AS PLANNED.
I WONDER IF HONEY WAS ABLE TO GET AWAY...?

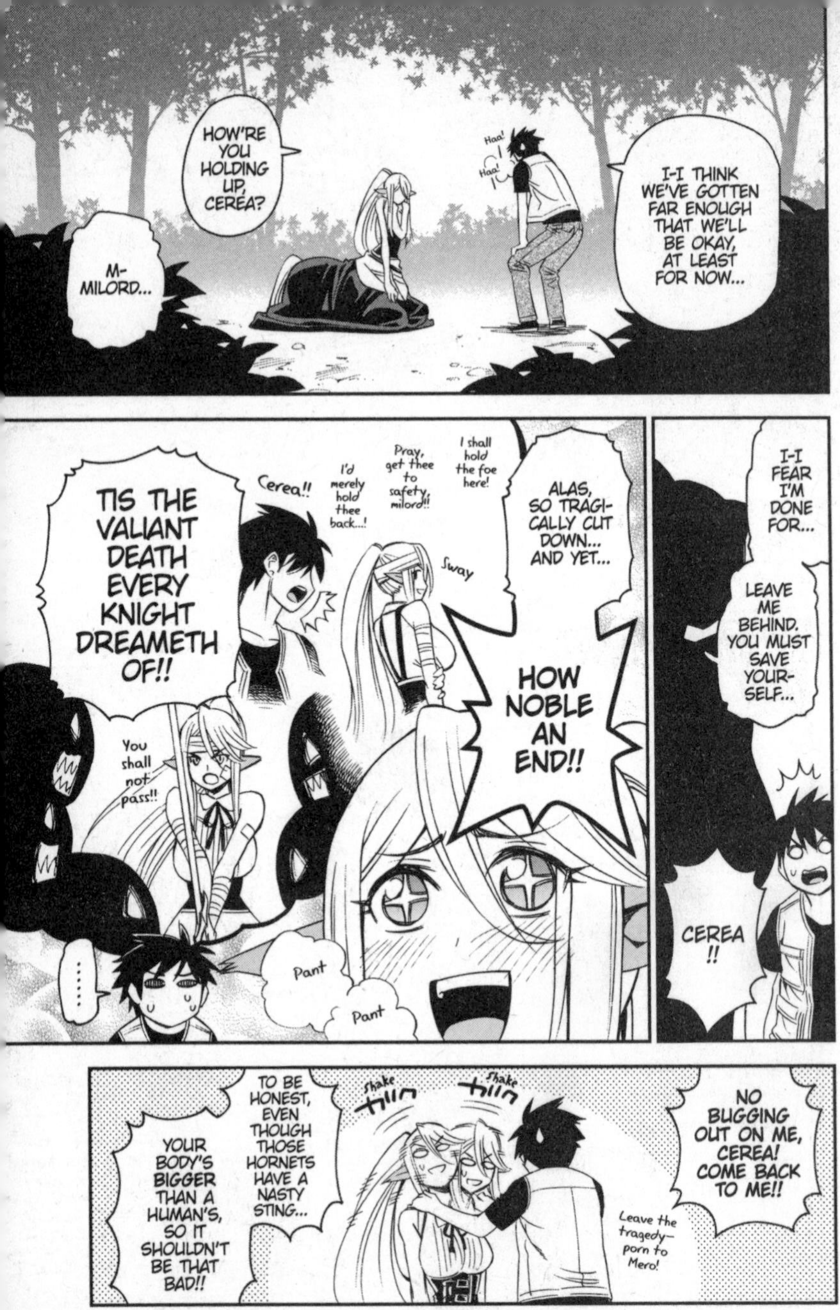
I-I THINK WE'VE GOTTEN FAR ENOUGH THAT WE'LL BE OKAY, AT LEAST FOR NOW...
Haa! Haa!
HOW'RE YOU HOLDING UP, CERÉA?
M-MILORD...
I-I FEAR I'M DONE FOR...
LEAVE ME BEHIND. YOU MUST SAVE YOURSELF...
CEREA!!
ALAS, SO TRAGICALLY CUT DOWN... AND YET...
HOW NOBLE AN END!!
I shall hold the foe here!
Pray, get thee to safety, milord!!
I'd merely hold thee back...!
Cerea!!
Sway
TIS THE VALIANT DEATH EVERY KNIGHT DREAMETH OF!!
You shall not pass!!
Pant
Pant
......
NO BUGGING OUT ON ME, CEREA! COME BACK TO ME!!
Leave the tragedy-porn to Mero!
Shake
Shake
TO BE HONEST, EVEN THOUGH THOSE HORNETS HAVE A NASTY STING...
YOUR BODY'S BIGGER THAN A HUMAN'S, SO IT SHOULDN'T BE THAT BAD!!

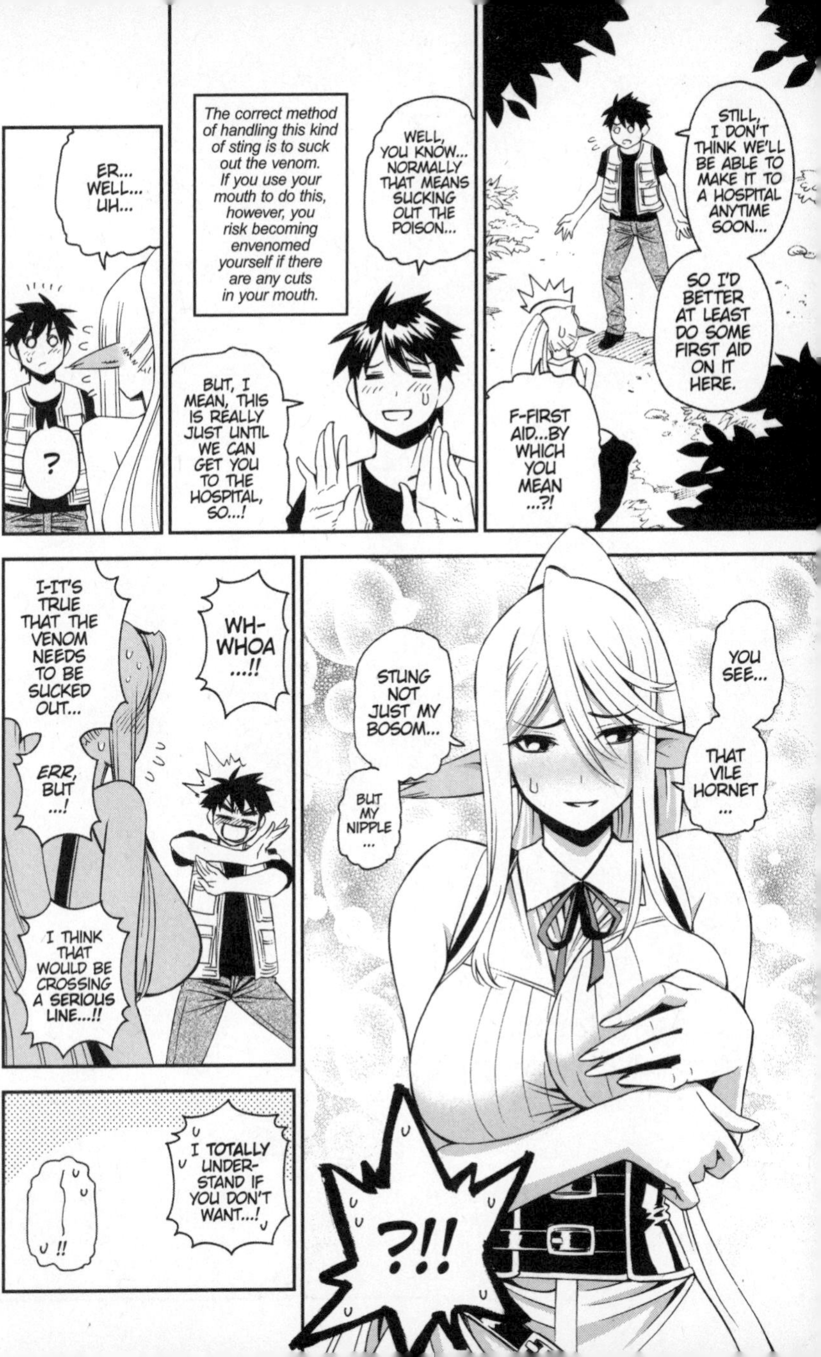
STILL, I DON'T THINK WE'LL BE ABLE TO MAKE IT TO A HOSPITAL ANYTIME SOON...
SO I'D BETTER AT LEAST DO SOME FIRST AID ON IT HERE.
F-FIRST AID...BY WHICH YOU MEAN ...?!
WELL, YOU KNOW... NORMALLY THAT MEANS SUCKING OUT THE POISON...
The correct method of handling this kind of sting is to suck out the venom. If you use your mouth to do this, however, you risk becoming envenomed yourself if there are any cuts in your mouth.
BUT, I MEAN, THIS IS REALLY JUST UNTIL WE CAN GET YOU TO THE HOSPITAL, SO...!
ER... WELL... UH...
?
YOU SEE...
THAT VILE HORNET ...
STUNG NOT JUST MY BOSOM...
BUT MY NIPPLE ...
?!!
WH- WHOA ...!!
I-IT'S TRUE THAT THE VENOM NEEDS TO BE SUCKED OUT...
ERR, BUT ...!
I THINK THAT WOULD BE CROSSING A SERIOUS LINE...!!
I TOTALLY UNDER- STAND IF YOU DON'T WANT...!
—!!

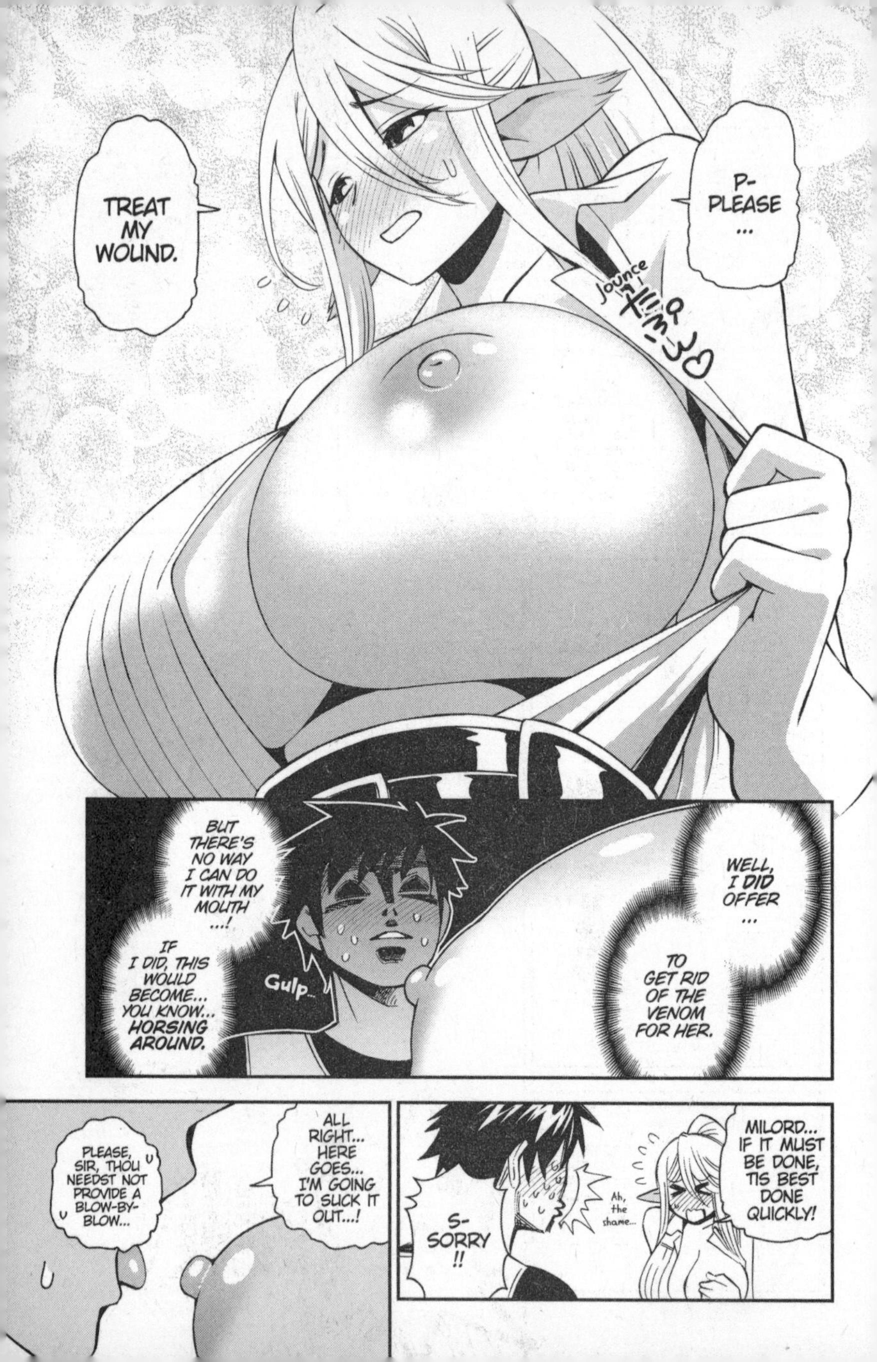
P-PLEASE...
TREAT MY WOUND.
jounce
WELL, I DID OFFER...
TO GET RID OF THE VENOM FOR HER.
BUT THERE'S NO WAY I CAN DO IT WITH MY MOUTH...!
IF I DID, THIS WOULD BECOME... YOU KNOW... HORSING AROUND.
Gulp...
MILORD... IF IT MUST BE DONE, TIS BEST DONE QUICKLY!
Ah, the shame...
S-SORRY!!
ALL RIGHT... HERE GOES... I'M GOING TO SUCK IT OUT...!
PLEASE, SIR, THOU NEEDST NOT PROVIDE A BLOW-BY-BLOW...

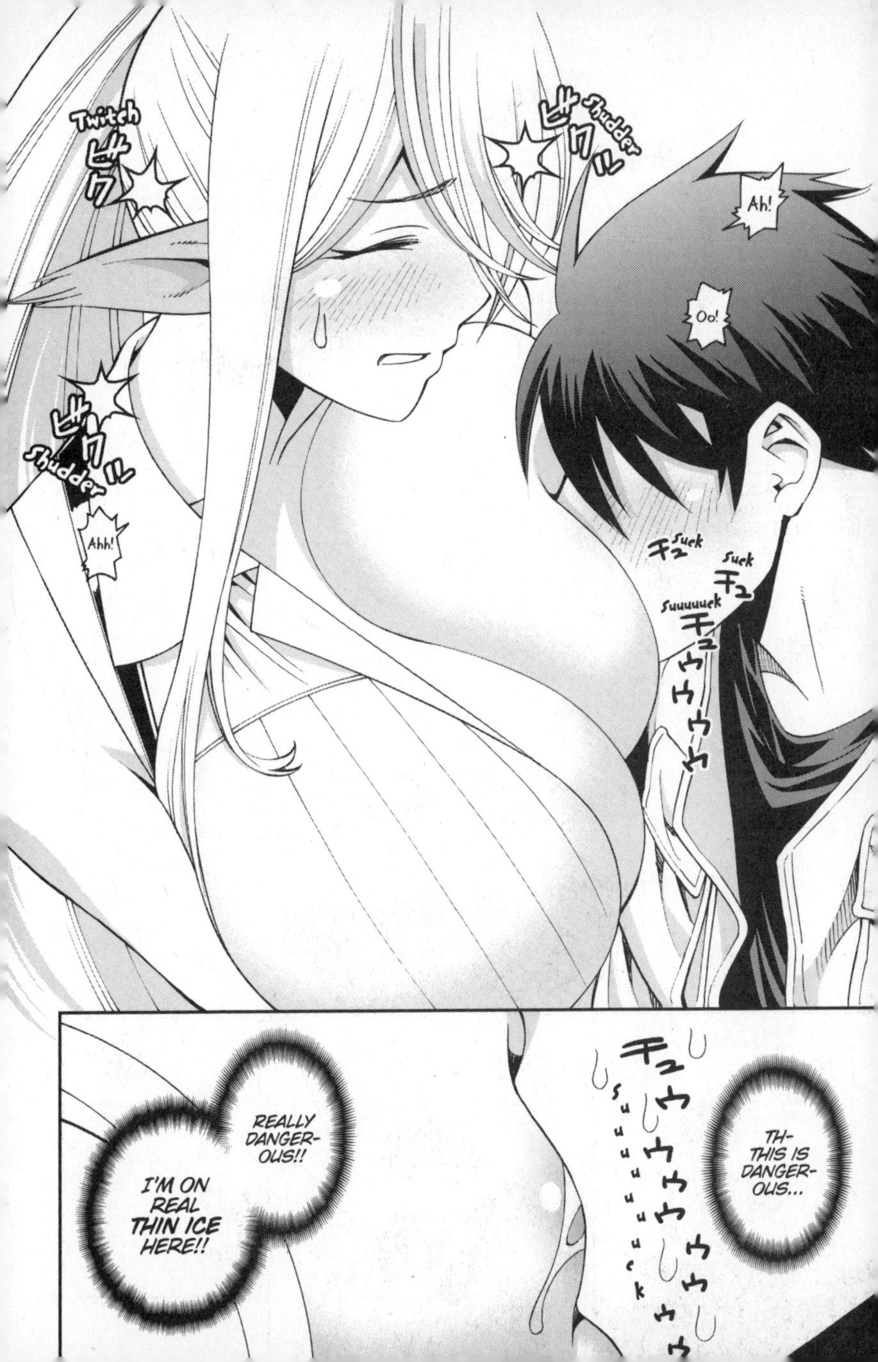

Shudder
Ah!
Oo!
Suck
Suck
Suuuuuck
Twitch
Shudder
Ahh!
TH- THIS IS DANGER-OUS...
Suuuuuuuuck
REALLY DANGER-OUS!!
I'M ON REAL THIN ICE HERE!!

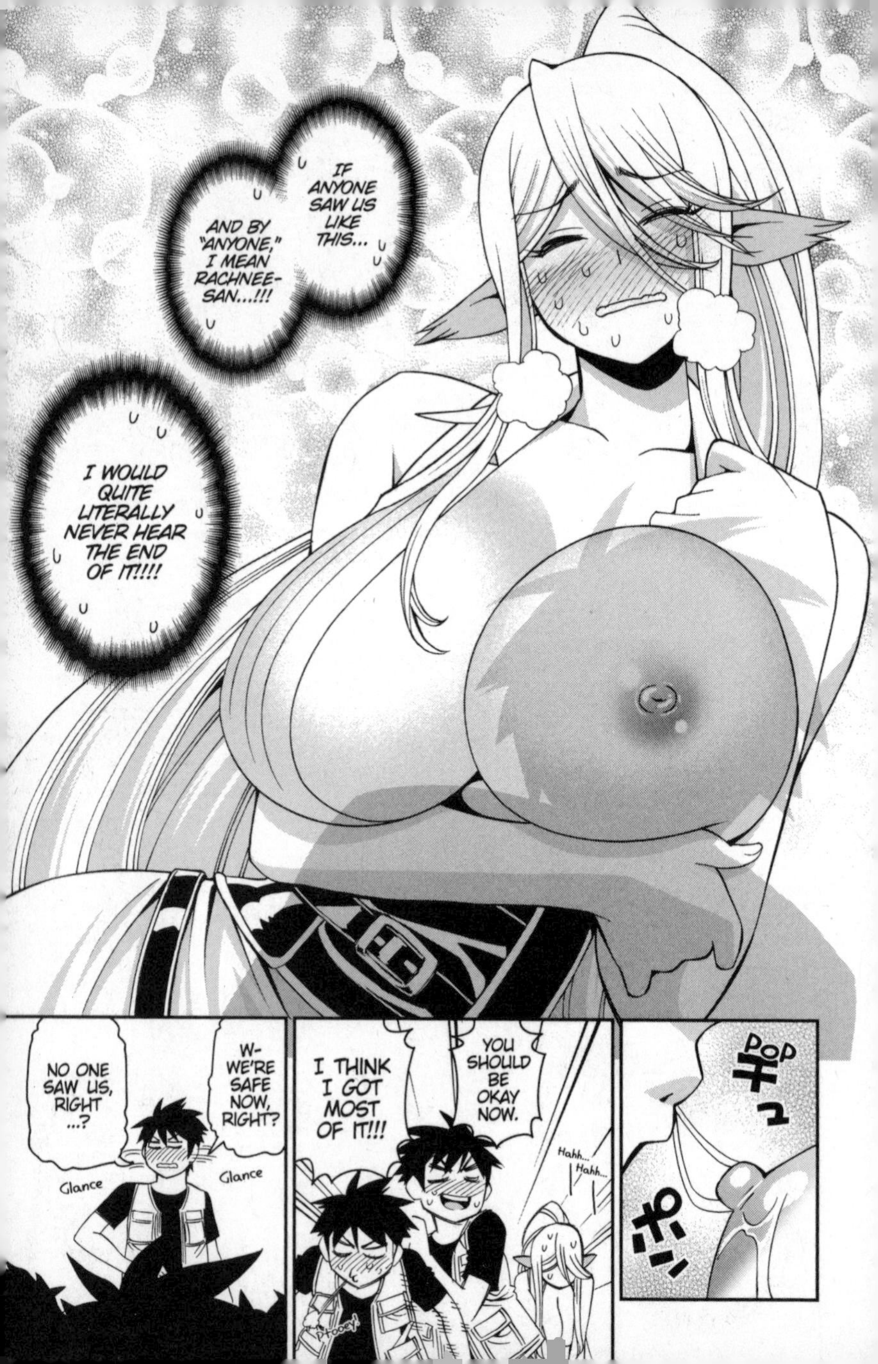
IF ANYONE SAW US LIKE THIS...
AND BY "ANYONE," I MEAN RACHNEE-SAN...!!!
I WOULD QUITE LITERALLY NEVER HEAR THE END OF IT!!!!
POP
YOU SHOULD BE OKAY NOW.
I THINK I GOT MOST OF IT!!!
Hahh... Hahh...
Ptooey!
W-WE'RE SAFE NOW, RIGHT?
NO ONE SAW US, RIGHT ...?
Glance
Glance

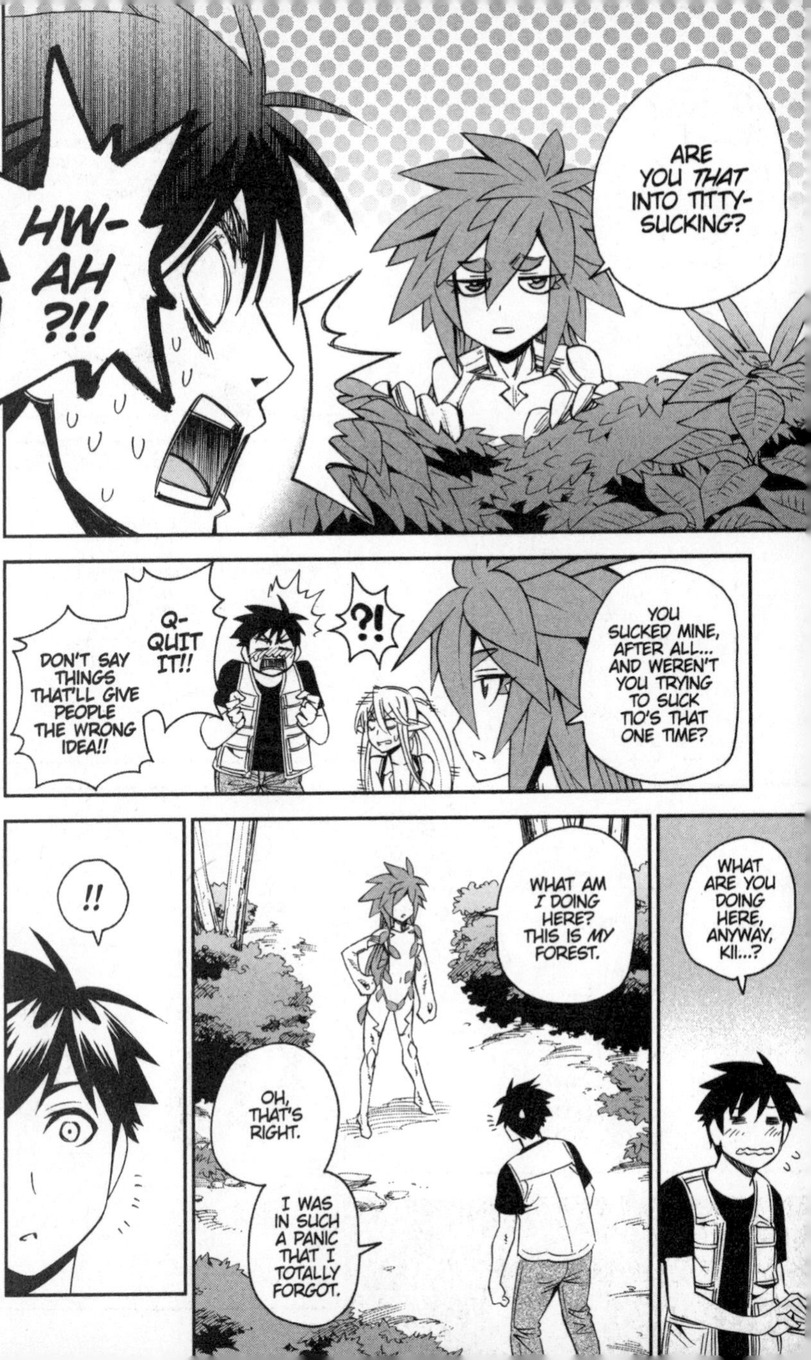
ARE YOU THAT INTO TITTY-SUCKING?
HW-AH?!!
YOU SUCKED MINE, AFTER ALL... AND WEREN'T YOU TRYING TO SUCK TIO'S THAT ONE TIME?
?!
Q-QUIT IT!!
DON'T SAY THINGS THAT'LL GIVE PEOPLE THE WRONG IDEA!!
WHAT ARE YOU DOING HERE, ANYWAY, KII...?
WHAT AM I DOING HERE? THIS IS MY FOREST.
OH, THAT'S RIGHT.
I WAS IN SUCH A PANIC THAT I TOTALLY FORGOT.
!!

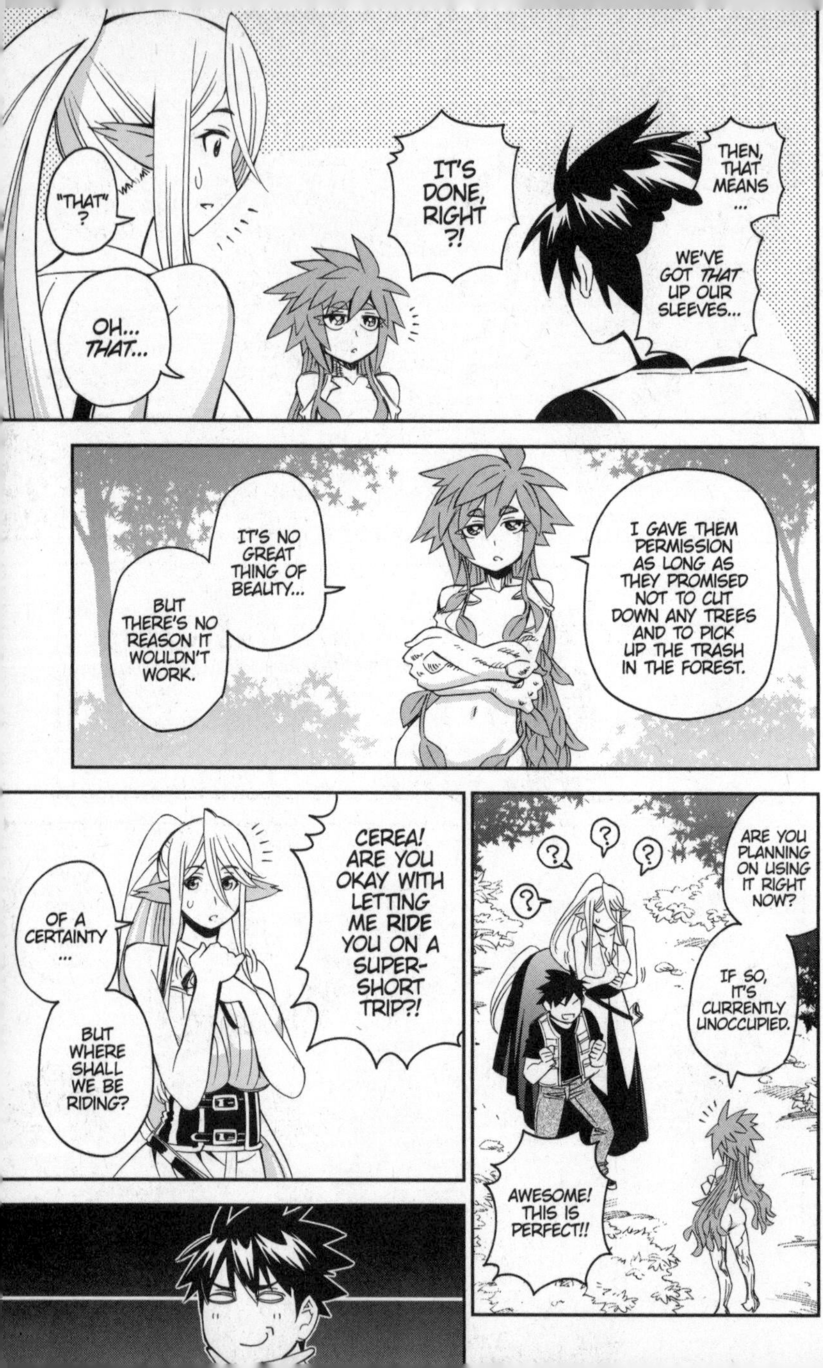
THEN, THAT MEANS ...
WE'VE GOT *THAT* UP OUR SLEEVES...
IT'S DONE, RIGHT ?!
"THAT" ?
OH... *THAT*...
I GAVE THEM PERMISSION AS LONG AS THEY PROMISED NOT TO CUT DOWN ANY TREES AND TO PICK UP THE TRASH IN THE FOREST.
IT'S NO GREAT THING OF BEAUTY...
BUT THERE'S NO REASON IT WOULDN'T WORK.
ARE YOU PLANNING ON USING IT RIGHT NOW?
IF SO, IT'S CURRENTLY UNOCCUPIED.
AWESOME! THIS IS PERFECT!!
CEREA! ARE YOU OKAY WITH LETTING ME RIDE YOU ON A SUPER-SHORT TRIP?!
OF A CERTAINTY ...
BUT WHERE SHALL WE BE RIDING?

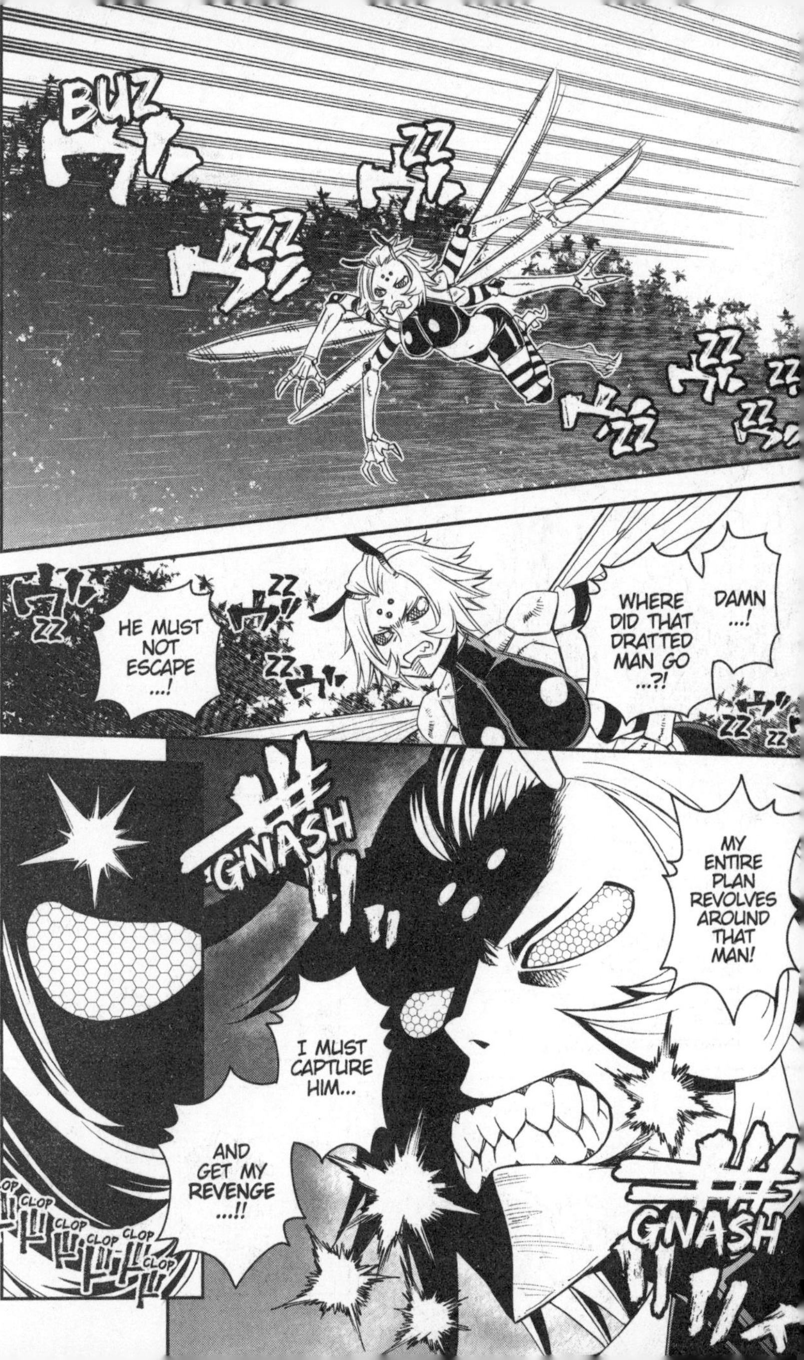
BUZ
ZZZ
ZZZ
ZZZ
ZZ
DAMN...!
WHERE DID THAT DRATTED MAN GO...?!
HE MUST NOT ESCAPE...!
MY ENTIRE PLAN REVOLVES AROUND THAT MAN!
GNASH
GNASH
I MUST CAPTURE HIM...
AND GET MY REVENGE...!!
CLOP CLOP CLOP CLOP CLOP CLOP

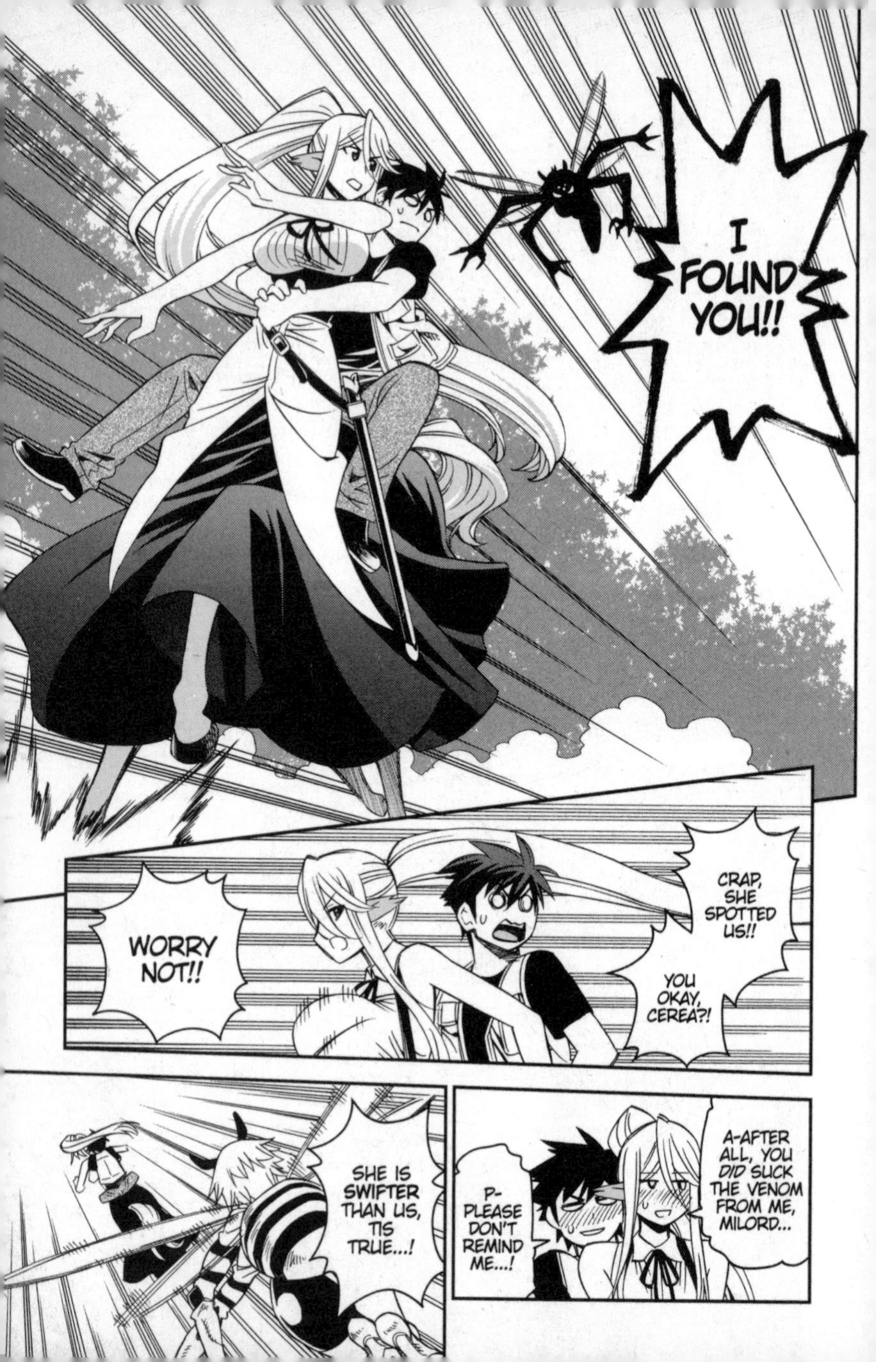
I FOUND YOU!!
CRAP, SHE SPOTTED US!!
YOU OKAY, CEREA?!
WORRY NOT!!
A-AFTER ALL, YOU *DID* SUCK THE VENOM FROM ME, MILORD...
P-PLEASE DON'T REMIND ME...!
SHE IS SWIFTER THAN US, TIS TRUE...!

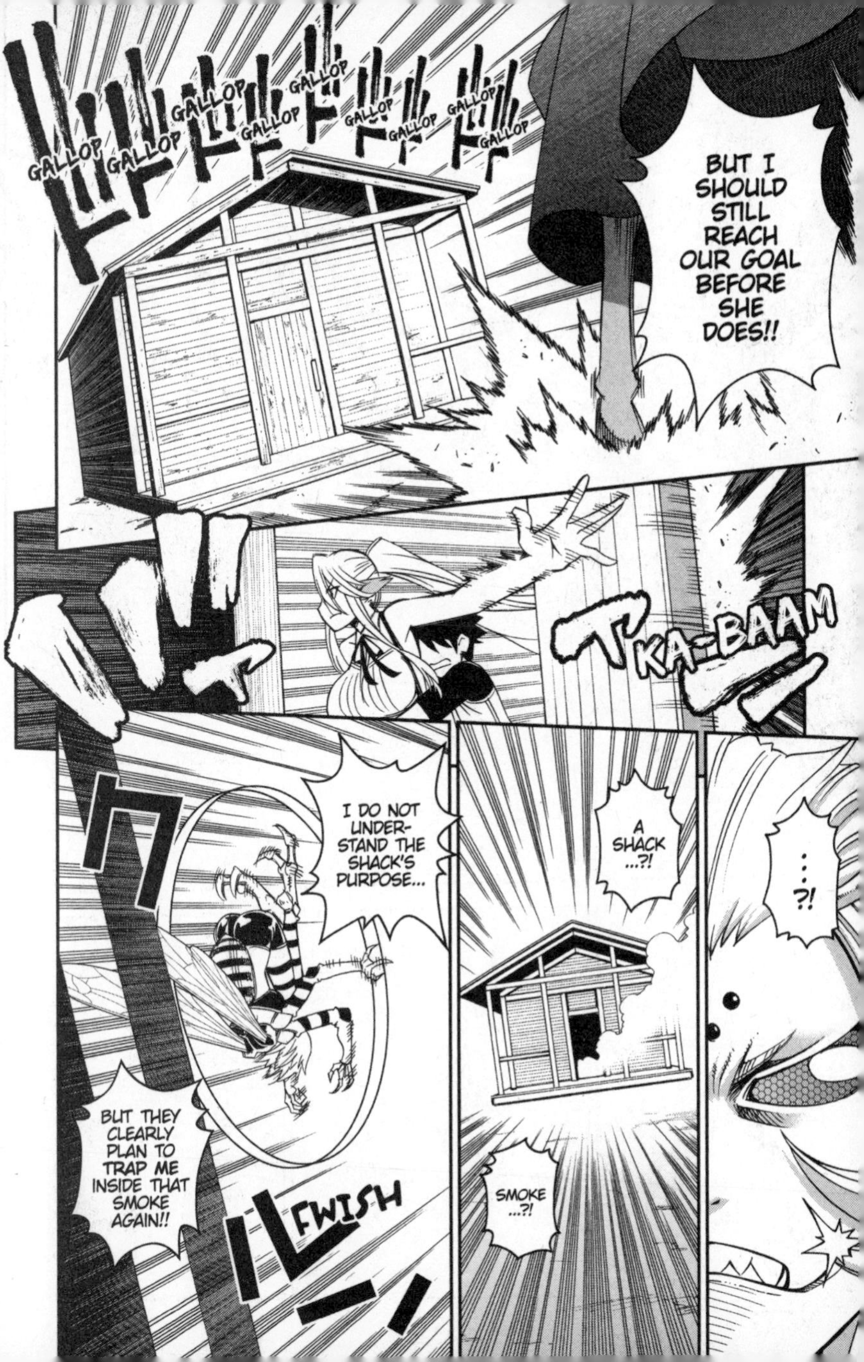
BUT I SHOULD STILL REACH OUR GOAL BEFORE SHE DOES!!
GALLOP GALLOP GALLOP GALLOP GALLOP GALLOP GALLOP GALLOP GALLOP
KA-BAAM
...?!
A SHACK ...?!
SMOKE ...?!
I DO NOT UNDER-STAND THE SHACK'S PURPOSE...
BUT THEY CLEARLY PLAN TO TRAP ME INSIDE THAT SMOKE AGAIN!!
FWISH

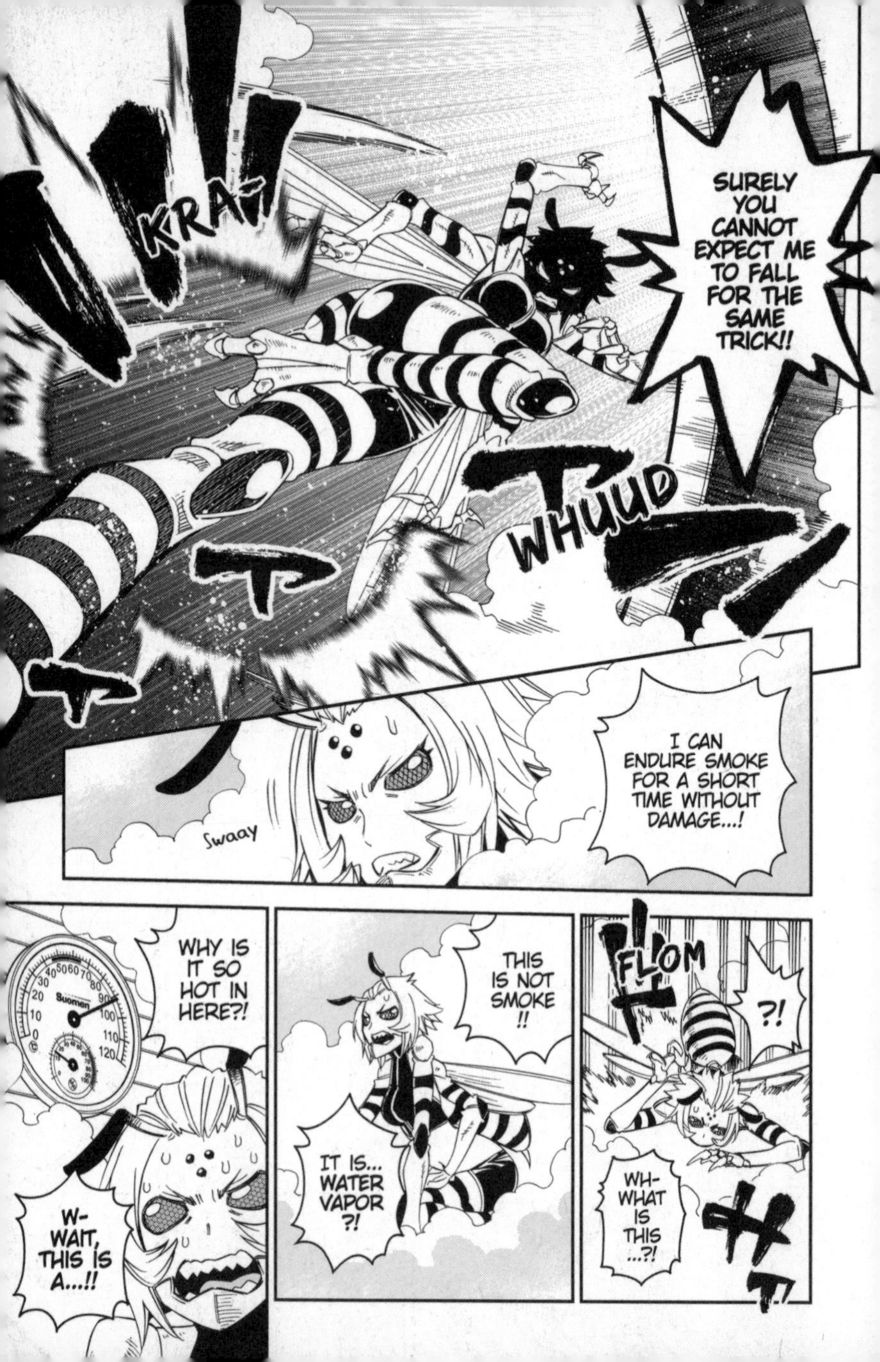
SURELY YOU CANNOT EXPECT ME TO FALL FOR THE SAME TRICK!!
KRA-
WHUUD
I CAN ENDURE SMOKE FOR A SHORT TIME WITHOUT DAMAGE...!
Swaay
FLOM
?!
WH- WHAT IS THIS ...?!
THIS IS NOT SMOKE !!
IT IS... WATER VAPOR ?!
WHY IS IT SO HOT IN HERE?!
Suomen
W- WAIT, THIS IS A...!!

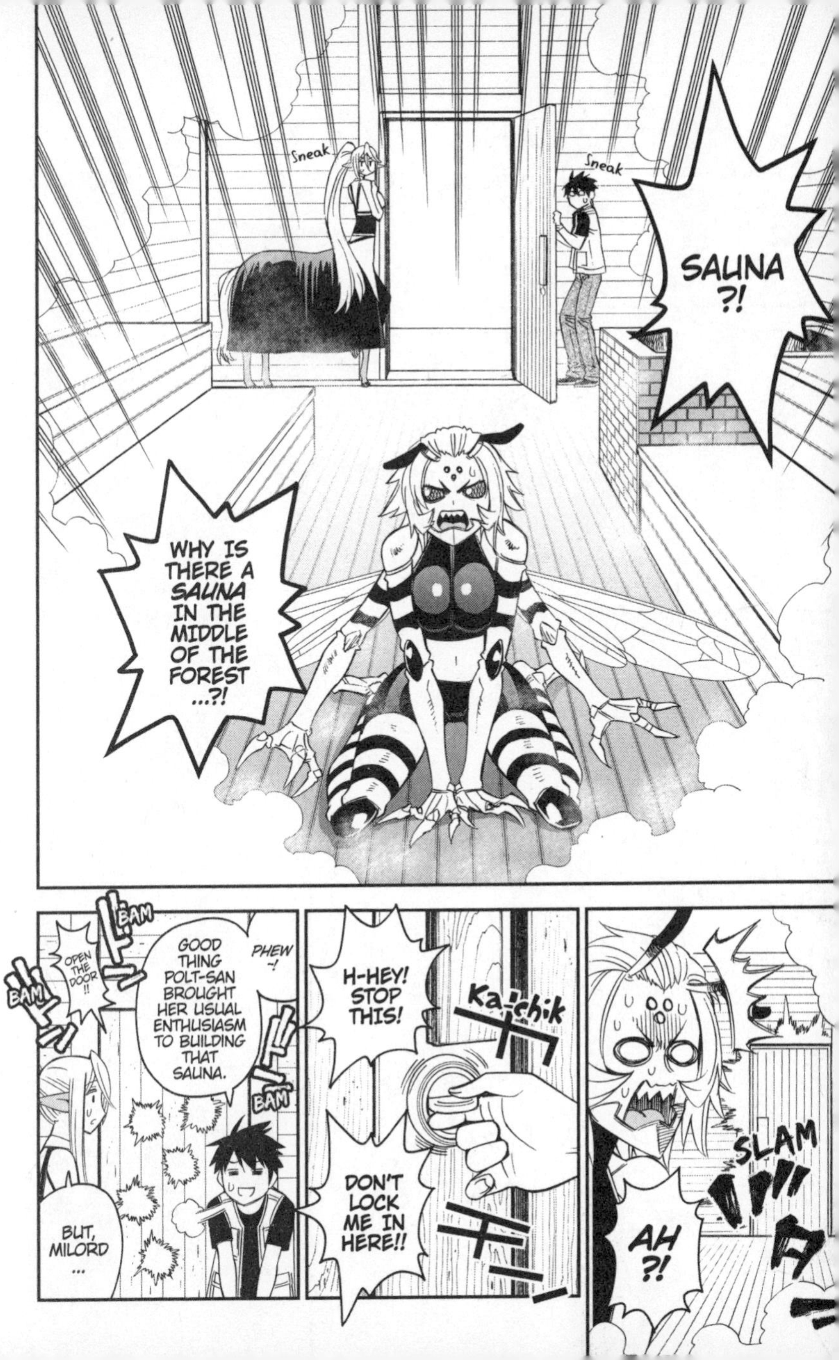
SAUNA ?!
Sneak
Sneak
WHY IS THERE A SAUNA IN THE MIDDLE OF THE FOREST ...?!
AH ?!
SLAM
H-HEY! STOP THIS!
Ka-chik
DON'T LOCK ME IN HERE!!
BAM
PHEW -!
GOOD THING POLT-SAN BROUGHT HER USUAL ENTHUSIASM TO BUILDING THAT SAUNA.
OPEN THE DOOR !!
BAM
BAM
BUT, MILORD ...

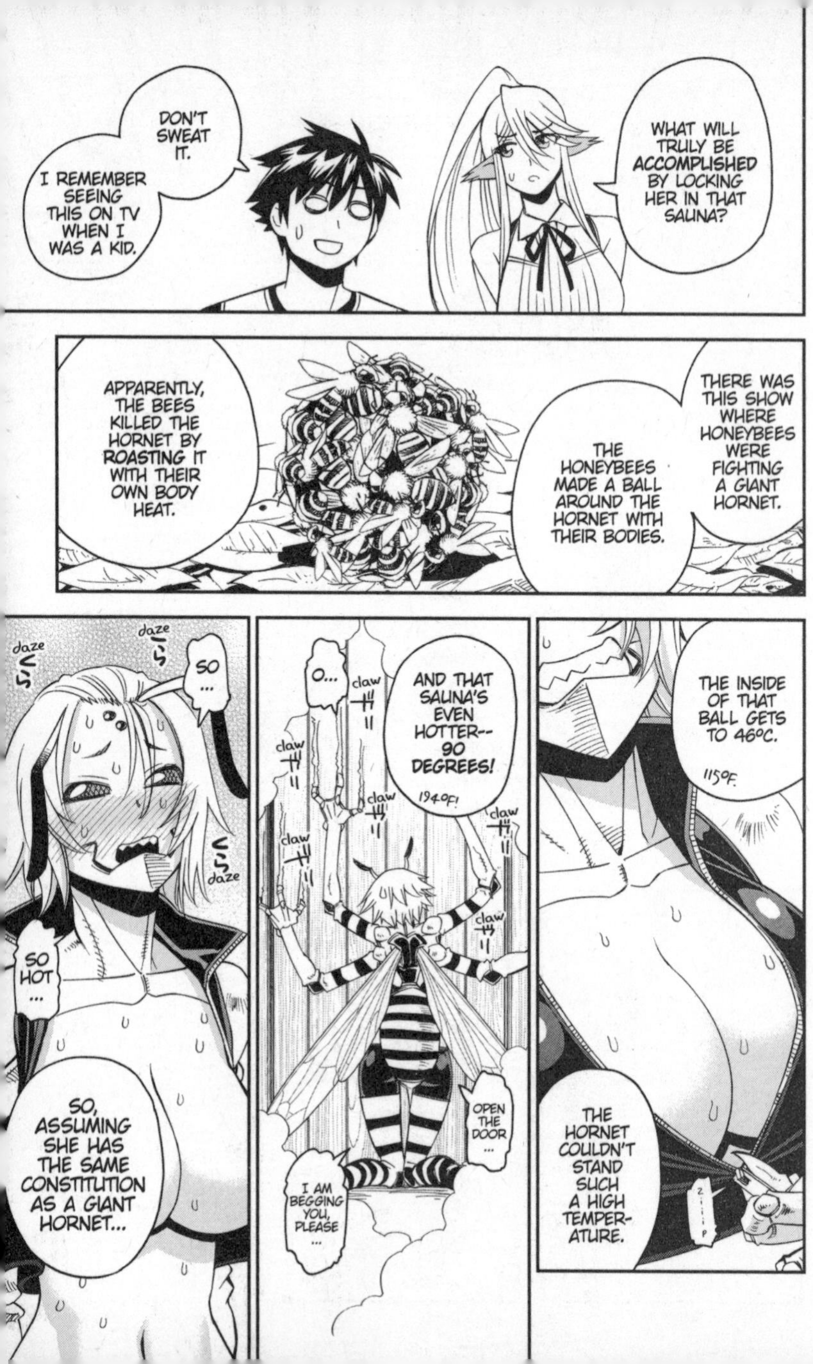
WHAT WILL TRULY BE ACCOMPLISHED BY LOCKING HER IN THAT SAUNA?
DON'T SWEAT IT.
I REMEMBER SEEING THIS ON TV WHEN I WAS A KID.
THERE WAS THIS SHOW WHERE HONEYBEES WERE FIGHTING A GIANT HORNET.
THE HONEYBEES MADE A BALL AROUND THE HORNET WITH THEIR BODIES.
APPARENTLY, THE BEES KILLED THE HORNET BY ROASTING IT WITH THEIR OWN BODY HEAT.
THE INSIDE OF THAT BALL GETS TO 46°C.
115°F.
THE HORNET COULDN'T STAND SUCH A HIGH TEMPER-ATURE.
z...p
AND THAT SAUNA'S EVEN HOTTER--90 DEGREES!
194°F!
O...
claw
claw
claw
claw
claw
claw
OPEN THE DOOR...
I AM BEGGING YOU, PLEASE...
daze
daze
SO...
daze
SO HOT...
SO, ASSUMING SHE HAS THE SAME CONSTITUTION AS A GIANT HORNET...

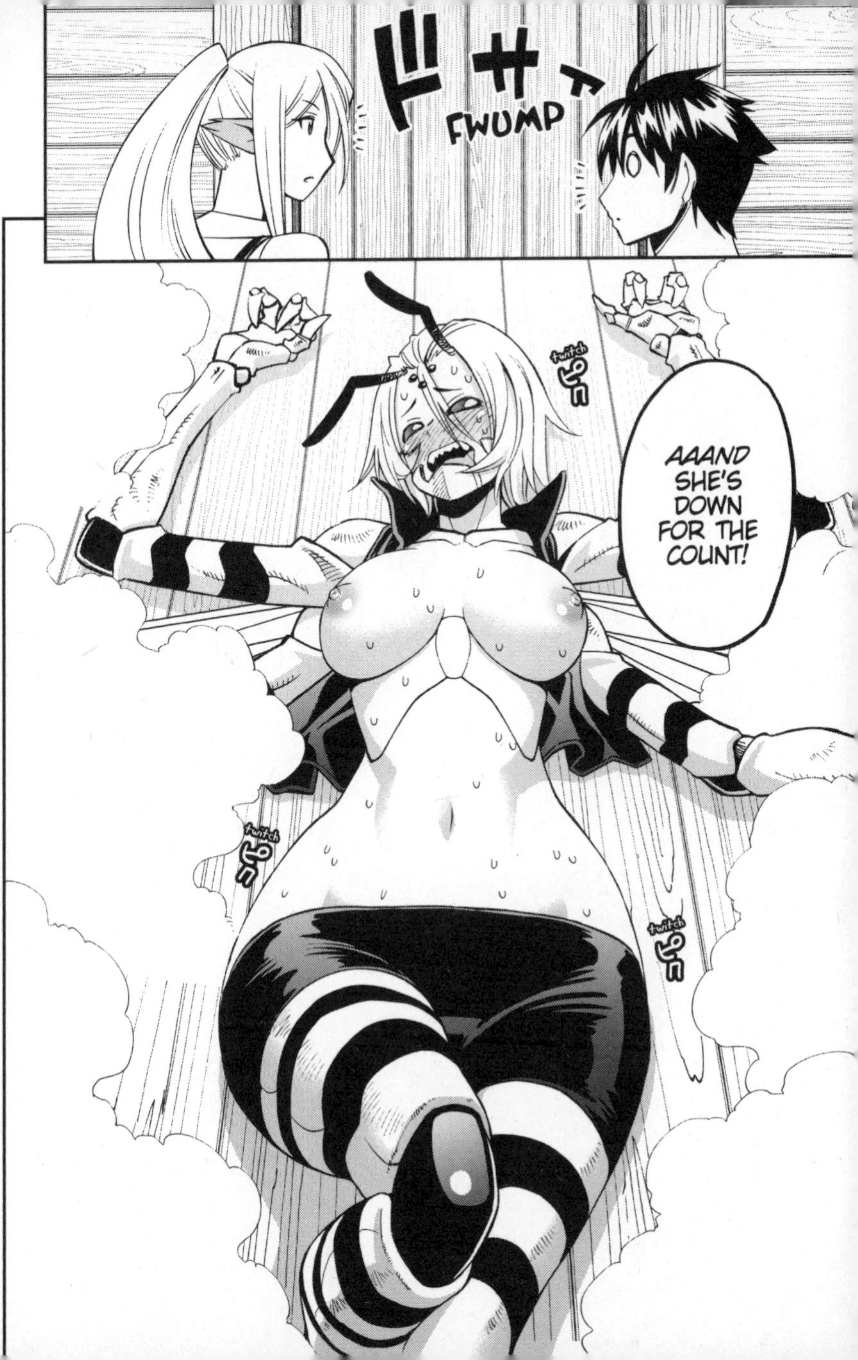
ドサァ
FWUMP
twitch
AAAND SHE'S DOWN FOR THE COUNT!
twitch
twitch

Monster Musume

Everyday Life with Monster Girls

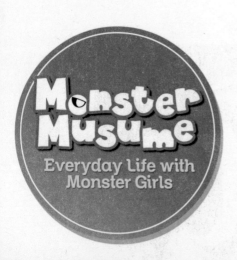

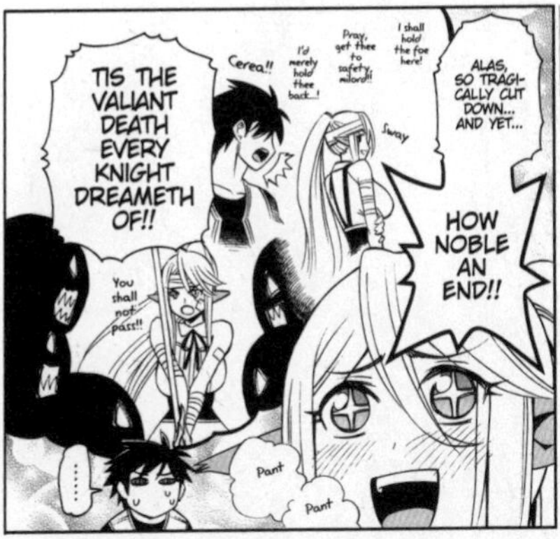
ALAS, SO TRAGI-CALLY CUT DOWN... AND YET...
I shall hold the foe here!
Pray, get thee to safety, milord!!
I'd merely hold thee back...!
Cerea!!
TIS THE VALIANT DEATH EVERY KNIGHT DREAMETH OF!!
HOW NOBLE AN END!!
Sway
You shall not pass!!
Pant
Pant
......

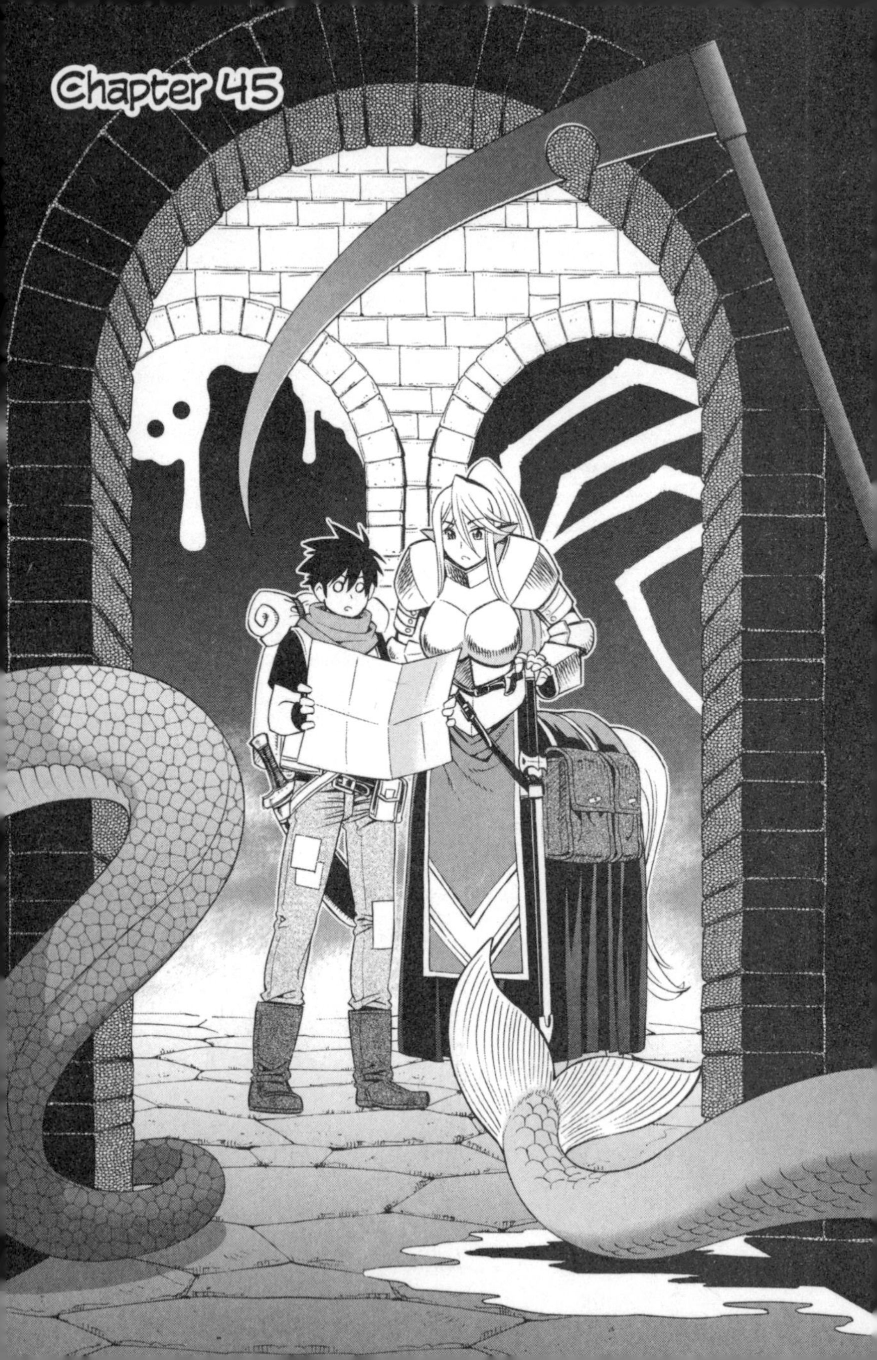
Chapter 45

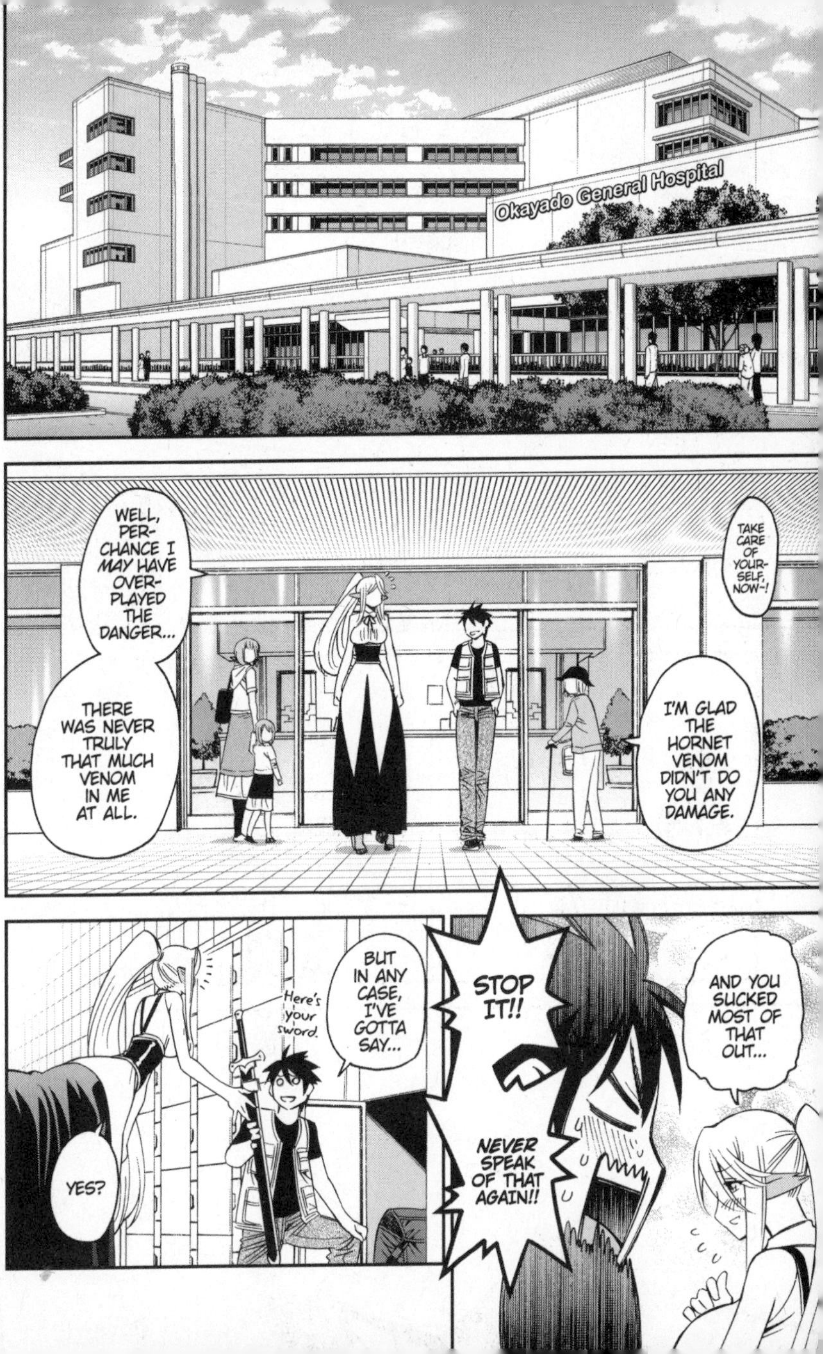
Okayado General Hospital
TAKE CARE OF YOURSELF, NOW~!
I'M GLAD THE HORNET VENOM DIDN'T DO YOU ANY DAMAGE.
WELL, PERCHANCE I *MAY* HAVE OVERPLAYED THE DANGER...
THERE WAS NEVER TRULY THAT MUCH VENOM IN ME AT ALL.
AND YOU SUCKED MOST OF THAT OUT...
STOP IT!!
NEVER SPEAK OF THAT AGAIN!!
BUT IN ANY CASE, I'VE GOTTA SAY...
Here's your sword.
YES?

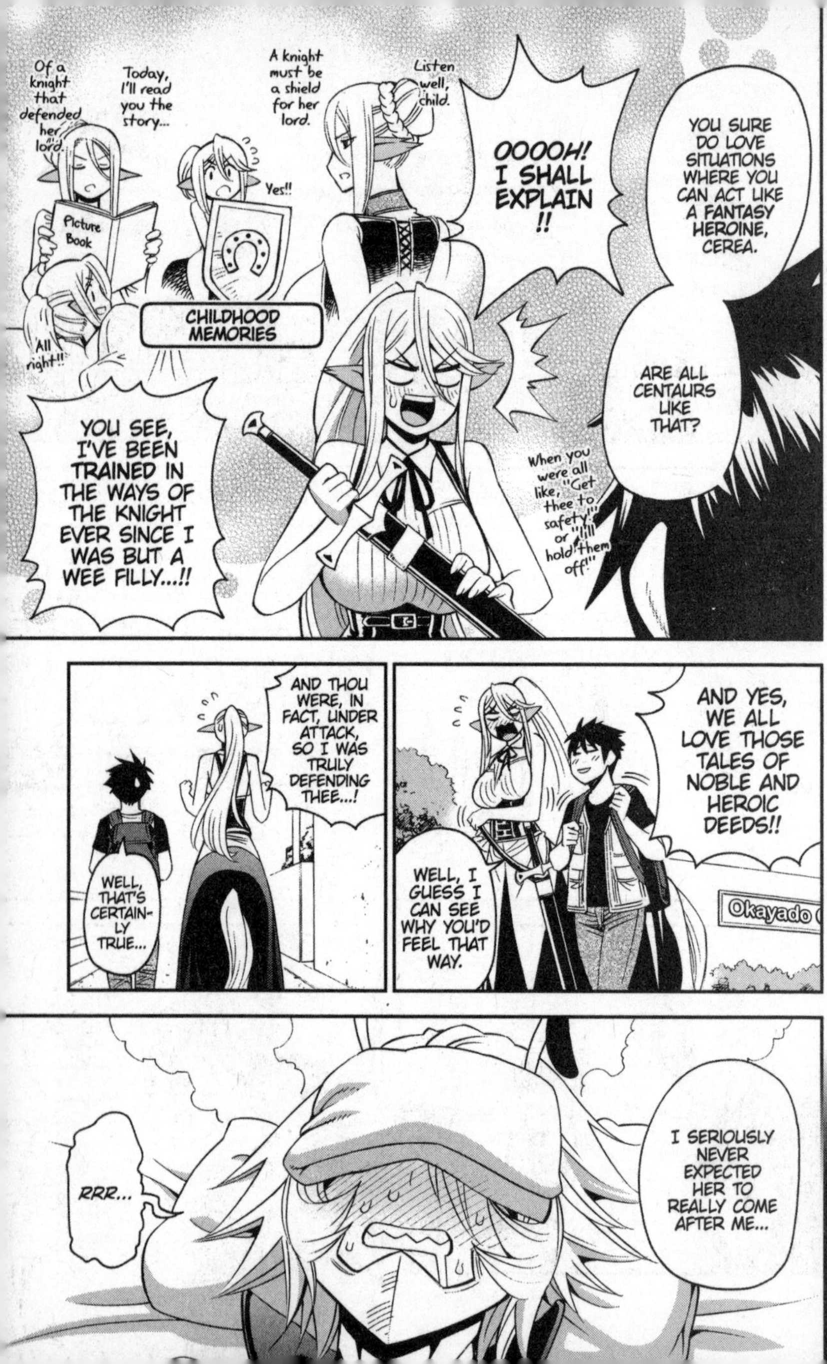
YOU SURE DO LOVE SITUATIONS WHERE YOU CAN ACT LIKE A FANTASY HEROINE, CEREA.
ARE ALL CENTAURS LIKE THAT?
When you were all like, "Get thee to safety!" or "I'll hold them off!"
OOOOH! I SHALL EXPLAIN!!
Listen well, child.
A knight must be a shield for her lord.
Yes!!
Today, I'll read you the story...
Of a knight that defended her lord.
Picture Book
All right!!
CHILDHOOD MEMORIES
YOU SEE, I'VE BEEN TRAINED IN THE WAYS OF THE KNIGHT EVER SINCE I WAS BUT A WEE FILLY...!!
AND YES, WE ALL LOVE THOSE TALES OF NOBLE AND HEROIC DEEDS!!
WELL, I GUESS I CAN SEE WHY YOU'D FEEL THAT WAY.
Okayado
AND THOU WERE, IN FACT, UNDER ATTACK, SO I WAS TRULY DEFENDING THEE...!
WELL, THAT'S CERTAINLY TRUE...
I SERIOUSLY NEVER EXPECTED HER TO REALLY COME AFTER ME...
RRR...

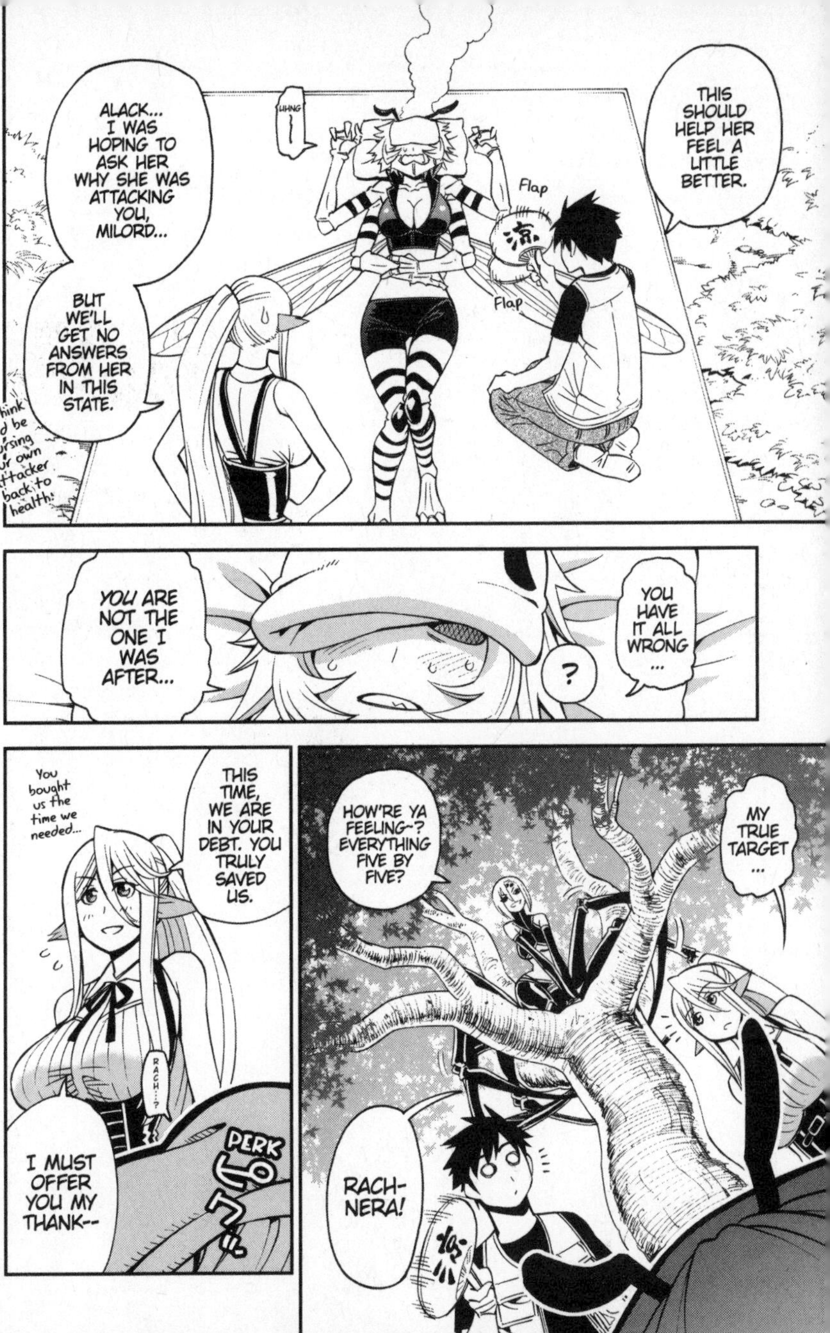

THIS SHOULD HELP HER FEEL A LITTLE BETTER.
Flap
Flap
UHNG
ALACK... I WAS HOPING TO ASK HER WHY SHE WAS ATTACKING YOU, MILORD...
BUT WE'LL GET NO ANSWERS FROM HER IN THIS STATE.
To think we'd be nursing our own attacker back to health.
YOU HAVE IT ALL WRONG ...
?
YOU ARE NOT THE ONE I WAS AFTER...
MY TRUE TARGET ...
HOW'RE YA FEELING~? EVERYTHING FIVE BY FIVE?
RACH-NERA!
THIS TIME, WE ARE IN YOUR DEBT. YOU TRULY SAVED US.
You bought us the time we needed...
RACH...?
PERK
I MUST OFFER YOU MY THANK--

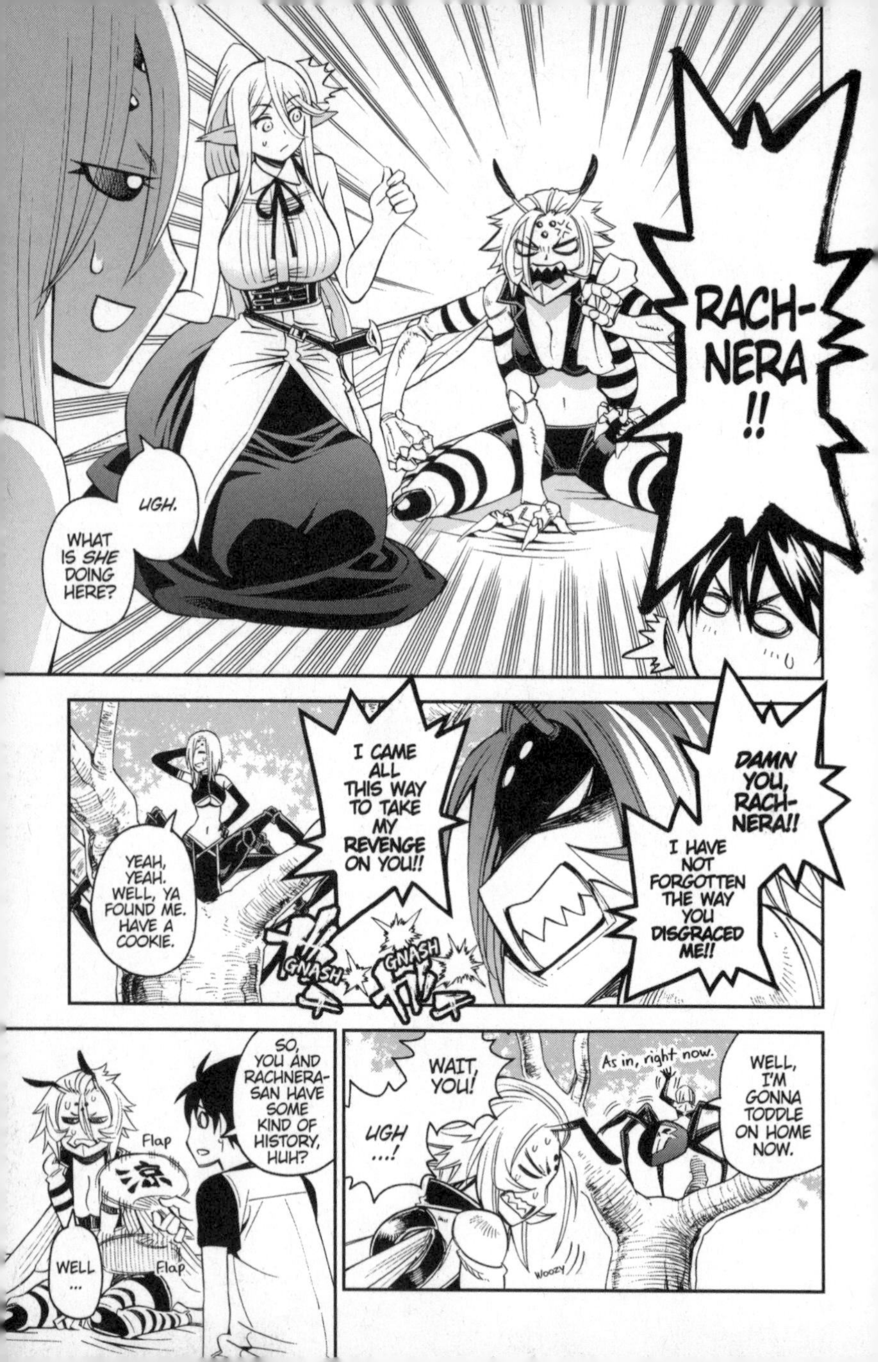
RACH-NERA!!
UGH.
WHAT IS SHE DOING HERE?
DAMN YOU, RACH-NERA!!
I HAVE NOT FORGOTTEN THE WAY YOU DISGRACED ME!!
I CAME ALL THIS WAY TO TAKE MY REVENGE ON YOU!!
GNASH
GNASH
YEAH, YEAH. WELL, YA FOUND ME. HAVE A COOKIE.
WELL, I'M GONNA TODDLE ON HOME NOW.
As in, right now.
WAIT, YOU!
UGH ...!
Woozy
SO, YOU AND RACHNERA-SAN HAVE SOME KIND OF HISTORY, HUH?
Flap
涼
Flap
WELL ...

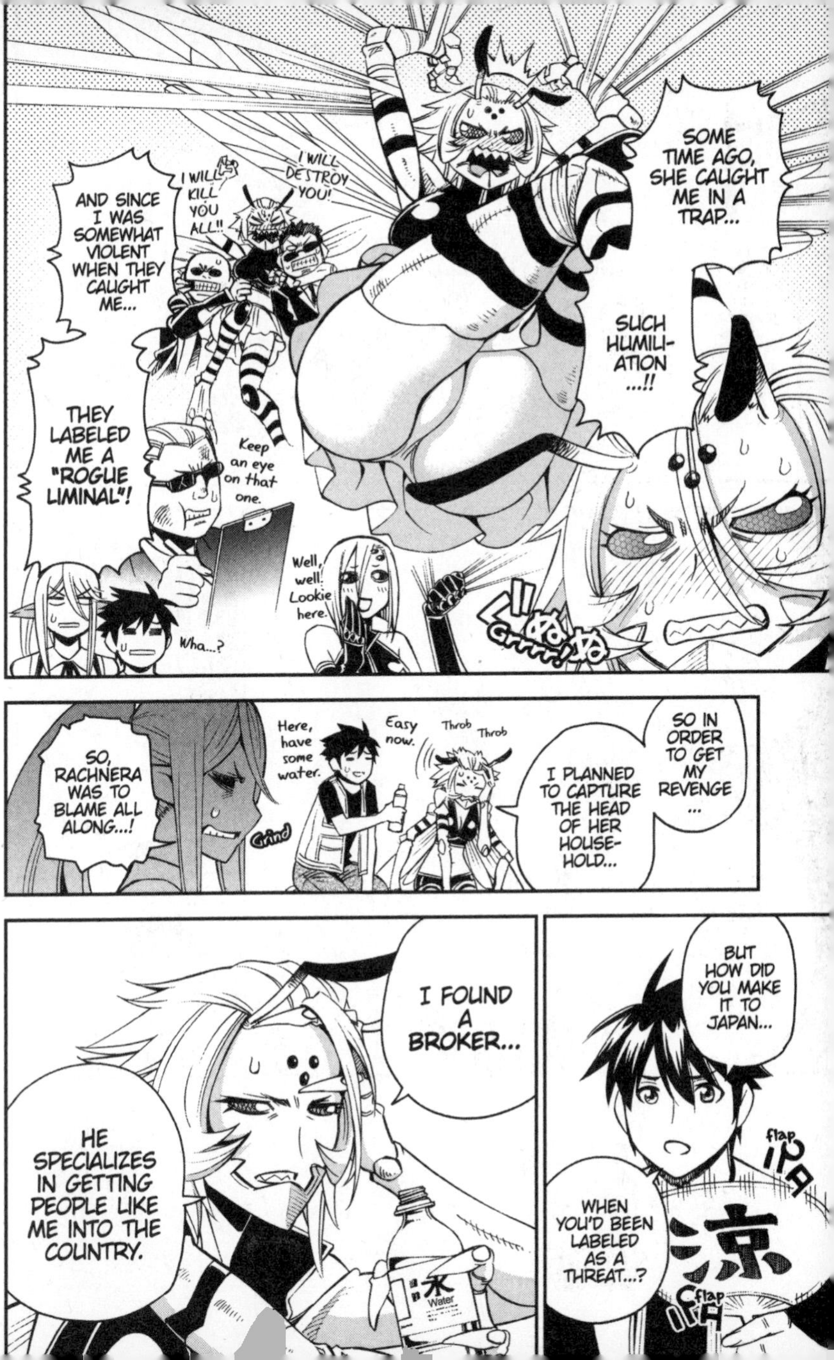
SOME TIME AGO, SHE CAUGHT ME IN A TRAP...
SUCH HUMILIATION...!!
Grrrr!
I WILL DESTROY YOU!
I WILL KILL YOU ALL!!
AND SINCE I WAS SOMEWHAT VIOLENT WHEN THEY CAUGHT ME...
THEY LABELED ME A "ROGUE LIMINAL"!
Keep an eye on that one.
Well, well! Lookie here.
Wha...?
SO IN ORDER TO GET MY REVENGE...
I PLANNED TO CAPTURE THE HEAD OF HER HOUSEHOLD...
Throb Throb
Easy now.
Here, have some water.
SO, RACHNERA WAS TO BLAME ALL ALONG...!
Grind
BUT HOW DID YOU MAKE IT TO JAPAN...
flap
WHEN YOU'D BEEN LABELED AS A THREAT...?
涼
flap
I FOUND A BROKER...
HE SPECIALIZES IN GETTING PEOPLE LIKE ME INTO THE COUNTRY.
水
Water

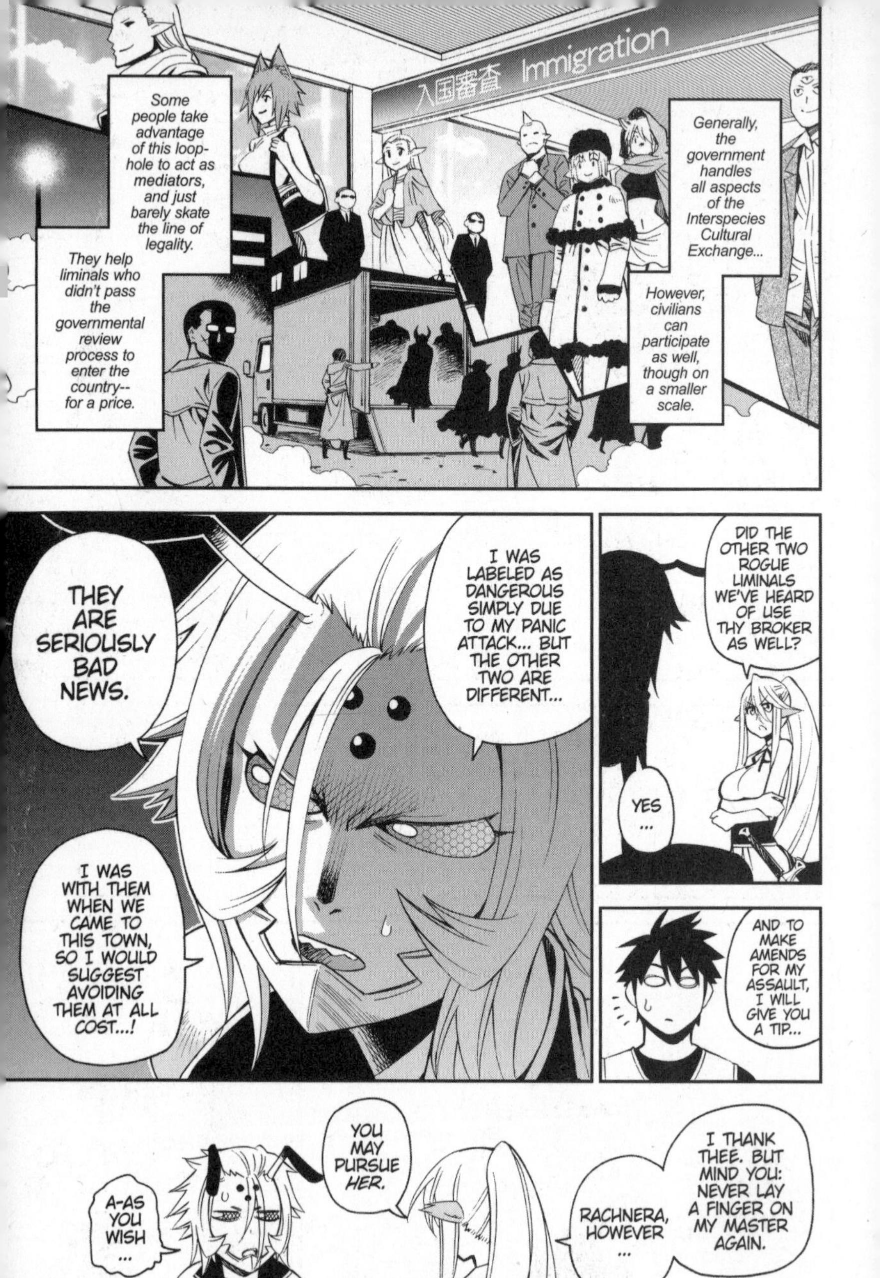
入国審査 Immigration
Generally, the government handles all aspects of the Interspecies Cultural Exchange...
However, civilians can participate as well, though on a smaller scale.
Some people take advantage of this loop-hole to act as mediators, and just barely skate the line of legality.
They help liminals who didn't pass the governmental review process to enter the country-- for a price.
DID THE OTHER TWO ROGUE LIMINALS WE'VE HEARD OF USE THY BROKER AS WELL?
YES ...
AND TO MAKE AMENDS FOR MY ASSAULT, I WILL GIVE YOU A TIP...
I WAS LABELED AS DANGEROUS SIMPLY DUE TO MY PANIC ATTACK... BUT THE OTHER TWO ARE DIFFERENT...
THEY ARE SERIOUSLY BAD NEWS.
I WAS WITH THEM WHEN WE CAME TO THIS TOWN, SO I WOULD SUGGEST AVOIDING THEM AT ALL COST...!
I THANK THEE. BUT MIND YOU: NEVER LAY A FINGER ON MY MASTER AGAIN.
RACHNERA, HOWEVER ...
YOU MAY PURSUE HER.
A-AS YOU WISH ...

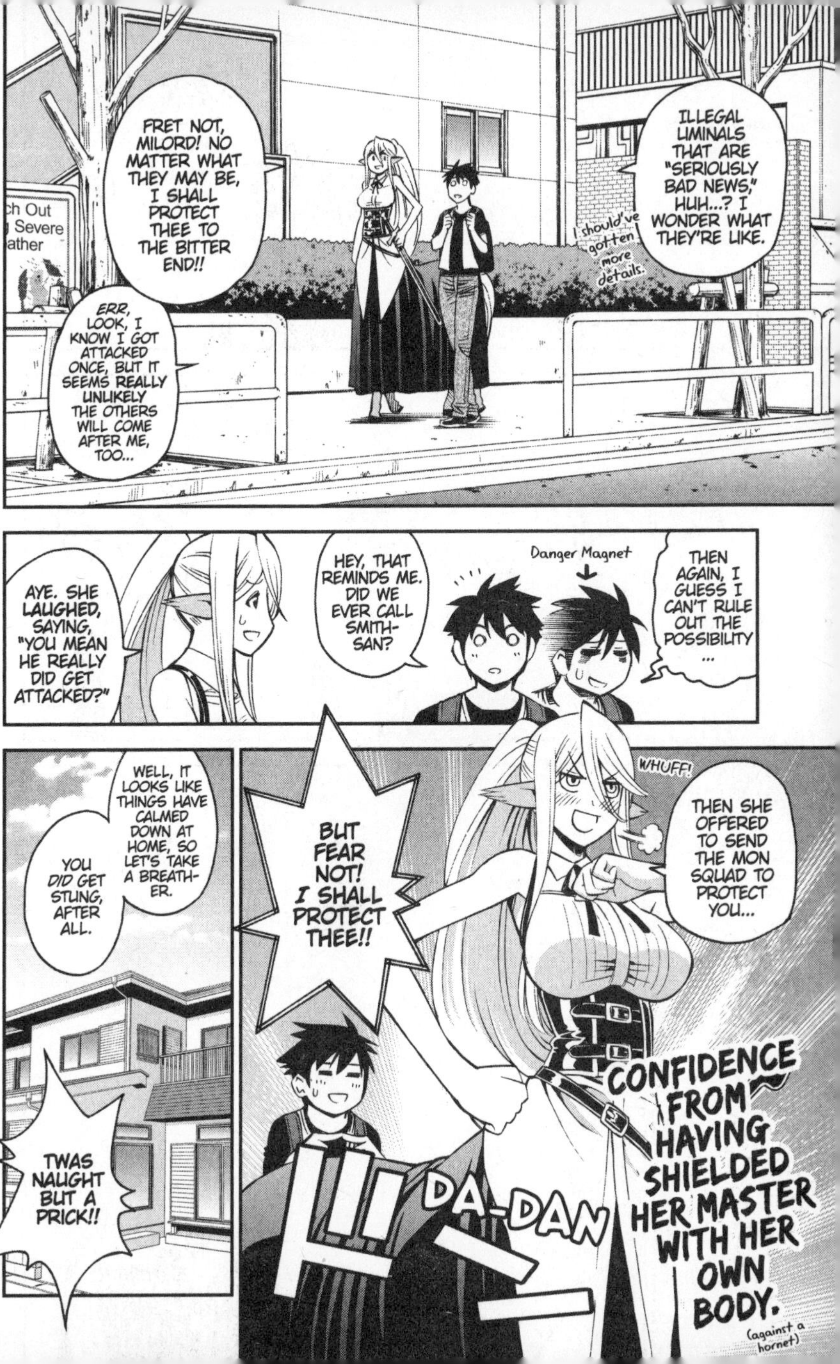
ILLEGAL LIMINALS THAT ARE "SERIOUSLY BAD NEWS," HUH...? I WONDER WHAT THEY'RE LIKE.
I should've gotten more details.
FRET NOT, MILORD! NO MATTER WHAT THEY MAY BE, I SHALL PROTECT THEE TO THE BITTER END!!
ERR, LOOK, I KNOW I GOT ATTACKED ONCE, BUT IT SEEMS REALLY UNLIKELY THE OTHERS WILL COME AFTER ME, TOO...
THEN AGAIN, I GUESS I CAN'T RULE OUT THE POSSIBILITY ...
Danger Magnet
HEY, THAT REMINDS ME. DID WE EVER CALL SMITH-SAN?
AYE. SHE LAUGHED, SAYING, "YOU MEAN HE REALLY DID GET ATTACKED?"
W'HUFF!
THEN SHE OFFERED TO SEND THE MON SQUAD TO PROTECT YOU...
BUT FEAR NOT! I SHALL PROTECT THEE!!
DA-DAN
CONFIDENCE FROM HAVING SHIELDED HER MASTER WITH HER OWN BODY.
(against a hornet)
WELL, IT LOOKS LIKE THINGS HAVE CALMED DOWN AT HOME, SO LET'S TAKE A BREATHER.
YOU DID GET STUNG, AFTER ALL.
TWAS NAUGHT BUT A PRICK!!

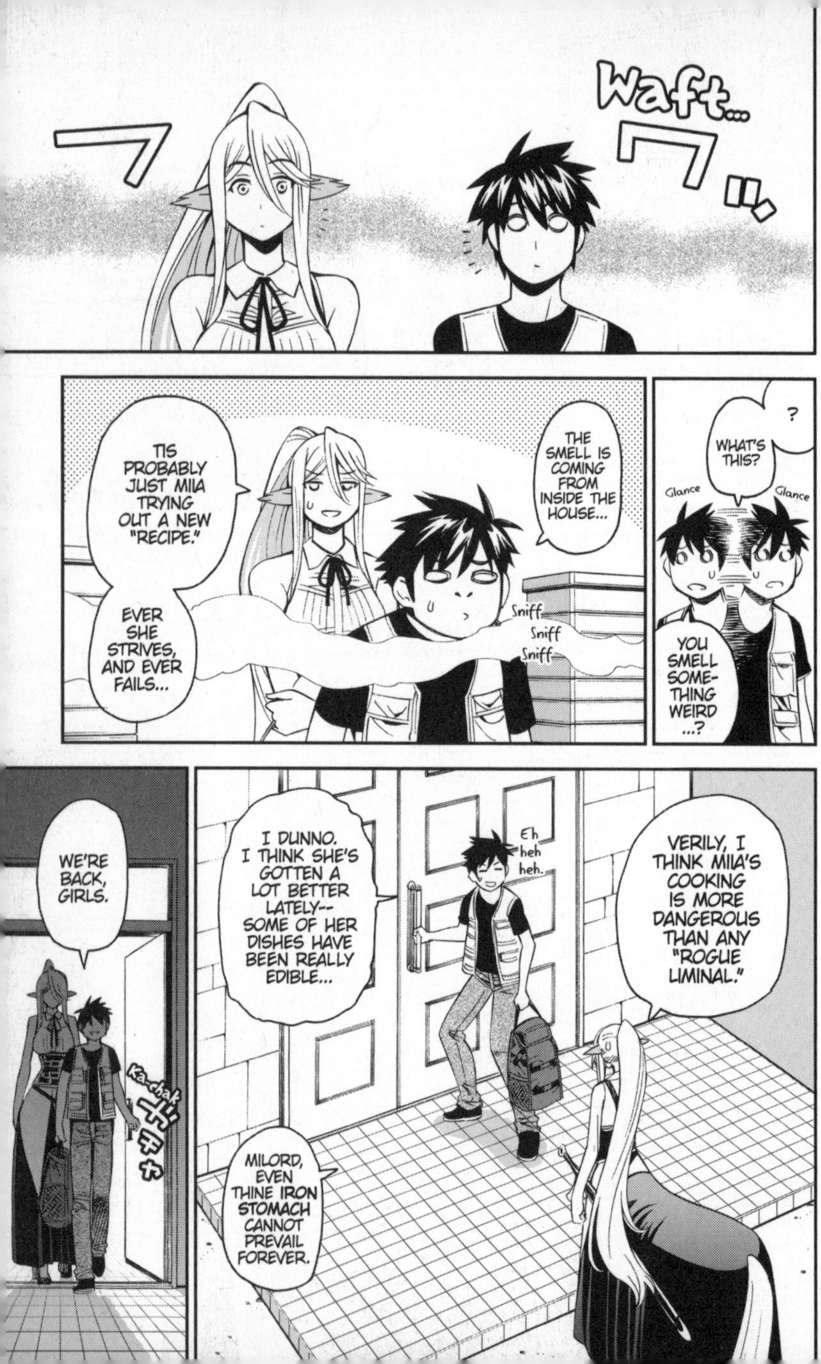
Waft...
?
WHAT'S THIS?
Glance
Glance
YOU SMELL SOMETHING WEIRD ...?
THE SMELL IS COMING FROM INSIDE THE HOUSE...
Sniff
Sniff
Sniff
TIS PROBABLY JUST MIIA TRYING OUT A NEW "RECIPE."
EVER SHE STRIVES, AND EVER FAILS...
VERILY, I THINK MIIA'S COOKING IS MORE DANGEROUS THAN ANY "ROGUE LIMINAL."
Eh heh heh.
I DUNNO. I THINK SHE'S GOTTEN A LOT BETTER LATELY-- SOME OF HER DISHES HAVE BEEN REALLY EDIBLE...
MILORD, EVEN THINE IRON STOMACH CANNOT PREVAIL FOREVER.
WE'RE BACK, GIRLS.
Ka-chak

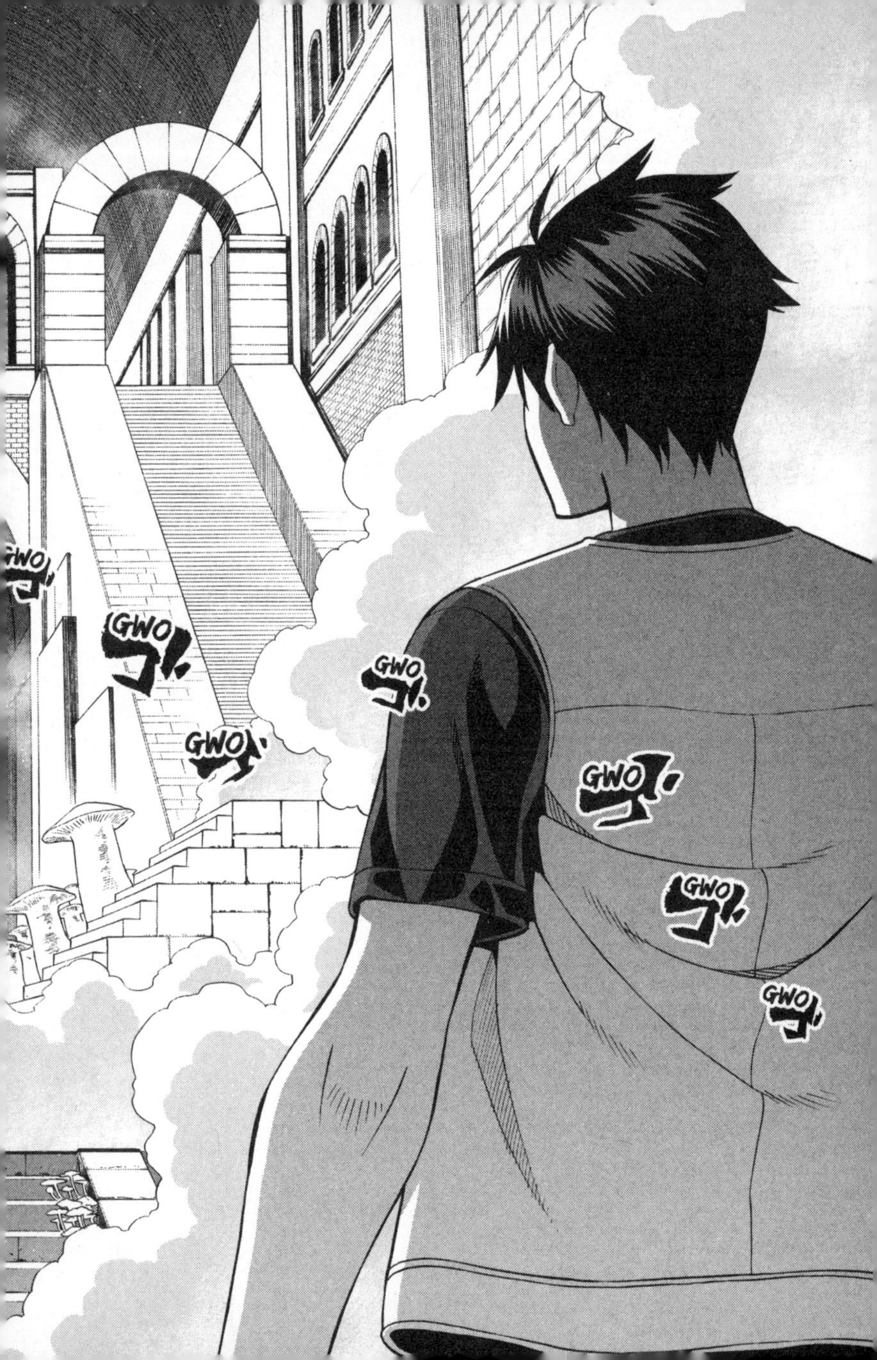
GWO
GWO
GWO
GWO
GWO
GWO
GWO

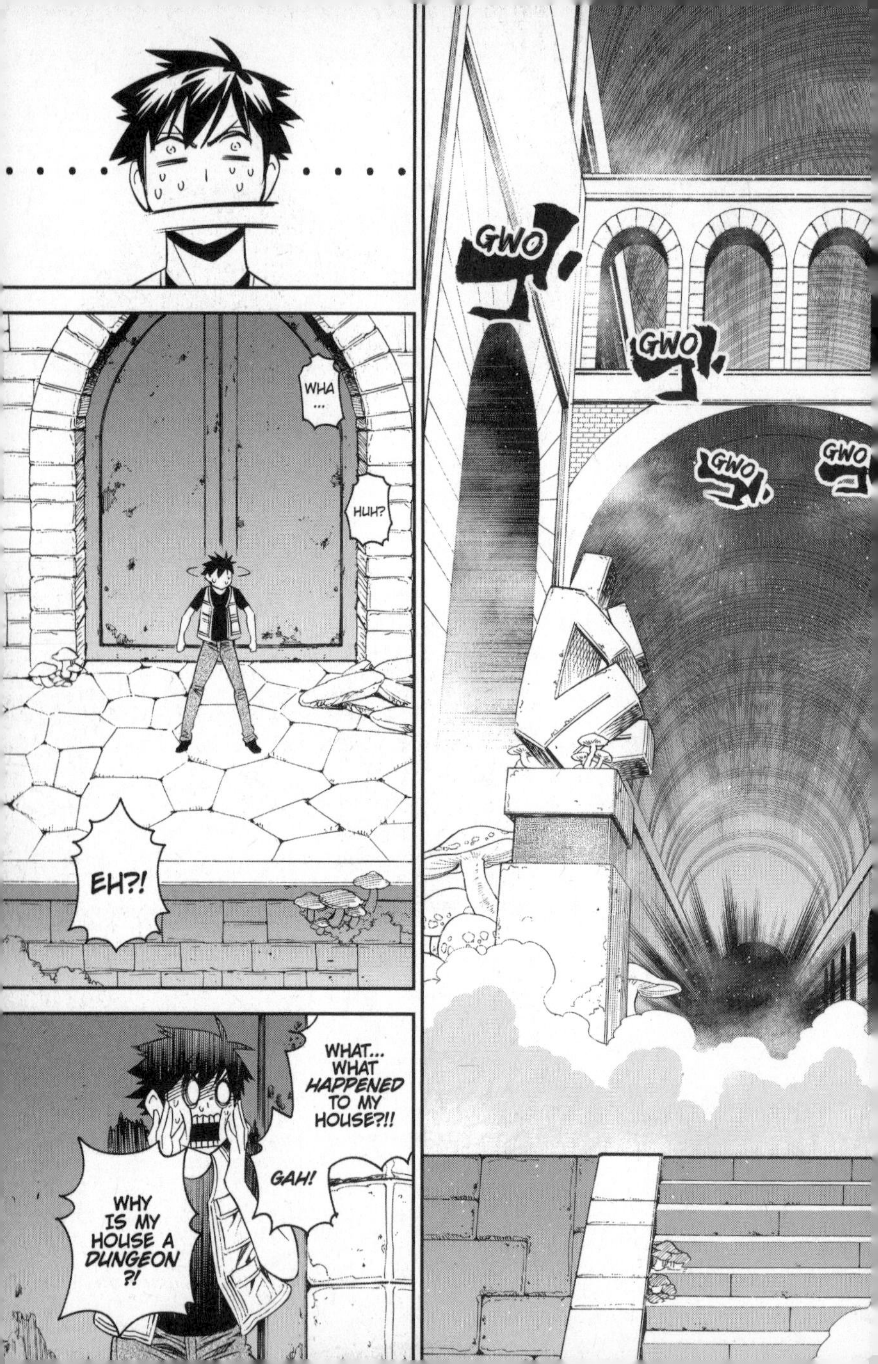
GWO
GWO
GWO
GWO
WHA...
HUH?
EH?!
WHAT... WHAT HAPPENED TO MY HOUSE?!!
GAH!
WHY IS MY HOUSE A DUNGEON?!

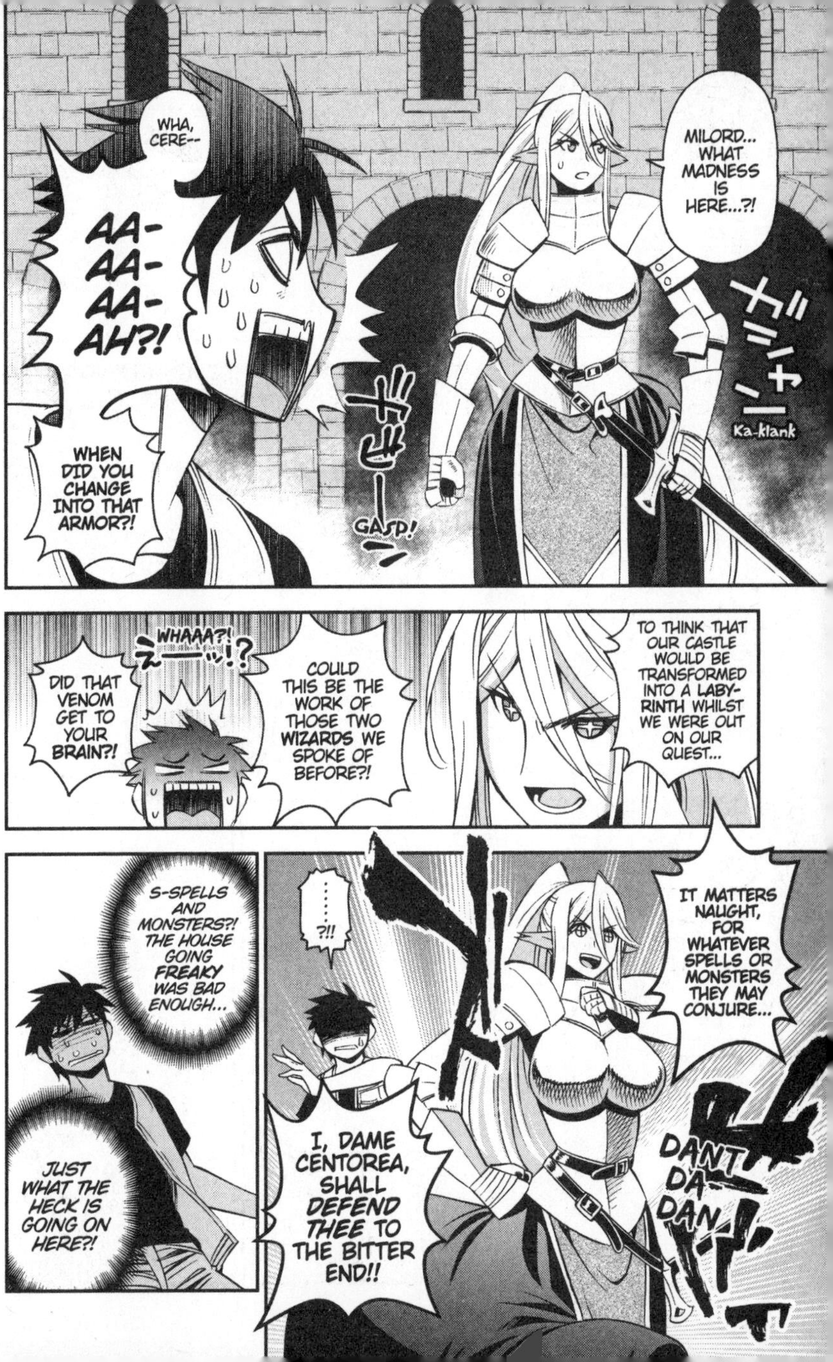
MILORD... WHAT MADNESS IS HERE...?!
Ka-klank
WHA, CERE--
AA-AA-AA-AH?!
GASP!
WHEN DID YOU CHANGE INTO THAT ARMOR?!
TO THINK THAT OUR CASTLE WOULD BE TRANSFORMED INTO A LABY-RINTH WHILST WE WERE OUT ON OUR QUEST...
COULD THIS BE THE WORK OF THOSE TWO WIZARDS WE SPOKE OF BEFORE?!
WHAAA?!
DID THAT VENOM GET TO YOUR BRAIN?!
IT MATTERS NAUGHT, FOR WHATEVER SPELLS OR MONSTERS THEY MAY CONJURE...
......?!!
I, DAME CENTOREA, SHALL DEFEND THEE TO THE BITTER END!!
DANT DA DAN
S-SPELLS AND MONSTERS?! THE HOUSE GOING FREAKY WAS BAD ENOUGH...
JUST WHAT THE HECK IS GOING ON HERE?!

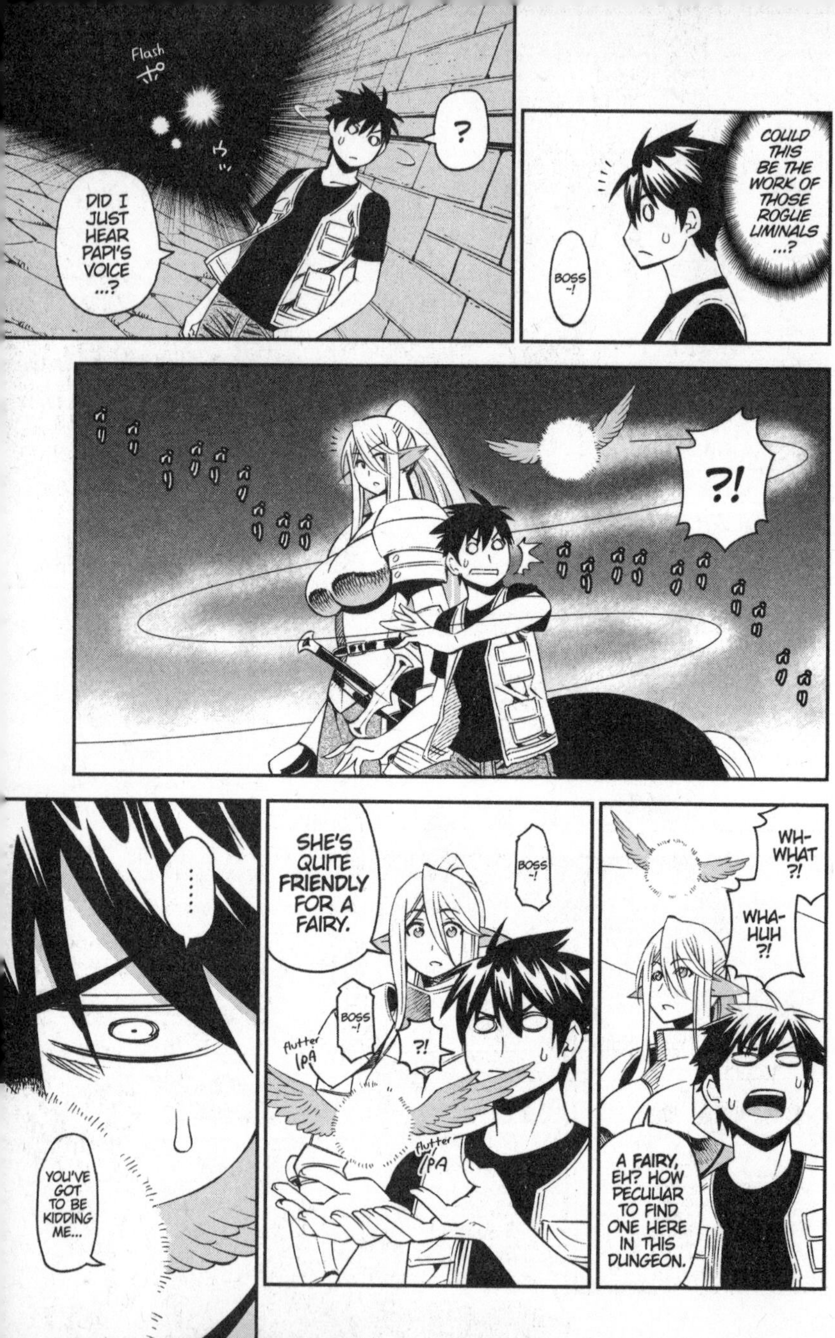
COULD THIS BE THE WORK OF THOSE ROGUE LIMINALS ...?
BOSS ~!
Flash
?
DID I JUST HEAR PAPI'S VOICE ...?
?!
WH-WHAT ?!
WHA-HUH ?!
A FAIRY, EH? HOW PECULIAR TO FIND ONE HERE IN THIS DUNGEON.
BOSS ~!
SHE'S QUITE FRIENDLY FOR A FAIRY.
BOSS ~!
flutter
?!
flutter
......
YOU'VE GOT TO BE KIDDING ME...

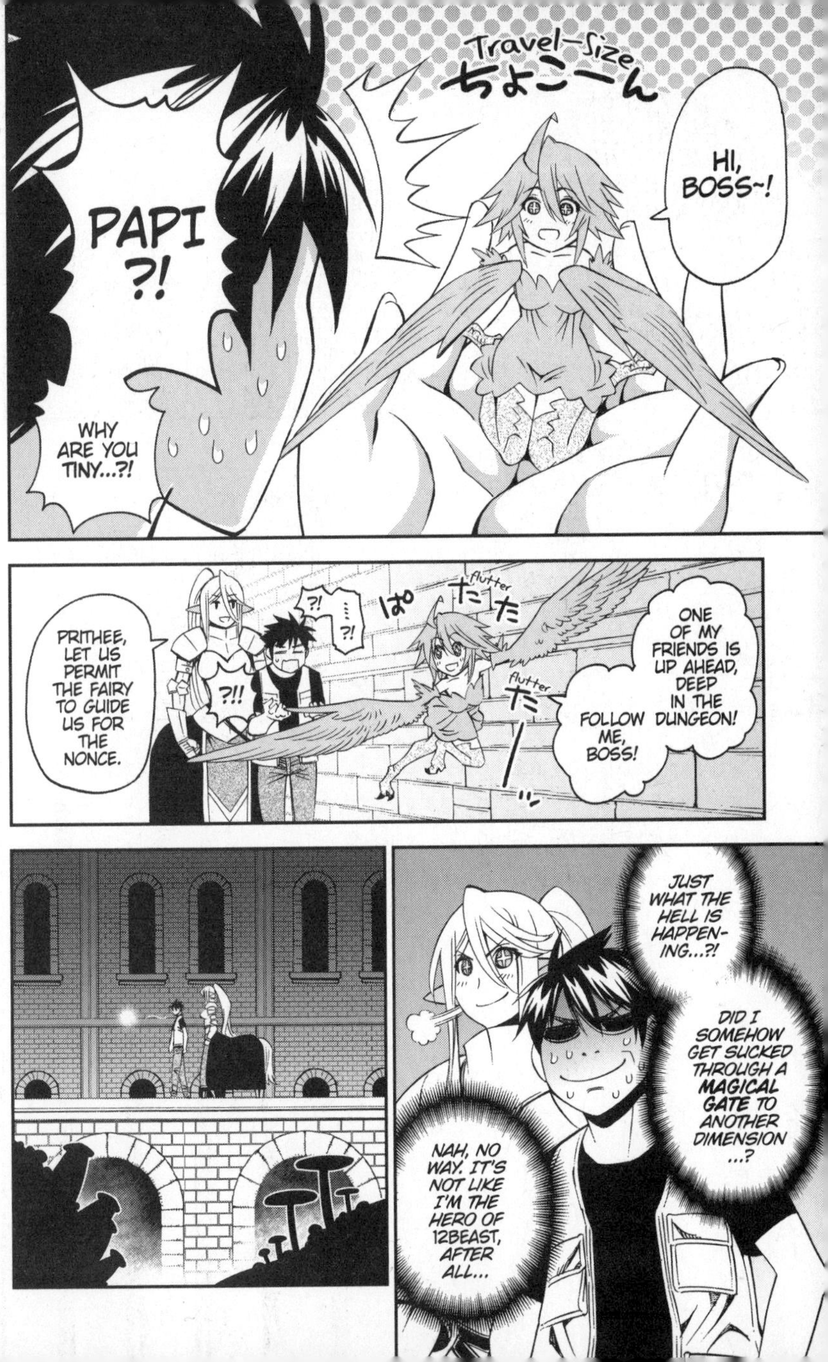
Travel-Size
ちょこーん
HI, BOSS~!
PAPI ?!
WHY ARE YOU TINY...?!
ONE OF MY FRIENDS IS UP AHEAD, DEEP IN THE DUNGEON!
FOLLOW ME, BOSS!
flutter
たた
flutter
た
ぱ
...?!
?!
?!!
PRITHEE, LET US PERMIT THE FAIRY TO GUIDE US FOR THE NONCE.
JUST WHAT THE HELL IS HAPPENING...?!
DID I SOMEHOW GET SUCKED THROUGH A **MAGICAL GATE** TO ANOTHER DIMENSION...?
NAH, NO WAY. IT'S NOT LIKE I'M THE HERO OF 12BEAST, AFTER ALL...

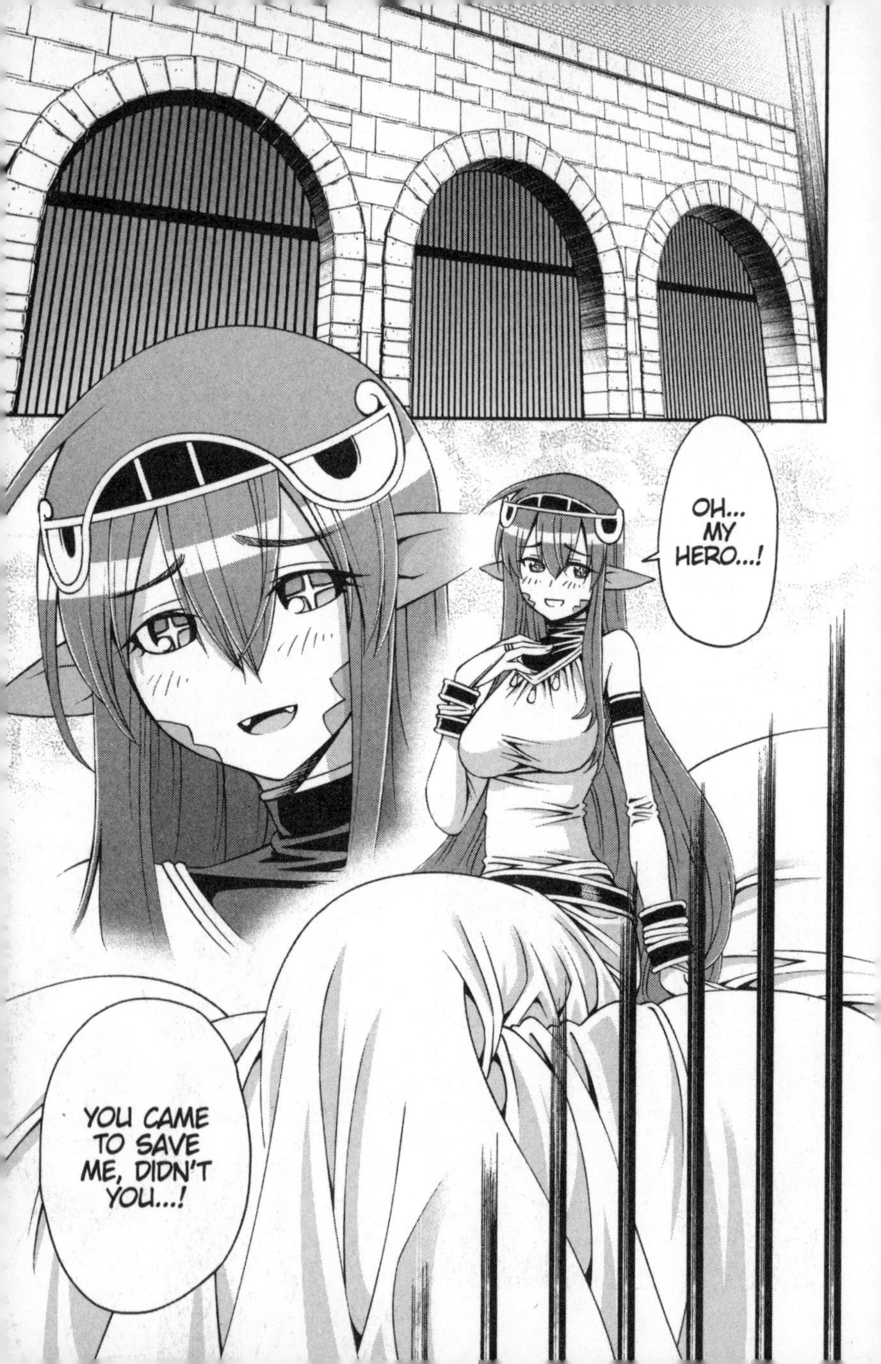
OH... MY HERO...!
YOU CAME TO SAVE ME, DIDN'T YOU...!

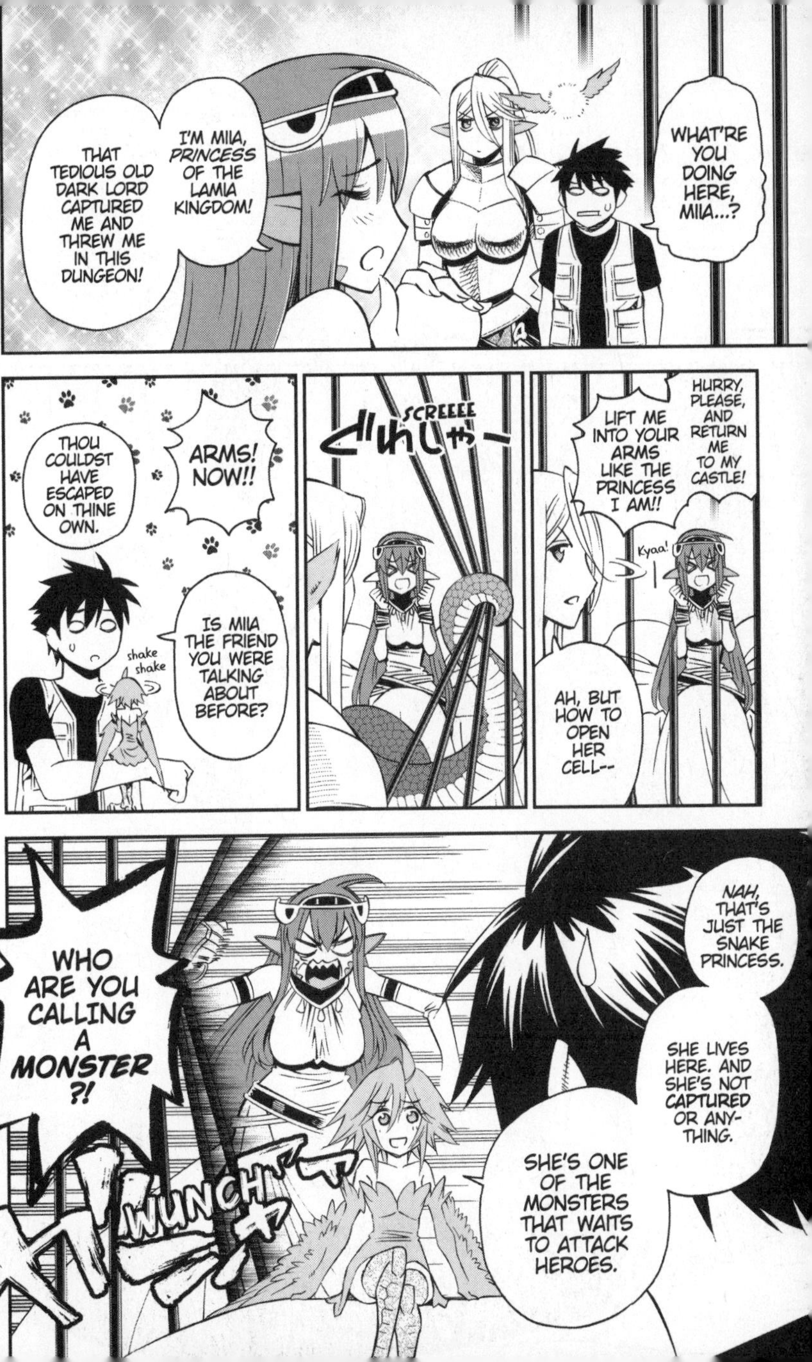
WHAT'RE YOU DOING HERE, MIIA...?
I'M MIIA, PRINCESS OF THE LAMIA KINGDOM!
THAT TEDIOUS OLD DARK LORD CAPTURED ME AND THREW ME IN THIS DUNGEON!
HURRY, PLEASE, AND RETURN ME TO MY CASTLE!
LIFT ME INTO YOUR ARMS LIKE THE PRINCESS I AM!!
Kyaa!
AH, BUT HOW TO OPEN HER CELL--
SCREEEE
ARMS! NOW!!
THOU COULDST HAVE ESCAPED ON THINE OWN.
IS MIIA THE FRIEND YOU WERE TALKING ABOUT BEFORE?
shake shake
NAH, THAT'S JUST THE SNAKE PRINCESS.
SHE LIVES HERE. AND SHE'S NOT CAPTURED OR ANY-THING.
SHE'S ONE OF THE MONSTERS THAT WAITS TO ATTACK HEROES.
WHO ARE YOU CALLING A MONSTER?!
WUNCH

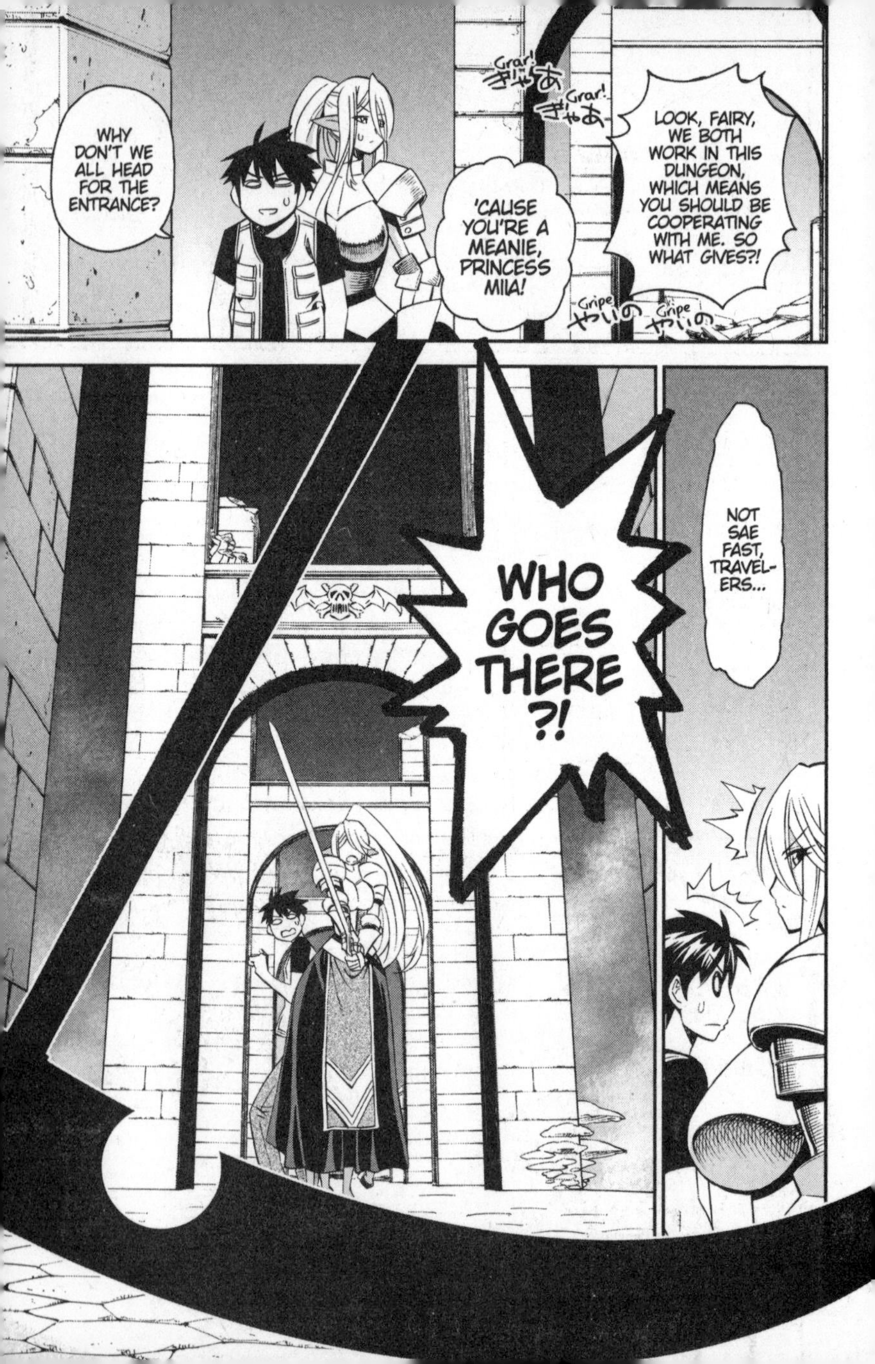
LOOK, FAIRY, WE BOTH WORK IN THIS DUNGEON, WHICH MEANS YOU SHOULD BE COOPERATING WITH ME. SO WHAT GIVES?!
Grar! ぎゃあ
Grar! ぎゃあ
'CAUSE YOU'RE A MEANIE, PRINCESS MIIA!
WHY DON'T WE ALL HEAD FOR THE ENTRANCE?
Gripe やいの
Gripe やいの
NOT SAE FAST, TRAVEL-ERS...
WHO GOES THERE?!

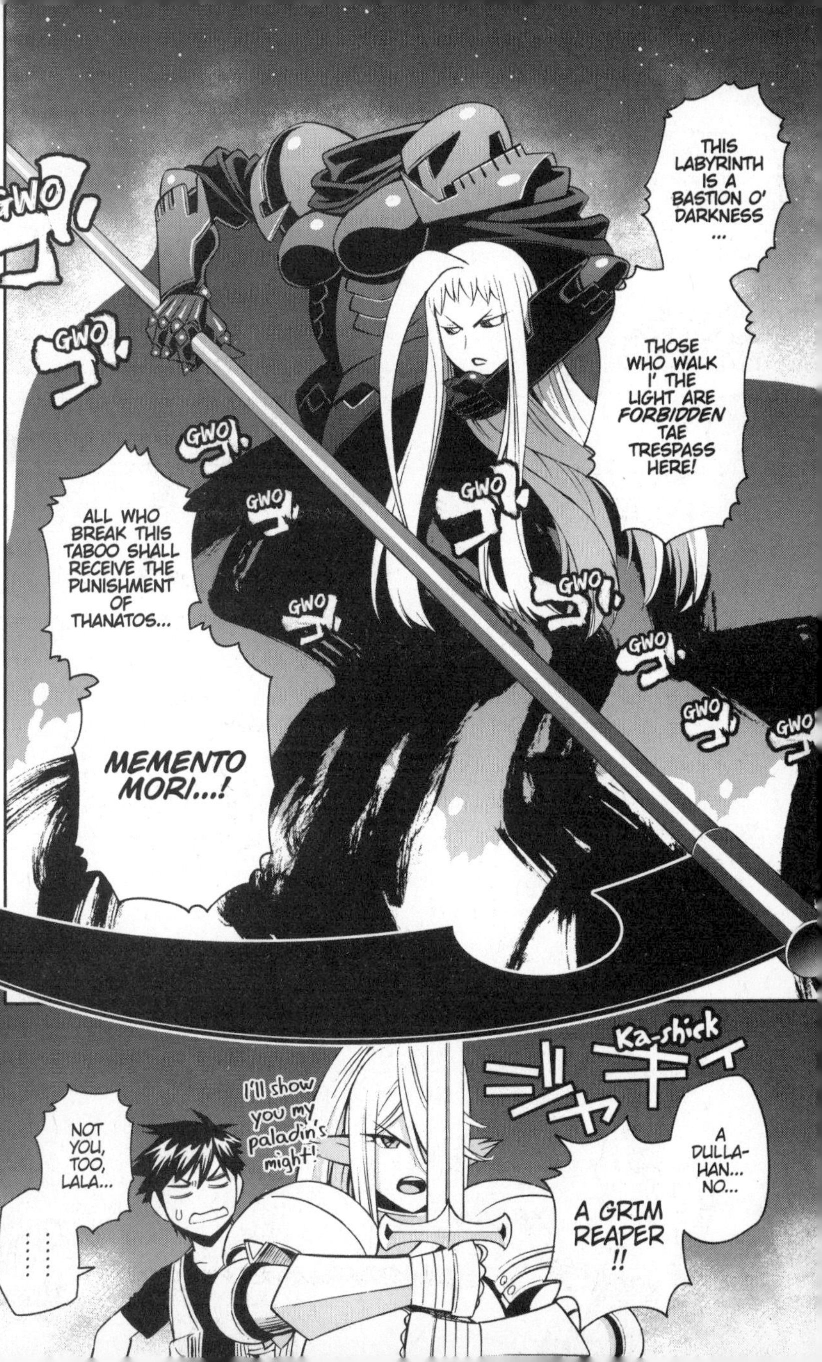
THIS LABYRINTH IS A BASTION O' DARKNESS...
GWO
THOSE WHO WALK I' THE LIGHT ARE *FORBIDDEN* TAE TRESPASS HERE!
GWO
GWO
GWO
GWO
GWO
GWO
GWO
GWO
GWO
ALL WHO BREAK THIS TABOO SHALL RECEIVE THE PUNISHMENT OF THANATOS...
MEMENTO MORI...!
Ka-shick
A DULLA-HAN... NO...
A GRIM REAPER!!
I'll show you my paladin's might!
NOT YOU, TOO, LALA...
......

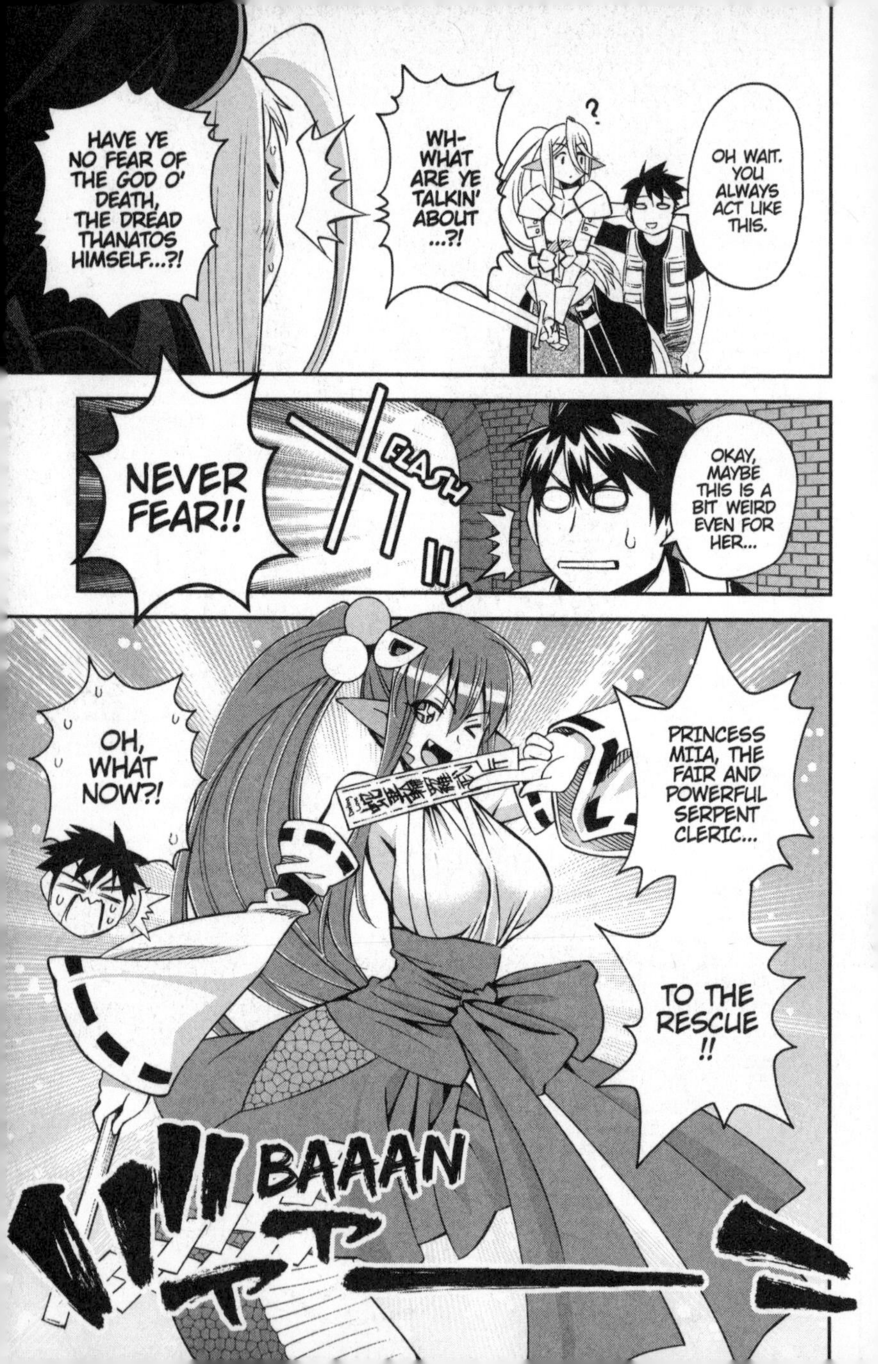
?
OH WAIT. YOU ALWAYS ACT LIKE THIS.
WH- WHAT ARE YE TALKIN' ABOUT ...?!
HAVE YE NO FEAR OF THE GOD O' DEATH, THE DREAD THANATOS HIMSELF...?!
OKAY, MAYBE THIS IS A BIT WEIRD EVEN FOR HER...
FLASH
NEVER FEAR!!
PRINCESS MIIA, THE FAIR AND POWERFUL SERPENT CLERIC...
TO THE RESCUE !!
OH, WHAT NOW?!
BAAAN

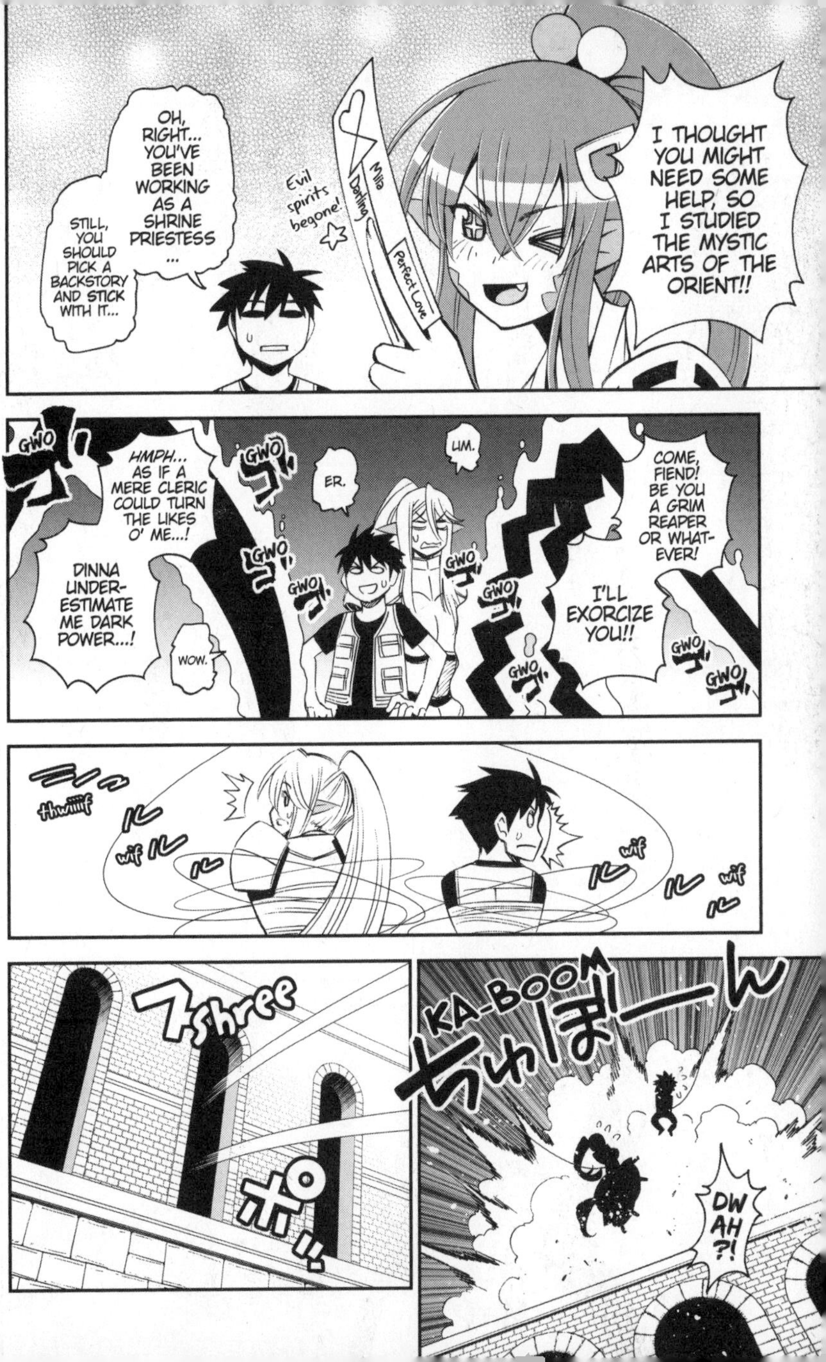
I THOUGHT YOU MIGHT NEED SOME HELP, SO I STUDIED THE MYSTIC ARTS OF THE ORIENT!!
Mia
Darling
Perfect Love
Evil spirits begone!
OH, RIGHT... YOU'VE BEEN WORKING AS A SHRINE PRIESTESS ...
STILL, YOU SHOULD PICK A BACKSTORY AND STICK WITH IT...
GWO
GWO
COME, FIEND! BE YOU A GRIM REAPER OR WHAT-EVER!
I'LL EXORCIZE YOU!!
GWO
GWO
GWO
UM.
ER.
GWO
GWO
GWO
HMPH... AS IF A MERE CLERIC COULD TURN THE LIKES O' ME...!
DINNA UNDER-ESTIMATE ME DARK POWER...!
WOW.
GWO
wif
wif
wif
thwiiiif
KA-BOOM
DWAH ?!
shree

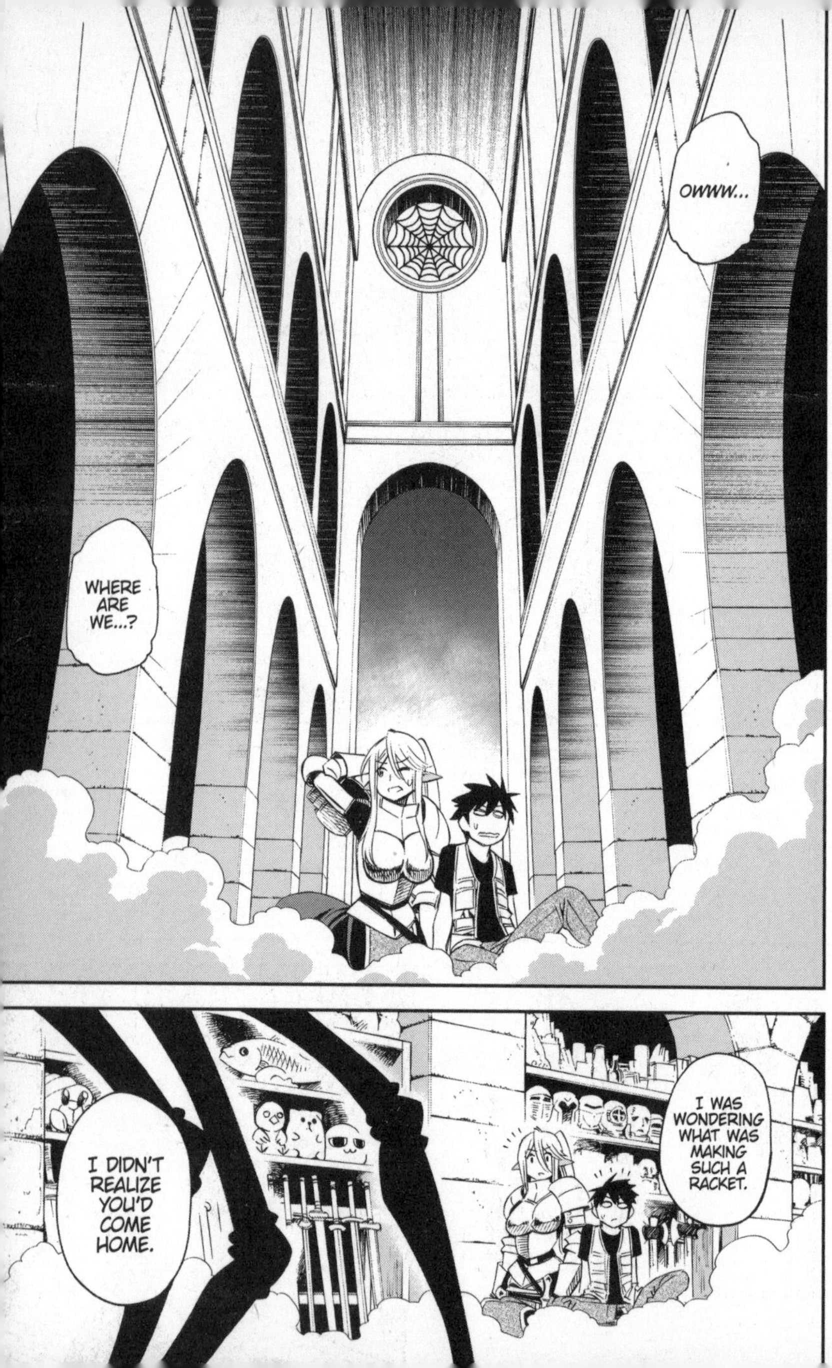
OWWW...
WHERE ARE WE...?
I WAS WONDERING WHAT WAS MAKING SUCH A RACKET.
I DIDN'T REALIZE YOU'D COME HOME.

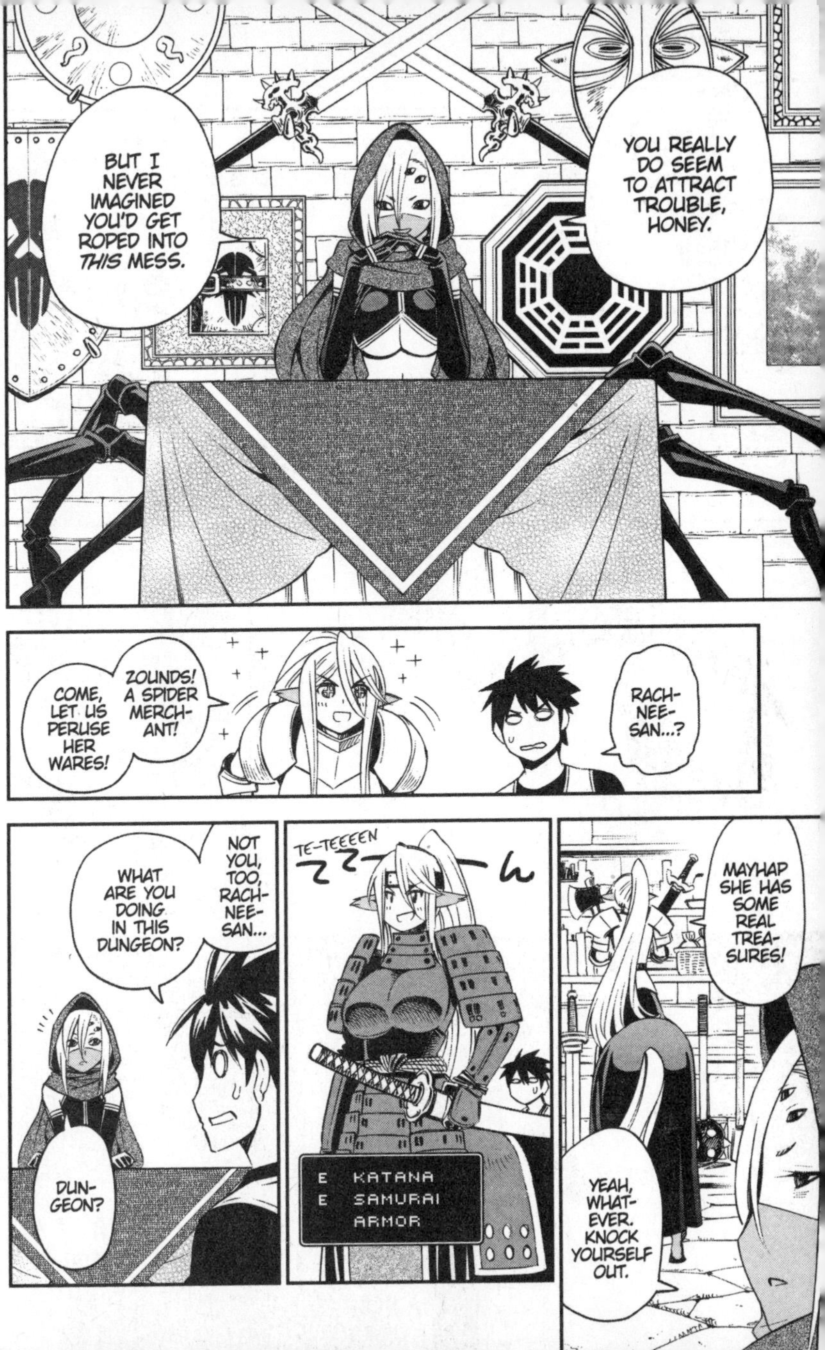
YOU REALLY DO SEEM TO ATTRACT TROUBLE, HONEY.
BUT I NEVER IMAGINED YOU'D GET ROPED INTO *THIS* MESS.
RACH-NEE-SAN...?
ZOUNDS! A SPIDER MERCH-ANT!
COME, LET US PERUSE HER WARES!
MAYHAP SHE HAS SOME REAL TREA-SURES!
YEAH, WHAT-EVER. KNOCK YOURSELF OUT.
TE-TEEEEN
E KATANA
E SAMURAI ARMOR
NOT YOU, TOO, RACH-NEE-SAN...
WHAT ARE YOU DOING IN THIS DUNGEON?
DUN-GEON?

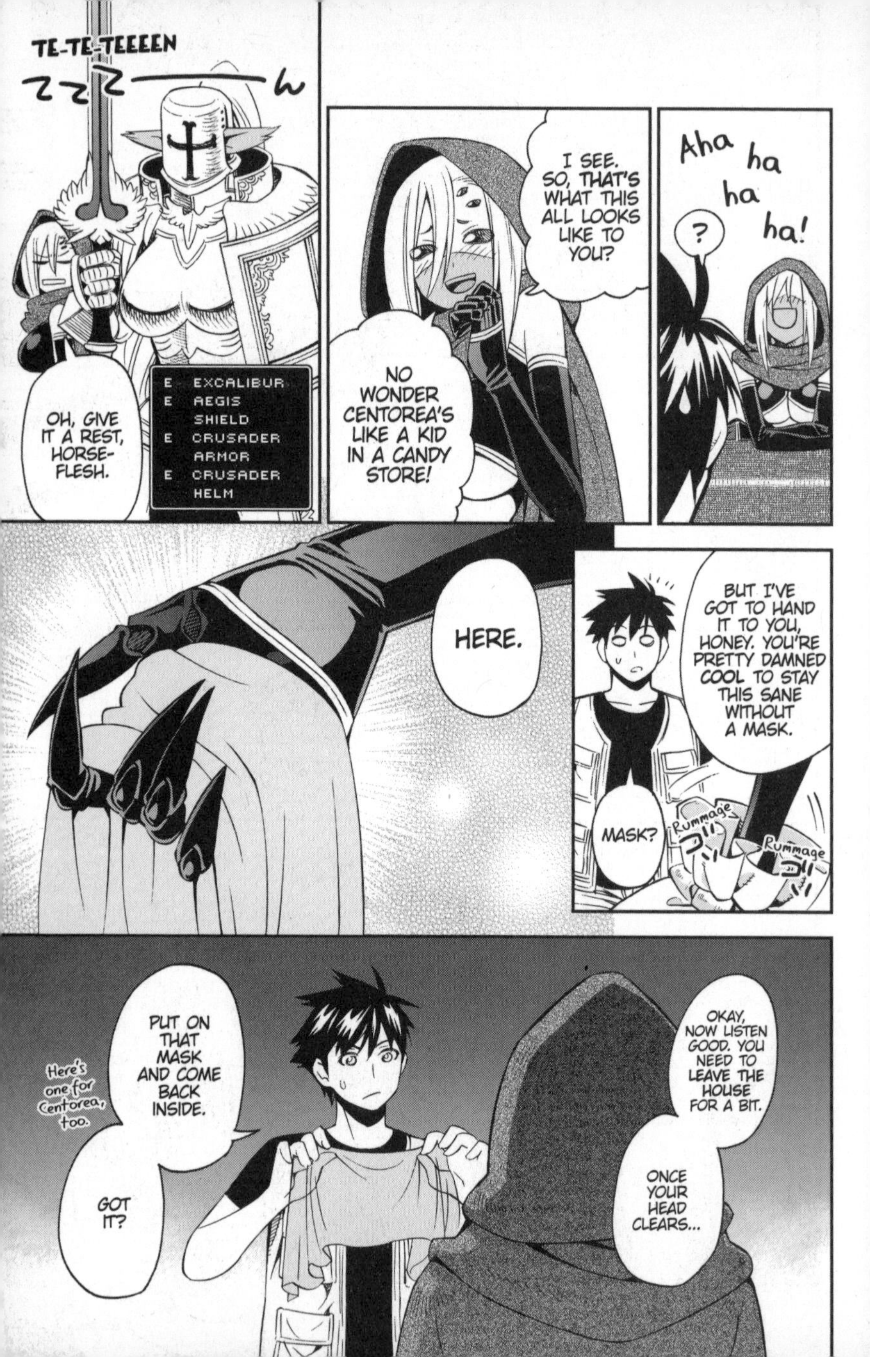
Aha ha ha ha!
?
I SEE. SO, THAT'S WHAT THIS ALL LOOKS LIKE TO YOU?
NO WONDER CENTOREA'S LIKE A KID IN A CANDY STORE!
TE-TE-TEEEEN
E EXCALIBUR
E AEGIS SHIELD
E CRUSADER ARMOR
E CRUSADER HELM
OH, GIVE IT A REST, HORSE-FLESH.
BUT I'VE GOT TO HAND IT TO YOU, HONEY. YOU'RE PRETTY DAMNED COOL TO STAY THIS SANE WITHOUT A MASK.
MASK?
Rummage
Rummage
HERE.
OKAY, NOW LISTEN GOOD. YOU NEED TO LEAVE THE HOUSE FOR A BIT.
ONCE YOUR HEAD CLEARS...
PUT ON THAT MASK AND COME BACK INSIDE.
GOT IT?
Here's one for Centorea, too.

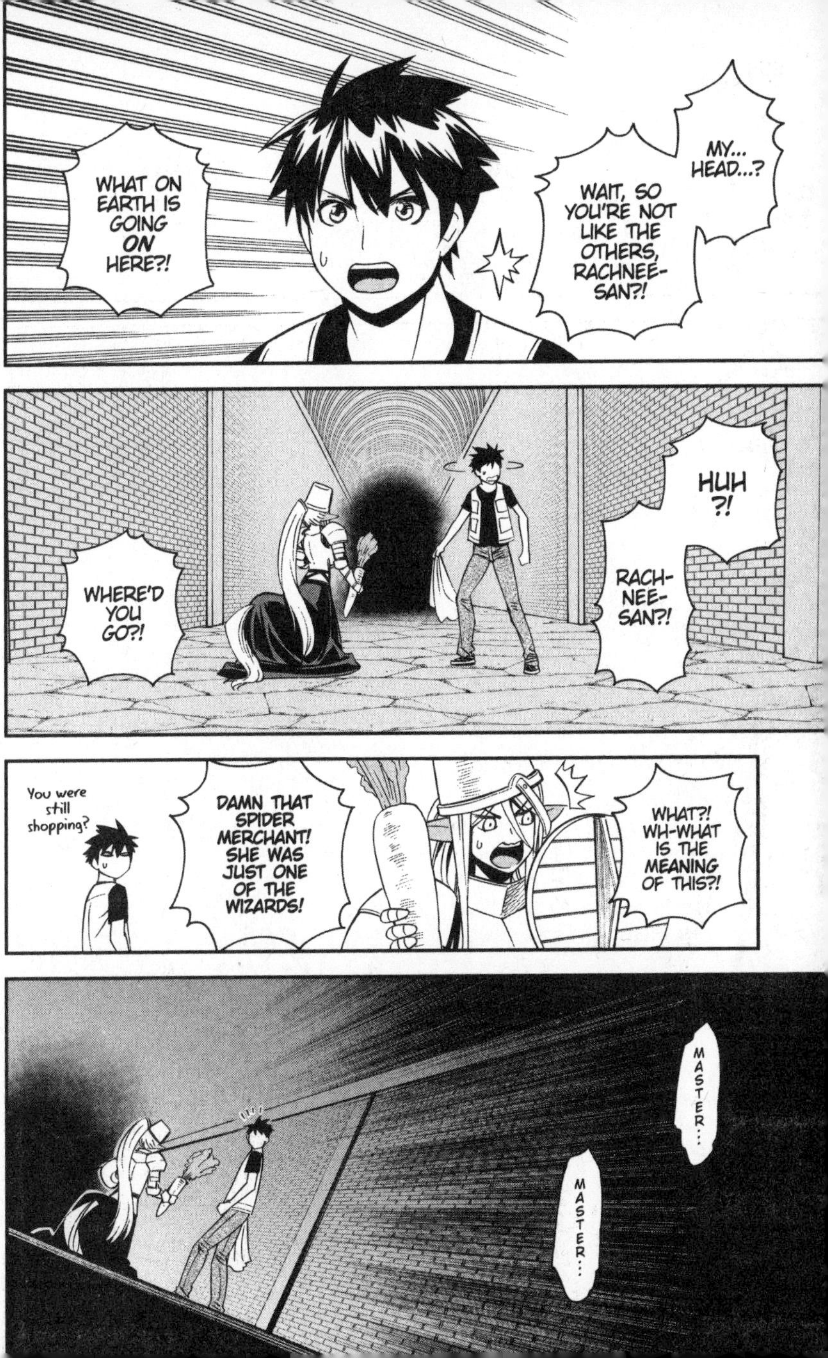
MY... HEAD...?
WAIT, SO YOU'RE NOT LIKE THE OTHERS, RACHNEE-SAN?!
WHAT ON EARTH IS GOING ON HERE?!
HUH?!
RACH-NEE-SAN?!
WHERE'D YOU GO?!
WHAT?! WH-WHAT IS THE MEANING OF THIS?!
DAMN THAT SPIDER MERCHANT! SHE WAS JUST ONE OF THE WIZARDS!
You were still shopping?
MASTER...
MASTER...

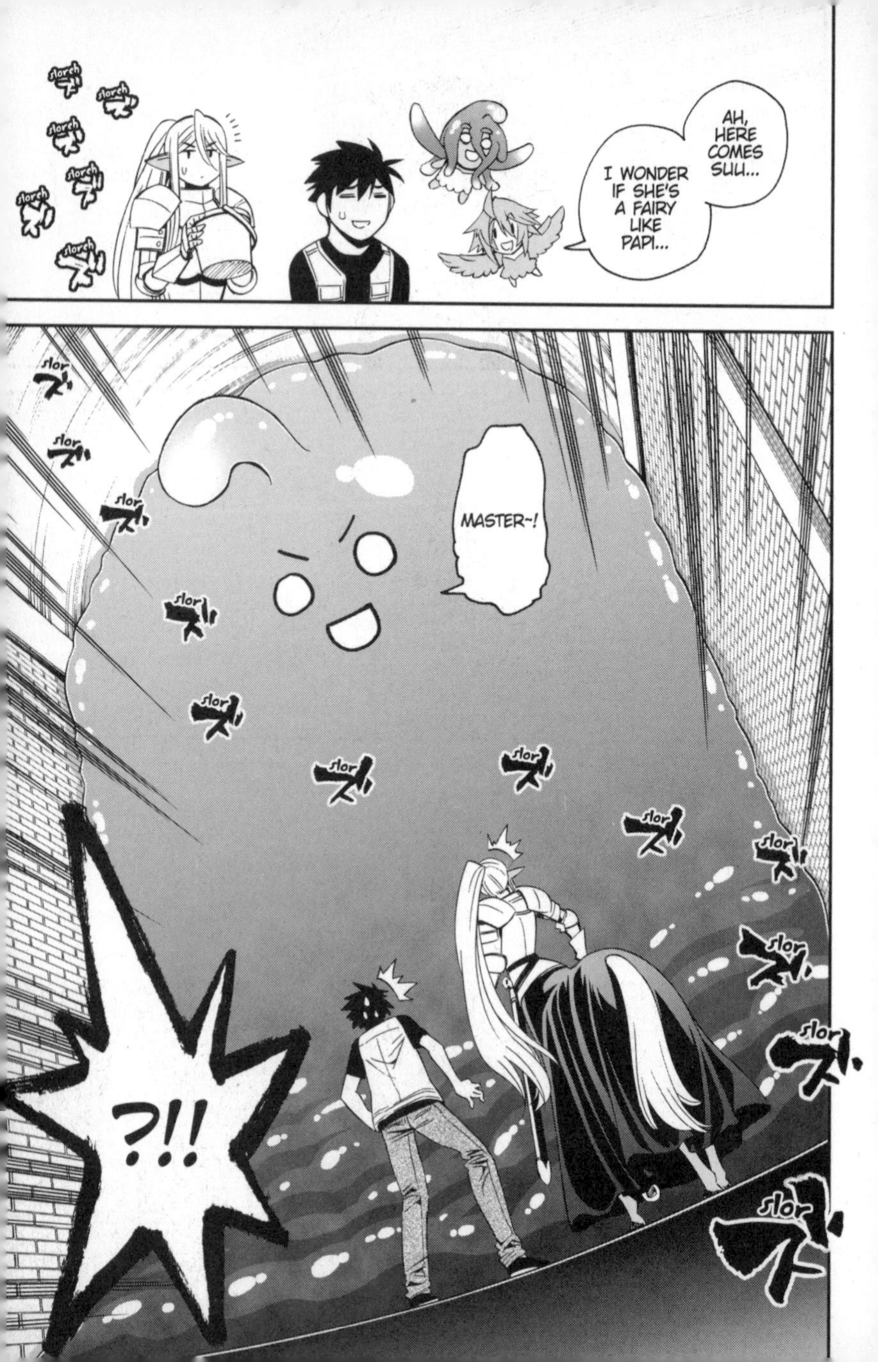
AH, HERE COMES SUU... I WONDER IF SHE'S A FAIRY LIKE PAPI...
slorch
slorch
slorch
slorch
slorch
slorch
MASTER~!
slor
slor
slor
slor
slor
slor
slor
slor
slor
slor
slor
slor
?!!

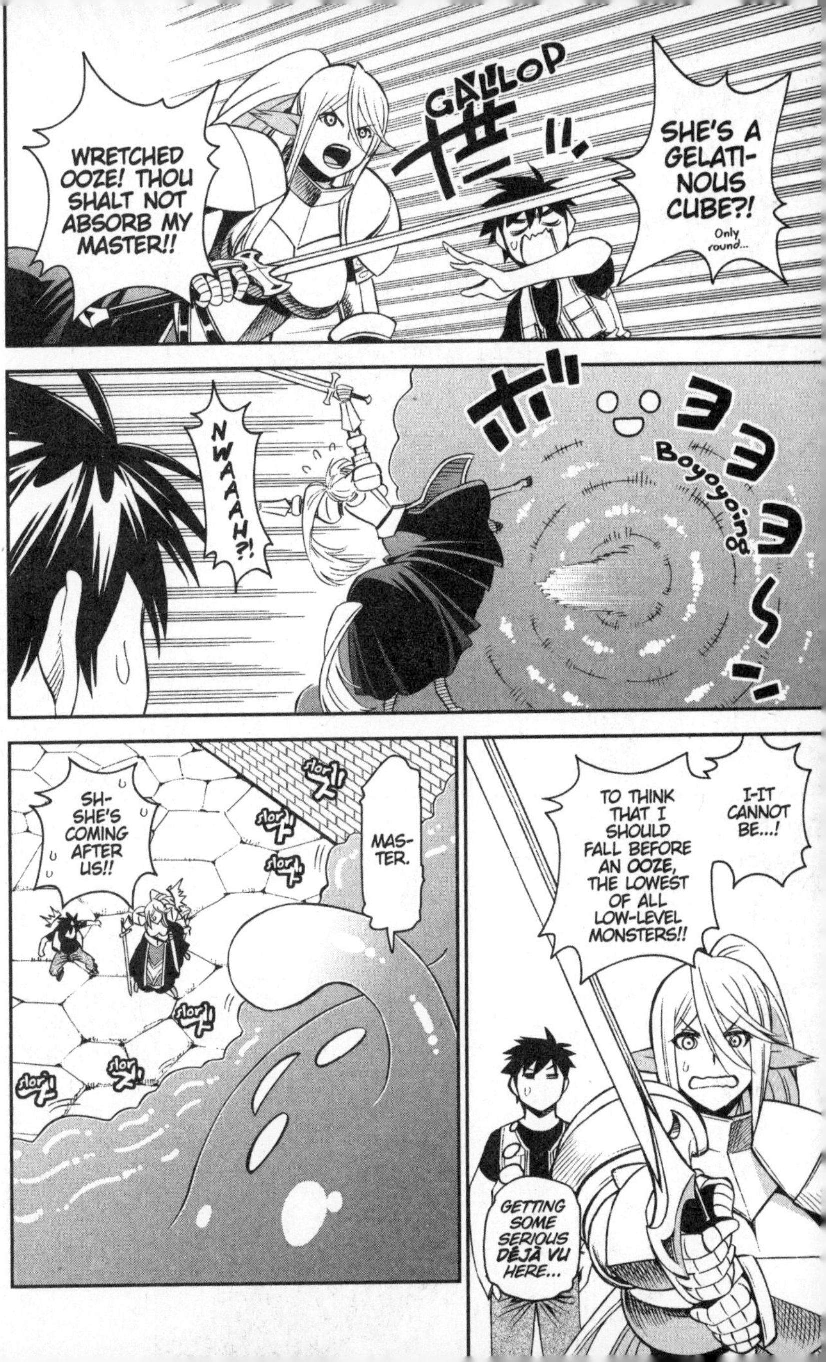
SHE'S A GELATINOUS CUBE?!
Only round...
GALLOP
WRETCHED OOZE! THOU SHALT NOT ABSORB MY MASTER!!
Boyoyoing
NWAAAAH?!
I-IT CANNOT BE...!
TO THINK THAT I SHOULD FALL BEFORE AN OOZE, THE LOWEST OF ALL LOW-LEVEL MONSTERS!!
GETTING SOME SERIOUS DÉJÀ VU HERE...
slorp
slorp
MASTER.
slorp
SH-SHE'S COMING AFTER US!!
slorp
slorp
slorp

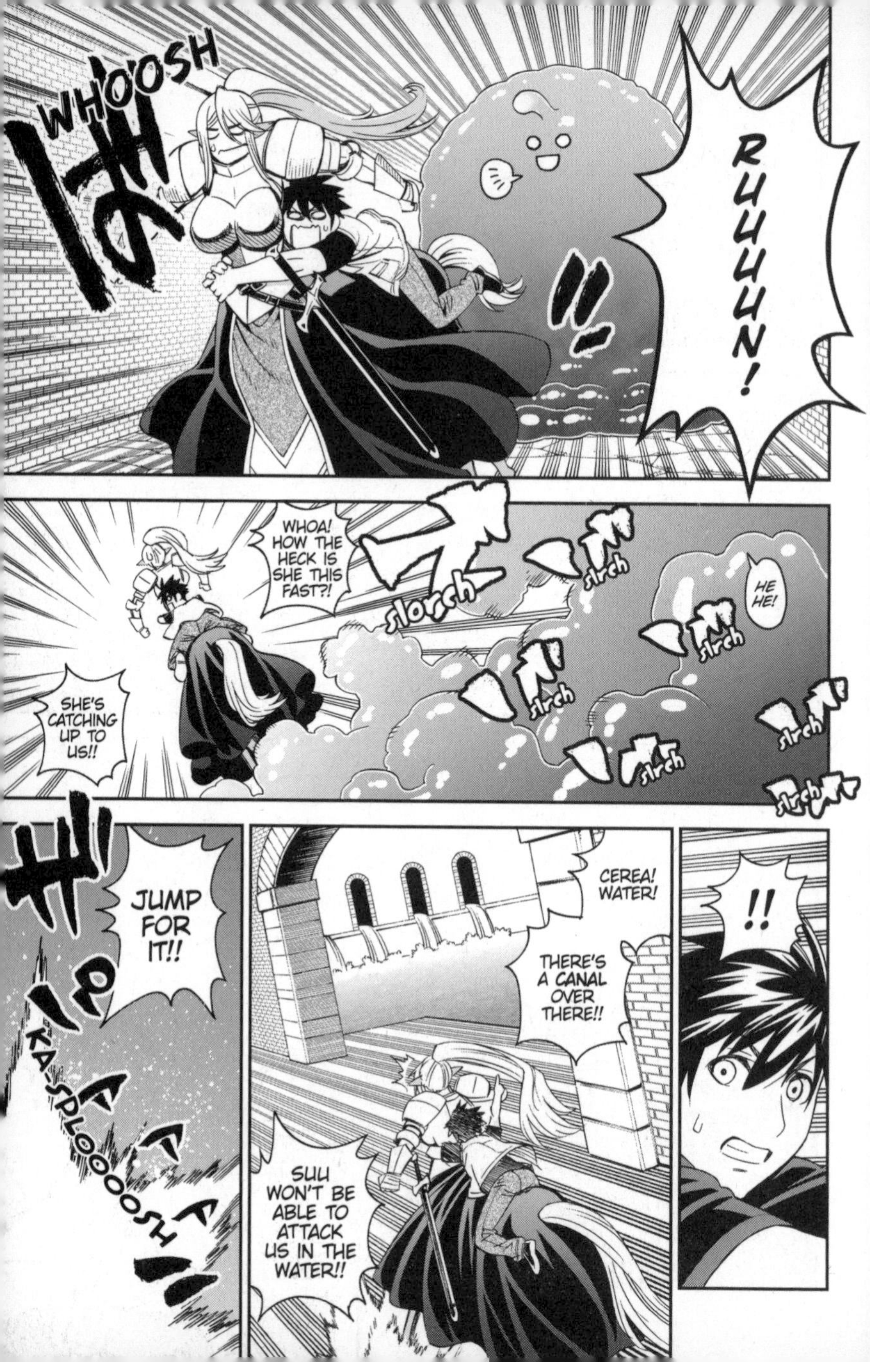
RUUUUUN!
WHOOSH
HE HE!
slrch
slrch
slrch
slrch
slrch
slrch
WHOA! HOW THE HECK IS SHE THIS FAST?!
slorch
SHE'S CATCHING UP TO US!!
!!
CEREA! WATER!
THERE'S A CANAL OVER THERE!!
SUU WON'T BE ABLE TO ATTACK US IN THE WATER!!
JUMP FOR IT!!
KA-SPLOOOOSH!!

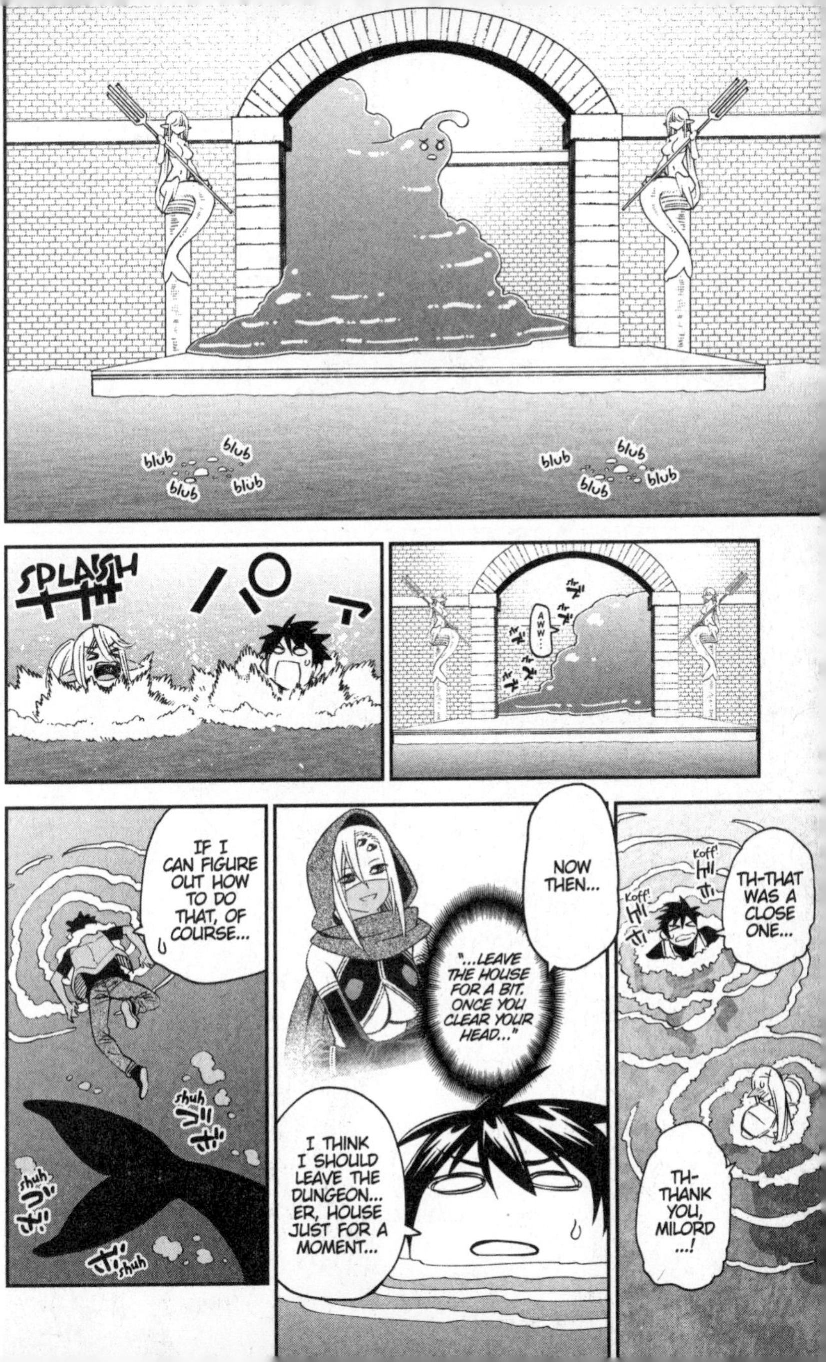
blub
blub
blub
blub
blub
blub
blub
blub
AWW...
SPLASH
Koff!
Koff!
TH-THAT WAS A CLOSE ONE...
TH-THANK YOU, MILORD...!
NOW THEN...
"...LEAVE THE HOUSE FOR A BIT. ONCE YOU CLEAR YOUR HEAD..."
I THINK I SHOULD LEAVE THE DUNGEON... ER, HOUSE JUST FOR A MOMENT...
IF I CAN FIGURE OUT HOW TO DO THAT, OF COURSE...
shuh
shuh
shuh

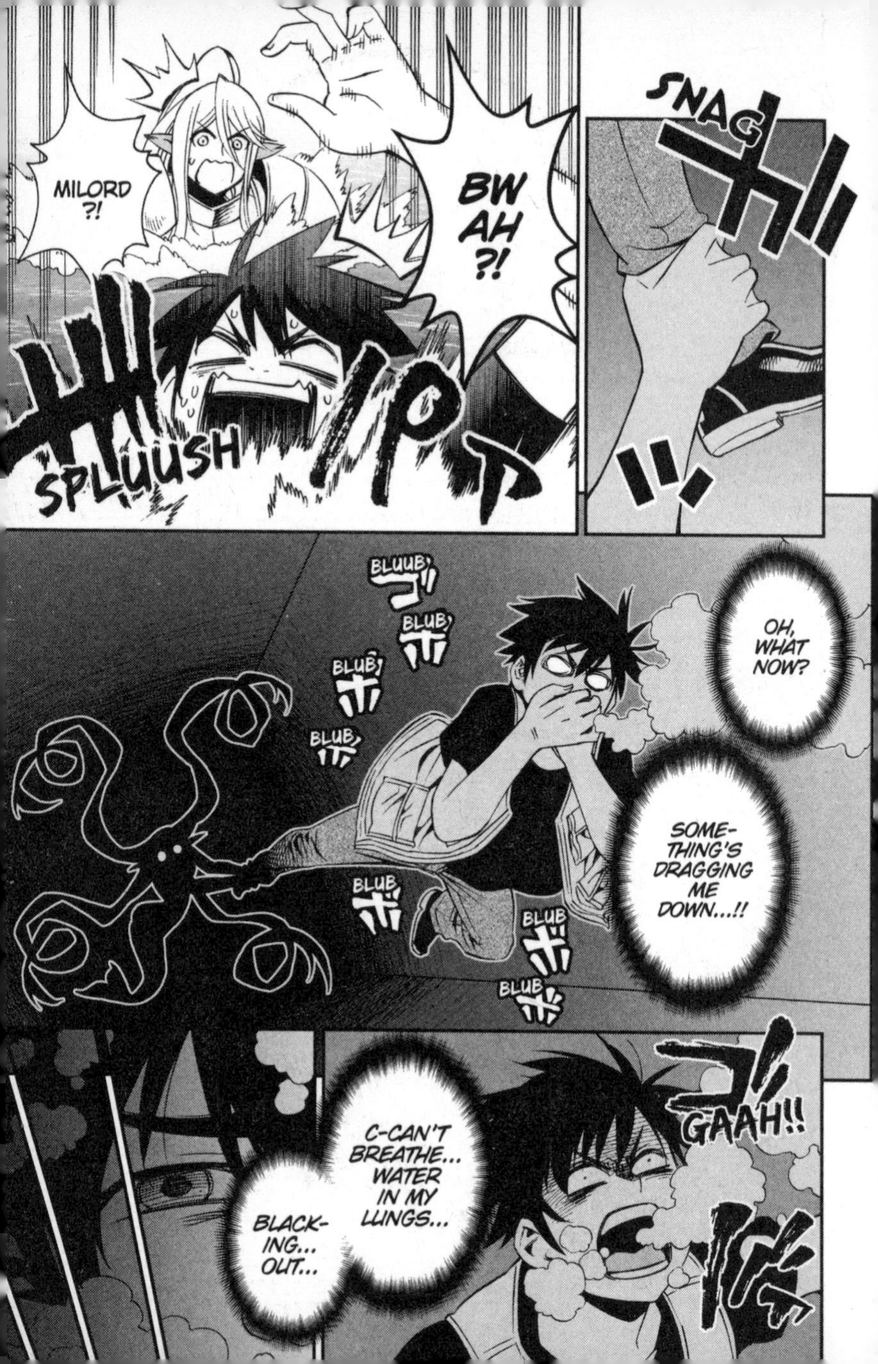
SNAG
BWAH ?!
MILORD ?!
SPLUUSH
OH, WHAT NOW?
BLUUB
BLUB
BLUB
BLUB
SOME-THING'S DRAGGING ME DOWN...!!
BLUB
BLUB
BLUB
GAAH!!
C-CAN'T BREATHE... WATER IN MY LUNGS...
BLACK-ING... OUT...

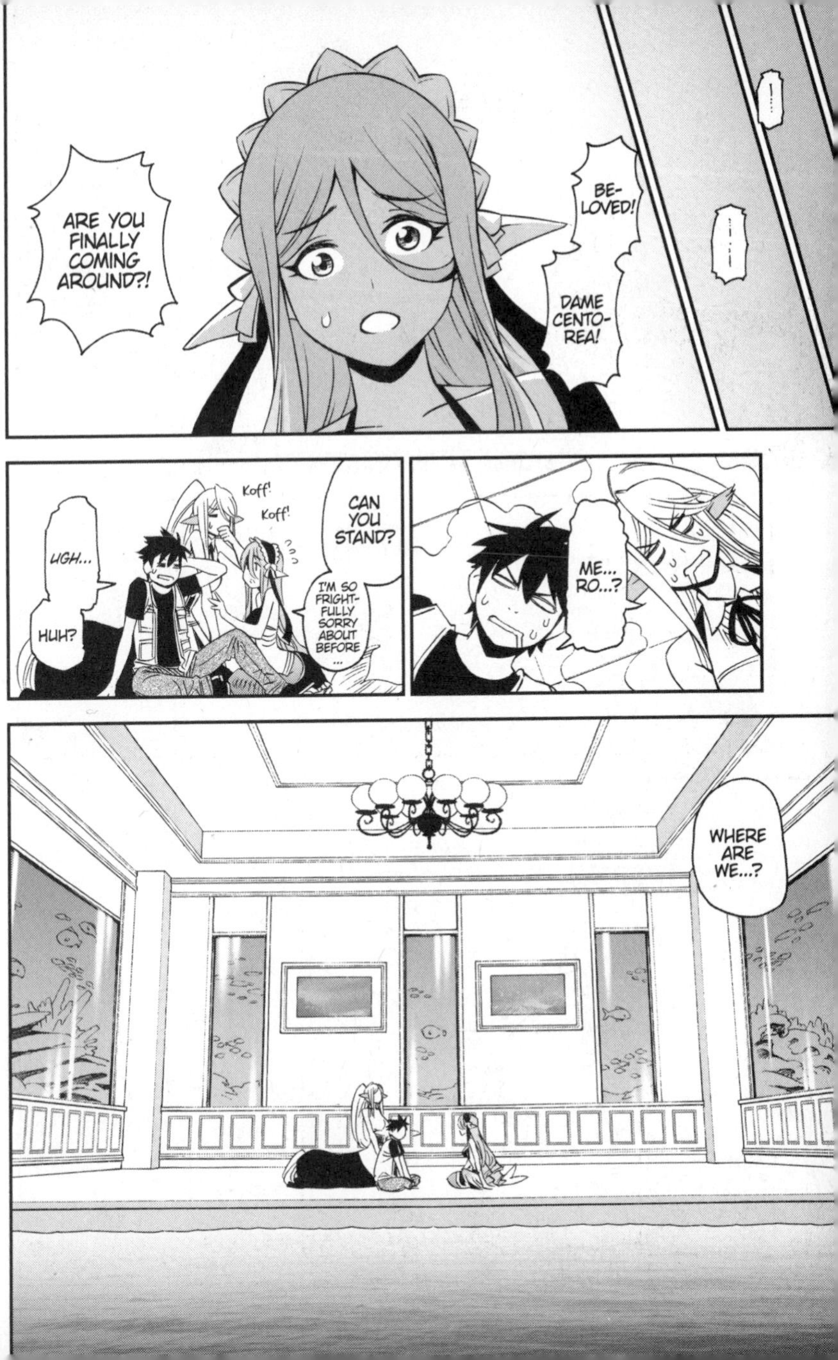
BE-
LOVED!
DAME
CENTO-
REA!
ARE YOU
FINALLY
COMING
AROUND?!
ME...
RO...?
CAN
YOU
STAND?
Koff!
Koff!
I'M SO
FRIGHT-
FULLY
SORRY
ABOUT
BEFORE
...
UGH...
HUH?
WHERE
ARE
WE...?

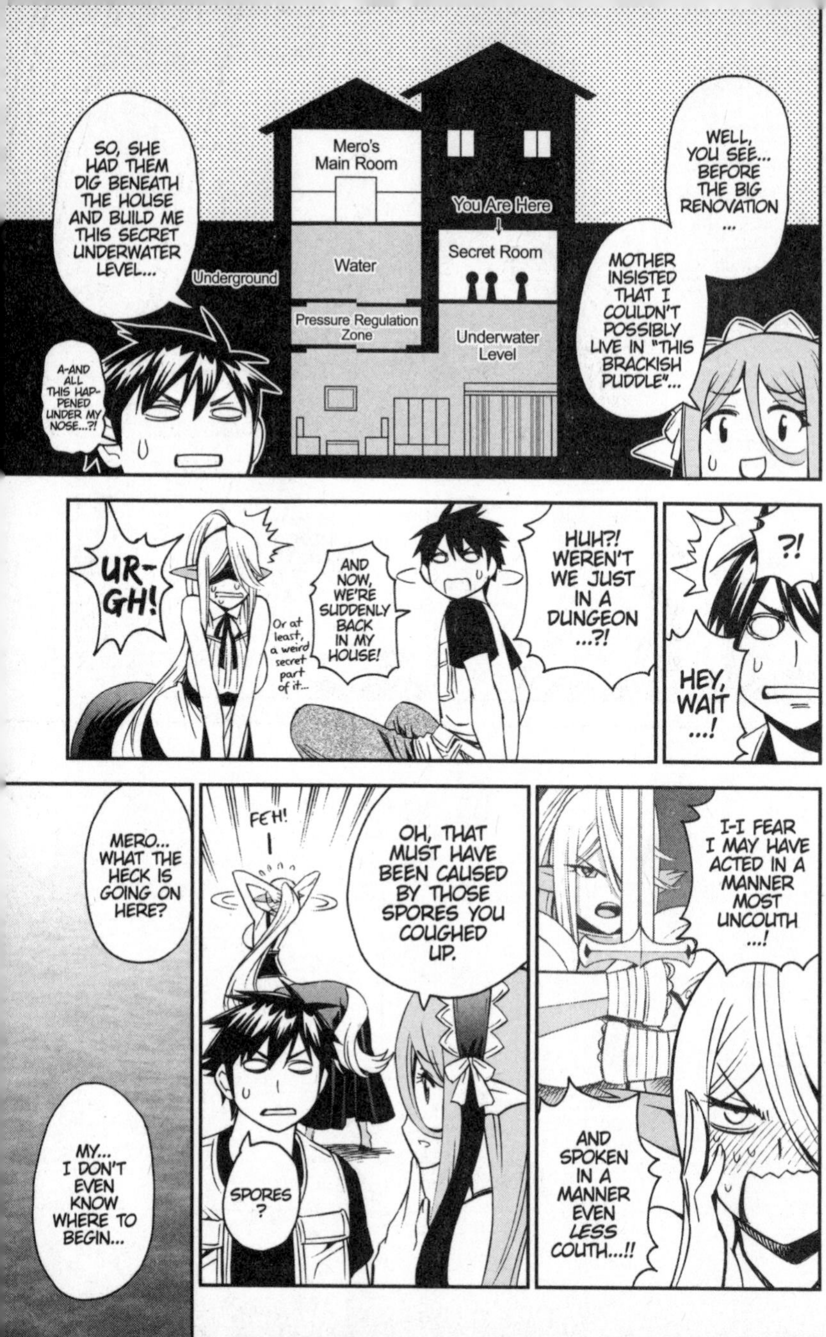
WELL, YOU SEE... BEFORE THE BIG RENOVATION ...
MOTHER INSISTED THAT I COULDN'T POSSIBLY LIVE IN "THIS BRACKISH PUDDLE"...
Mero's Main Room
You Are Here
Secret Room
Water
Underground
Pressure Regulation Zone
Underwater Level
SO, SHE HAD THEM DIG BENEATH THE HOUSE AND BUILD ME THIS SECRET UNDERWATER LEVEL...
A-AND ALL THIS HAP-PENED UNDER MY NOSE...?!
?!
HEY, WAIT ...!
HUH?! WEREN'T WE JUST IN A DUNGEON ...?!
AND NOW, WE'RE SUDDENLY BACK IN MY HOUSE!
Or at least, a weird secret part of it...
UR-GH!
I-I FEAR I MAY HAVE ACTED IN A MANNER MOST UNCOUTH ...!
AND SPOKEN IN A MANNER EVEN LESS COUTH...!!
FEH!
OH, THAT MUST HAVE BEEN CAUSED BY THOSE SPORES YOU COUGHED UP.
SPORES ?
MERO... WHAT THE HECK IS GOING ON HERE?
MY... I DON'T EVEN KNOW WHERE TO BEGIN...

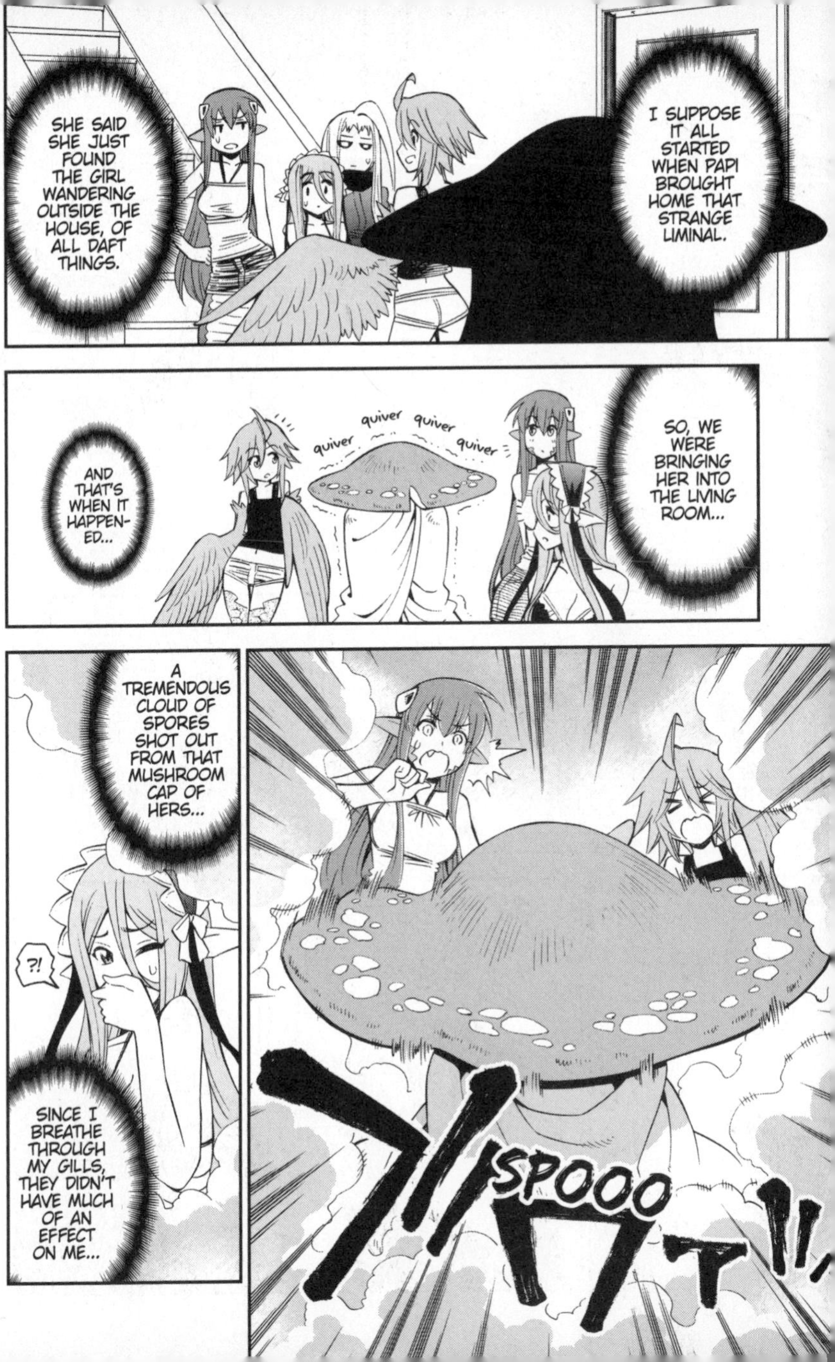
I SUPPOSE IT ALL STARTED WHEN PAPI BROUGHT HOME THAT STRANGE LIMINAL.
SHE SAID SHE JUST FOUND THE GIRL WANDERING OUTSIDE THE HOUSE, OF ALL DAFT THINGS.
SO, WE WERE BRINGING HER INTO THE LIVING ROOM...
quiver quiver quiver quiver
AND THAT'S WHEN IT HAPPEN-ED...
SPOOOT
A TREMENDOUS CLOUD OF SPORES SHOT OUT FROM THAT MUSHROOM CAP OF HERS...
?!
SINCE I BREATHE THROUGH MY GILLS, THEY DIDN'T HAVE MUCH OF AN EFFECT ON ME...

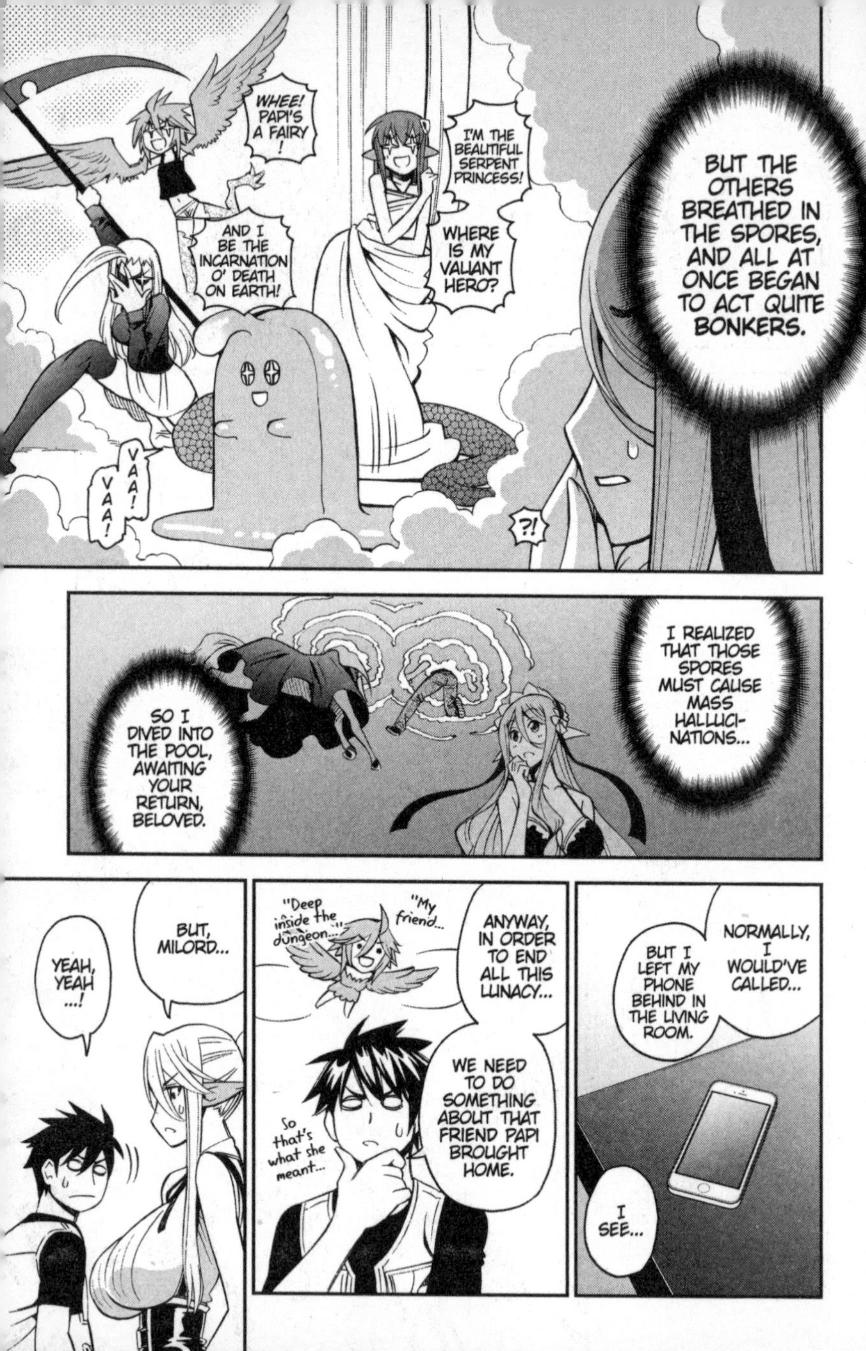
BUT THE OTHERS BREATHED IN THE SPORES, AND ALL AT ONCE BEGAN TO ACT QUITE BONKERS.
I'M THE BEAUTIFUL SERPENT PRINCESS!
WHERE IS MY VALIANT HERO?
WHEE! PAPI'S A FAIRY!
AND I BE THE INCARNATION O' DEATH ON EARTH!
?!
VAA! VAA!
I REALIZED THAT THOSE SPORES MUST CAUSE MASS HALLUCI-NATIONS...
SO I DIVED INTO THE POOL, AWAITING YOUR RETURN, BELOVED.
NORMALLY, I WOULD'VE CALLED...
BUT I LEFT MY PHONE BEHIND IN THE LIVING ROOM.
I SEE...
ANYWAY, IN ORDER TO END ALL THIS LUNACY...
"My friend...
"Deep inside the dungeon..."
WE NEED TO DO SOMETHING ABOUT THAT FRIEND PAPI BROUGHT HOME.
So that's what she meant...
BUT, MILORD...
YEAH, YEAH...!

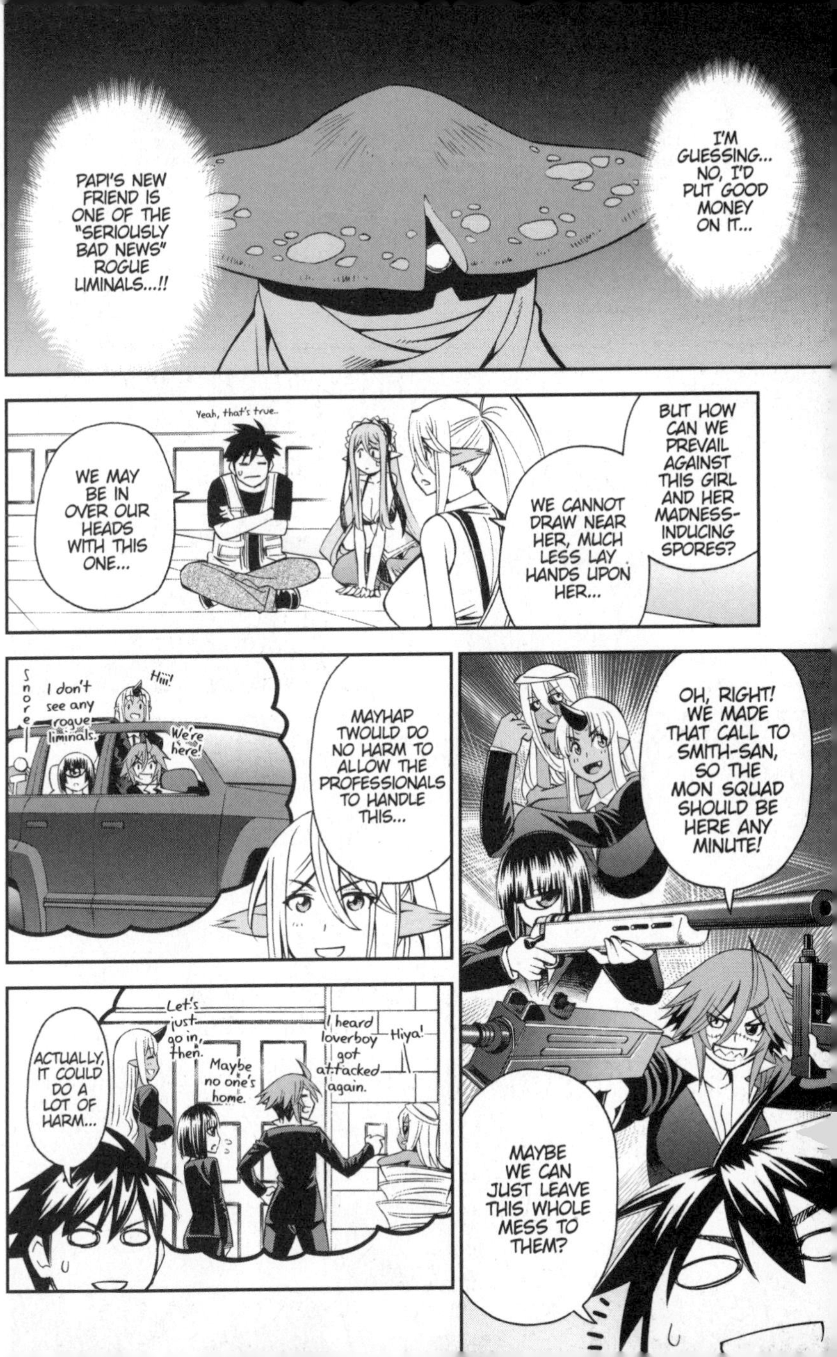
I'M GUESSING... NO, I'D PUT GOOD MONEY ON IT...
PAPI'S NEW FRIEND IS ONE OF THE "SERIOUSLY BAD NEWS" ROGUE LIMINALS...!!
BUT HOW CAN WE PREVAIL AGAINST THIS GIRL AND HER MADNESS-INDUCING SPORES?
WE CANNOT DRAW NEAR HER, MUCH LESS LAY HANDS UPON HER...
Yeah, that's true..
WE MAY BE IN OVER OUR HEADS WITH THIS ONE...
OH, RIGHT! WE MADE THAT CALL TO SMITH-SAN, SO THE MON SQUAD SHOULD BE HERE ANY MINUTE!
MAYBE WE CAN JUST LEAVE THIS WHOLE MESS TO THEM?
MAYHAP TWOULD DO NO HARM TO ALLOW THE PROFESSIONALS TO HANDLE THIS...
Hiii!
We're here!
I don't see any rogue liminals.
Snore
I heard loverboy got attacked again.
Hiya!
Let's just go in, then.
Maybe no one's home.
ACTUALLY, IT COULD DO A LOT OF HARM...

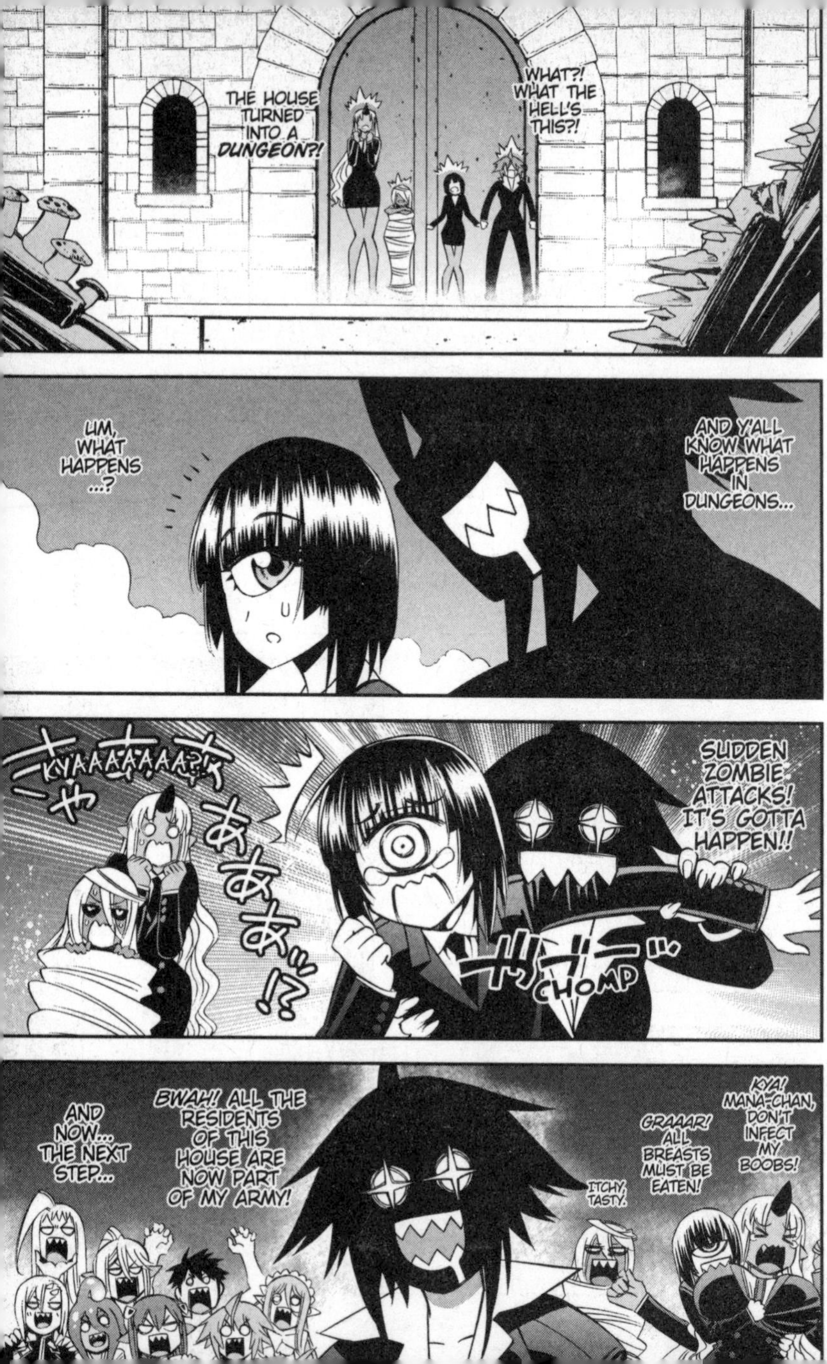
WHAT?! WHAT THE HELL'S THIS?!
THE HOUSE TURNED INTO A DUNGEON?!
AND Y'ALL KNOW WHAT HAPPENS IN DUNGEONS...
UM, WHAT HAPPENS ...?
SUDDEN ZOMBIE ATTACKS! IT'S GOTTA HAPPEN!!
CHOMP
KYAAAAAAA?!
KYA! MANA-CHAN, DON'T INFECT MY BOOBS!
GRAAAR! ALL BREASTS MUST BE EATEN!
ITCHY, TASTY.
BWAH! ALL THE RESIDENTS OF THIS HOUSE ARE NOW PART OF MY ARMY!
AND NOW... THE NEXT STEP...

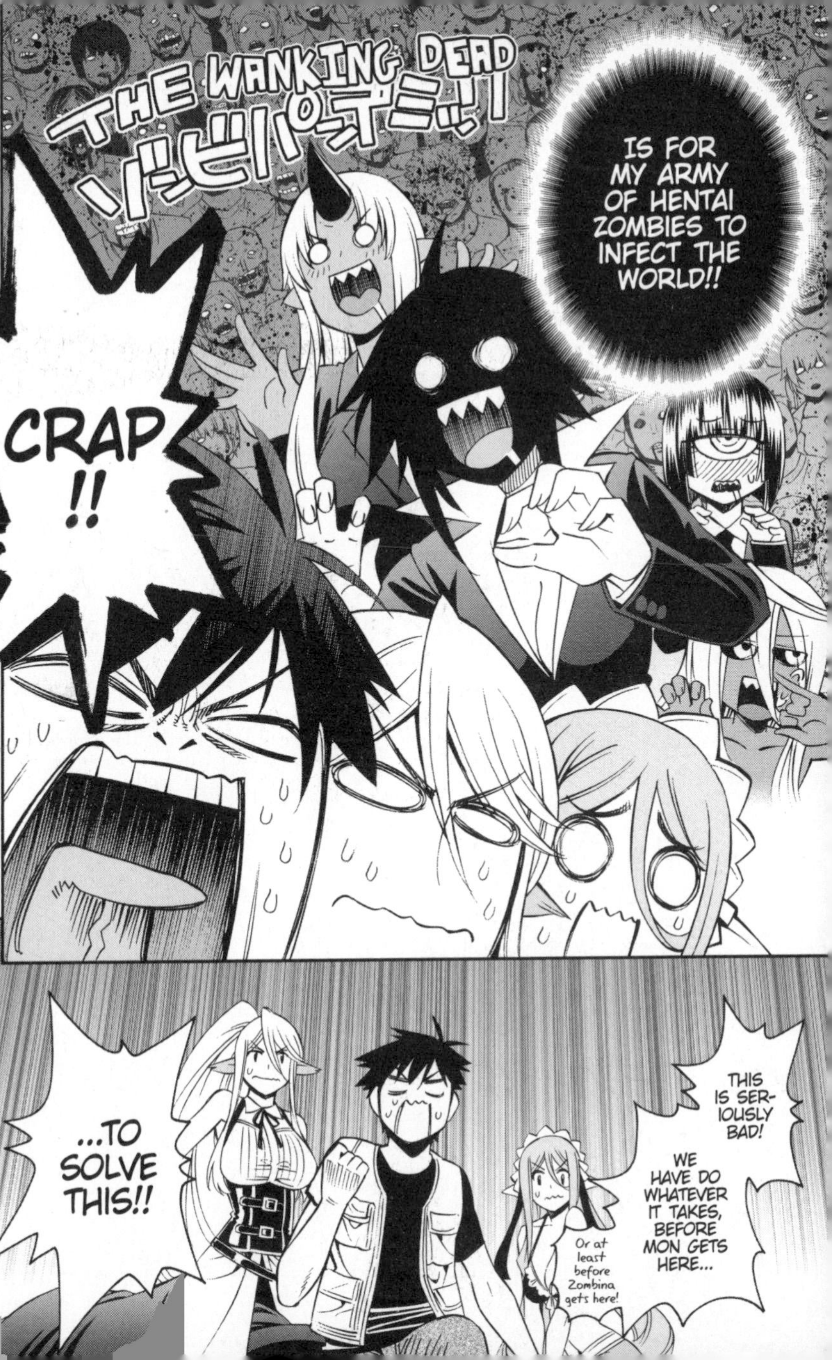
IS FOR MY ARMY OF HENTAI ZOMBIES TO INFECT THE WORLD!!
THE WANKING DEAD
CRAP!!
THIS IS SERIOUSLY BAD!
WE HAVE DO WHATEVER IT TAKES, BEFORE MON GETS HERE...
Or at least before Zombina gets here!
...TO SOLVE THIS!!

Monster Musume
Everyday Life with Monster Girls

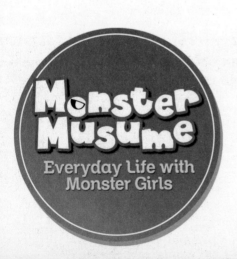

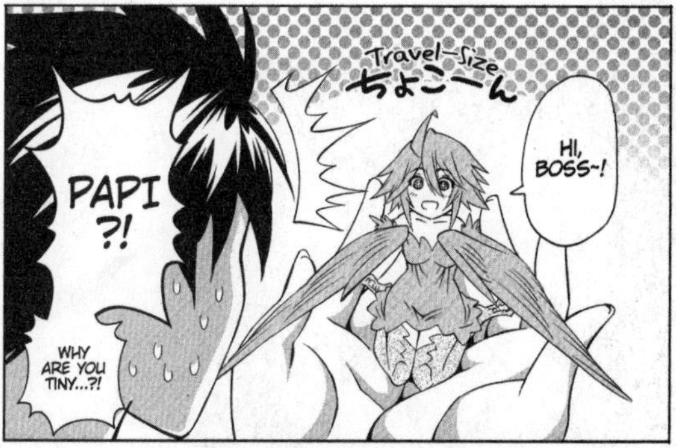HI, BOSS~!
Travel-Size
ちょこーん
PAPI ?!
WHY ARE YOU TINY...?!

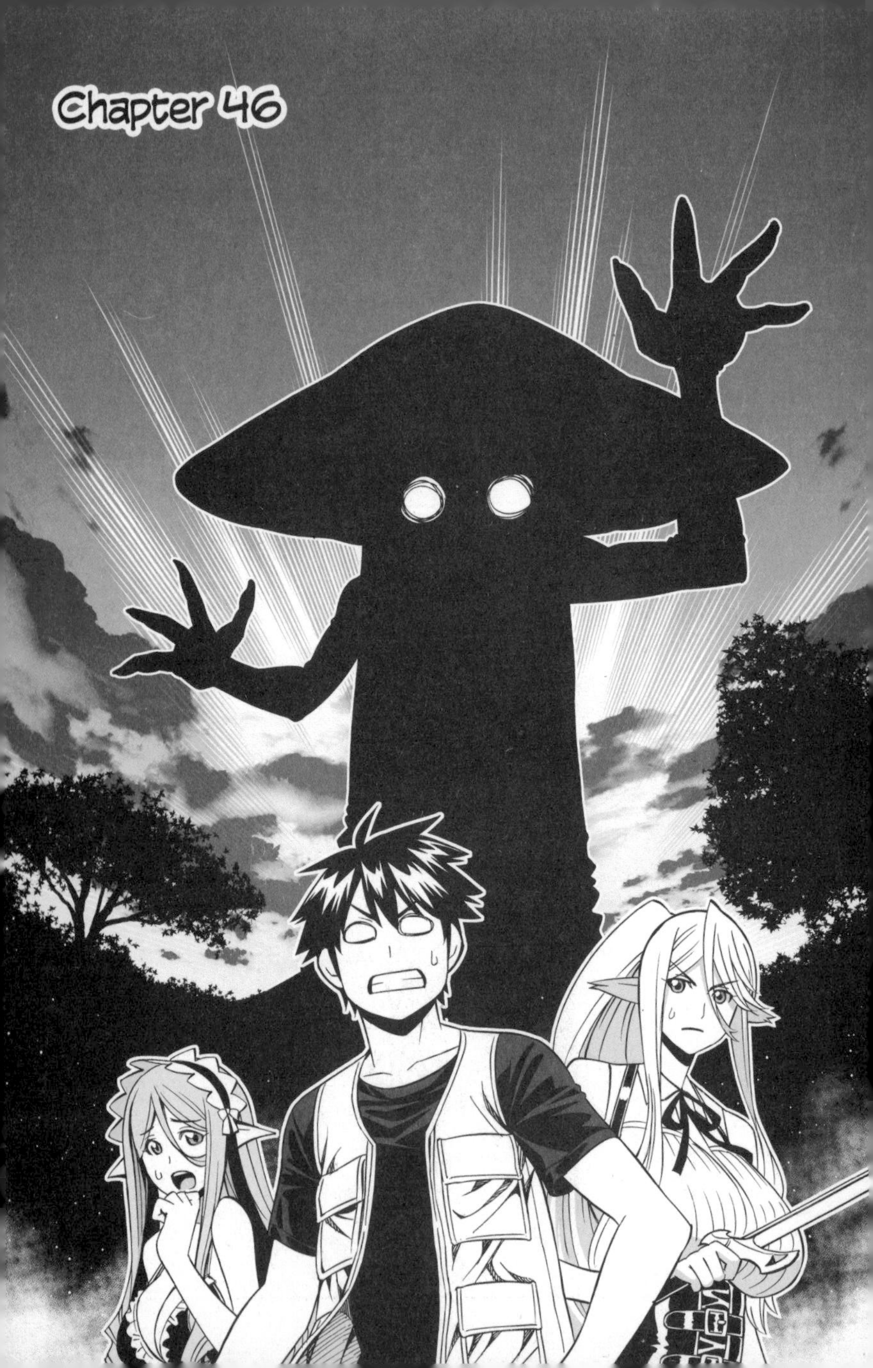
Chapter 46

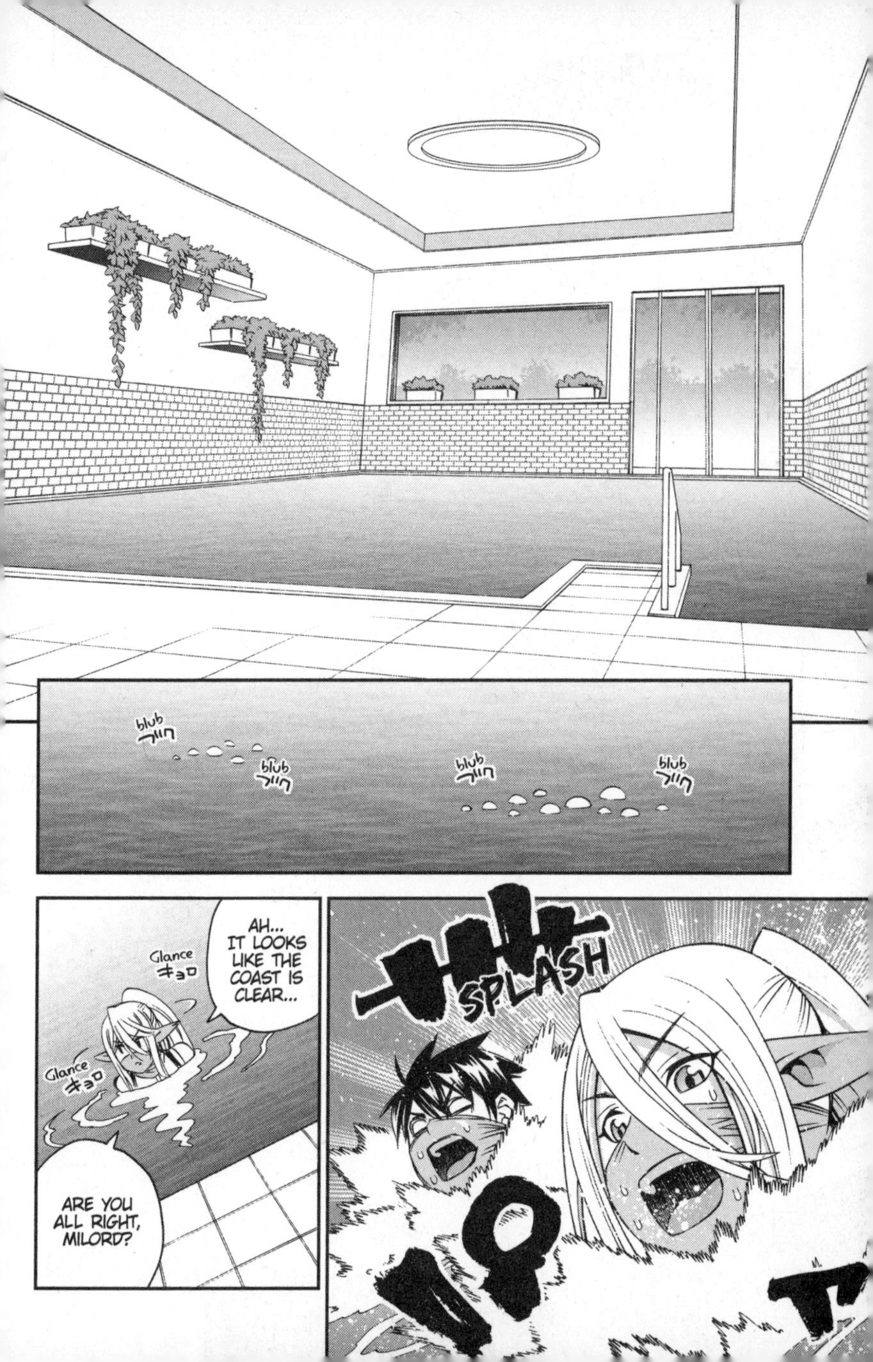
blub
blub
blub
blub
SPLASH
AH... IT LOOKS LIKE THE COAST IS CLEAR...
Glance キョロ
Glance キョロ
ARE YOU ALL RIGHT, MILORD?

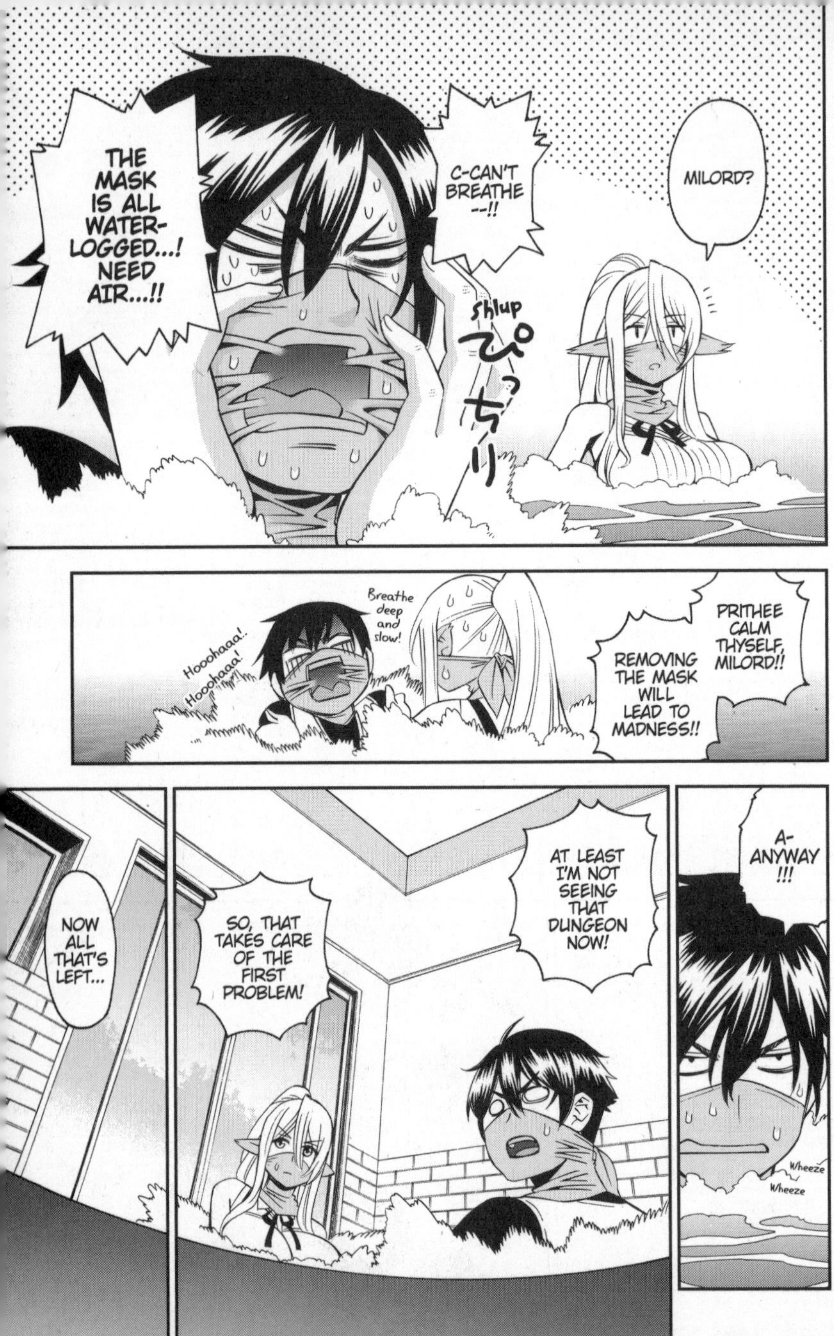
MILORD?
C-CAN'T BREATHE--!!
THE MASK IS ALL WATER-LOGGED...! NEED AIR...!!
shlup
ぴっちり
PRITHEE CALM THYSELF, MILORD!!
REMOVING THE MASK WILL LEAD TO MADNESS!!
Breathe deep and slow!
Hooohaaa! Hooohaaa!
A- ANYWAY !!!
Wheeze
Wheeze
AT LEAST I'M NOT SEEING THAT DUNGEON NOW!
SO, THAT TAKES CARE OF THE FIRST PROBLEM!
NOW ALL THAT'S LEFT...

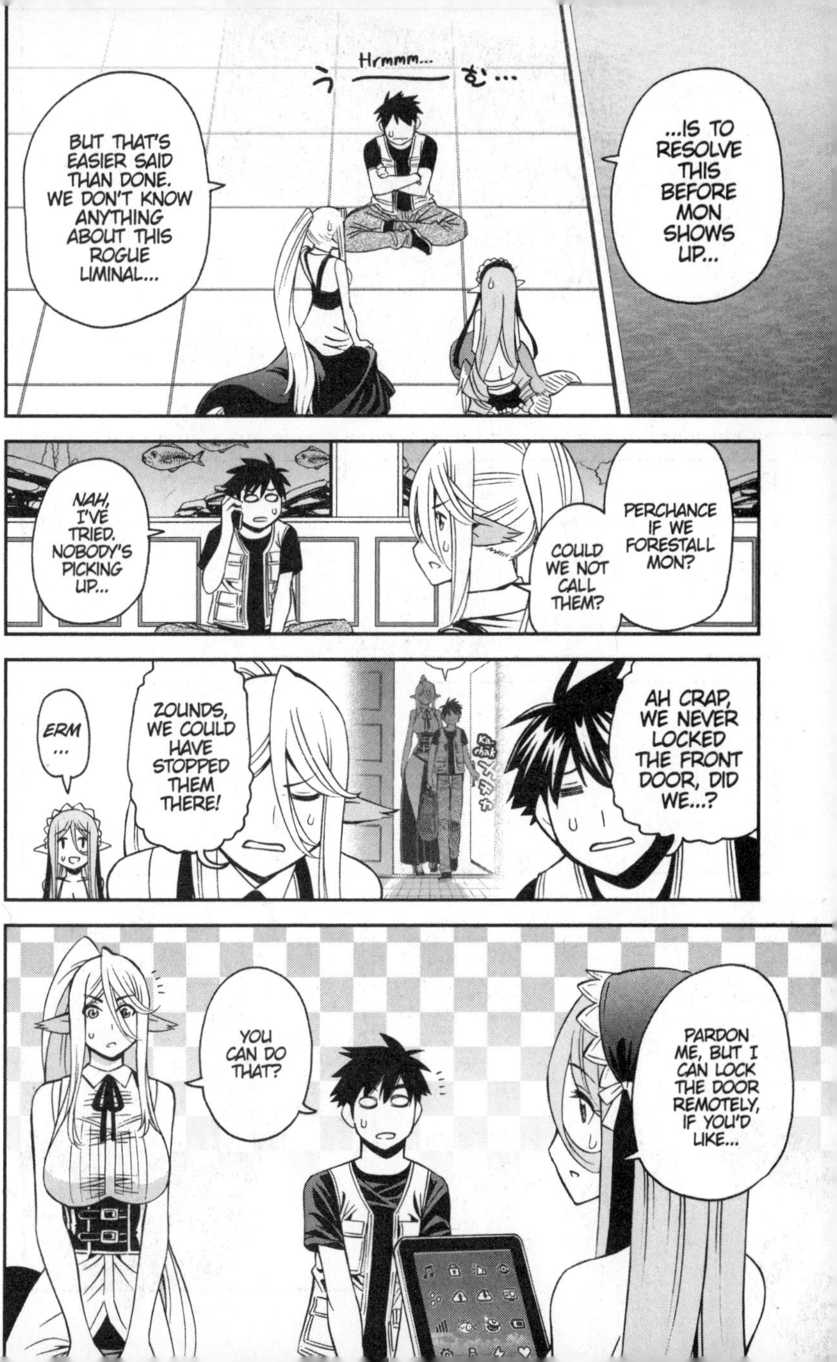
...IS TO RESOLVE THIS BEFORE MON SHOWS UP...
Hrmmm...
う——む...
BUT THAT'S EASIER SAID THAN DONE. WE DON'T KNOW ANYTHING ABOUT THIS ROGUE LIMINAL...
PERCHANCE IF WE FORESTALL MON?
COULD WE NOT CALL THEM?
NAH, I'VE TRIED. NOBODY'S PICKING UP...
AH CRAP, WE NEVER LOCKED THE FRONT DOOR, DID WE...?
Ka-chak
ZOUNDS, WE COULD HAVE STOPPED THEM THERE!
ERM ...
PARDON ME, BUT I CAN LOCK THE DOOR REMOTELY, IF YOU'D LIKE...
YOU CAN DO THAT?

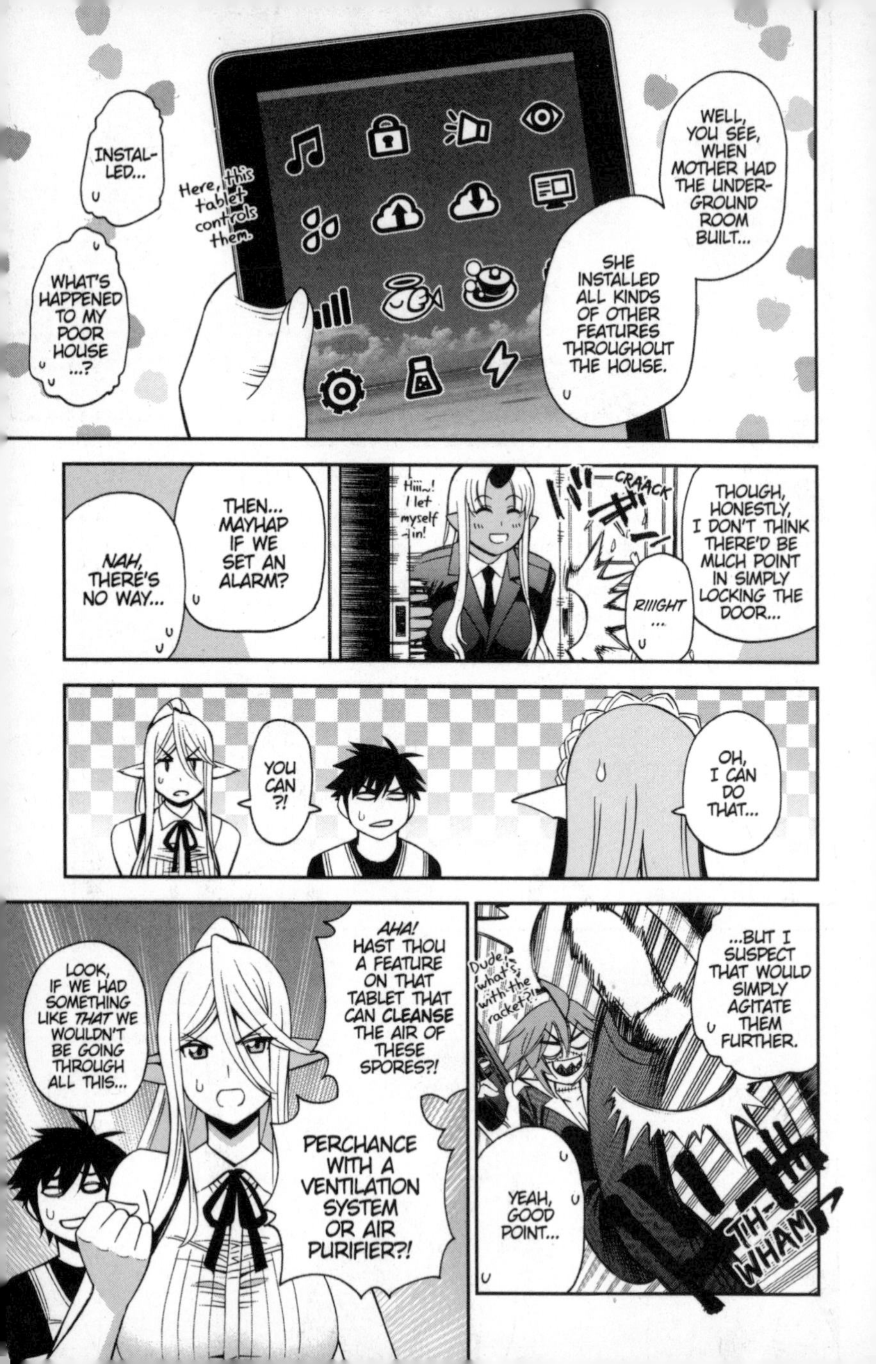

WELL, YOU SEE, WHEN MOTHER HAD THE UNDER-GROUND ROOM BUILT...
SHE INSTALLED ALL KINDS OF OTHER FEATURES THROUGHOUT THE HOUSE.
Here, this tablet controls them.
INSTAL-LED...
WHAT'S HAPPENED TO MY POOR HOUSE ...?
THOUGH, HONESTLY, I DON'T THINK THERE'D BE MUCH POINT IN SIMPLY LOCKING THE DOOR...
RIIIGHT ...
CRA'ACK
Hiii~! I let myself in!
THEN... MAYHAP IF WE SET AN ALARM?
NAH, THERE'S NO WAY...
OH, I CAN DO THAT...
YOU CAN ?!
...BUT I SUSPECT THAT WOULD SIMPLY AGITATE THEM FURTHER.
Dude, what's with the racket?!
YEAH, GOOD POINT...
TH-WHAM
AHA! HAST THOU A FEATURE ON THAT TABLET THAT CAN CLEANSE THE AIR OF THESE SPORES?!
PERCHANCE WITH A VENTILATION SYSTEM OR AIR PURIFIER?!
LOOK, IF WE HAD SOMETHING LIKE *THAT* WE WOULDN'T BE GOING THROUGH ALL THIS...

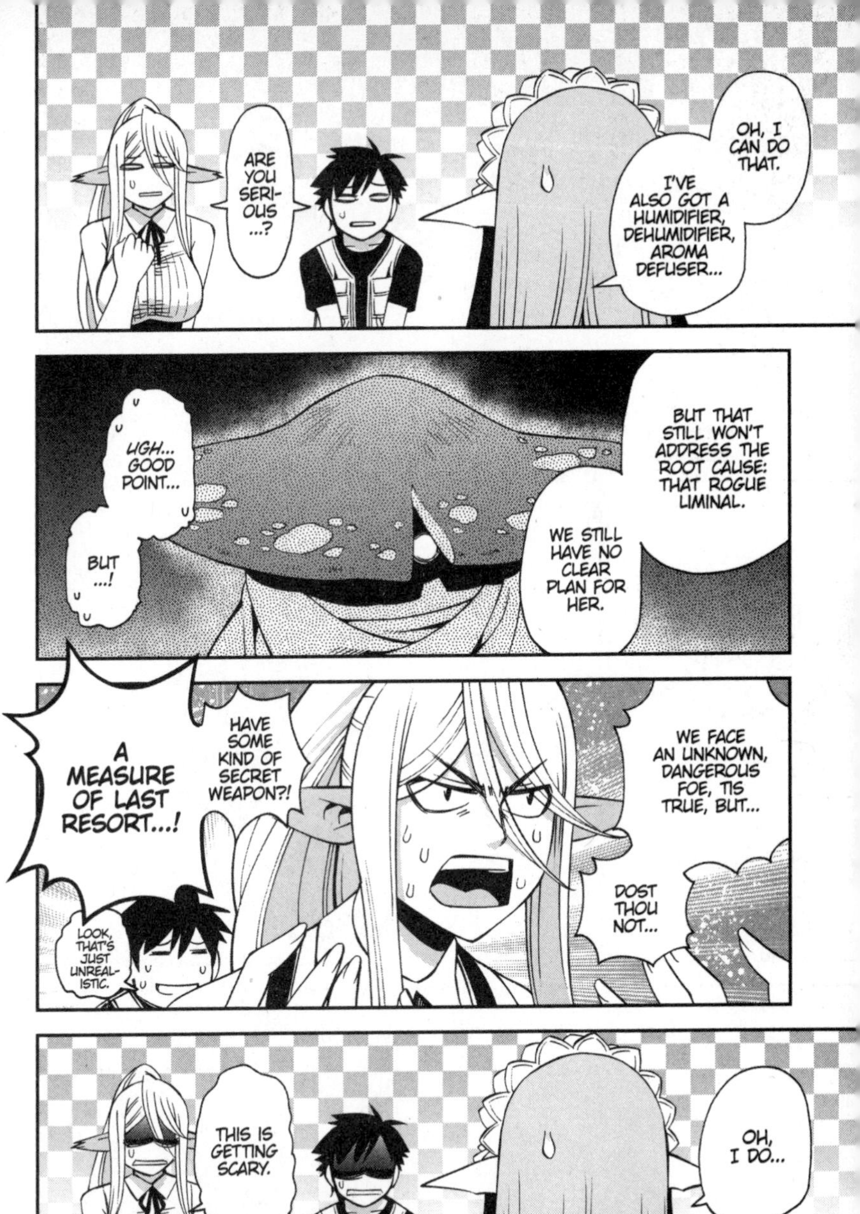

OH, I CAN DO THAT.
I'VE ALSO GOT A HUMIDIFIER, DEHUMIDIFIER, AROMA DEFUSER...
ARE YOU SERI-OUS ...?
BUT THAT STILL WON'T ADDRESS THE ROOT CAUSE: THAT ROGUE LIMINAL.
WE STILL HAVE NO CLEAR PLAN FOR HER.
UGH... GOOD POINT...
BUT ...!
WE FACE AN UNKNOWN, DANGEROUS FOE, TIS TRUE, BUT...
DOST THOU NOT...
HAVE SOME KIND OF SECRET WEAPON?!
A MEASURE OF LAST RESORT...!
LOOK, THAT'S JUST UNREAL-ISTIC.
OH, I DO...
THIS IS GETTING SCARY.

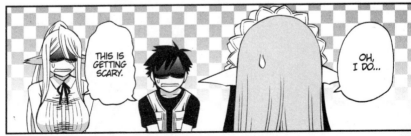

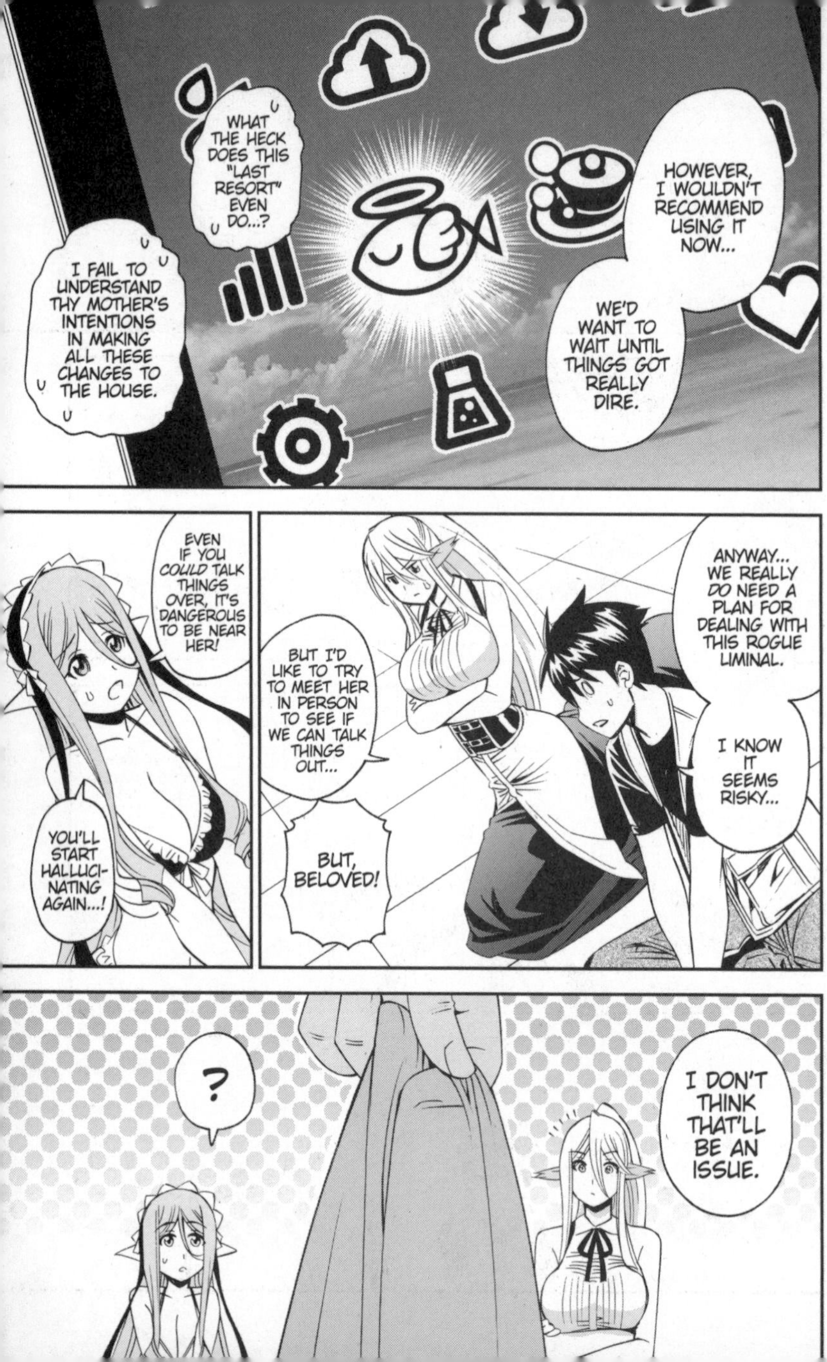
HOWEVER, I WOULDN'T RECOMMEND USING IT NOW...
WE'D WANT TO WAIT UNTIL THINGS GOT REALLY DIRE.
WHAT THE HECK DOES THIS "LAST RESORT" EVEN DO...?
I FAIL TO UNDERSTAND THY MOTHER'S INTENTIONS IN MAKING ALL THESE CHANGES TO THE HOUSE.
ANYWAY... WE REALLY DO NEED A PLAN FOR DEALING WITH THIS ROGUE LIMINAL.
I KNOW IT SEEMS RISKY...
BUT I'D LIKE TO TRY TO MEET HER IN PERSON TO SEE IF WE CAN TALK THINGS OUT...
BUT, BELOVED!
EVEN IF YOU COULD TALK THINGS OVER, IT'S DANGEROUS TO BE NEAR HER!
YOU'LL START HALLUCI-NATING AGAIN...!
I DON'T THINK THAT'LL BE AN ISSUE.
?

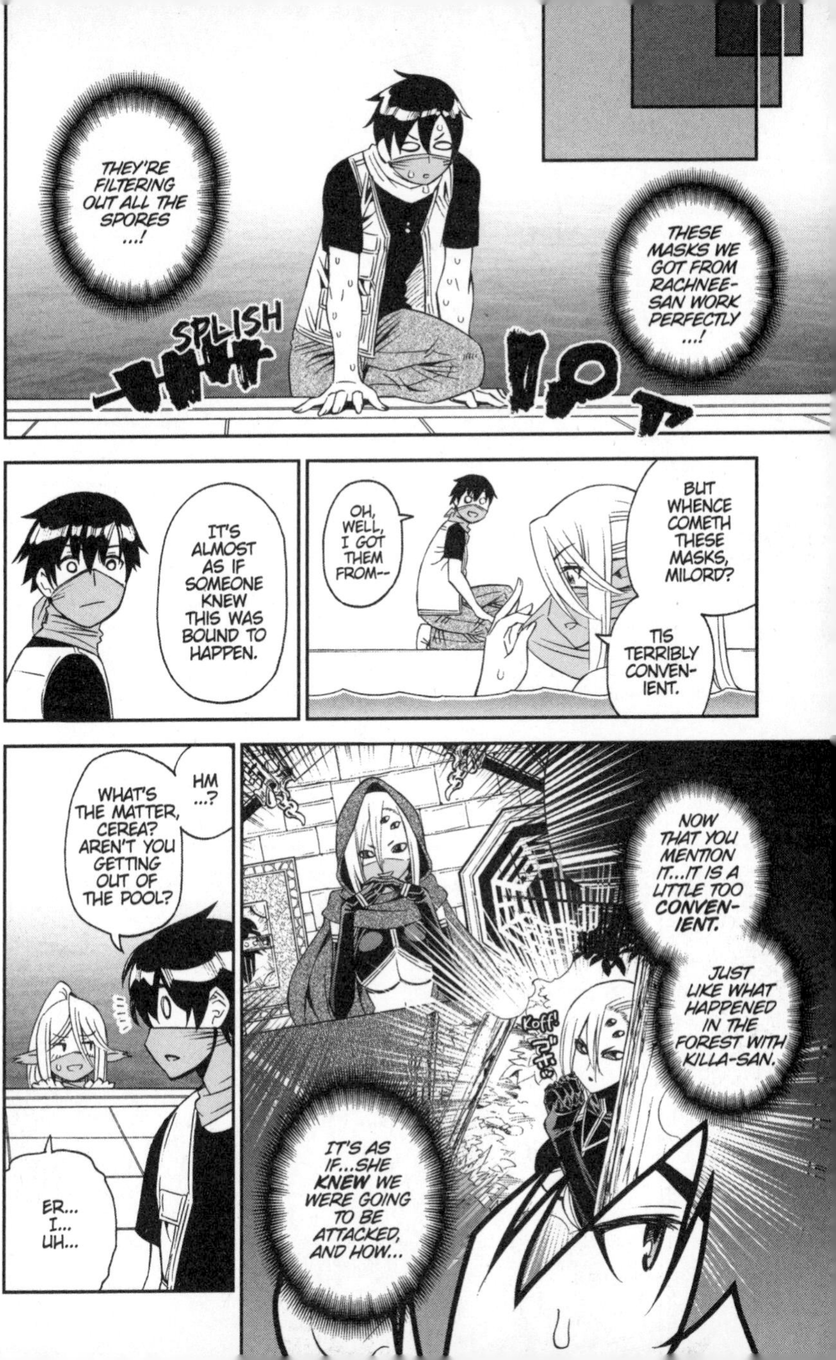
THESE MASKS WE GOT FROM RACHNEE-SAN WORK PERFECTLY ...!
THEY'RE FILTERING OUT ALL THE SPORES ...!
SPLISH
BUT WHENCE COMETH THESE MASKS, MILORD?
'TIS TERRIBLY CONVEN-IENT.
OH, WELL, I GOT THEM FROM--
IT'S ALMOST AS IF SOMEONE KNEW THIS WAS BOUND TO HAPPEN.
NOW THAT YOU MENTION IT...IT IS A LITTLE TOO CONVEN-IENT.
JUST LIKE WHAT HAPPENED IN THE FOREST WITH KILLA-SAN.
Koff!
IT'S AS IF...SHE KNEW WE WERE GOING TO BE ATTACKED, AND HOW...
HM ...?
WHAT'S THE MATTER, CEREA? AREN'T YOU GETTING OUT OF THE POOL?
ER... I... UH...

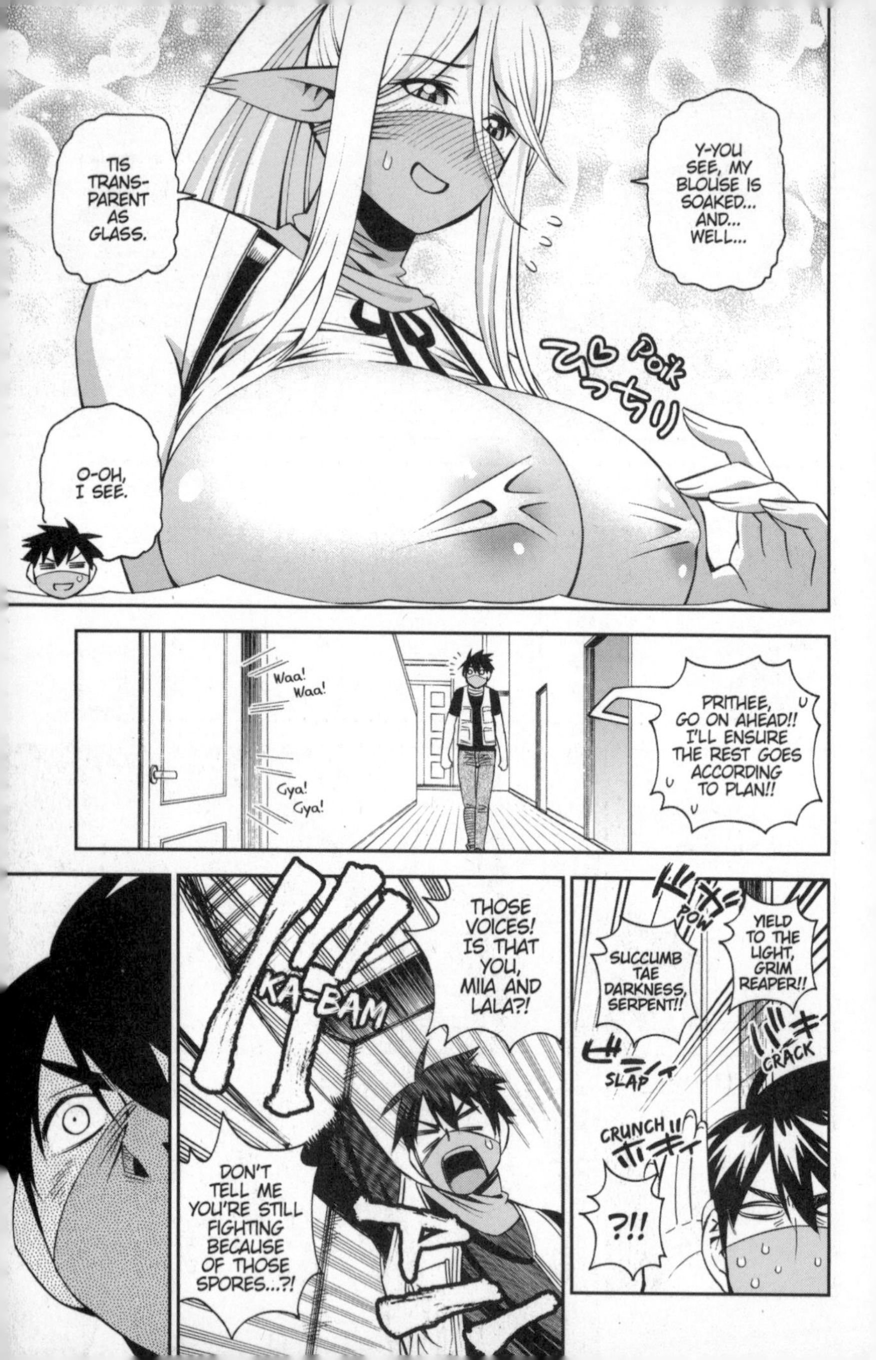
Y-YOU SEE, MY BLOUSE IS SOAKED... AND... WELL...
Poik
TIS TRANSPARENT AS GLASS.
O-OH, I SEE.
PRITHEE, GO ON AHEAD!! I'LL ENSURE THE REST GOES ACCORDING TO PLAN!!
Waa! Waa!
Gya! Gya!
POW
YIELD TO THE LIGHT, GRIM REAPER!!
SUCCUMB TAE DARKNESS, SERPENT!!
CRACK
SLAP
CRUNCH
?!!
THOSE VOICES! IS THAT YOU, MIIA AND LALA?!
KA-BAM
DON'T TELL ME YOU'RE STILL FIGHTING BECAUSE OF THOSE SPORES...?!

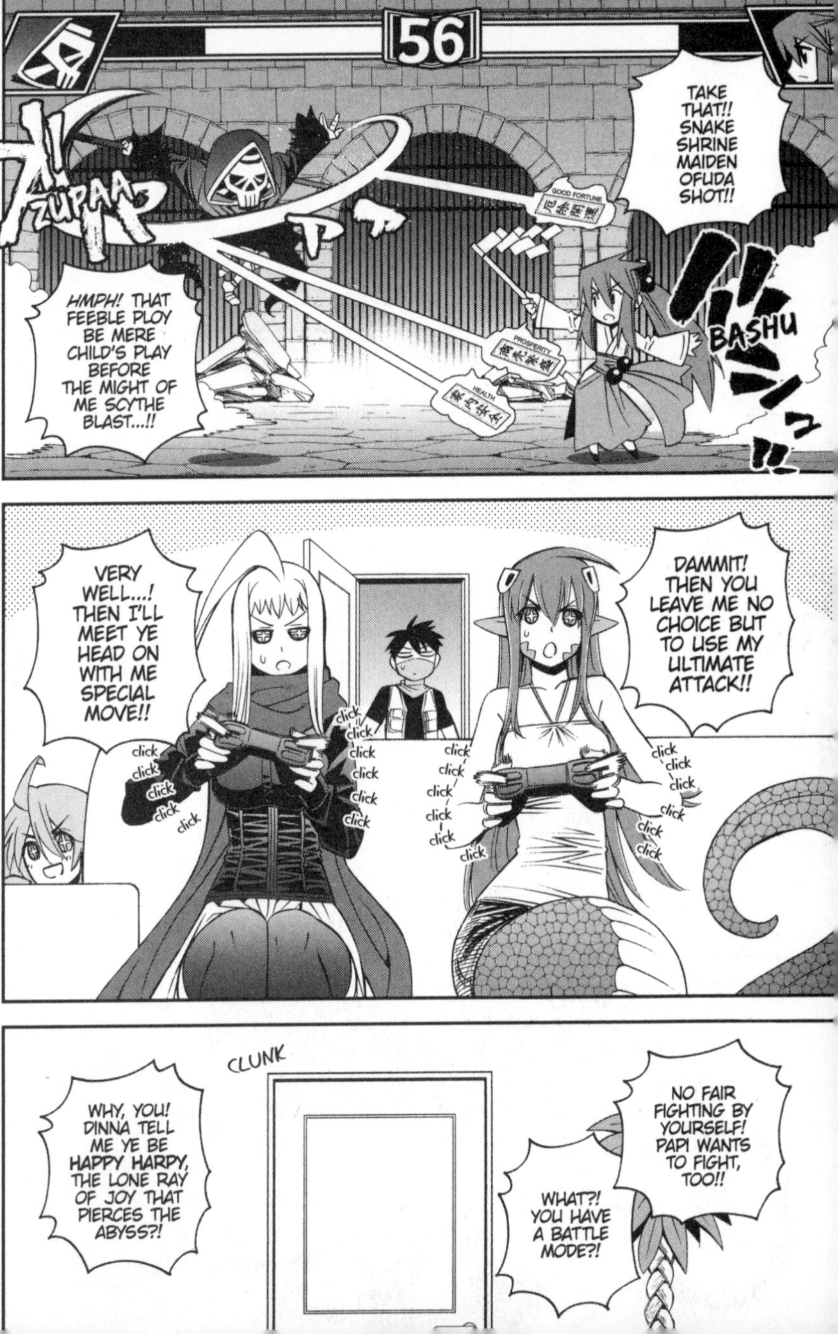
56
TAKE THAT!! SNAKE SHRINE MAIDEN OFUDA SHOT!!
GOOD FORTUNE
BASHU
PROSPERITY
HEALTH
ZUPAA
HMPH! THAT FEEBLE PLOY BE MERE CHILD'S PLAY BEFORE THE MIGHT OF ME SCYTHE BLAST...!!
DAMMIT! THEN YOU LEAVE ME NO CHOICE BUT TO USE MY ULTIMATE ATTACK!!
click click click click click click
click click click click click click
click click click click click
VERY WELL...! THEN I'LL MEET YE HEAD ON WITH ME SPECIAL MOVE!!
click click click click click
NO FAIR FIGHTING BY YOURSELF! PAPI WANTS TO FIGHT, TOO!!
WHAT?! YOU HAVE A BATTLE MODE?!
CLUNK
WHY, YOU! DINNA TELL ME YE BE HAPPY HARPY, THE LONE RAY OF JOY THAT PIERCES THE ABYSS?!

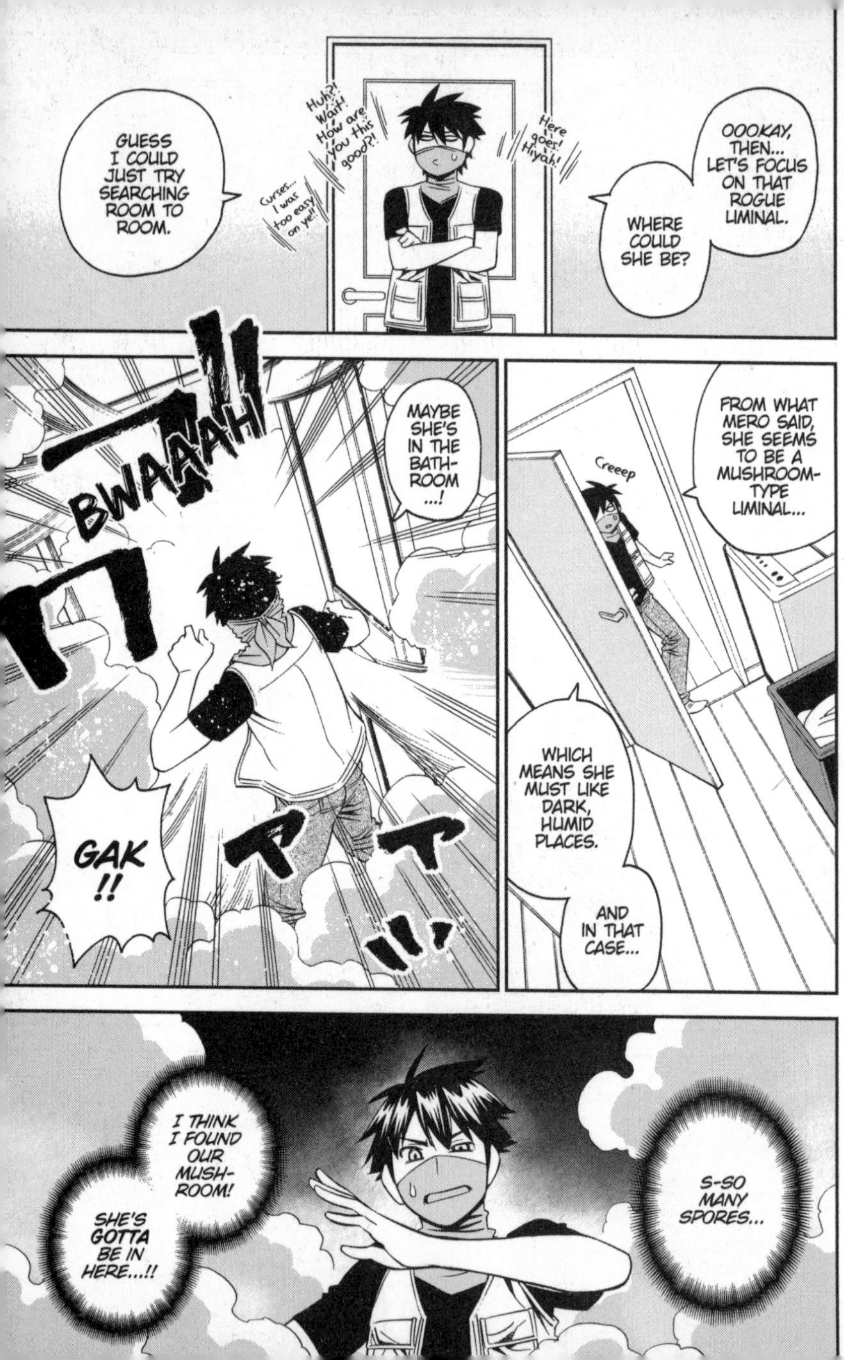
OOOKAY, THEN... LET'S FOCUS ON THAT ROGUE LIMINAL.
WHERE COULD SHE BE?
Here goes! Hiyah!
Huh?! Wait! How are you this good?!
Curses... I was too easy on ye!!
GUESS I COULD JUST TRY SEARCHING ROOM TO ROOM.
FROM WHAT MERO SAID, SHE SEEMS TO BE A MUSHROOM-TYPE LIMINAL...
Creeep
WHICH MEANS SHE MUST LIKE DARK, HUMID PLACES.
AND IN THAT CASE...
MAYBE SHE'S IN THE BATH-ROOM ...!
BWAAAAH!!
GAK !!
S-SO MANY SPORES...
I THINK I FOUND OUR MUSH-ROOM!
SHE'S GOTTA BE IN HERE...!!

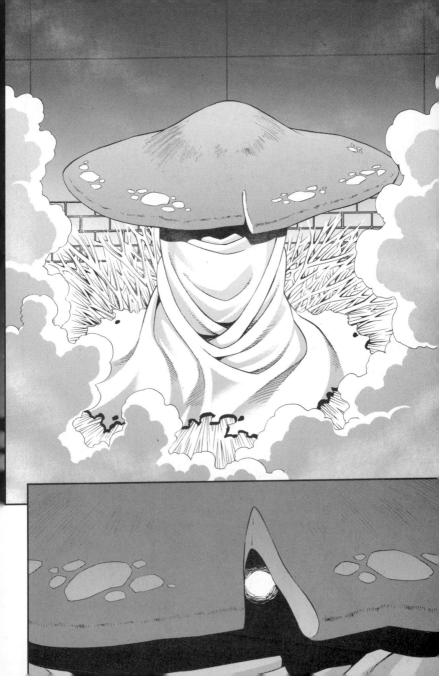

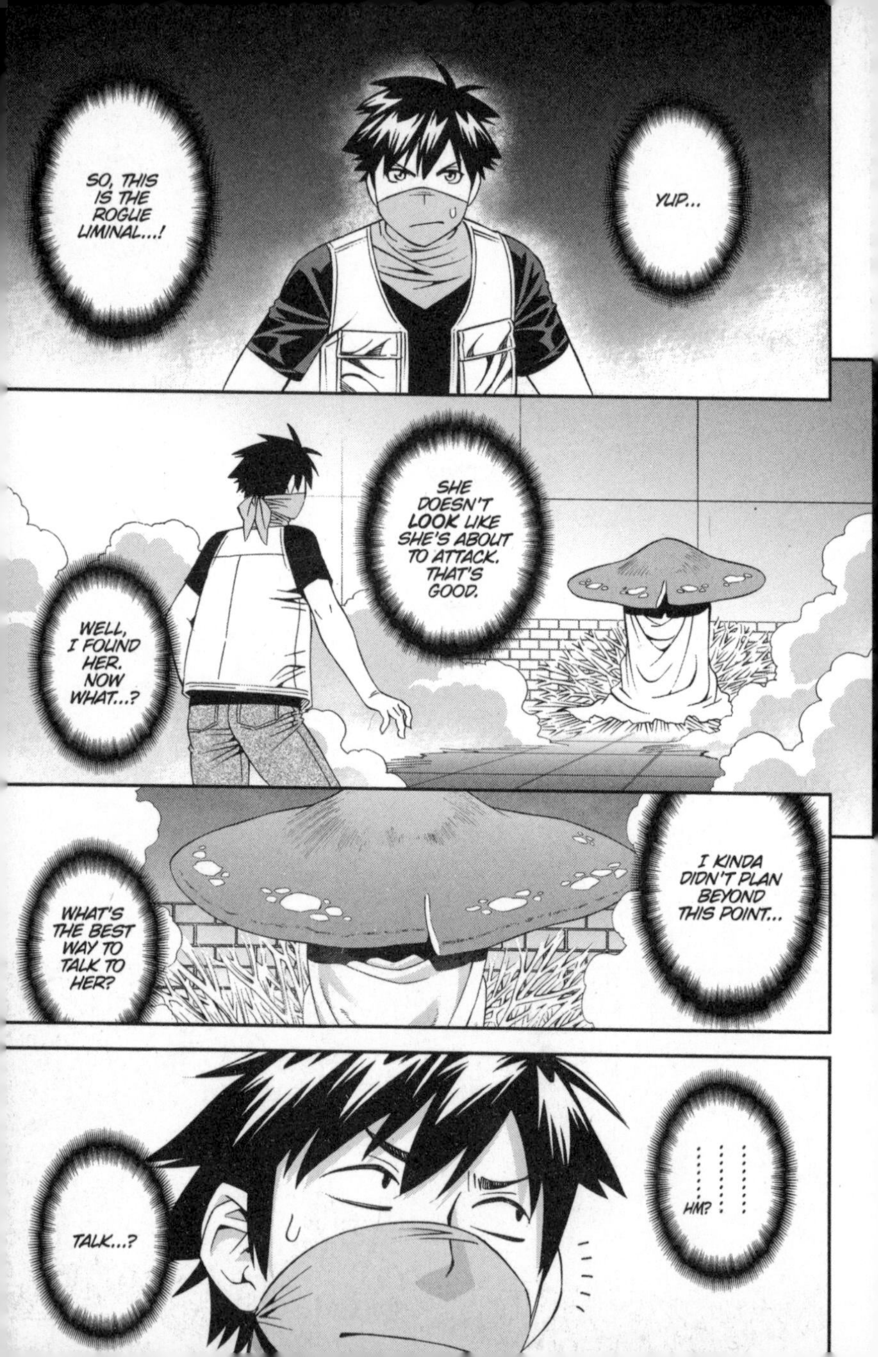
SO, THIS IS THE ROGUE LIMINAL...!
YUP...
SHE DOESN'T LOOK LIKE SHE'S ABOUT TO ATTACK. THAT'S GOOD.
WELL, I FOUND HER. NOW WHAT...?
I KINDA DIDN'T PLAN BEYOND THIS POINT...
WHAT'S THE BEST WAY TO TALK TO HER?
......HM?
TALK...?

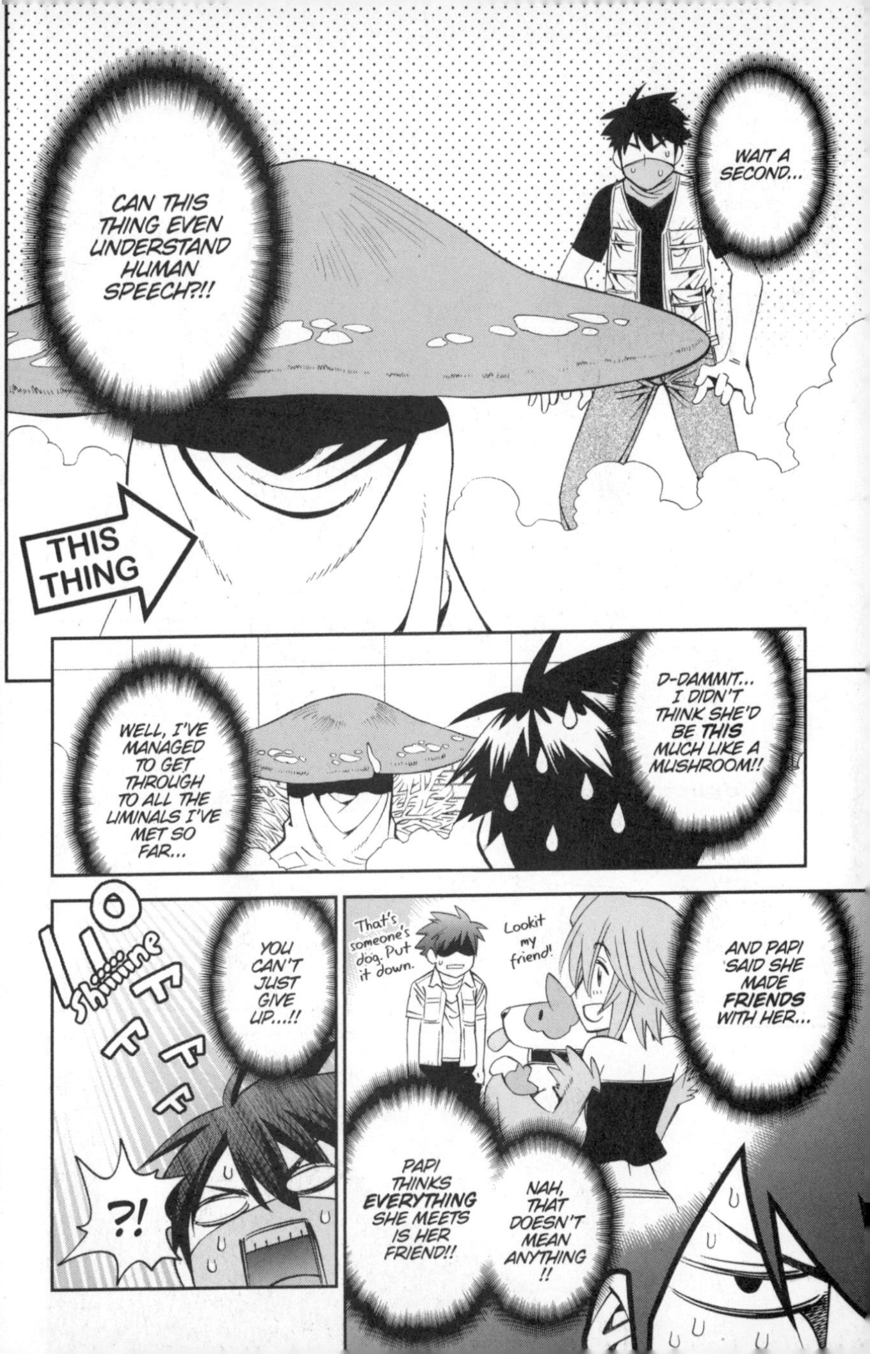
WAIT A SECOND...
CAN THIS THING EVEN UNDERSTAND HUMAN SPEECH?!!
THIS THING
D-DAMMIT... I DIDN'T THINK SHE'D BE THIS MUCH LIKE A MUSHROOM!!
WELL, I'VE MANAGED TO GET THROUGH TO ALL THE LIMINALS I'VE MET SO FAR...
AND PAPI SAID SHE MADE FRIENDS WITH HER...
Lookit my friend!
That's someone's dog. Put it down.
NAH, THAT DOESN'T MEAN ANYTHING!!
PAPI THINKS EVERYTHING SHE MEETS IS HER FRIEND!!
YOU CAN'T JUST GIVE UP...!!
Shiiiine
?!

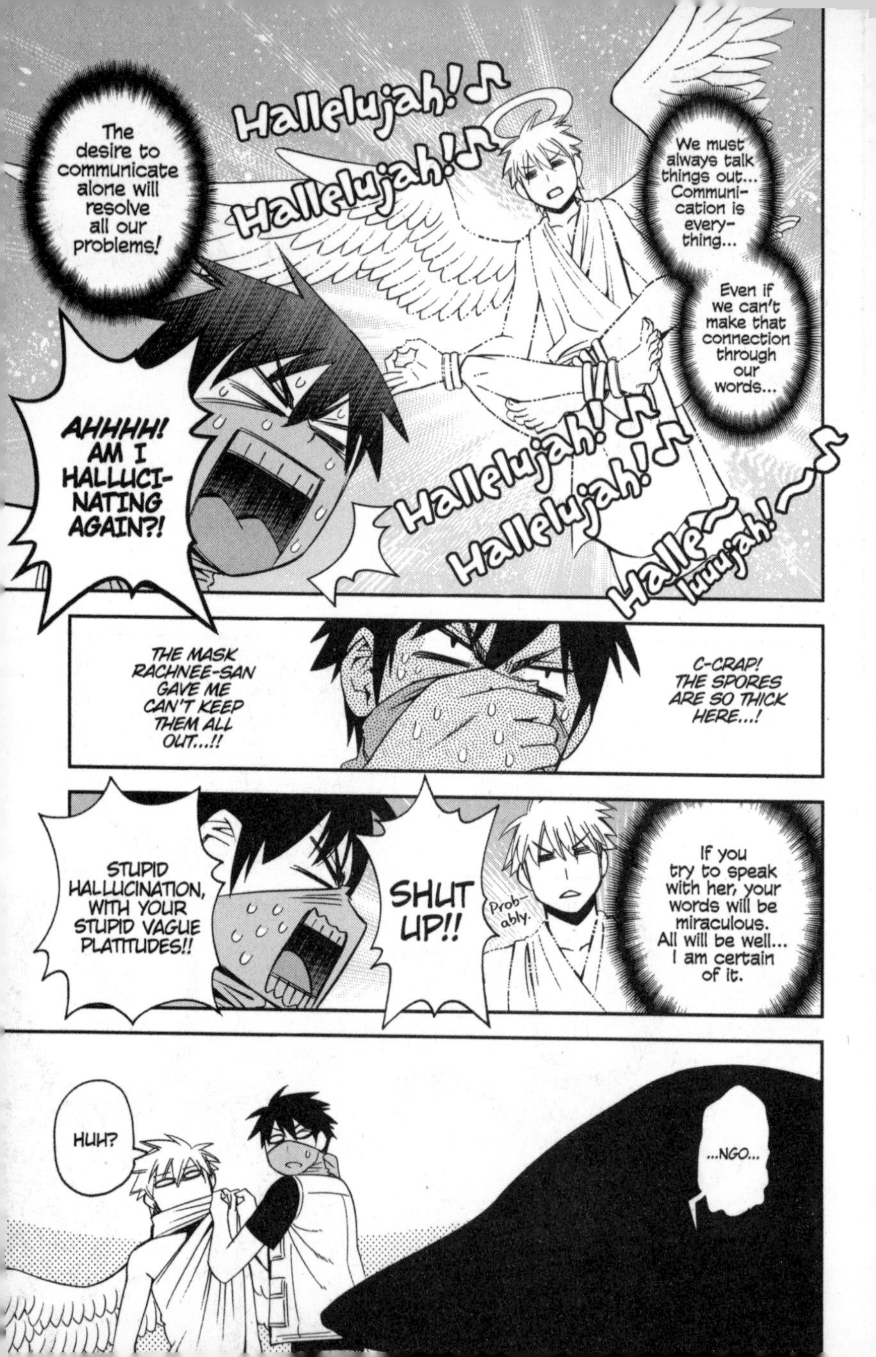
We must always talk things out... Communication is everything...
Even if we can't make that connection through our words...
Hallelujah!♪
Hallelujah!♪
The desire to communicate alone will resolve all our problems!
Hallelujah!♪
Hallelujah!♪
Halle~luuujah!~♪
AHHHH! AM I HALLUCINATING AGAIN?!
C-CRAP! THE SPORES ARE SO THICK HERE...!
THE MASK RACHNEE-SAN GAVE ME CAN'T KEEP THEM ALL OUT...!!
If you try to speak with her, your words will be miraculous. All will be well... I am certain of it.
Probably.
SHUT UP!!
STUPID HALLUCINATION, WITH YOUR STUPID VAGUE PLATITUDES!!
...NGO...
HUH?

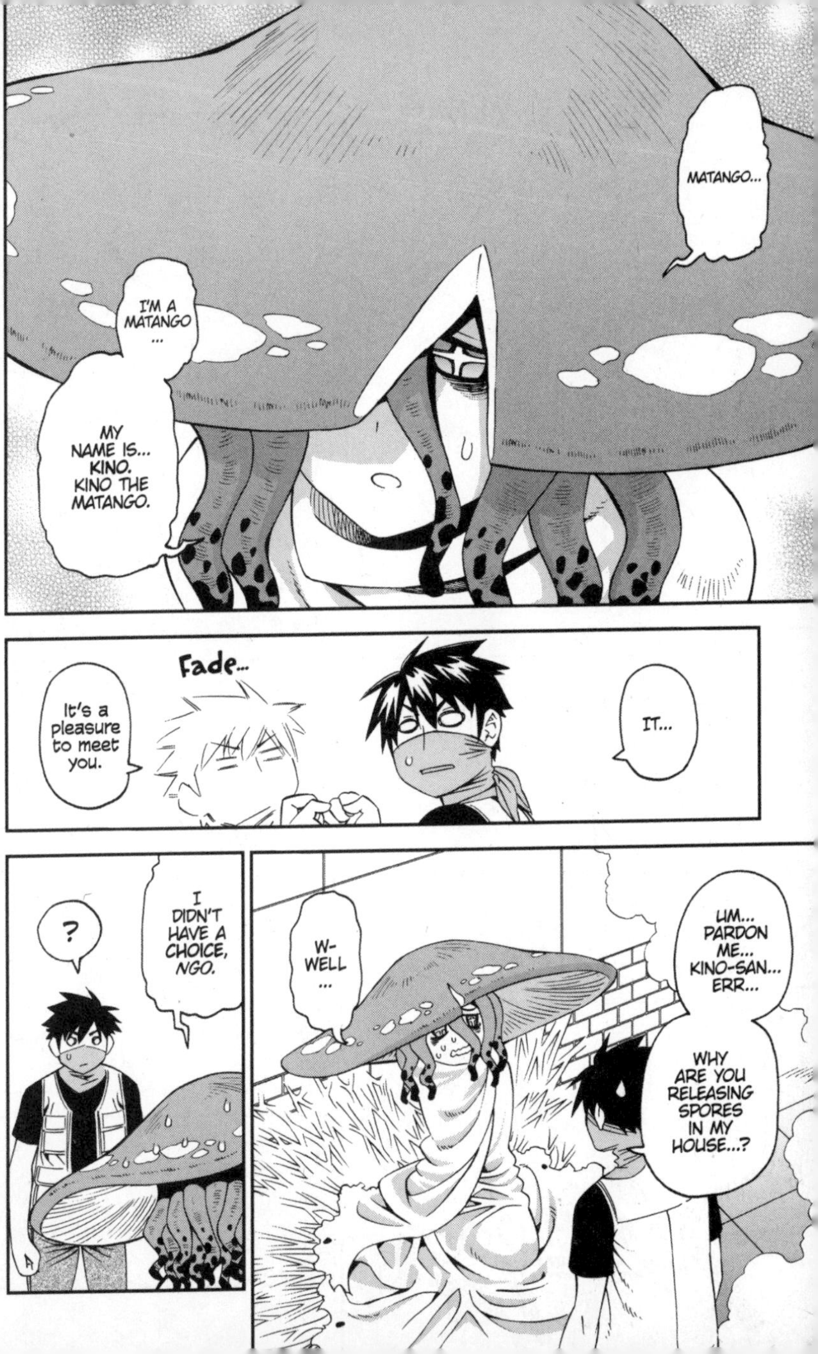
MATANGO...
I'M A MATANGO ...
MY NAME IS... KINO. KINO THE MATANGO.
IT...
Fade...
It's a pleasure to meet you.
UM... PARDON ME... KINO-SAN... ERR...
WHY ARE YOU RELEASING SPORES IN MY HOUSE...?
W-WELL ...
I DIDN'T HAVE A CHOICE, NGO.
?

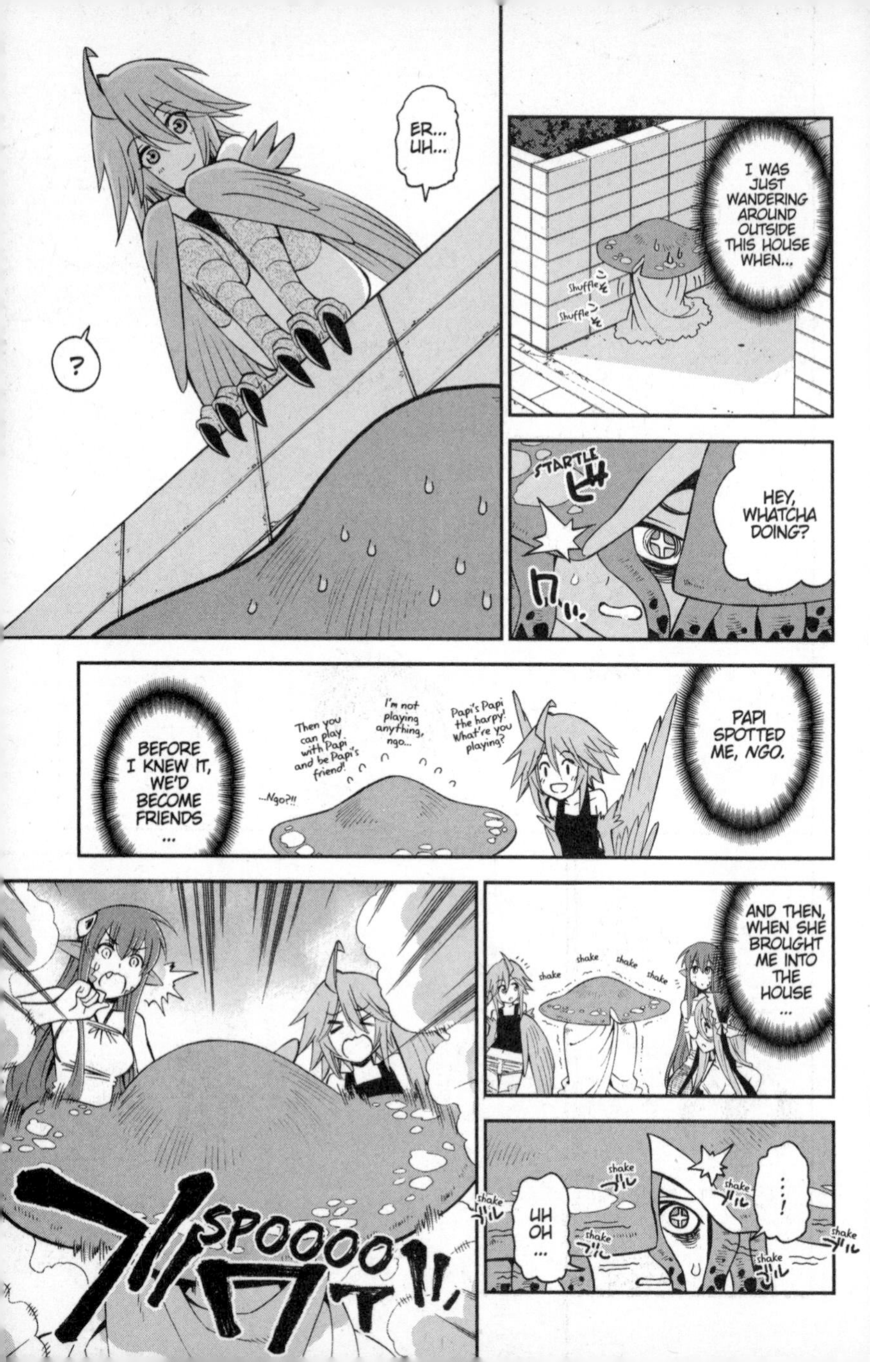
I WAS JUST WANDERING AROUND OUTSIDE THIS HOUSE WHEN...
Shuffle
Shuffle
STARTLE
HEY, WHATCHA DOING?
ER... UH...
?
PAPI SPOTTED ME, NGO.
Papi's Papi the harpy! What're you playing?
I'm not playing anything, ngo...
Then you can play with Papi and be Papi's friend!
...Ngo?!!
BEFORE I KNEW IT, WE'D BECOME FRIENDS ...
AND THEN, WHEN SHE BROUGHT ME INTO THE HOUSE ...
shake
shake
shake
shake
...!
shake
shake
shake
UH OH ...
shake
shake
SPOOOOO

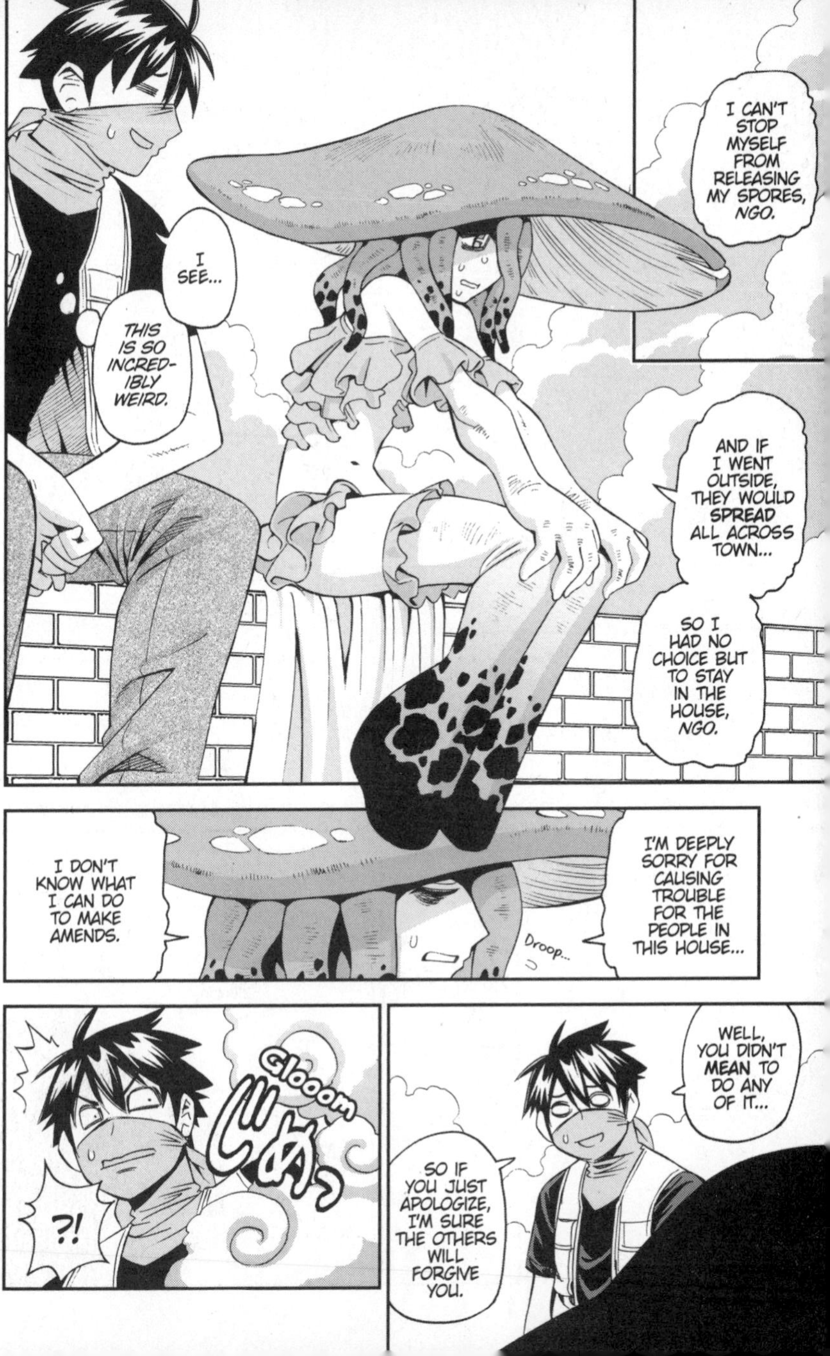
I CAN'T STOP MYSELF FROM RELEASING MY SPORES, NGO.
AND IF I WENT OUTSIDE, THEY WOULD SPREAD ALL ACROSS TOWN...
SO I HAD NO CHOICE BUT TO STAY IN THE HOUSE, NGO.
I SEE...
THIS IS SO INCREDIBLY WEIRD.
I'M DEEPLY SORRY FOR CAUSING TROUBLE FOR THE PEOPLE IN THIS HOUSE...
Droop...
I DON'T KNOW WHAT I CAN DO TO MAKE AMENDS.
WELL, YOU DIDN'T MEAN TO DO ANY OF IT...
SO IF YOU JUST APOLOGIZE, I'M SURE THE OTHERS WILL FORGIVE YOU.
Glooom
じめっ
?!

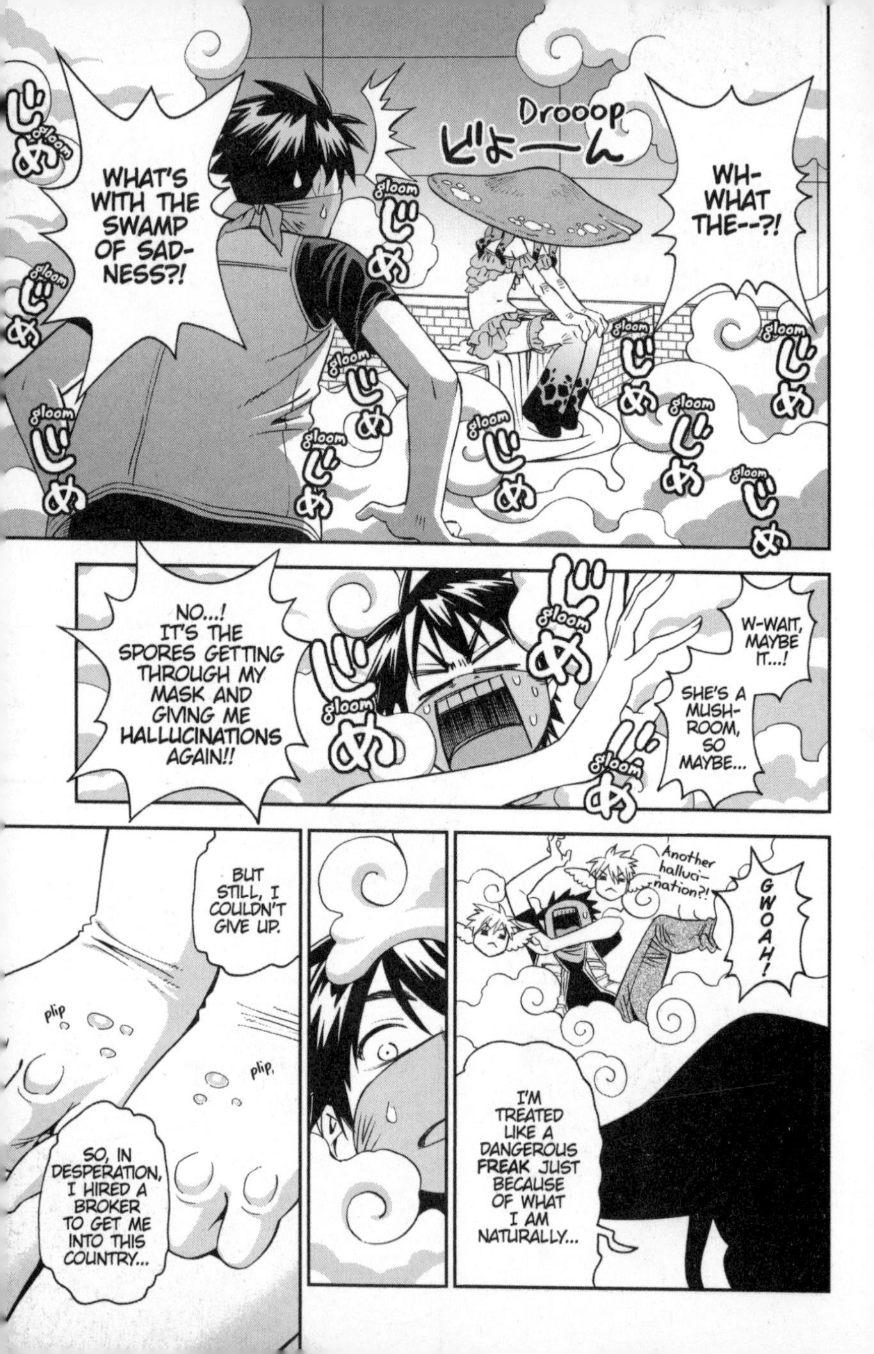
WH-WHAT THE--?!
Drooop
びよーーん
WHAT'S WITH THE SWAMP OF SADNESS?!
gloom じめ
W-WAIT, MAYBE IT...!
SHE'S A MUSH-ROOM, SO MAYBE...
gloom じめ
NO...! IT'S THE SPORES GETTING THROUGH MY MASK AND GIVING ME HALLUCINATIONS AGAIN!!
GWOAH!
Another halluci-nation?!
I'M TREATED LIKE A DANGEROUS FREAK JUST BECAUSE OF WHAT I AM NATURALLY...
BUT STILL, I COULDN'T GIVE UP.
plip
plip,
SO, IN DESPERATION, I HIRED A BROKER TO GET ME INTO THIS COUNTRY...

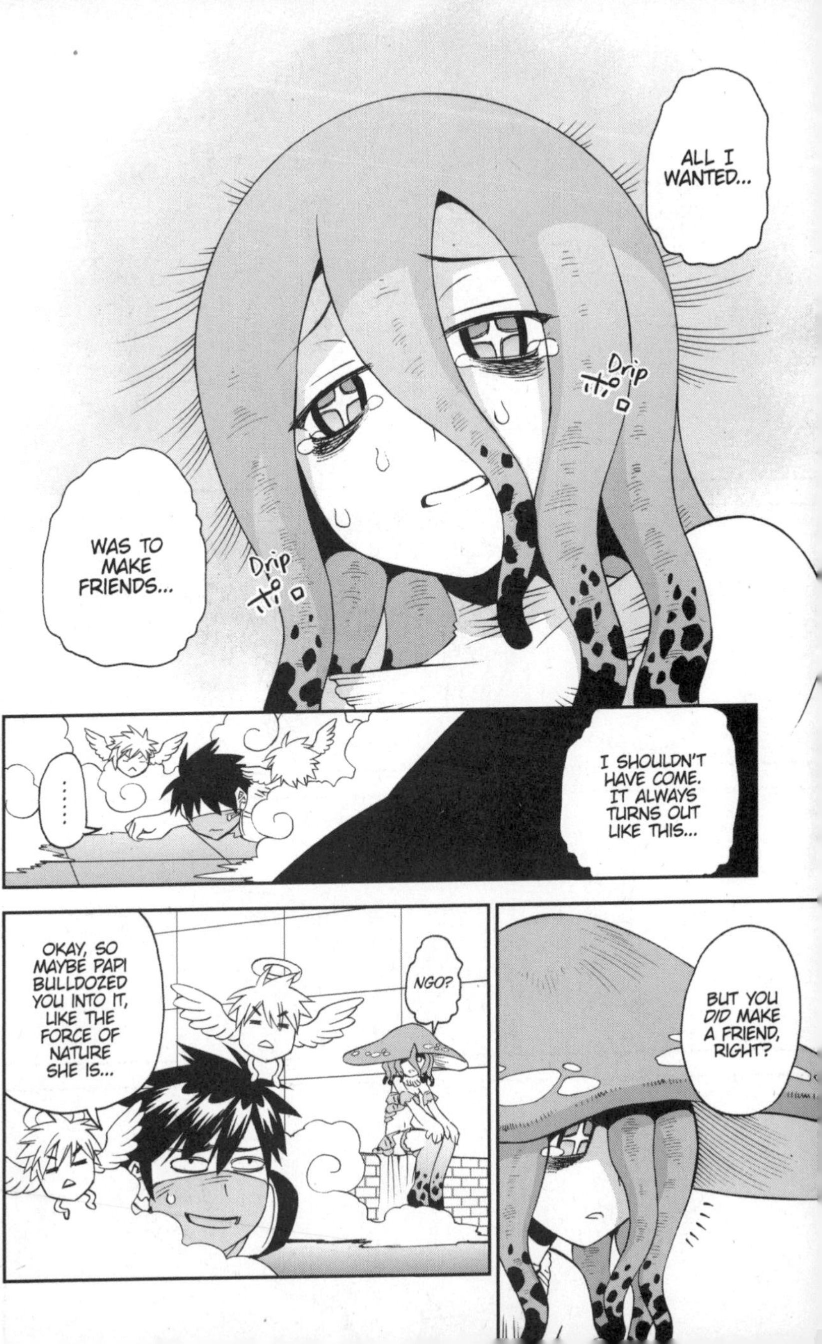
ALL I WANTED...
Drip
WAS TO MAKE FRIENDS...
Drip
I SHOULDN'T HAVE COME. IT ALWAYS TURNS OUT LIKE THIS...
......
BUT YOU *DID* MAKE A FRIEND, RIGHT?
NGO?
OKAY, SO MAYBE PAPI BULLDOZED YOU INTO IT, LIKE THE FORCE OF NATURE SHE IS...

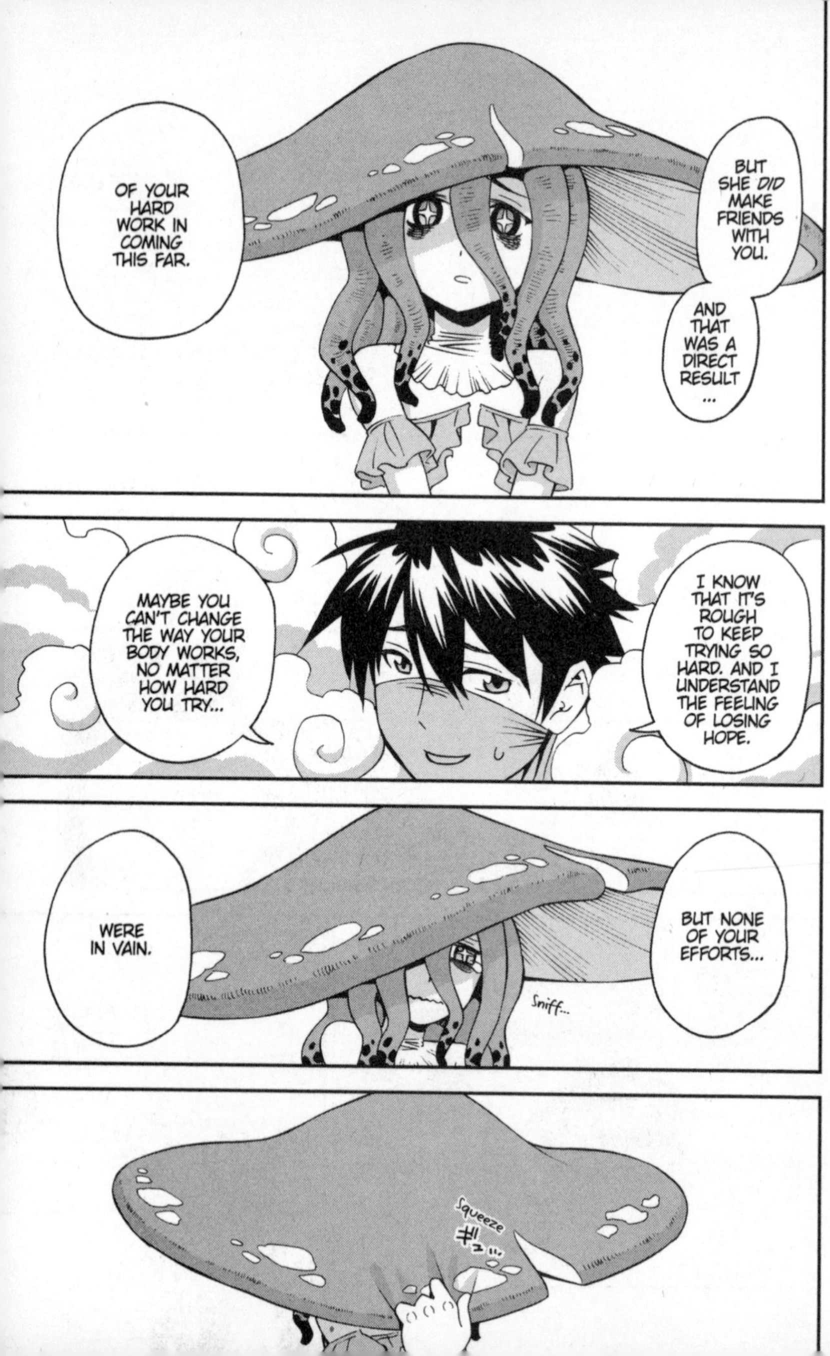
BUT SHE *DID* MAKE FRIENDS WITH YOU.
AND THAT WAS A DIRECT RESULT ...
OF YOUR HARD WORK IN COMING THIS FAR.
I KNOW THAT IT'S ROUGH TO KEEP TRYING SO HARD. AND I UNDERSTAND THE FEELING OF LOSING HOPE.
MAYBE YOU CAN'T CHANGE THE WAY YOUR BODY WORKS, NO MATTER HOW HARD YOU TRY...
BUT NONE OF YOUR EFFORTS...
Sniff...
WERE IN VAIN.
Squeeze

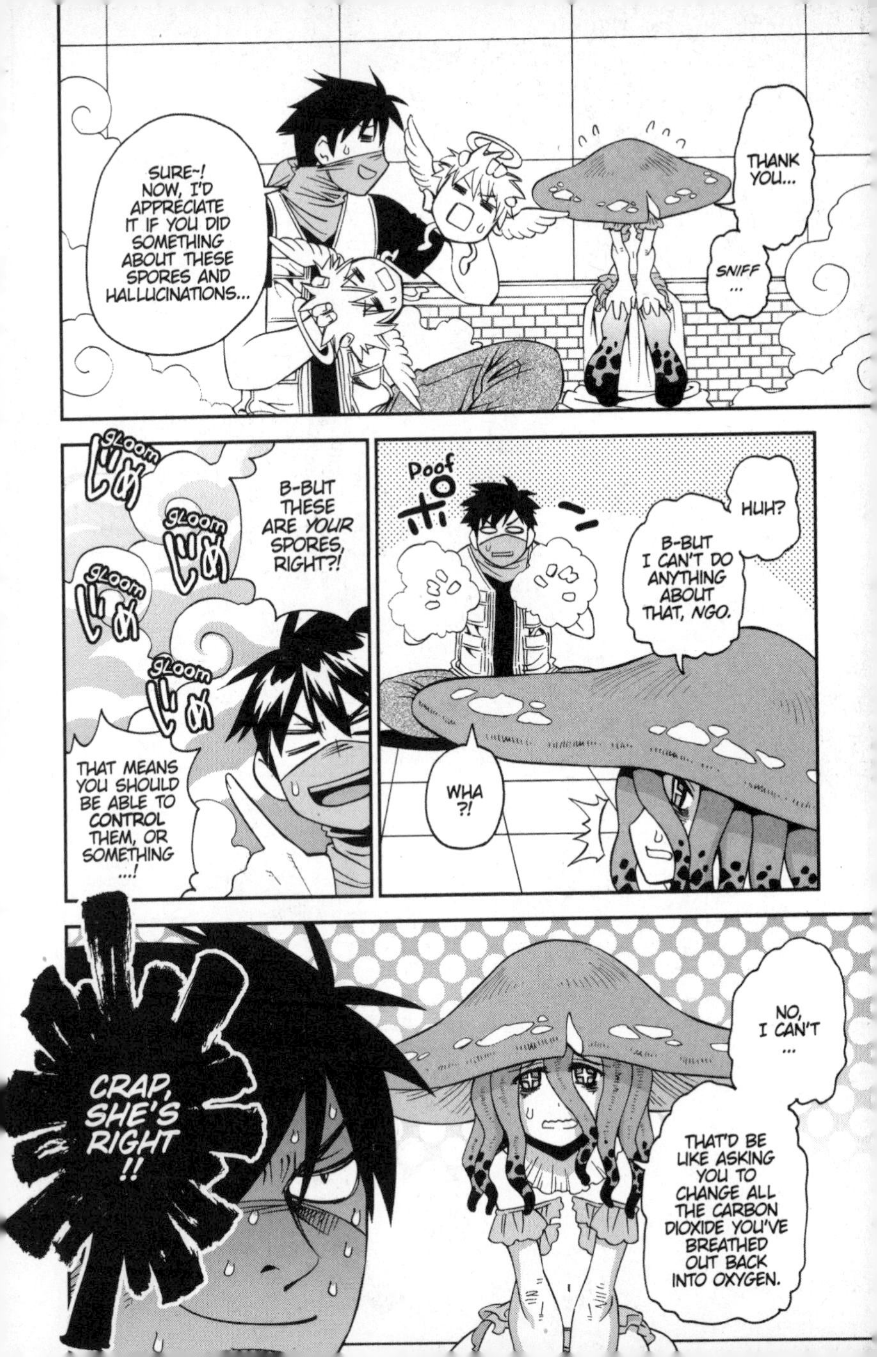
THANK YOU...
SNIFF ...
SURE~! NOW, I'D APPRECIATE IT IF YOU DID SOMETHING ABOUT THESE SPORES AND HALLUCINATIONS...
HUH?
B-BUT I CAN'T DO ANYTHING ABOUT THAT, *NGO*.
Poof
ポ
WHA ?!
B-BUT THESE ARE *YOUR* SPORES, RIGHT?!
gloom じめ
gloom じめ
gloom じめ
gloom じめ
THAT MEANS YOU SHOULD BE ABLE TO CONTROL THEM, OR SOMETHING ...!
NO, I CAN'T ...
THAT'D BE LIKE ASKING YOU TO CHANGE ALL THE CARBON DIOXIDE YOU'VE BREATHED OUT BACK INTO OXYGEN.
CRAP, SHE'S RIGHT !!

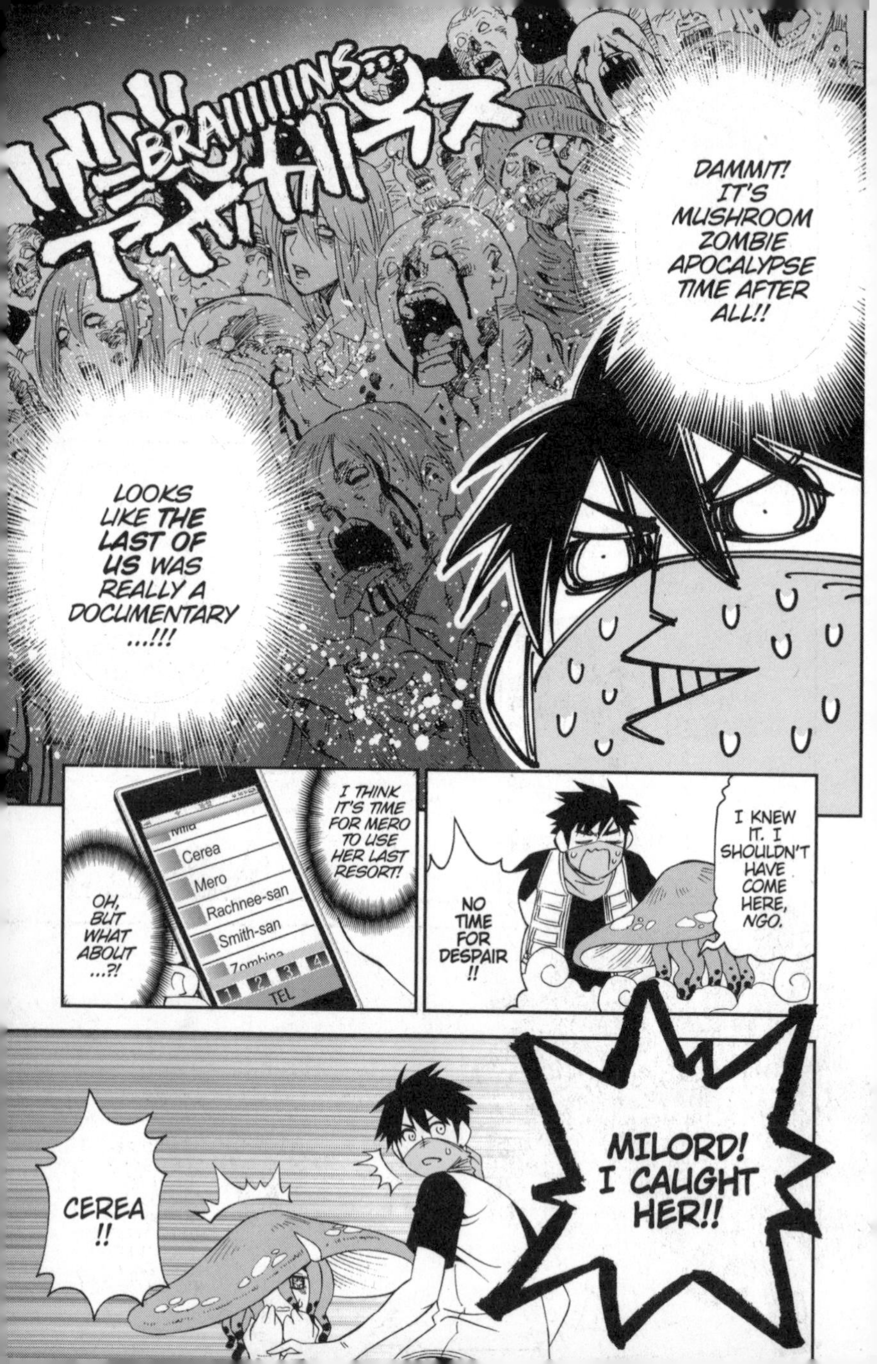
BRAIIIIIINS...
DAMMIT! IT'S MUSHROOM ZOMBIE APOCALYPSE TIME AFTER ALL!!
LOOKS LIKE THE LAST OF US WAS REALLY A DOCUMENTARY ...!!!
I KNEW IT. I SHOULDN'T HAVE COME HERE, NGO.
NO TIME FOR DESPAIR !!
I THINK IT'S TIME FOR MERO TO USE HER LAST RESORT!
Cerea
Mero
Rachnee-san
Smith-san
1 2 3 4
TEL
OH, BUT WHAT ABOUT ...?!
MILORD! I CAUGHT HER!!
CEREA !!

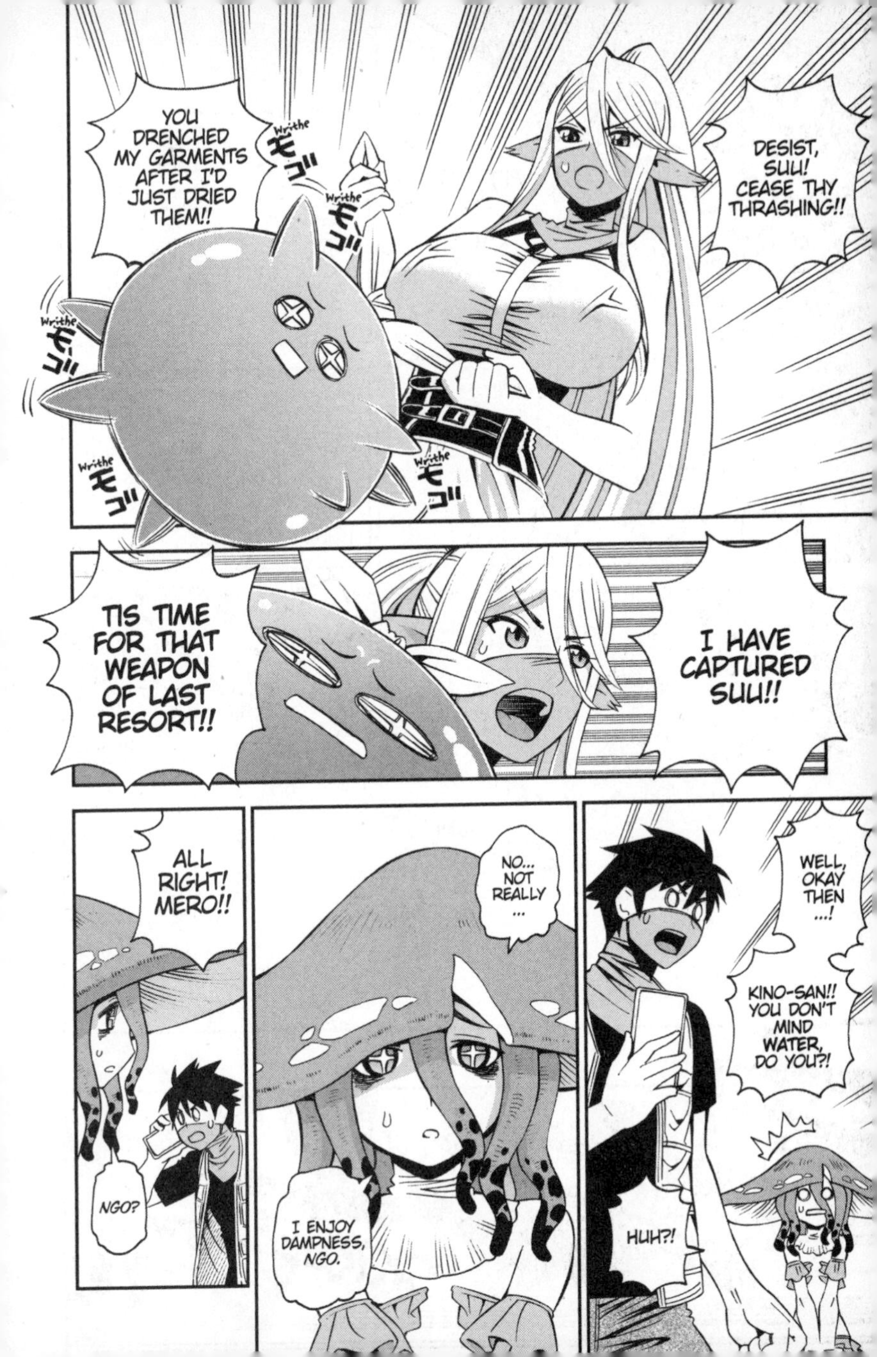
DESIST, SUU! CEASE THY THRASHING!!
YOU DRENCHED MY GARMENTS AFTER I'D JUST DRIED THEM!!
Writhe モゴ
Writhe モゴ
Writhe モゴ
Writhe モゴ
Writhe モゴ
I HAVE CAPTURED SUU!!
TIS TIME FOR THAT WEAPON OF LAST RESORT!!
WELL, OKAY THEN ...!
KINO-SAN!! YOU DON'T MIND WATER, DO YOU?!
HUH?!
NO... NOT REALLY ...
I ENJOY DAMPNESS, NGO.
ALL RIGHT! MERO!!
NGO?

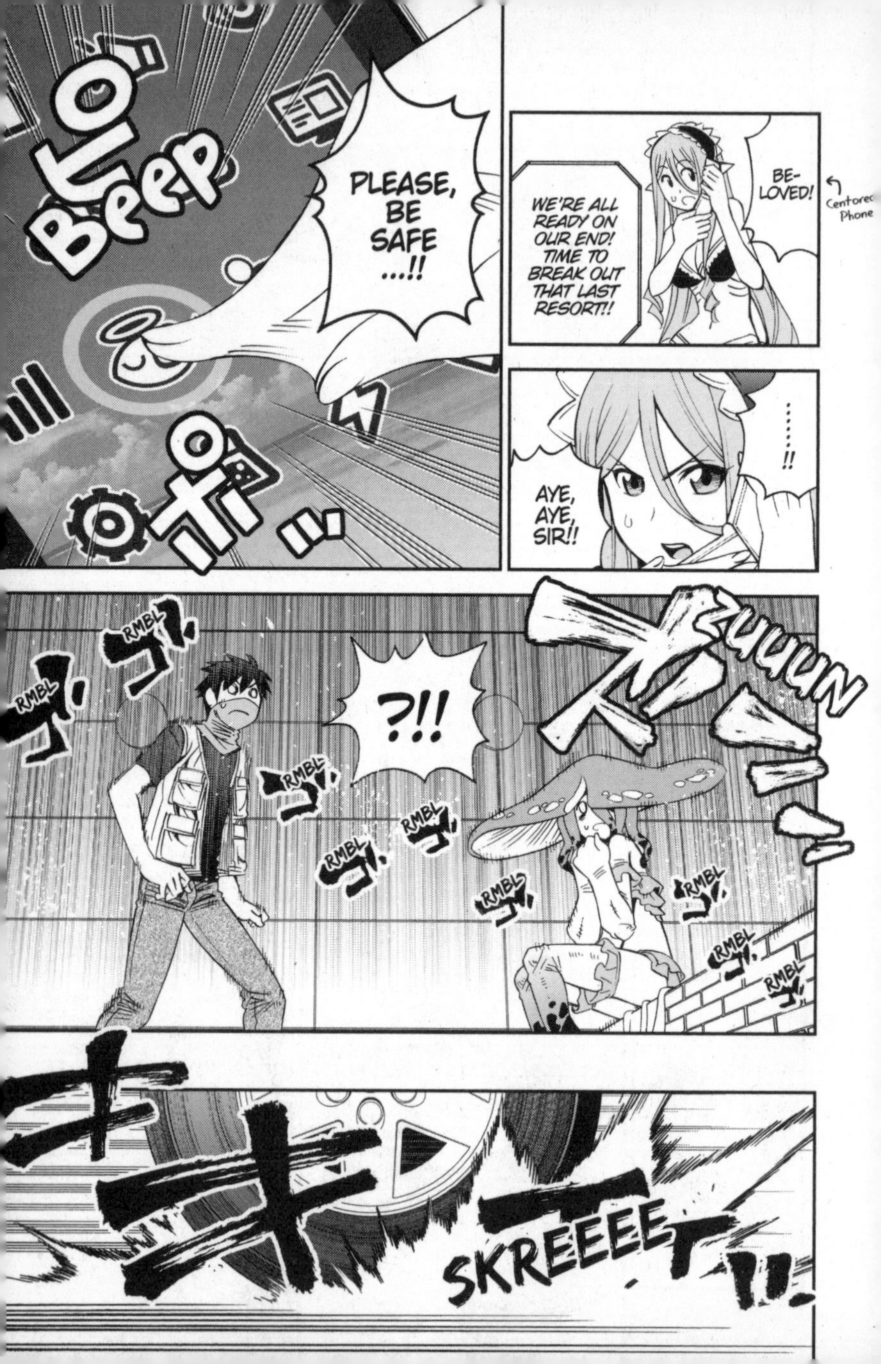
BE-LOVED!
Centorec Phone
WE'RE ALL READY ON OUR END! TIME TO BREAK OUT THAT LAST RESORT!!
......!!
AYE, AYE, SIR!!
Beep
PLEASE, BE SAFE ...!!
ZUUUUN
?!!
RMBL
RMBL
RMBL
RMBL
RMBL
RMBL
RMBL
RMBL
RMBL
RMBL
SKREEEEE!!

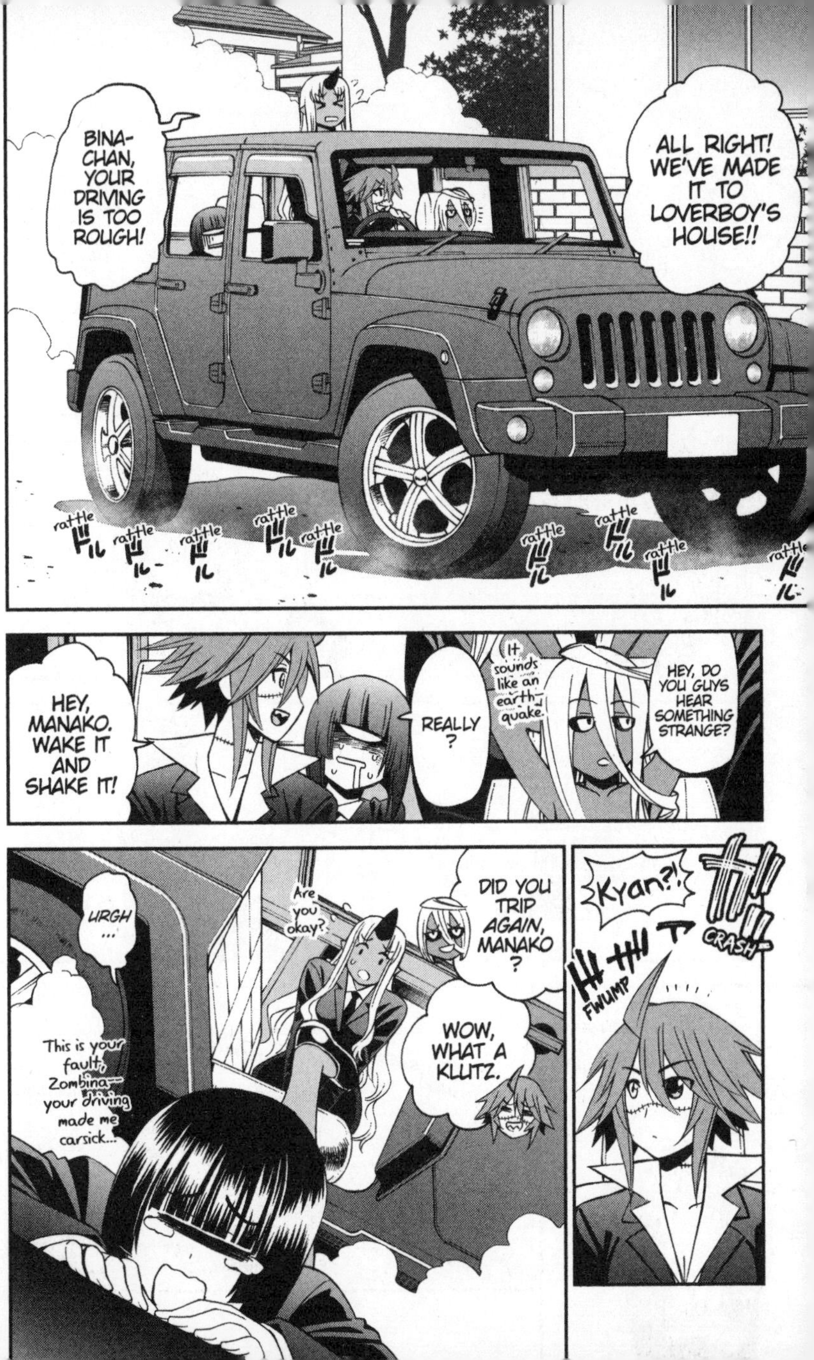
ALL RIGHT! WE'VE MADE IT TO LOVERBOY'S HOUSE!!
BINA-CHAN, YOUR DRIVING IS TOO ROUGH!
rattle ドル
rattle ドル
rattle ドル
rattle ドル
rattle ドル
rattle ドル
rattle ドル
rattle ドル
rattle ドル
HEY, DO YOU GUYS HEAR SOMETHING STRANGE?
It sounds like an earthquake.
REALLY?
HEY, MANAKO. WAKE IT AND SHAKE IT!
Kyan?!
CRASH
FWUMP
DID YOU TRIP AGAIN, MANAKO?
Are you okay?
URGH...
WOW, WHAT A KLUTZ.
This is your fault, Zombina—your driving made me carsick...

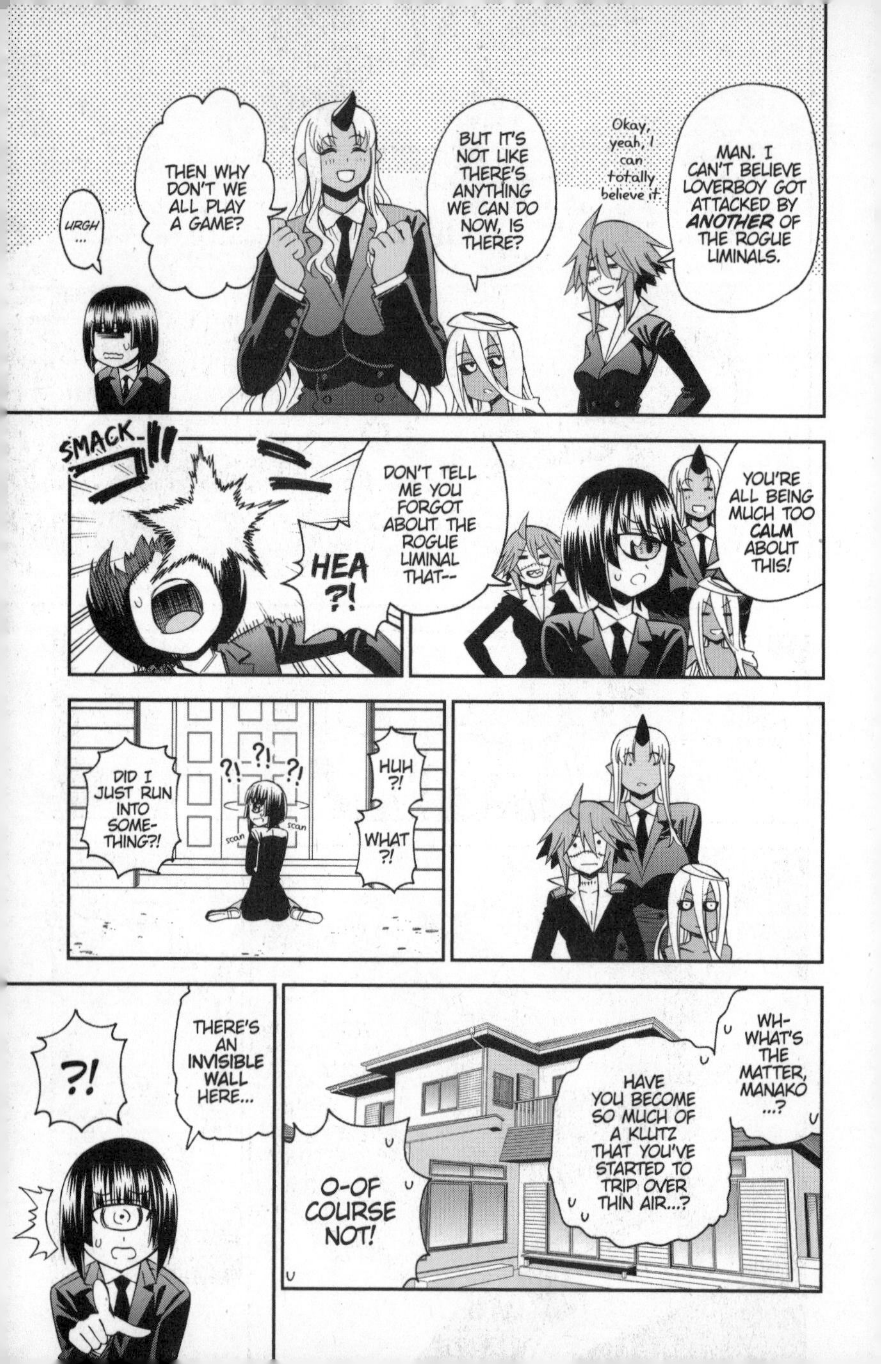
MAN. I CAN'T BELIEVE LOVERBOY GOT ATTACKED BY ANOTHER OF THE ROGUE LIMINALS.
Okay, yeah, I can totally believe it.
BUT IT'S NOT LIKE THERE'S ANYTHING WE CAN DO NOW, IS THERE?
THEN WHY DON'T WE ALL PLAY A GAME?
URGH ...
YOU'RE ALL BEING MUCH TOO CALM ABOUT THIS!
DON'T TELL ME YOU FORGOT ABOUT THE ROGUE LIMINAL THAT--
HEA ?!
SMACK
HUH ?!
WHAT ?!
?! ?! ?!
scan
scan
DID I JUST RUN INTO SOME-THING?!
WH-WHAT'S THE MATTER, MANAKO ...?
HAVE YOU BECOME SO MUCH OF A KLUTZ THAT YOU'VE STARTED TO TRIP OVER THIN AIR...?
O-OF COURSE NOT!
THERE'S AN INVISIBLE WALL HERE...
?!

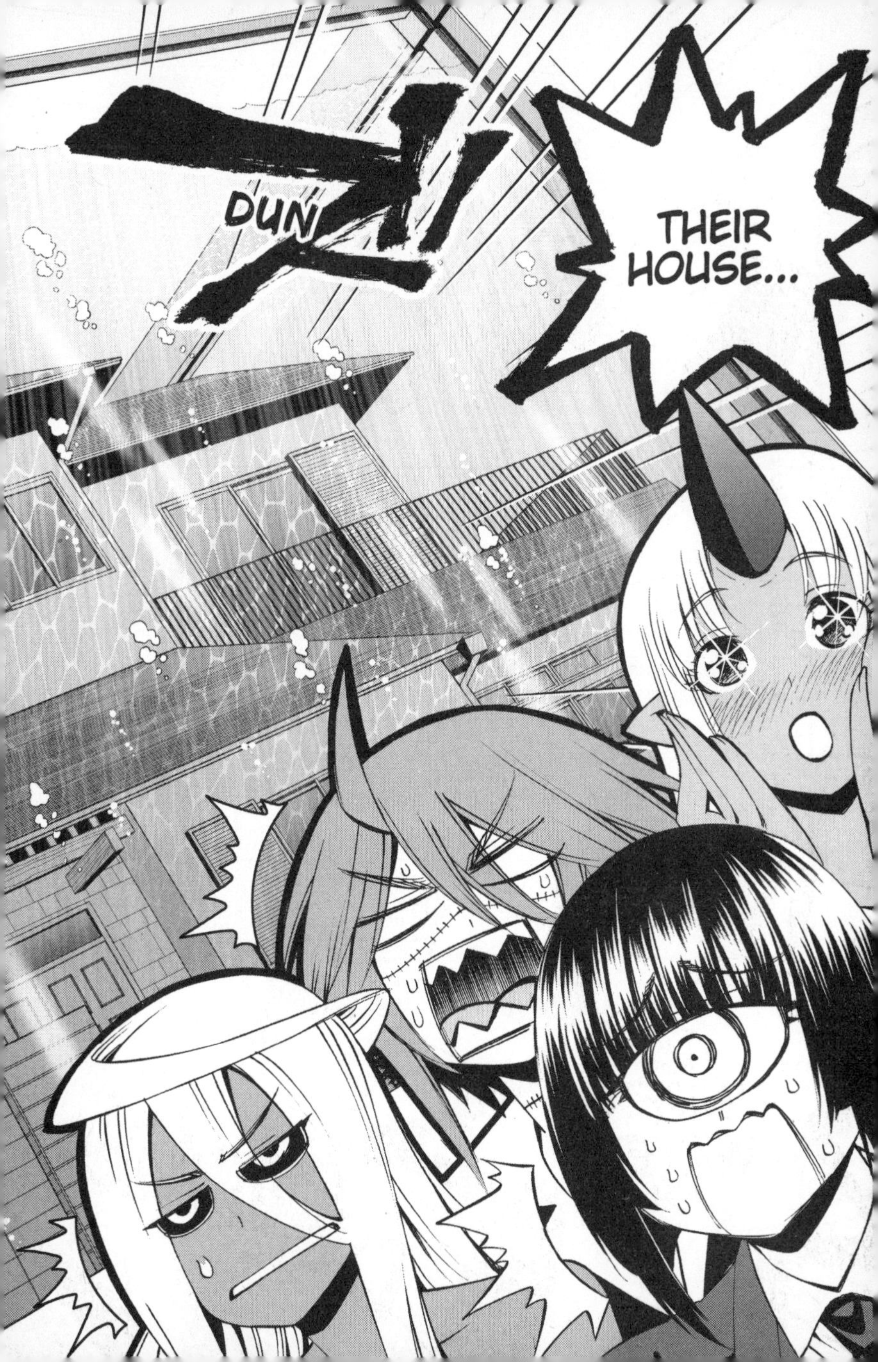
THEIR HOUSE...
DUN

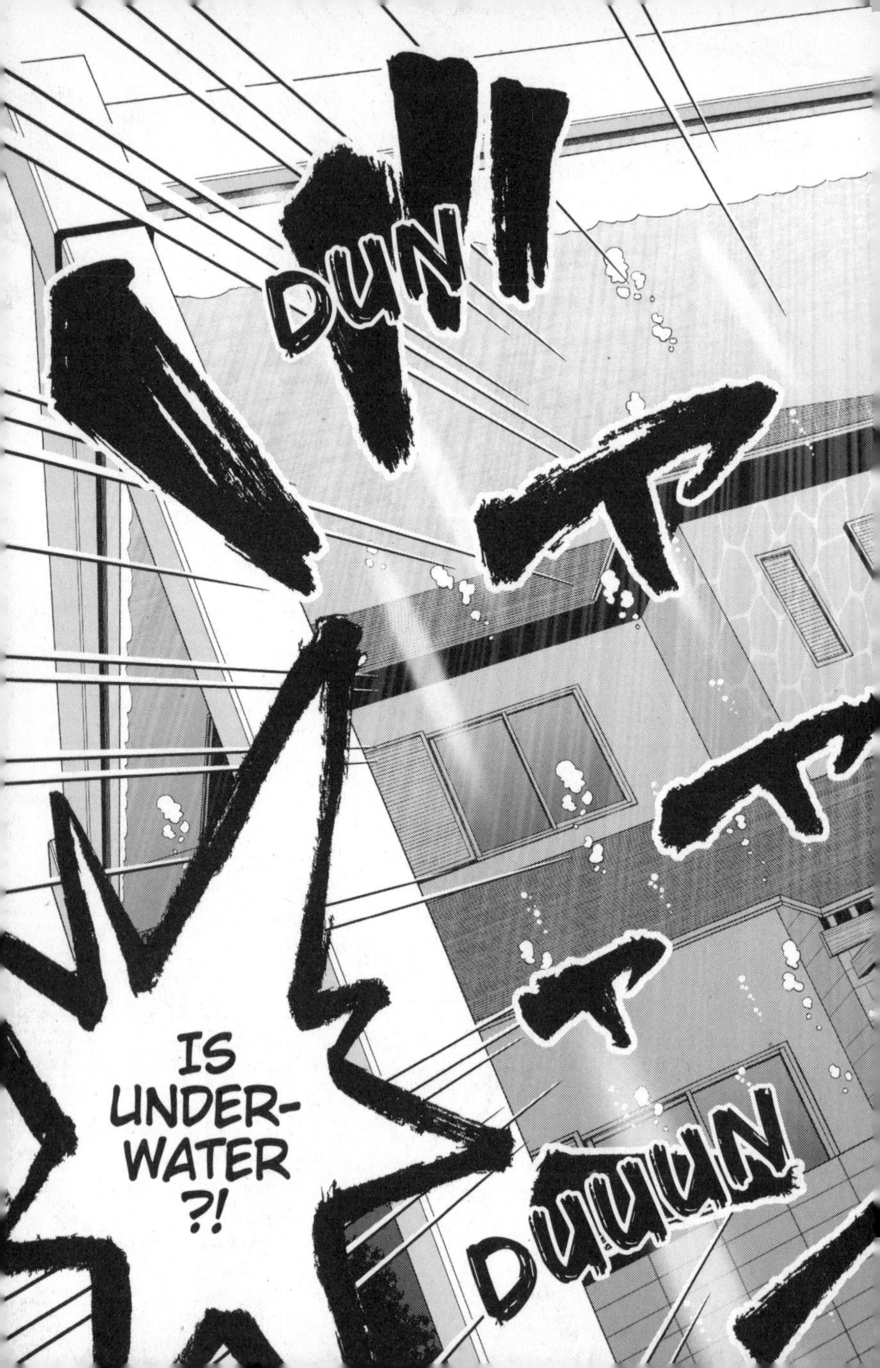
DUN
IS UNDER-WATER?!
DUUUUN

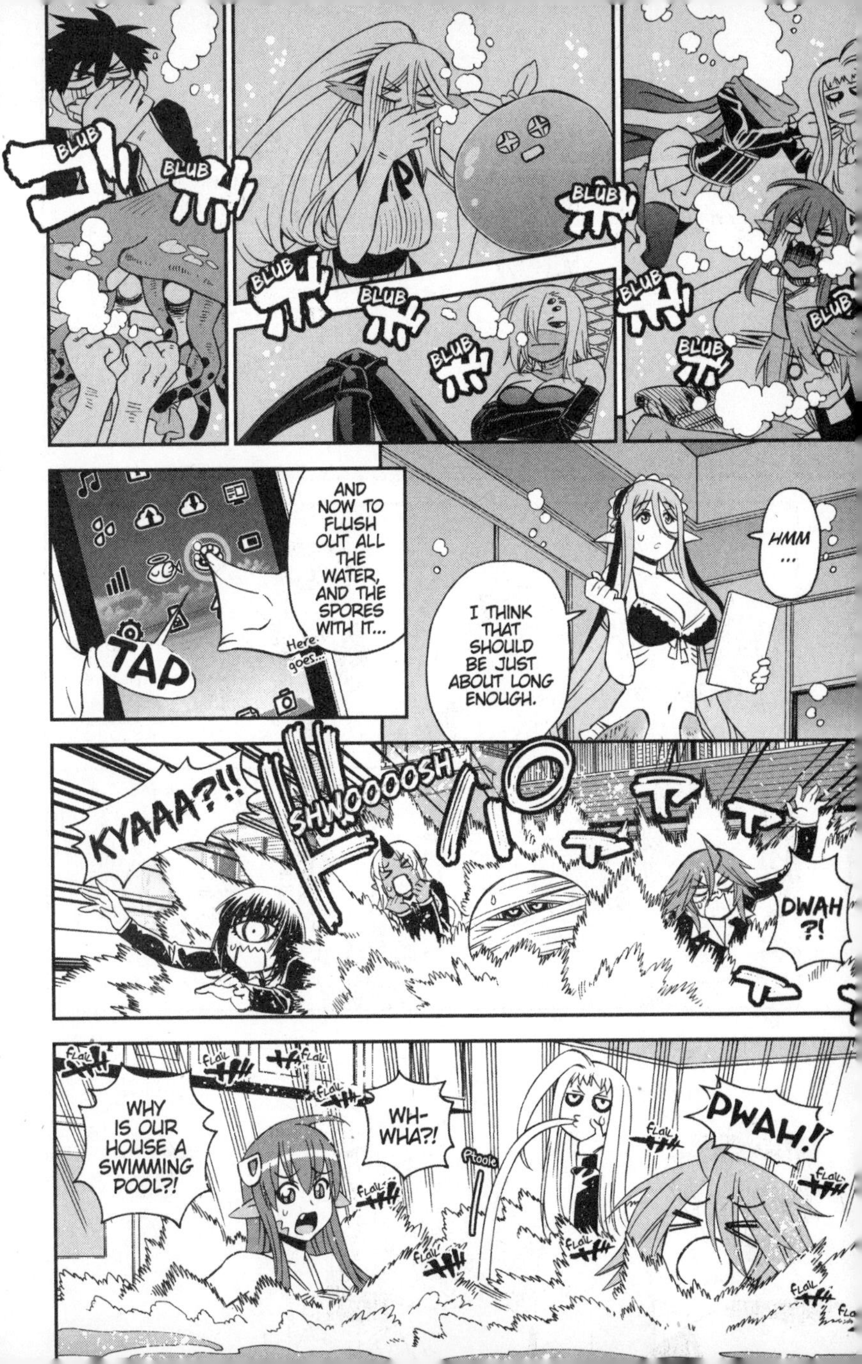

BLUB
BLUB
BLUB
BLUB
BLUB
BLUB
BLUB
BLUB
BLUB
BLUB
HMM ...
I THINK THAT SHOULD BE JUST ABOUT LONG ENOUGH.
AND NOW TO FLUSH OUT ALL THE WATER, AND THE SPORES WITH IT...
Here goes...
TAP
DWAH ?!
SHWOOOOSH
KYAAA?!!
PWAH!
FLAK
FLAK
FLAK
FLAK
Ptooie
WH-WHA?!
FLAK
FLAK
FLAK
FLAK
WHY IS OUR HOUSE A SWIMMING POOL?!
FLAK
FLAK
FLAK

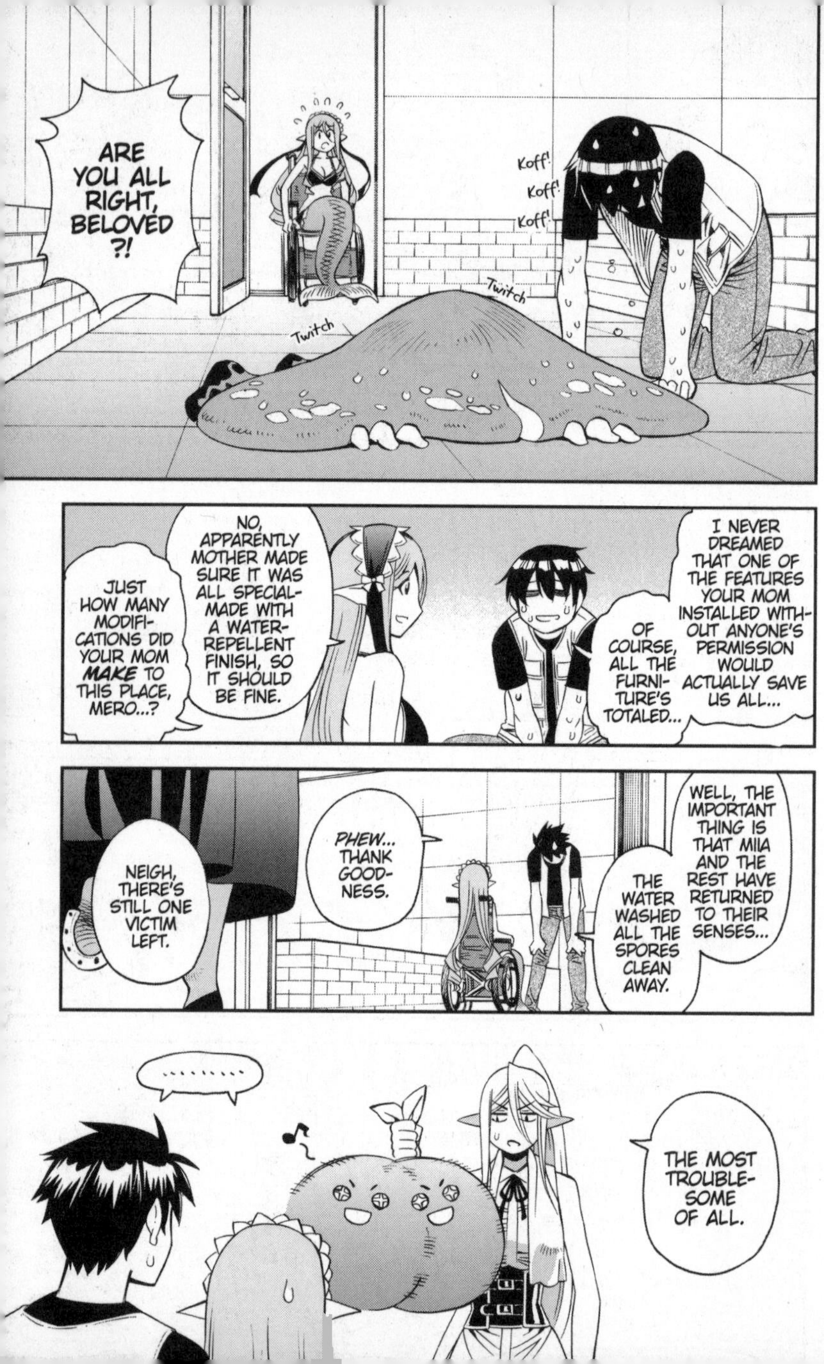
Koff!
Koff!
Koff!
Twitch
ARE YOU ALL RIGHT, BELOVED?!
Twitch
I NEVER DREAMED THAT ONE OF THE FEATURES YOUR MOM INSTALLED WITH-OUT ANYONE'S PERMISSION WOULD ACTUALLY SAVE US ALL...
OF COURSE, ALL THE FURNI-TURE'S TOTALED...
NO, APPARENTLY MOTHER MADE SURE IT WAS ALL SPECIAL-MADE WITH A WATER-REPELLENT FINISH, SO IT SHOULD BE FINE.
JUST HOW MANY MODIFI-CATIONS DID YOUR MOM *MAKE* TO THIS PLACE, MERO...?
WELL, THE IMPORTANT THING IS THAT MIIA AND THE REST HAVE RETURNED TO THEIR SENSES...
THE WATER WASHED ALL THE SPORES CLEAN AWAY.
PHEW... THANK GOOD-NESS.
NEIGH, THERE'S STILL ONE VICTIM LEFT.
THE MOST TROUBLE-SOME OF ALL.
....

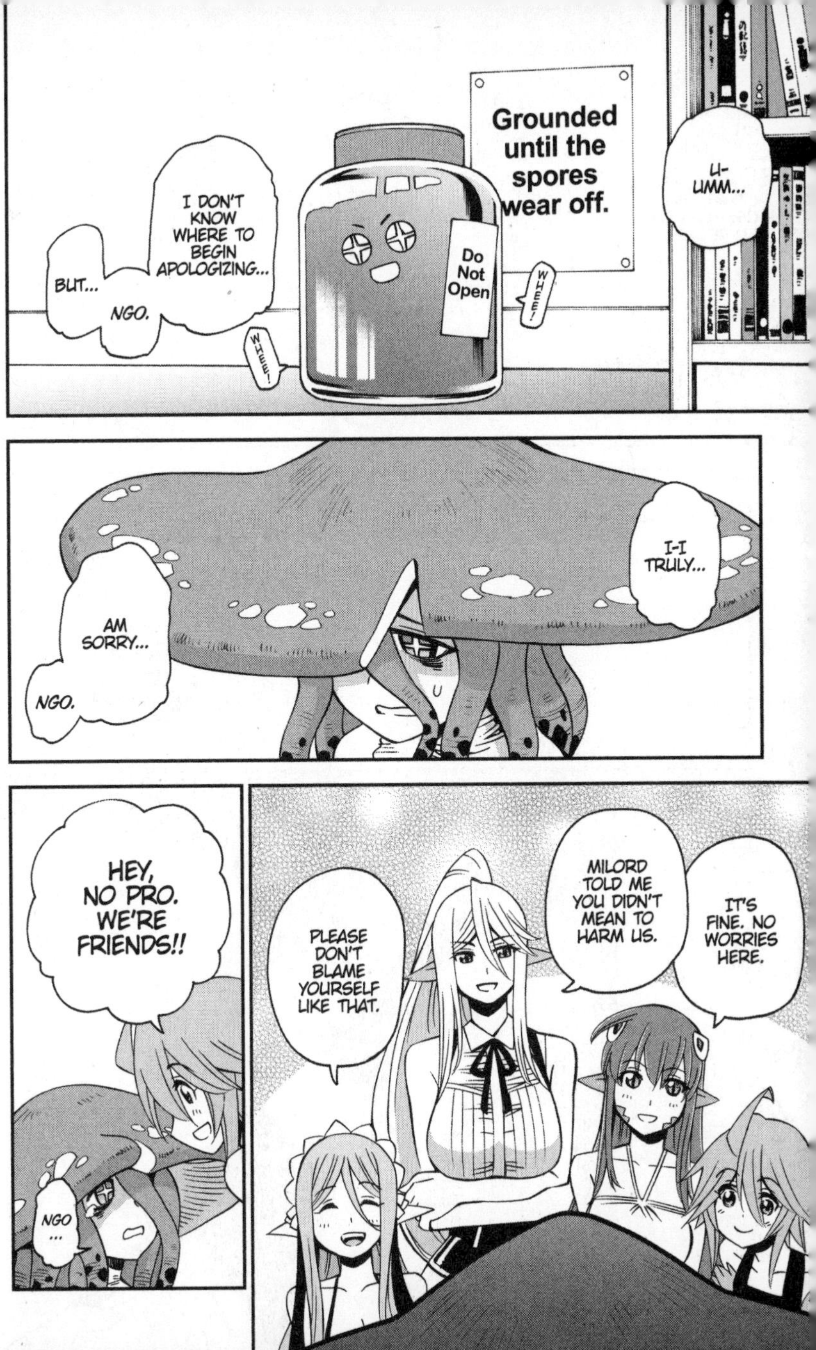
U-UMM...
Grounded until the spores wear off.
Do Not Open
WHEE!
WHEE!
I DON'T KNOW WHERE TO BEGIN APOLOGIZING...
BUT...
NGO.
I-I TRULY...
AM SORRY...
NGO.
IT'S FINE. NO WORRIES HERE.
MILORD TOLD ME YOU DIDN'T MEAN TO HARM US.
PLEASE DON'T BLAME YOURSELF LIKE THAT.
HEY, NO PRO. WE'RE FRIENDS!!
NGO...

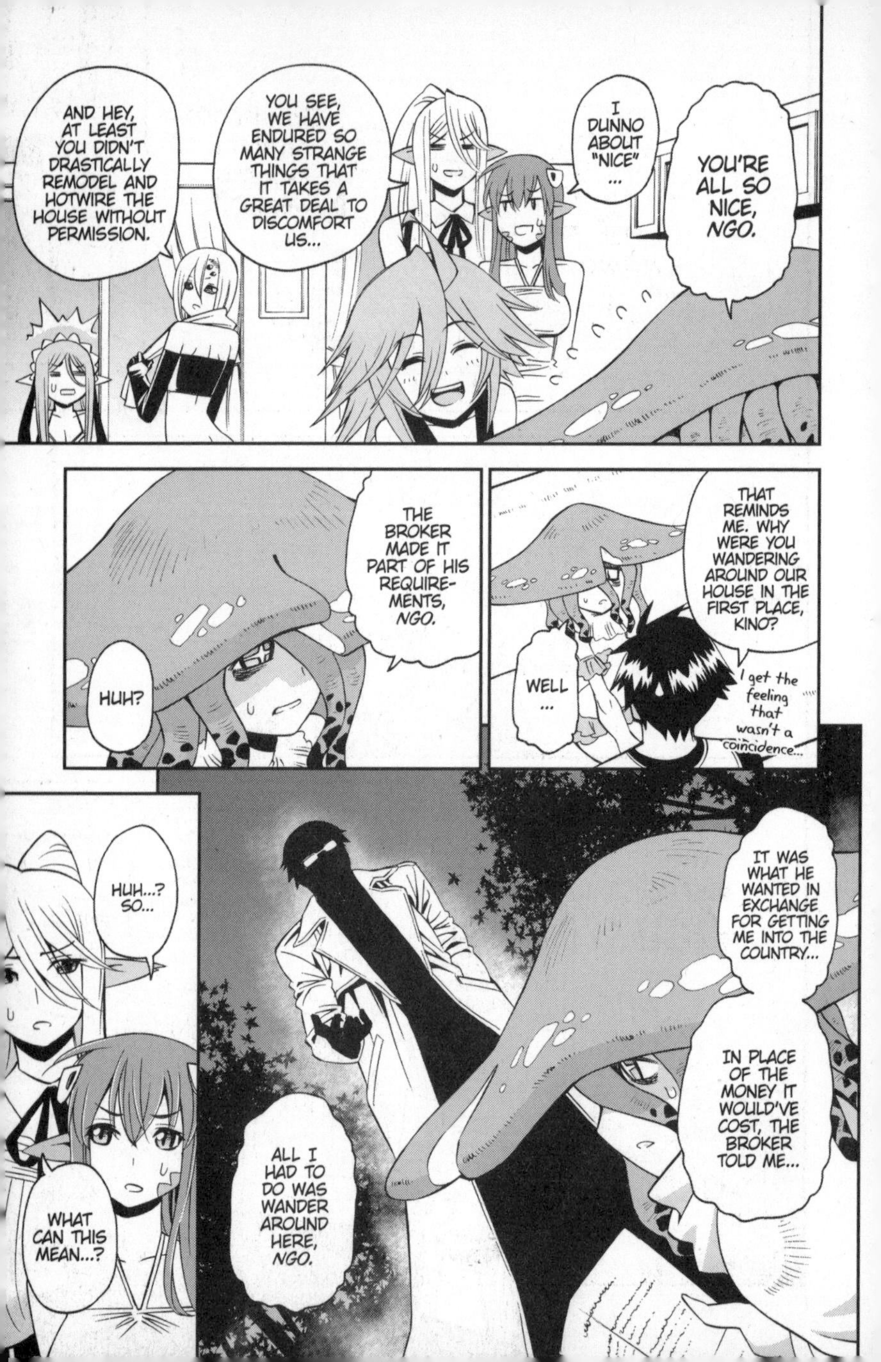
YOU'RE ALL SO NICE, *NGO.*
I DUNNO ABOUT "NICE" ...
YOU SEE, WE HAVE ENDURED SO MANY STRANGE THINGS THAT IT TAKES A GREAT DEAL TO DISCOMFORT US...
AND HEY, AT LEAST YOU DIDN'T DRASTICALLY REMODEL AND HOTWIRE THE HOUSE WITHOUT PERMISSION.
THAT REMINDS ME. WHY WERE YOU WANDERING AROUND OUR HOUSE IN THE FIRST PLACE, KINO?
I get the feeling that wasn't a coincidence...
WELL ...
THE BROKER MADE IT PART OF HIS REQUIRE-MENTS, *NGO.*
HUH?
IT WAS WHAT HE WANTED IN EXCHANGE FOR GETTING ME INTO THE COUNTRY...
IN PLACE OF THE MONEY IT WOULD'VE COST, THE BROKER TOLD ME...
ALL I HAD TO DO WAS WANDER AROUND HERE, *NGO.*
HUH...? SO...
WHAT CAN THIS MEAN...?

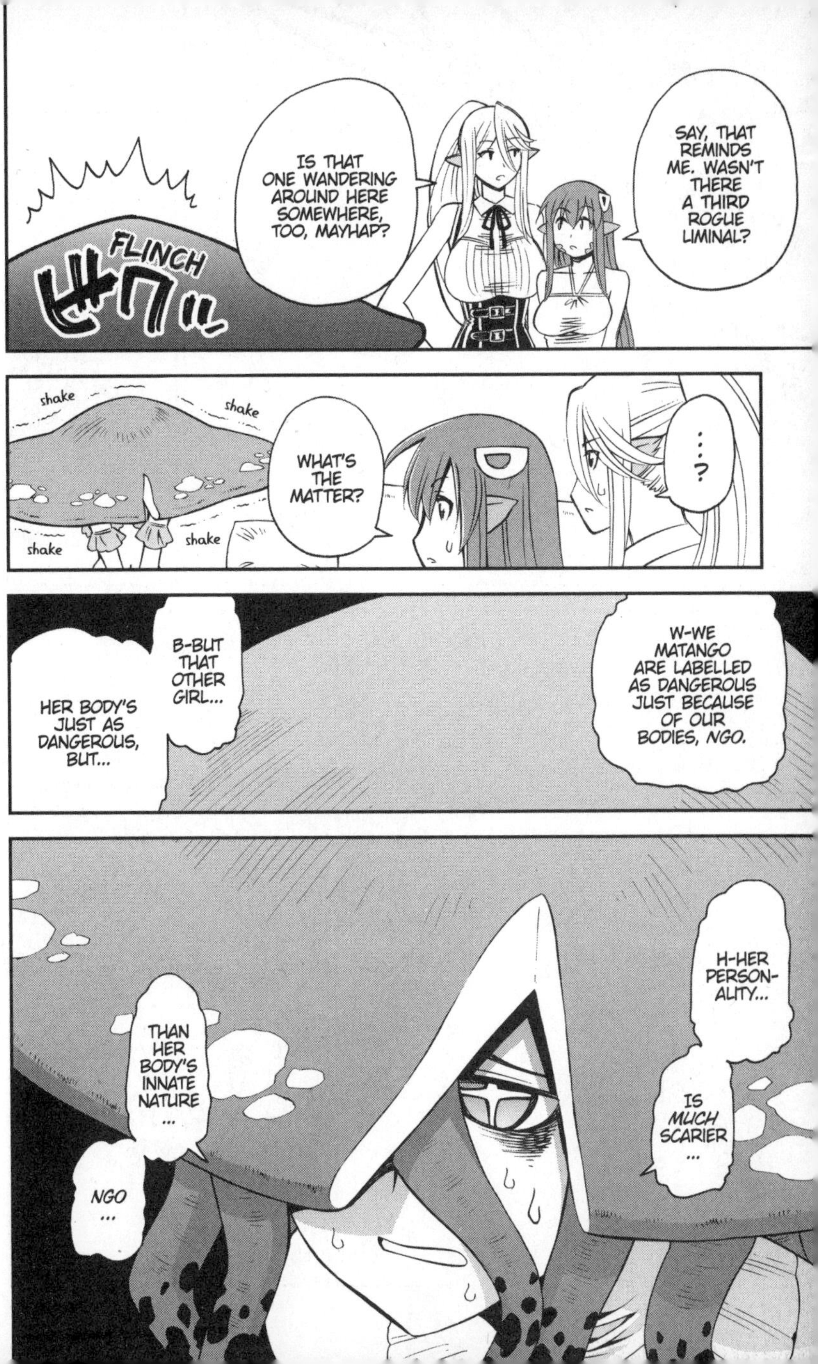
SAY, THAT REMINDS ME. WASN'T THERE A THIRD ROGUE LIMINAL?
IS THAT ONE WANDERING AROUND HERE SOMEWHERE, TOO, MAYHAP?
FLINCH
ビクッ
...?
WHAT'S THE MATTER?
shake
shake
shake
shake
W-WE MATANGO ARE LABELLED AS DANGEROUS JUST BECAUSE OF OUR BODIES, *NGO.*
B-BUT THAT OTHER GIRL...
HER BODY'S JUST AS DANGEROUS, BUT...
H-HER PERSON-ALITY...
IS *MUCH* SCARIER...
THAN HER BODY'S INNATE NATURE...
NGO...

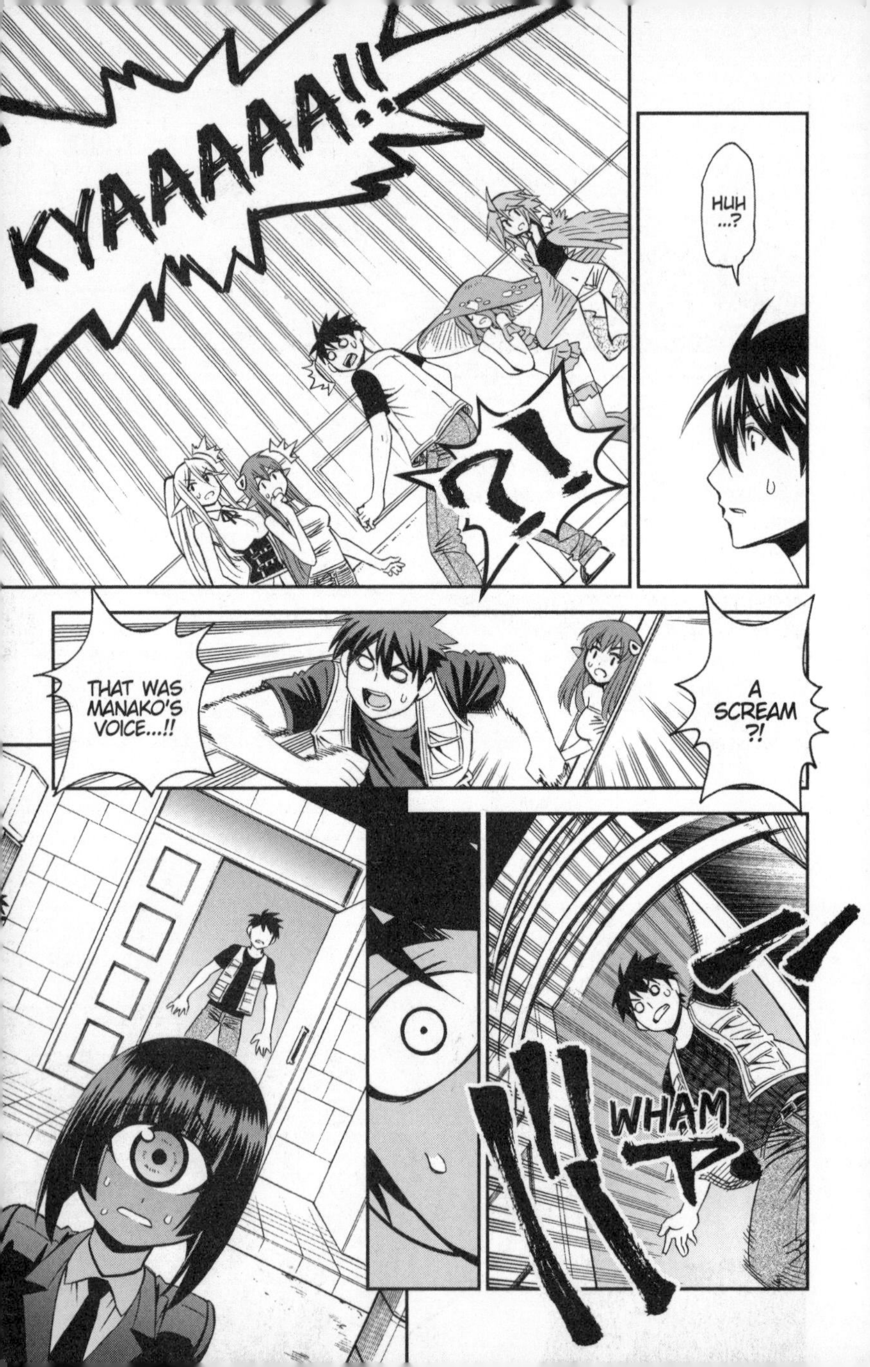
HUH ...?
KYAAAAA!!
?!
A SCREAM ?!
THAT WAS MANAKO'S VOICE...!!
WHAM

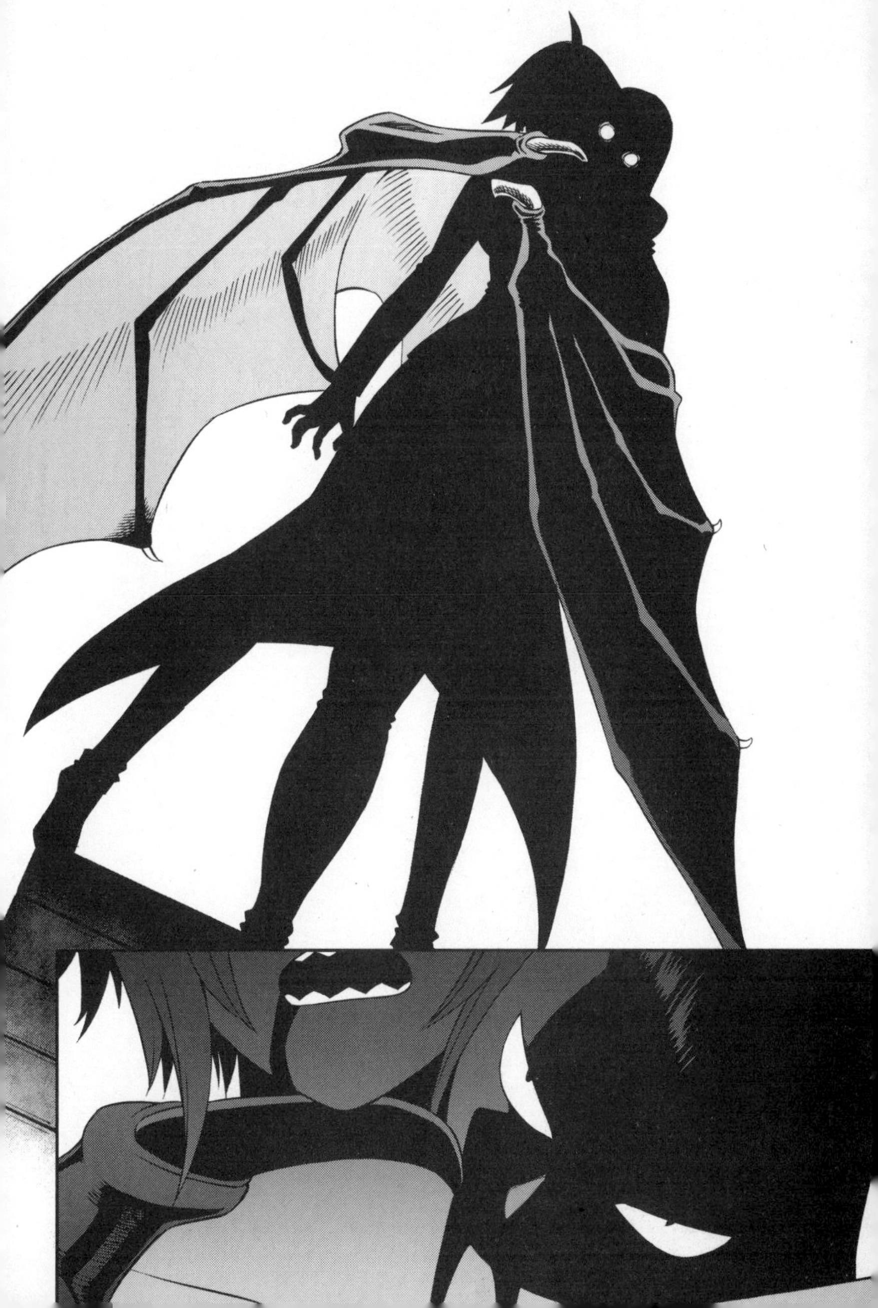

Monster Musume

Everyday Life with Monster Girls

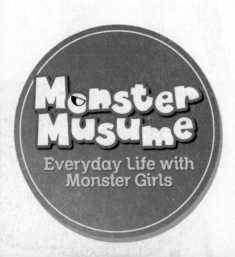

ORIGIN STORY

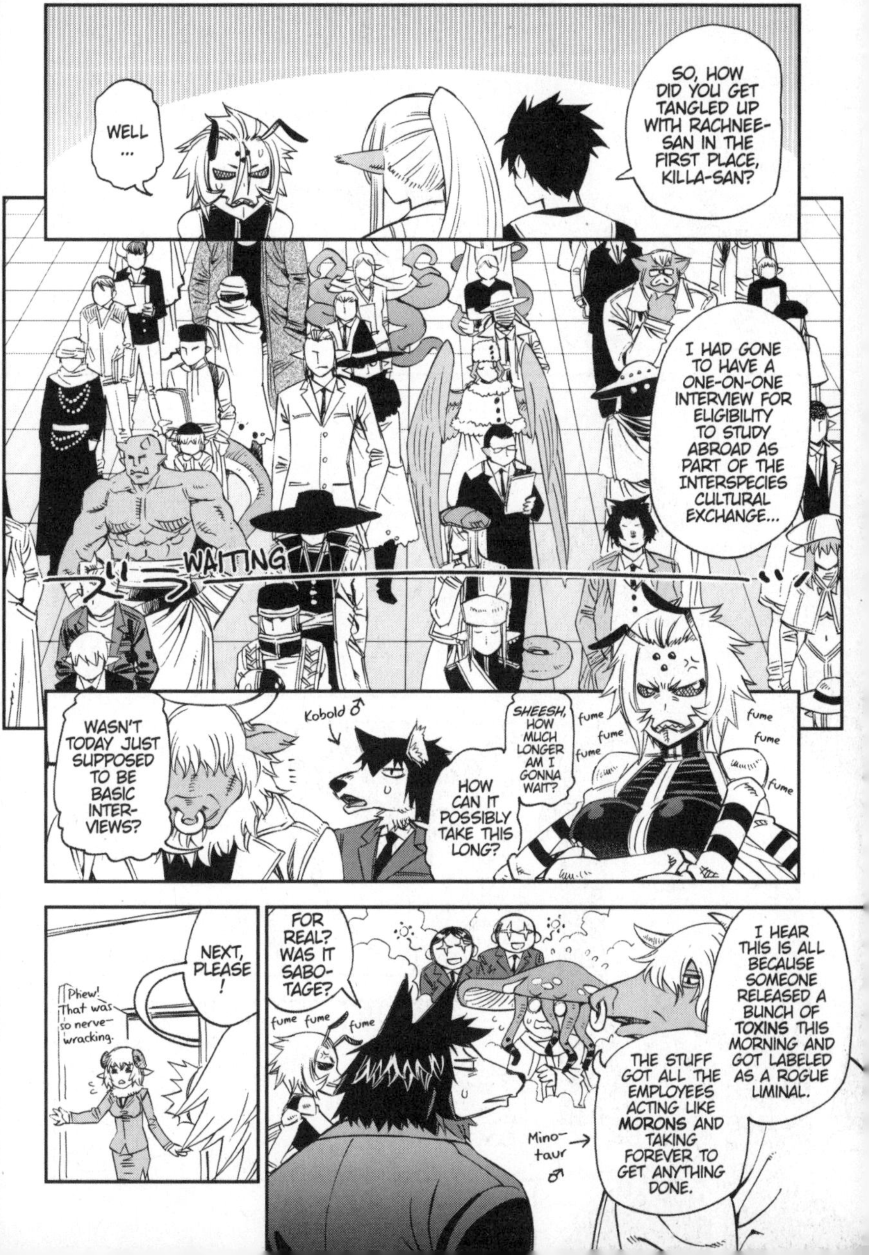

SO, HOW DID YOU GET TANGLED UP WITH RACHNEE-SAN IN THE FIRST PLACE, KILLA-SAN?
WELL ...
I HAD GONE TO HAVE A ONE-ON-ONE INTERVIEW FOR ELIGIBILITY TO STUDY ABROAD AS PART OF THE INTERSPECIES CULTURAL EXCHANGE...
WAITING
fume fume fume fume fume fume
SHEESH, HOW MUCH LONGER AM I GONNA WAIT?
HOW CAN IT POSSIBLY TAKE THIS LONG?
Kobold ♂
WASN'T TODAY JUST SUPPOSED TO BE BASIC INTER-VIEWS?
I HEAR THIS IS ALL BECAUSE SOMEONE RELEASED A BUNCH OF TOXINS THIS MORNING AND GOT LABELED AS A ROGUE LIMINAL.
THE STUFF GOT ALL THE EMPLOYEES ACTING LIKE MORONS AND TAKING FOREVER TO GET ANYTHING DONE.
Mino-taur ♂
FOR REAL? WAS IT SABO-TAGE?
fume fume fume
NEXT, PLEASE!
Phew! That was so nerve-wracking.

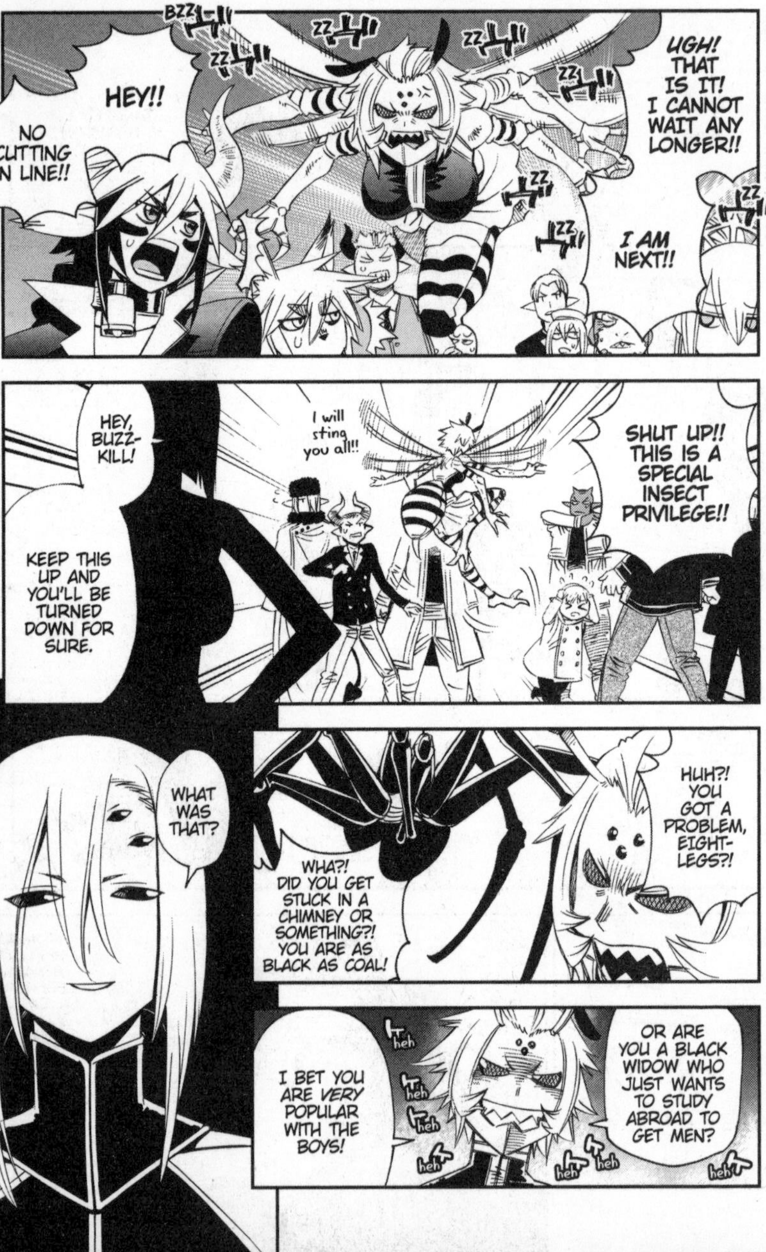

UGH! THAT IS IT! I CANNOT WAIT ANY LONGER!!
ZZ
ZZ
ZZ
ZZ
ZZ
ZZ
I AM NEXT!!
ZZ
ZZ
BZZ
HEY!!
NO CUTTING IN LINE!!
SHUT UP!! THIS IS A SPECIAL INSECT PRIVILEGE!!
I will sting you all!!
HEY, BUZZ-KILL!
KEEP THIS UP AND YOU'LL BE TURNED DOWN FOR SURE.
HUH?! YOU GOT A PROBLEM, EIGHT-LEGS?!
WHA?! DID YOU GET STUCK IN A CHIMNEY OR SOMETHING?! YOU ARE AS BLACK AS COAL!
OR ARE YOU A BLACK WIDOW WHO JUST WANTS TO STUDY ABROAD TO GET MEN?
heh heh heh heh heh heh heh heh
I BET YOU ARE *VERY* POPULAR WITH THE BOYS!
WHAT WAS THAT?

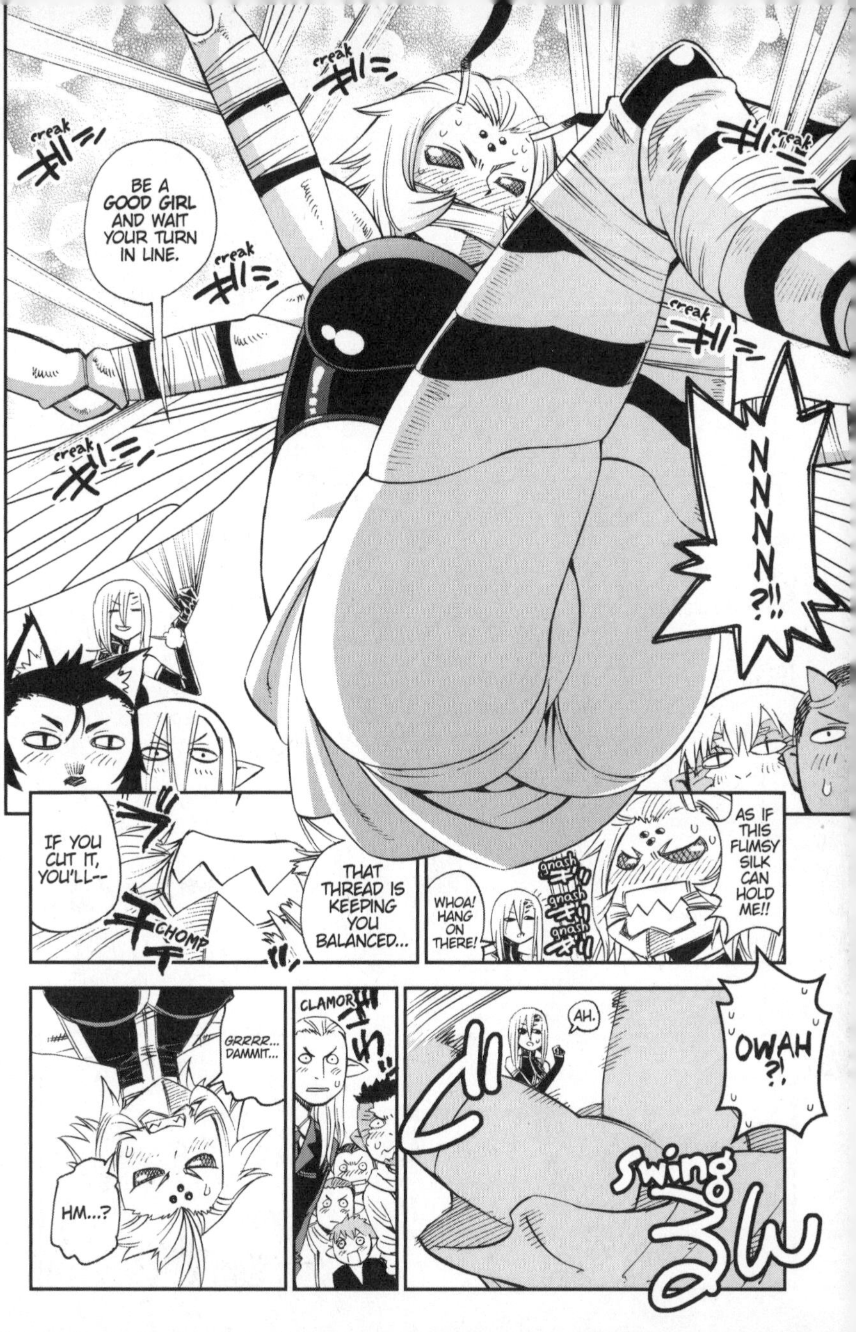
creak
creak
creak
NNNN?!!
creak
BE A GOOD GIRL AND WAIT YOUR TURN IN LINE.
creak
creak
AS IF THIS FLIMSY SILK CAN HOLD ME!!
gnash
gnash
gnash
WHOA! HANG ON THERE!
THAT THREAD IS KEEPING YOU BALANCED...
IF YOU CUT IT, YOU'LL--
CHOMP
OWAH?!
AH.
swing
CLAMOR
GRRRR... DAMMIT...
HM...?

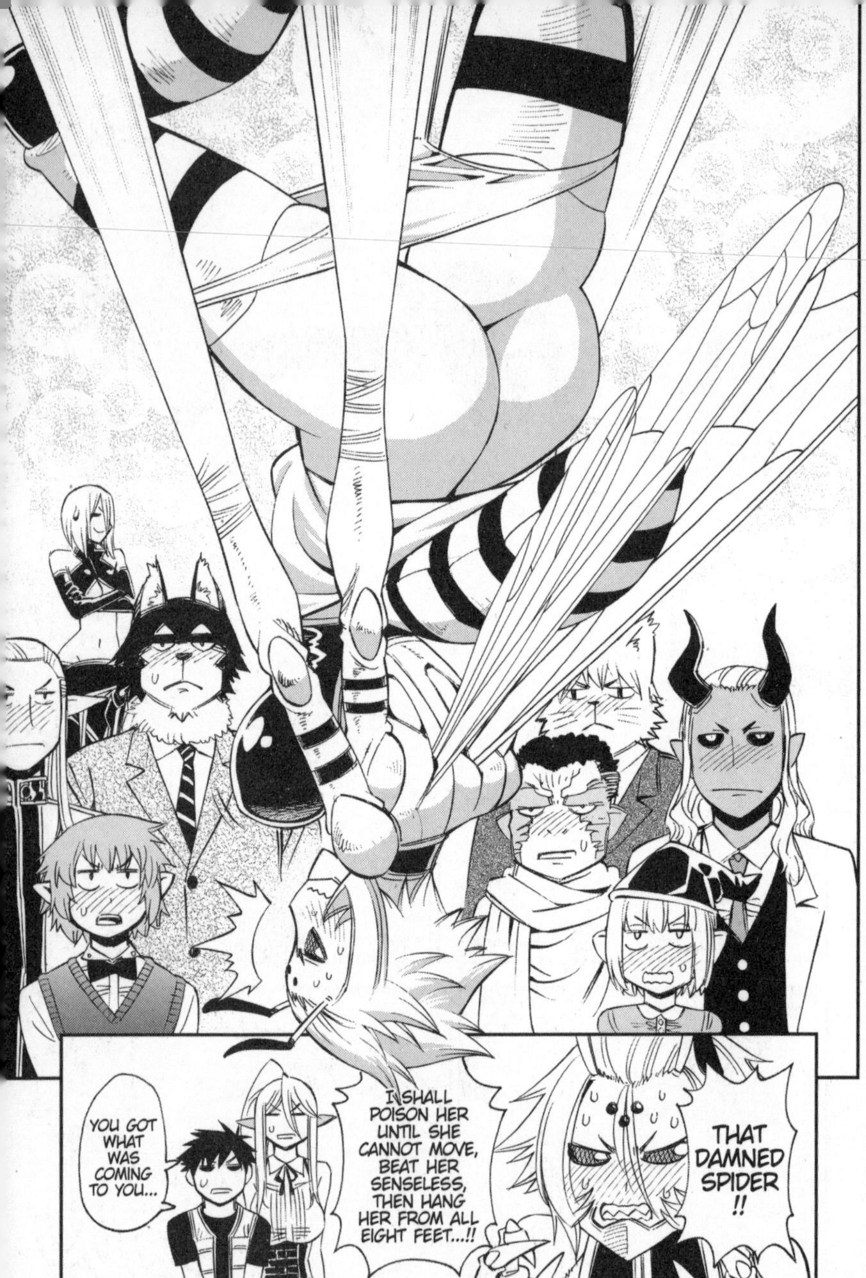
THAT DAMNED SPIDER!!
I SHALL POISON HER UNTIL SHE CANNOT MOVE, BEAT HER SENSELESS, THEN HANG HER FROM ALL EIGHT FEET...!!
YOU GOT WHAT WAS COMING TO YOU...

The Buzz on Killa the Killer Bee

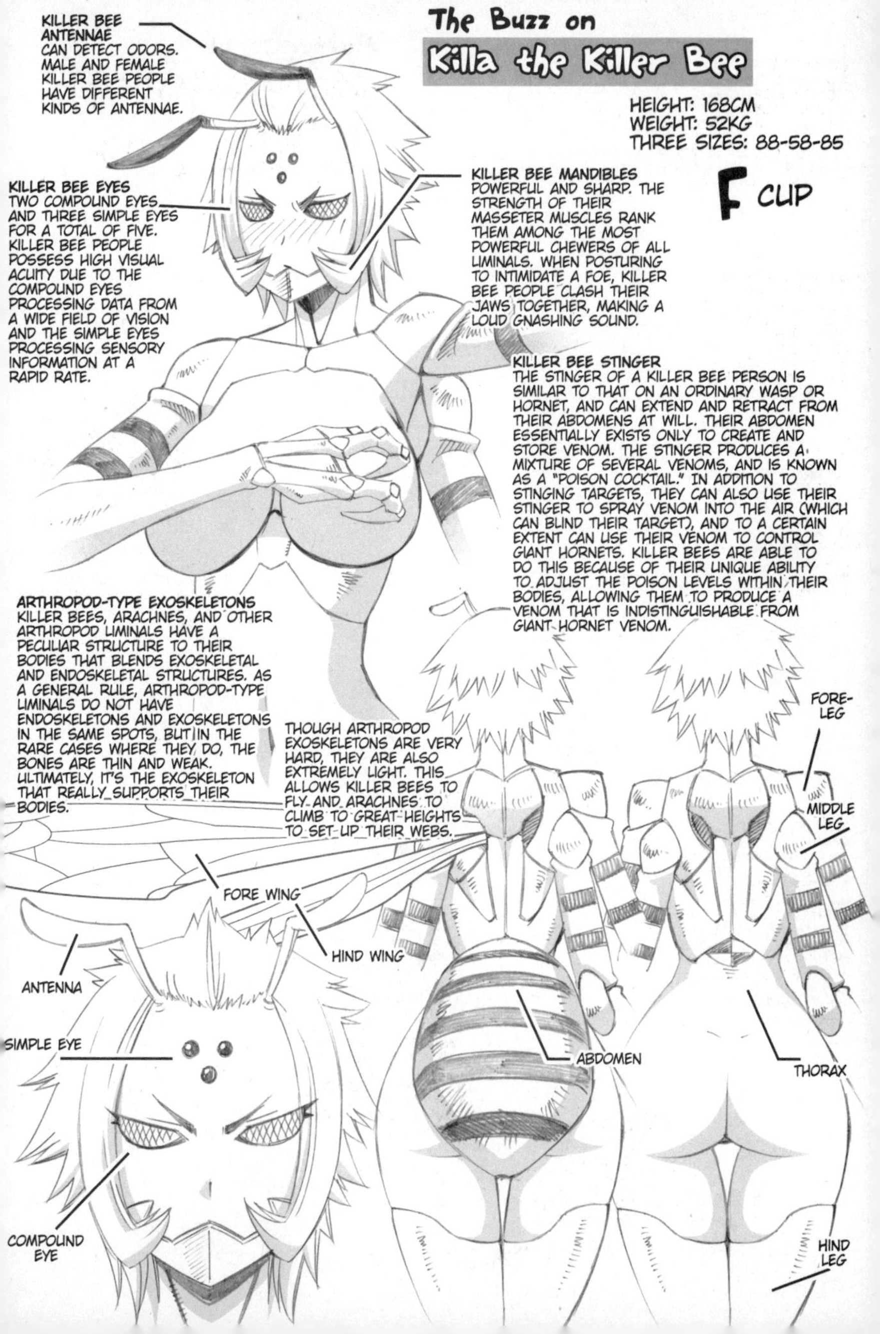
HEIGHT: 168CM
WEIGHT: 52KG
THREE SIZES: 88-58-85
F CUP
KILLER BEE ANTENNAE CAN DETECT ODORS. MALE AND FEMALE KILLER BEE PEOPLE HAVE DIFFERENT KINDS OF ANTENNAE.
KILLER BEE EYES TWO COMPOUND EYES AND THREE SIMPLE EYES FOR A TOTAL OF FIVE. KILLER BEE PEOPLE POSSESS HIGH VISUAL ACUITY DUE TO THE COMPOUND EYES PROCESSING DATA FROM A WIDE FIELD OF VISION AND THE SIMPLE EYES PROCESSING SENSORY INFORMATION AT A RAPID RATE.
KILLER BEE MANDIBLES POWERFUL AND SHARP. THE STRENGTH OF THEIR MASSETER MUSCLES RANK THEM AMONG THE MOST POWERFUL CHEWERS OF ALL LIMINALS. WHEN POSTURING TO INTIMIDATE A FOE, KILLER BEE PEOPLE CLASH THEIR JAWS TOGETHER, MAKING A LOUD GNASHING SOUND.
KILLER BEE STINGER THE STINGER OF A KILLER BEE PERSON IS SIMILAR TO THAT ON AN ORDINARY WASP OR HORNET, AND CAN EXTEND AND RETRACT FROM THEIR ABDOMENS AT WILL. THEIR ABDOMEN ESSENTIALLY EXISTS ONLY TO CREATE AND STORE VENOM. THE STINGER PRODUCES A MIXTURE OF SEVERAL VENOMS, AND IS KNOWN AS A "POISON COCKTAIL." IN ADDITION TO STINGING TARGETS, THEY CAN ALSO USE THEIR STINGER TO SPRAY VENOM INTO THE AIR (WHICH CAN BLIND THEIR TARGET), AND TO A CERTAIN EXTENT CAN USE THEIR VENOM TO CONTROL GIANT HORNETS. KILLER BEES ARE ABLE TO DO THIS BECAUSE OF THEIR UNIQUE ABILITY TO ADJUST THE POISON LEVELS WITHIN THEIR BODIES, ALLOWING THEM TO PRODUCE A VENOM THAT IS INDISTINGUISHABLE FROM GIANT HORNET VENOM.
ARTHROPOD-TYPE EXOSKELETONS KILLER BEES, ARACHNES, AND OTHER ARTHROPOD LIMINALS HAVE A PECULIAR STRUCTURE TO THEIR BODIES THAT BLENDS EXOSKELETAL AND ENDOSKELETAL STRUCTURES. AS A GENERAL RULE, ARTHROPOD-TYPE LIMINALS DO NOT HAVE ENDOSKELETONS AND EXOSKELETONS IN THE SAME SPOTS, BUT IN THE RARE CASES WHERE THEY DO, THE BONES ARE THIN AND WEAK. ULTIMATELY, IT'S THE EXOSKELETON THAT REALLY SUPPORTS THEIR BODIES.
THOUGH ARTHROPOD EXOSKELETONS ARE VERY HARD, THEY ARE ALSO EXTREMELY LIGHT. THIS ALLOWS KILLER BEES TO FLY AND ARACHNES TO CLIMB TO GREAT HEIGHTS TO SET UP THEIR WEBS.
FORE-LEG
MIDDLE LEG
FORE WING
HIND WING
ANTENNA
SIMPLE EYE
ABDOMEN
THORAX
COMPOUND EYE
HIND LEG

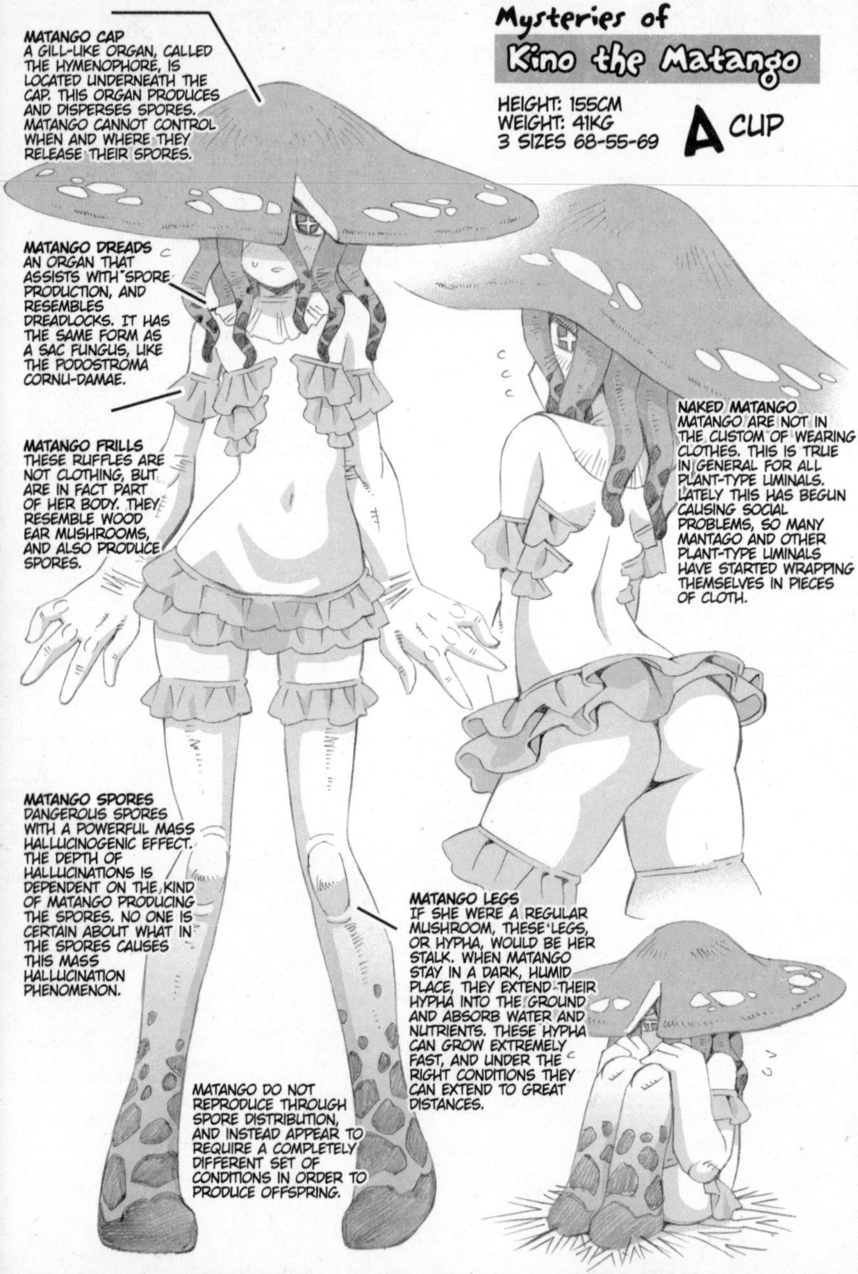
Mysteries of
Kino the Matango
HEIGHT: 155CM
WEIGHT: 41KG
3 SIZES 68-55-69
A CUP
MATANGO CAP
A GILL-LIKE ORGAN, CALLED THE HYMENOPHORE, IS LOCATED UNDERNEATH THE CAP. THIS ORGAN PRODUCES AND DISPERSES SPORES. MATANGO CANNOT CONTROL WHEN AND WHERE THEY RELEASE THEIR SPORES.
MATANGO DREADS
AN ORGAN THAT ASSISTS WITH SPORE PRODUCTION, AND RESEMBLES DREADLOCKS. IT HAS THE SAME FORM AS A SAC FUNGUS, LIKE THE PODOSTROMA CORNU-DAMAE.
MATANGO FRILLS
THESE RUFFLES ARE NOT CLOTHING, BUT ARE IN FACT PART OF HER BODY. THEY RESEMBLE WOOD EAR MUSHROOMS, AND ALSO PRODUCE SPORES.
NAKED MATANGO
MATANGO ARE NOT IN THE CUSTOM OF WEARING CLOTHES. THIS IS TRUE IN GENERAL FOR ALL PLANT-TYPE LIMINALS. LATELY THIS HAS BEGUN CAUSING SOCIAL PROBLEMS, SO MANY MANTAGO AND OTHER PLANT-TYPE LIMINALS HAVE STARTED WRAPPING THEMSELVES IN PIECES OF CLOTH.
MATANGO SPORES
DANGEROUS SPORES WITH A POWERFUL MASS HALLUCINOGENIC EFFECT. THE DEPTH OF HALLUCINATIONS IS DEPENDENT ON THE KIND OF MATANGO PRODUCING THE SPORES. NO ONE IS CERTAIN ABOUT WHAT IN THE SPORES CAUSES THIS MASS HALLUCINATION PHENOMENON.
MATANGO LEGS
IF SHE WERE A REGULAR MUSHROOM, THESE LEGS, OR HYPHA, WOULD BE HER STALK. WHEN MATANGO STAY IN A DARK, HUMID PLACE, THEY EXTEND THEIR HYPHA INTO THE GROUND AND ABSORB WATER AND NUTRIENTS. THESE HYPHA CAN GROW EXTREMELY FAST, AND UNDER THE RIGHT CONDITIONS THEY CAN EXTEND TO GREAT DISTANCES.
MATANGO DO NOT REPRODUCE THROUGH SPORE DISTRIBUTION, AND INSTEAD APPEAR TO REQUIRE A COMPLETELY DIFFERENT SET OF CONDITIONS IN ORDER TO PRODUCE OFFSPRING.

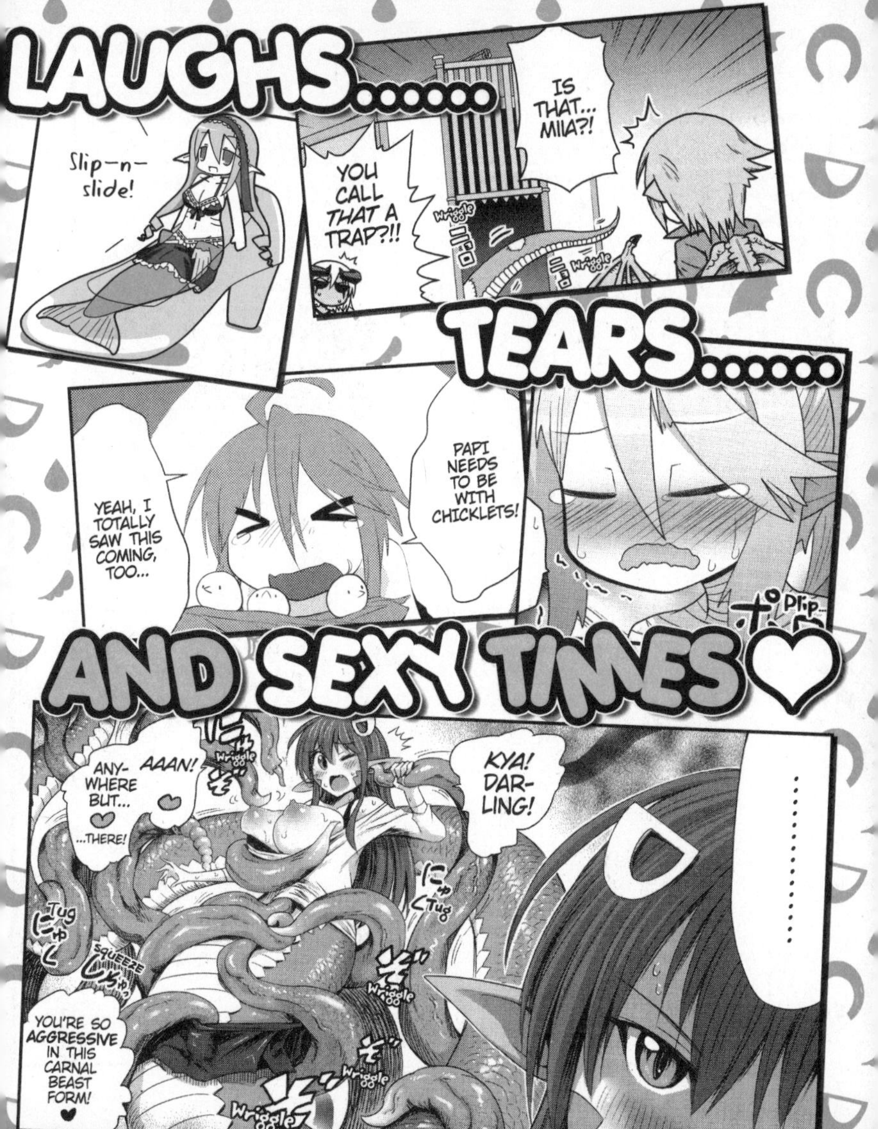

LAUGHS......
IS THAT... MIIA?!
YOU CALL THAT A TRAP?!!
Wriggle
Wriggle
Slip-n-slide!
TEARS......
Drip...
PAPI NEEDS TO BE WITH CHICKLETS!
YEAH, I TOTALLY SAW THIS COMING, TOO...
AND SEXY TIMES♥
......
KYA! DARLING!
AAAN!
Wriggle
ANY-WHERE BUT... ♥ ...THERE!
Tug
Tug
Squeeze
Wriggle
Wriggle
Wriggle
YOU'RE SO AGGRESSIVE IN THIS CARNAL BEAST FORM! ♥